Japan and the New Silk Road

This book presents a study of Japanese involvement in post-Soviet Central Asia since the independence of these countries in 1991, examining the reasons for progress and stagnation in this multi-lateral relationship.

Featuring interviews with decision-makers and experts from Japan, China, Kazakhstan, Uzbekistan, Azerbaijan, and the Philippines, this book argues that Japan's impact on Central Asia and its connectivity has been underappreciated. It demonstrates that Japan's infrastructural footprint in the New Silk Road significantly pre-dated China's Belt and Road Initiative, and that the financial and policy contribution driven by Japanese officials was of a similar order of magnitude. It also goes on to show that Japan was the first major power outside of post-Soviet Central Asia to articulate a dedicated Silk Road diplomacy vis-à-vis the region before the United States and China, and the first to sponsor pivotal assistance.

Being the first detailed analytical account of the diplomatic impact made on the New Silk Road by various Japanese actors beyond formal diplomacy, this book will be useful to students and scholars of Japanese politics, as well as Asian politics and international politics more generally.

Nikolay Murashkin is a visiting fellow at the Griffith Asia Institute, Griffith University and a sessional lecturer at the School of Political Sciences and International Studies, University of Queensland, Australia. His research interests include Japan's economic statecraft and politics of connectivity infrastructure and finance in the Indo-Pacific and Eurasia.

The Nissan Institute/Routledge Japanese Studies Series

Series Editors:
Roger Goodman, *Nissan Professor of Modern Japanese Studies, University of Oxford, Fellow, St Antony's College*
J.A.A. Stockwin, *formerly Nissan Professor of Modern Japanese Studies and former Director of the Nissan Institute of Japanese Studies, University of Oxford, Emeritus Fellow, St Antony's College*

Japan's World Power
Assessment, Outlook and Vision
Edited by Guibourg Delamotte

Friendship and Work Culture of Women Managers in Japan
Tokyo After Ten
Swee-Lin Ho

The Dilemma of Faith in Modern Japanese Literature
Metaphors of Christianity
Massimiliano Tomasi

Understanding Japanese Society
Fifth edition
Joy Hendry

The Liberal Democratic Party of Japan
The realities of 'power'
Nakakita Kōji

Japan's New Ruralities
Coping with decline in the periphery
Edited by Wolfram Manzenreiter, Ralph Lützeler, and Sebastian Polak-Rottmann

Japan and the New Silk Road
Diplomacy, Development, and Connectivity
Nikolay Murashkin

For more information about this series, please visit: www.routledge.com/Nissan-Institute-Routledge-Japanese-Studies/book-series/SE0022

Japan and the New Silk Road
Diplomacy, Development, and Connectivity

Nikolay Murashkin

LONDON AND NEW YORK

First published 2020
by Routledge
2 Park Square, Milton Park, Abingdon, Oxon OX14 4RN

and by Routledge
605 Third Avenue, New York, NY 10017

Routledge is an imprint of the Taylor & Francis Group, an informa business

First issued in paperback 2021

© 2020 Nikolay Murashkin

The right of Nikolay Murashkin to be identified as author of this work
has been asserted by him in accordance with sections 77 and 78 of the
Copyright, Designs and Patents Act 1988.

All rights reserved. No part of this book may be reprinted or reproduced
or utilised in any form or by any electronic, mechanical, or other
means, now known or hereafter invented, including photocopying and
recording, or in any information storage or retrieval system, without
permission in writing from the publishers.

Trademark notice: Product or corporate names may be trademarks
or registered trademarks, and are used only for identification and
explanation without intent to infringe.

Publisher's Note
The publisher has gone to great lengths to ensure the quality of this
reprint but points out that some imperfections in the original copies
may be apparent.

British Library Cataloguing-in-Publication Data
A catalogue record for this book is available from the British Library

Library of Congress Cataloging-in-Publication Data
A catalog record has been requested for this book

ISBN 13: 978-0-367-10990-5 (hbk)
ISBN 13: 978-0-429-02418-4 (ebk)
ISBN 13: 978-1-03-223853-1 (pbk)

DOI: 10.4324/9780429024184

Typeset in Times New Roman
by Lumina Datamatics Limited

To Evgeniya, Yuri, Seraphima, and Boris

Contents

List of illustrations	viii
Series editors' preface	ix
Notes on style	xi
Acknowledgements	xii
List of abbreviations and acronyms	xiv
Introduction: Japan, the New Great Game, and New Silk Road	1
1 Central Asia on Japan's diplomatic agenda: security, resources, and humanitarianism	19
2 Silk Road diplomacy of the DPJ cabinets: continuity, inertia, and change	64
3 Japan's aid in the New Silk Road: developmentalism, securitisation, and likely prototype for Belt and Road?	89
4 Energy Silk Road: anticipation and adaption in Japan's resource diplomacy	141
5 Japan, China, and Asian connectivity: competition, cooperation, and the weaponisation of infrastructure finance?	191
Conclusion	215
Glossary	221
Index	223

Illustrations

Figures

1.1	JICA loan aid to major Silk Road countries in 1995–2011	34
3.1	Japan's bilateral ODA in Central Asia (FY1993–2009), 100 million yen	105
3.2	A vision of Central Asia's regional connectivity and cooperation, 1998	120
3.3	CAREC corridors in 2008	120
3.4	Central Asia Regional Economic Cooperation, designated rail corridors	125
4.1	Japan–Central Asia two-way trade	148

Tables

I.1	Selected key data on CA states (2018)	8
1.1	Milestones of Japan–CA diplomatic relations	20
4.1	2005 forecast of Japanese energy consumption	153

Series editors' preface

The Nissan Institute/Routledge Japanese Studies Series is now well past its 100th volume and has published across a wide variety of areas relating to Japan, including political science, social anthropology, sociology, international relations, modern history, education, economics, and the arts. The broad aim of the series is to inform readers of the many aspects of Japan and the Japanese people, using objective and, where necessary, critical methodologies. We believe that the rest of the world can learn much from the experience of what is now the third largest economy in the world and is heir to sophisticated national traditions.

The present volume, by Nikolay Murashkin, is a pioneering work exploring the relationships between Japan and the five former central Asian republics of the Soviet Union, all of which became independent republics in 1991: Kazakhstan, Kyrgyzstan, Tajikistan, Turkmenistan, and Uzbekistan. (He also touches on Azerbaijan, to the west of the Caspian Sea.) These republics are prominent in the well-known Chinese 'Belt and Road' Initiative, but Murashkin shows that Japan was actually ahead of China in developing the romantic notion of the 'Silk Road' into a coherent relationship between East Asia and Central Asia. Of the five countries concerned, two stand out as crucially important. Kazakhstan to the north is an enormous country, stretching from the Chinese border on the east to the Caspian Sea to the west, comparable in size with the bulk of Western Europe, and having a population of about 18 million. The double-landlocked Uzbekistan further south is much smaller, but has a population of some 33 million. Of the two, Kazakhstan, in Murashkin's opinion, has gone the furthest out of the five in modernising its infrastructure and economy more generally. The three smaller countries have suffered from internal instability and poor governance, and so have been less prominent in Japanese foreign policy calculations. Murashkin shows that although Central Asia does not figure in Japanese foreign policy calculations as prominently as does Southeast Asia, nevertheless, successive Japanese governments have treated it quite seriously since the late 1990s, and it has been an area of significant interest to Japanese business.

Murashkin is encyclopaedic in his coverage of security issues, party politics, financial assistance, natural resources, and connectivity infrastructure. He analyses in depth the influence of a certain number of individuals, both on the Japanese and on the Central Asian side, that have been particularly influential in cementing

x *Series editors' preface*

relationships between Japan and Central Asia. He discusses the internal politics of these countries, paying attention to the 'clans' that are an important feature of some, though not all of them. He likens these to the factions (habatsu) that are well known in Japanese politics, suggesting that this similarity makes it easier for the two sides to understand each other's politics.

One of the most important issues that he grapples with is interactions in the region between Japan and China. He argues against the widespread 'zero-sum' understanding of this bilateral relationship, showing that to a considerable extent Japan and China have in practice co-operated in their initiatives in the region, including those of infrastructural and concessional lending.

Nobody in the years to come, who is interested in Japanese foreign policy or in the politics and economics of the former Soviet republics of Central Asia, will be able to ignore this book, based as it is on exceptionally wide-ranging scholarship and valuable insight into an important, but hitherto little-studied set of relationships.

Arthur Stockwin
Roger Goodman

Notes on style

Japanese, Chinese, and Korean names are not italicised and are given with the surname first, so in the case of Abe Shinzō, Abe is the family name and Shinzō is the first name. Other Japanese and Russian terms are italicised and written in *romaji* and transliteration from Russian Cyrillic. Emphatic italicisation in quotations is entirely mine. For the sake of clarity, words commonly used in English are usually chosen in preference to their local counterparts; for example, 'Bukhara' (a city in Uzbekistan) is used in preference to the Uzbek 'Buxoro,' and 'Itochu' is used in preference to 'Itōchū.' The spelling standard used is British English, except when quoting English-language Japanese documents and other sources predominantly using American English spelling (for instance, 'defense' rather than 'defence').

A character glossary of the most important Japanese terms is provided. A list of abbreviations used in the text is at the beginning of this book. Dates in the footnotes are presented in abbreviated British format, such that 26 December 1991 becomes 26/12/91. Amounts in dollars refer to American dollars and are indicated with '$,' while amounts in yen are indicated with '¥.'

Many of the officials interviewed for this research did so on the condition that they remain anonymous. Interviews in this study therefore follow the format whereby the name of the interviewee is included only when she or he agrees to be named. Full interview transcripts are available upon request.

Acknowledgements

This journey began when I was studying at Waseda University as a Russian exchange student from Sciences Po Paris. At Waseda, I met Russian-speaking Central Asian students and Japanese academics, many of whom ultimately became my friends, who introduced me to growing ties between Japan and the New Silk Road region. The term guro:baru (global) in Japan still held some euphoric and romantic connotations back then, applying both to my unforgettable experience of discovering Tokyo and exposure to the reconfiguration of Asian and post-Soviet spaces at the level of human exchanges. The proliferation of regional ties and integration seemed logical and natural, while relations between Japan and Central Asia represented a new kind of inter-Asian linkage. As a result, my graduate experience turned into a doctoral and post-doctoral research project, throughout which I have become greatly indebted to a large number of people in Japan, Central Asia, Russia, the United Kingdom, and across the world.

First and foremost, I would like to thank my doctoral supervisor, Dr John Nilsson-Wright. It is thanks to his insight, advice, and developmental feedback that I was able to write this dissertation. Other people also kindly read through various versions of the manuscript and made many insightful comments, in particular Dr Tony Brooks. Special thanks also go to my advisor Dr Barak Kushner for his help at various stages of practical research. Professor Siddharth Saxena, Dr Prajakti Kalra, and the team of Cambridge Central Asia Forum greatly supported me in many ways. I was extremely lucky and privileged to work with Professor Kitamura Toshiharu, who kindly agreed to be my advisor at Waseda University, where I was made to feel most welcome, greatly facilitated my field research in Tokyo, Manila, and Tashkent, and expanded my understanding of the subject in a way that would not have been possible otherwise. Dr Paik Keun-Wook kindly provided particularly valuable insights into Asian energy geopolitics and helped with field research in East Asia. Reviews and comments by Professor Arthur Stockwin and Professor Marie Söderberg were crucial at the final stage of my doctoral research. I am most grateful to St. Catharine's College Cambridge, the Faculty of Asian and Middle Eastern Studies, Cambridge Central Asia Forum, Griffith Asia Institute, Cambridge Overseas Trusts, Centre

Acknowledgements xiii

for East European Language-Based Area Studies, the Great Britain Sasakawa Foundation, the Japan Foundation, the Open Society Foundation, and Cambridge Oriental Culture Association for the support of my research project, allowing me to make research trips to Azerbaijan, China, Japan, Kazakhstan, the Philippines, and Uzbekistan, and also to present my work at numerous conferences.

I am also heavily indebted to the following individuals in the United Kingdom, Japan, Azerbaijan, Kazakhstan, Uzbekistan, Russia, Australia, France, and elsewhere who gave generously of their time and helped in various ways (in alphabetical order): Professor Abe Yoshiaki, Dr Tristam Barrett, Professor Caitlin Byrne, Geraldine Dunbar, Professor Hervé Fradet, Professor Ian Hall, Honma Masaru, Murad Ismayilov, Iio Akitoshi, Professor Purnendra Jain, Tatyana Kan, Ambassador Kawatō Akio, Kayum Khaydarov, Olga Kozlova, Dr Lam Peng Er, Dr Chokan Laumulin, Dr Murat Laumulin, Dr Peter Layton, Professor Abdurakhim Mannanov, Professor Vassily Molodiakov, Professor Elgena Molodiakova, Giuseppe Morta, Dr Sherzod Muminov, Nihei Naoki, Dr Bekzod Ochilov, Dr Oka Natsuko, Dr Giulio Pugliese, Elena Pyanova, Zhamilya Rymzhanova, Dr Jamshed Safarov, Xenia Smertina, Tania Sollogoub, Dr Alexander Sotnichenko, Yulia Stonogina, Mark Suleymanov, Dr Konstantin Syroezhkin, Professor Natalia Vassilyeva, Olga Volodkina, Professor Shukhrat Yovkochev, and Dr Yu Ka-ho.

Finally, I am extremely grateful to my family in Russia and Australia and friends across the world for all the invaluable support they have been kindly providing, especially at the final stages of writing up. Without them, this would not have been possible.

Abbreviations and acronyms

ADB	Asian Development Bank
AFP	Arc of Freedom and Prosperity
AIIB	Asian Infrastructure Investment Bank
BOJ	Bank of Japan
BRI	Belt and Road Initiative
CA	Central Asia
CAREC	Central Asian Regional Economic Cooperation
CICA	Conference on Interaction and Confidence-Building Measures in Asia
CPSU	Communist Party of the Soviet Union
CSTO	Collective Security Treaty Organisation
DAC	Development Assistance Committee (OECD, see below)
DPJ	Democratic Party of Japan
EAC	East Asian Community
EDB	Eurasian Development Bank
EAEC	Eurasian Economic Community
EBRD	European Bank for Reconstruction and Development
ETC	Early Transition Countries
IMF	International Monetary Fund
ISAF	International Security Assistance Forces (Afghanistan)
IsDB	Islamic Development Bank
JBIC	Japanese Bank for International Cooperation
JCA	Japan–Central Asia, Japanese–Central Asian
JICA	Japanese International Cooperation Agency
JNOC	Japanese National Oil Corporation (now part of JOGMEC)
JOGMEC	Japan Oil, Gas, and Metals National Corporation
LDP	Liberal Democratic Party of Japan
METI	Ministry of Economy, Trade, and Industry (Japan)
MOF	Ministry of Finance (Japan)
MOFA	Ministry of Foreign Affairs (Japan)
ODA	Official Development Assistance
OECD	Organisation for Economic Cooperation and Development

OECF	Overseas Economic Cooperation Fund (Japan, now JBIC)
OSCE	Organisation for Security and Cooperation in Europe
PRC	People's Republic of China
ROK	Republic of Korea
SCO	Shanghai Cooperation Organisation
SRF	Silk Road Fund
WB	World Bank

Introduction

Japan, the New Great Game, and New Silk Road

The 2013 announcement of China's Belt and Road Initiative (BRI) became a watershed for contemporary academic, political, and media discourse on Asian connectivity infrastructure and for our understanding of incipient regionalisation in Asia, including various New Silk Road (NSR) concepts. One of this 'post-BRI' era's effects was the increasing perception and reinterpretation of connectivity infrastructure and finance projects predating the BRI through the lens of the BRI. Another effect of the BRI on the NSR discourse was that it brought securitisation to the fore and sidelined functionalism by shifting the focus from development and macroeconomics towards statecraft and geo-economics. A somewhat similar phenomenon occurred in the 1990s–2000s, when the post-Cold War reopening of Central Asia was reductively interpreted through the New Great Game paradigm – the realpolitik interplay of great powers in the region.[1]

The resulting New Silk Road discourse, produced by politicians, pundits, and academics, tended to overemphasise the originality of the BRI and to contextualise it within China's rivalry with the United States and Japan. Furthermore, these interpretations reductively misconstrued Japan's initiatives and its long-established track record in development and infrastructure finance in Asia and the NSR as either secondary or purely reactive to China's advances. While the risk perceptions and opportunity perceptions of the BRI and other connectivity infrastructure projects go through cycles of euphoria and fatigue – similarly to foreign aid in the late twentieth century – the question remains on Japan's evolving policy in the NSR: what is its nature, what are its drivers, and how and why did it change before and after BRI?

This book seeks to fill the gap on the role of Japan, while nuancing and repudiating its Procrustean interpretations. I showcase Japan's diplomatic, financial, and resource activities in Central Asia (CA) and wider Asia since the end of the Cold War, including the first detailed account of Japan's pivotal role in regional infrastructure finance. In doing so, I seek to tackle the topical issues of contemporary international relations in the NSR. What consequences do Sino-Japanese infrastructure rivalry and cooperation portend for Asia and emerging regionalisation between Central, East, and, to an extent, South Asian sub-regions? Is Asian

2 *From New Great Games to New Silk Roads*

infrastructure becoming a mere continuation of policy by other means – economic ones, in this case? In the early twentieth century, two Eurasian trans-regional connectivity projects – the Berlin-Baghdad Railway and the China Eastern Railway – contributed to tensions and, ultimately, conflict between major powers. Do Sino-Japanese relations and Japanese foreign policy run similar risks in the NSR, especially now that this concept encompasses various Asian sub-regions beyond CA?

First and foremost, this book focuses on the study of Japanese involvement in post-Soviet CA since the independence of these countries in 1991 and examines the reasons for progress and stagnation in this multi-lateral relationship, where Japanese policy oscillated between proactivity and reactivity. It argues that Japan's impact on CA and its connectivity is underappreciated and under-researched, as Japan's infrastructural footprint in the NSR significantly pre-dates China's Belt and Road Initiative, while the Japan-led financial and policy contribution is of the same order of magnitude. Japan was the first major power outside post-Soviet Central Asia to articulate a dedicated Silk Road diplomacy vis-à-vis the region before the United States and China and the first to provide pivotal, but under-recognised aid. I stress the fact that Japan's foreign policy in Asian infrastructure finance featured both cooperative and competitive postures towards China, especially within multi-lateral development banks such as the Asian Development Bank. The research contributes to emerging scholarship on connectivity infrastructure in Asia – often shaped by strategic communications and projections – by highlighting Japan's regional role and shows how our understanding of international relations and political economy in Asia can be better informed by economic history and area studies.

Abe Shinzō's 2015 visit as an illustration of the relationship

When Japanese Prime Minister Abe Shinzō visited five CA republics in October 2015, his trip came across as both long-awaited and surprising news. Abe's voyage followed then-Secretary of State John Kerry's trip to CA and took place two years after Chinese President Xi Jinping announced the Silk Road Economic Belt initiative in Kazakhstan. Due to this timing, commentary on Abe's trip contextualised it within Tokyo's relations with either Beijing or Washington, thus underestimating the history and depth of Japan's own involvement in CA.

Abe's visit was long-awaited in some quarters of Japan and CA, as well as among some Japan watchers, because, since returning to power in December 2012, Abe had made proactive diplomacy and natural resources a priority for his cabinet, frequenting a record number of 50 countries – but not CA. This contradicted CA's strategic role and abundant mineral riches consistently noted in Japan's Diplomatic Bluebook, a key doctrinal document of the Ministry of Foreign Affairs.[2] Until Abe's trip, Koizumi Jun'ichirō was the only Japanese prime minister to ever visit post-Soviet CA (in 2006) since its independence in 1991. Meanwhile, during the first three years of Abe's second premiership

From New Great Games to New Silk Roads   3

(2012–present), more Japanese officials have travelled to the region than in the entire preceding decade.[3] Abe's visit had been discussed for many months, but remained sidelined by more important priorities, according to Japanese experts.[4]

In this light, the three-year delay of the visit appeared as a paradox, given the region's prima facie importance as recipient of Japanese aid, source of commodity procurement for Japan, and key element of both the securitisation of Afghanistan and China's BRI. When the visit finally took place in 2015, it produced additional spark in material terms, as the value of signed commodity, aid, and infrastructure agreements totalled an impressive $27 billion. This surprisingly large order of magnitude challenged CA's characterisation as periphery for Japan, since in terms of scale, it was comparable to Japan's cumulative investment in CA since 1991, and to jumbo projects, such as the Beijing-led Silk Road Fund and Central Asian Regional Economic Cooperation (CAREC), led by the Asian Development Bank.[5] Another novelty was that Turkmenistan and Uzbekistan accounted for the bulk of this deal value with $18 billion and nearly $9 billion, respectively. Prima facie, this suggested a revival of stagnating Japan–Uzbek business ties and a spark in Japan's commercial interest in Turkmenistan. At the same time, the visit's symbolic value exceeded the tangible one, as subsequent business cooperation between Japan and Uzbekistan was below the expectations of Japanese stakeholders.

The above illustration goes well beyond Abe's second premiership and captures a larger paradox in the history of relations between Japan and post-Soviet CA. Namely, these relations underwent steady, but on-and-off development and combined both declaratively strategic importance and a peripheral level of priority attached in diplomatic practice. In other words, the Japanese government demonstrated its willingness to stress the strategic importance of the relationship in rhetoric, while in practice, various cabinets have assigned relatively low priority to the region compared with other foreign policy interests.[6]

Japanese diplomacy towards CA has evolved considerably and proactively since 1991, when the region became independent. A decade and a half later and despite these developments, however, Japanese relationship-building with the region appeared to stagnate and prompted the usual questions about Japanese foreign policy-making in general. Did the relationship stagnate then and, if so, why? Did it lack strategy and coherence due to its dependence on ebbs and flows? Was Japanese foreign policy in CA reactive, proactive, transactional, or alternating between these contrasting postures? Was it influenced by rigidities in Japan's domestic politics? What significance did institutional inertia, external pressure, and the external environment have? Are factionalism and personal factors relevant? Certain Japanese experts on the matter, such as Kawatō Akio or Uyama Tomohiko, justified Japan's lack of strategy by the relatively peripheral place CA occupies on Tokyo's diplomatic agenda. It is therefore important to examine whether and why the patterns of Japanese foreign policy governing central concerns also apply to peripheral ones.

Going back to Abe's 2015 visit, both the prime minister and many key members of his second cabinet have been seen by Japanese diplomats and experts

4 *From New Great Games to New Silk Roads*

with knowledge of CA as politicians with a comparatively better understanding of regional matters than their peers. This difference stems from their past personal experience with the region, a rarity for Japanese top officials, and, to an extent, from affiliations with the *Seiwa Seisaku Kenkyūkai* faction (Seiwa Policy Research Council, or Seiwaken). The faction was founded by Abe's grandfather Prime Minister Kishi Nobusuke and known for its conservative attitude towards Beijing (as opposed to Taipei) and support of Japan's economic involvement in the Union of Soviet Socialist Republics (USSR).[7]

Furthermore, Abe's prioritisation of natural resources was reflected in his numerous international trips to Africa, the Middle East, and Russia that were a part of the response to the impact of the Fukushima nuclear accident and a wider push for Japan's higher international status. The Middle East has long been the traditional energy provider to Japan, unlike African countries, and Abe's attention to Russia and Africa was also interpreted as part of a wider China balancing act.

Sino-Japanese rivalry also resurged in the field of international finance. After Chinese President Xi Jinping had announced the BRI, involving Central and Southeast Asia in 2013, as well as Chinese funding via the newly established Asian Infrastructure Investment Bank and dedicated Silk Road Fund, Abe countered in May 2015 by promising to pour a total of $110 billion in Asian infrastructure projects, both bilaterally and via augmented financial contributions to the Asian Development Bank.[8]

In the logic of balancing China by Japan, CA warrants special recognition as both a source of raw materials and a region not only bordering China, but also experiencing an increase in Chinese presence.[9] At the previous peak of Sino-Japanese tensions in the mid-2000s, CA was covered by the Arc of Freedom and Prosperity – a (non-event) concept generally regarded as balancing China, reportedly devised by such key members of Abe's team as Foreign Minister Asō Tarō and diplomacy masterminds Yachi Shōtarō and Kanehara Nobukatsu.[10]

And yet, CA remained off Abe's diplomatic agenda until long into his second premiership, despite its unexpected continuity with preceding revolving-door governments. The delay in Abe's CA trip was particularly counter-intuitive at the backdrop of another cooling off in Sino-Japanese relations and of the expectations harboured by Japanese bureaucrats and corporate officers involved in CA matters.[11] These stakeholders were unhappy with the previous handling of the CA relationship by the Democratic Party of Japan (DPJ) and hoped for its revival now that the Liberal Democratic Party (LDP) was back in power and the government included officials with a past CA experience: Amari Akira, Asō, Kuroda Haruhiko, Kanehara, and Yachi.[12]

Moreover, as part of an attempt to normalise the Russo-Japanese ties made in 2013, the Japanese leader offered to Moscow a prospective bilateral cooperation in CA border control in light of the withdrawal of International Security Assistance Force (ISAF) that was at the time scheduled for 2014. Bringing Russia, CA's former imperial metropolis, into the relationship between Japan and CA, by a Japanese leader, was unprecedented and struck a contrast with Koizumi's and

From New Great Games to New Silk Roads   5

Abe's own policies a decade earlier. Furthermore, although Abe's trip to CA was interpreted by the media as another Japanese balancing act vis-à-vis China, during the prime minister's tenure, Tokyo made several attempts at a rapprochement with Beijing. So what are the motivations behind Japan's engagement with CA?

I seek to clarify whether, after a strong start in the 1990s, Japan–CA relations had 'run out of gas' in the late 2000s or remained intentionally dormant under a stage of laying groundwork (*nemawashi*), only to resurface at a time considered opportune by both parties.[13] In providing reasons for observed developments, my answer to the questions above both emphasises the structural role of the changing external environment and showcases individual and group agency by unpacking the 'black box' of Japanese foreign-policy making from inside. The thematic structure is fivefold in accordance with the main aspects of the relationship: the evolution of Japanese diplomatic strategy per se, its dependence on domestic partisan and bureaucratic politics in Japan and CA, Japanese development finance in the region, CA natural resources, and, connectivity infrastructure more specifically. More particularly, I argue that:

1. Japanese foreign policy in CA has oscillated, displaying both proactivity and reactivity, the degree of which was a function of the actions of the key three Japanese ministries and the macroeconomic and geopolitical climate rather than as a result of external pressure from another country.
2. Although the proactivity of Japanese foreign policy in CA depended on party politics in Japan, as witnessed by changes under the DPJ and bureaucratic continuities, these changes were due not so much to differences in the parties' ideologies as to lack of experience in foreign policy, intra-party factionalism, and external environment.
3. The autonomous agency and neo-patrimonialist domestic politics of CA states, in particular Uzbekistan, driven by the motivations of regime survival and multi-lateralism at times contributed to the relationship's stagnation and pragmatisation.
4. Development and infrastructure finance as well as the personal commitment of administrators at the Ministry of Finance were more important drivers of the overall policy than previously assumed and expanded the relationship beyond simple donor-recipient structure.
5. Conversely, structural factors mattered more than the personal actions of individual politicians or bureaucrats to the attractiveness of CA's natural resources for Japan, which was largely a function of relations with Russia and China, of cyclic macroeconomic junctures such as the 1990s cheap oil era, the 2000–15 commodity boom which finally ended with a drop in commodity prices in 2015, and, to a smaller extent, a 'black swan' event, such as the Fukushima nuclear incident.

The strategic character of Japanese Silk Road diplomacy has been often questioned by both Western and Japanese scholars, but less so by their CA colleagues.[14] Japanese strategy towards CA has been characterised by former diplomats and

6 *From New Great Games to New Silk Roads*

scholars as 'on-and-off diplomacy,' or 'colourless diplomacy,' either as a result of intentional choices made by Japanese policy-makers or due to structural specifics and the bureaucratic impediments of Japanese policy-making.[15]

What distinguishes CA from East Asian countries is the absence of a post-World War II legacy vis-à-vis Japan. On the contrary, the CA public and elites tend to have a consistently positive attitude towards Japan, as well as a shared concern over a rising China. Japan's soft power in the region has been consistently strong, alongside with its developmental credentials and promotion of human ties: in 1992–2017, Japan sent 2587 specialists to CA and trained 9668 interns from CA in various fields, many of whom went on to hold high-ranking government offices.[16] And yet one can hardly characterise the relationship between Japan and the region as an alliance, or even a partnership. Viewing CA thus as either 'low-hanging fruit' for Japan from the realist perspective or as a natural partner from the idealist mercantile perspective, the scholars of international relations may ask the question: does Japan as a major Asian power fail to maximise its influence in CA where it may naturally do so, and if so, why? Is the Japanese policy of 'punching below its weight' a premeditated action, inertia, a result of pressure, or presumably a structurally or culturally determined feature of Japanese foreign policy in general?[17] The case studies of this book also attempt to draw wider conclusions about Japanese foreign policy in general, especially under the Abe cabinets.

In my argument, I test a working hypothesis according to which, throughout Japan's recent two-decade history of involvement in CA (1991–2017), different and competing constituencies of Japanese officials have oscillated between proactive and reactive courses of action. They adapted to changing macroeconomic and geopolitical contexts, occasionally displaying both assertiveness and anticipation.[18]

In order to metaphorically nuance this kind of oscillation, I utilise the term 'damping' borrowed from physics. In physics, damping stands for a decreasing of a wave's amplitude, or, in other words, an influence within an oscillatory system that has the effect of reducing, restricting, or preventing its oscillations. The presence of such 'damping' would imply less oscillation and a firmer course of action. For instance, Abe's second premiership (2012–present) demonstrates how this oscillation or change of attitude towards CA took place even within a single government term and evolved towards a straightforward proactivity. In my view, the second decade of the observed period, that is, 2005–14, was marked by alternation with either decreasing or plateauing involvement due to structural reasons both inside Japan and CA.

Consequently, the more specific issue this book addresses is what kind of oscillation occurred in Japanese Silk Road diplomacy: oscillation between proactivity and reactivity or also between other policy options? What explains its causation and the 'damping' effect? What stimulated a firmer course of action?

I highlight the combination of both internal and external causes. Personal factors, lack of inter-agency coordination, and inertia inside Japanese bureaucratic politics were accompanied and reinforced by independent variables,

From New Great Games to New Silk Roads 7

such as the external macroeconomic context and the multi-vector foreign policies of CA regimes, whose shifting priorities and demands shaped Japanese involvement.

Multi-vectorism is a recurrent term used by numerous scholars of CA to characterise the foreign policies of the region's states that are balancing between the interests of larger players without aligning too closely with any of them.[19] It can be viewed as a brand of multi-lateralism or multi-alignment and was disputed by some Japanese scholars.[20] In this book, I use the term 'multi-vectorism' for three reasons. Firstly, multi-vectorism has solidified its use in the official and academic discourse of post-Soviet countries and, for that reason, the representatives of the region often literally translate it into English from Russian *mnogovektornost'* (for instance, see the work by Anuar Ayazbekov).[21] Secondly, multi-vectorism in the case of CA refers to a particular type of multi-lateralism, where the region's states pursue so-called multi-vector diplomacies towards external great powers in order to diversify their dependency on them, but often remain bilateral and almost anti-multi-lateral in dealings between each other due to strained intra-regional relations. Finally, as multi-vectorism stresses the direction of vectors, it also highlights the autonomous agency of CA.

Clarifying Central Asia's geography

The term 'Central Asia' is somewhat ambiguous, since its current administrative borders are a Soviet geographic legacy, and the region is still 'in the making' and susceptible to change.[22] By modern convention, 'CA' refers to five post-Soviet countries between the Caspian Sea and China's western border: Kazakhstan, Kyrgyzstan, Tajikistan, Turkmenistan, and Uzbekistan. By the 'Silk Road region,' officially, Tokyo initially designated the newly independent states of not only CA, but also the Caucasus, referring to their historic involvement in the Silk Road trade.[23]

In contemporary business language focusing on the geography of Caspian oil and gas operations and littoral states hosting those operations, Azerbaijan is sometimes added to Central Asia despite being formally in Caucasus – this is perhaps due to rich resource endowment, a similar political regime, and a shared Turco-Persian cultural heritage. The Japanese scholars of the area are increasingly using such terms as Central Eurasia and Slavic Eurasia, splitting the Eurasian mainland into two sub-spaces with different language groups.[24] Central Eurasia thus includes not only the aforementioned five 'Stans' of Central Asia, but also Afghanistan, Azerbaijan, China, Iran, Mongolia, Pakistan, and Turkic-speaking territories of Russia (Table I.1).

The nuances of Japanese foreign policy in this developing region reflected the latter's geographic ambiguity. On the one hand, official diplomacy dealt with newly independent states within given borders. On the other hand, multi-lateral projects with indirect Japanese participation (such as the Asian Development Bank (ADB)-led Central Asian Regional Economic Cooperation involving Xinjiang and Afghanistan), region-wide initiatives (such as 'Central Asia plus Japan'),

Table I.1 Selected key data on CA states (2018)

Country	Kazakhstan	Kyrgyzstan	Tajikistan	Turkmenistan	Uzbekistan
GDP, current $ billion	164.3	8.0	7.5	42.4	49.7
Population, million	18.2	6.3	9.1	5.8	32.9
Area, km²	2,724,900	199,951	143,100	488,100	447,400
Dominant mineral resources	Oil & gas, metals	Metals	Metals	Oil & gas	Oil & gas, metals
Trans-border river position	Downstream	Upstream	Upstream	Downstream	Downstream
Commentary on strategic aspects and location vis-à-vis external powers.	Largest area in the region; a Caspian littoral state.	A Ferghana Valley state.	A Ferghana Valley state.	A Caspian littoral state.	Largest population and military in the region; a Ferghana Valley state.

Source: World Bank.

From New Great Games to New Silk Roads 9

and less formal interactions located in these states in various cross-regional and multi-lateral contexts going beyond formal administrative boundaries are also happening.

The internal classification of CA states inside the Japanese government varies depending on the institution involved, reflecting their ambiguous place on Japan's foreign policy agenda. They are part of Europe in the organigrams of the Japanese Ministry of Foreign Affairs (MOFA) and the Japanese Bank for International Cooperation, but the Japanese International Cooperation Agency (JICA) places them under the East and Central Asia and Caucasus Department, thus distinguishing them from Eastern European aid recipients in transition. The Ministry of Finance's (MOF) and the Ministry of Economy, Trade, and Industry's (METI) dealings with CA are sector-based – through, respectively, the International Bureau's Development Institutions Division and Trade Policy Bureau's Russia, CA, and Caucasus Division. MOF-affiliated Japanese officials at the European Bank for Reconstruction and Development (EBRD) occasionally use the term 'Silk Road.'[25] The ADB, where Japan's role is paramount, places the region within the Central and West Asia Department.

In this work, the terms 'Central Asia' and 'Silk Road Countries' are synonymous and designate five former Soviet republics: Kazakhstan, Kyrgyzstan, Tajikistan, Turkmenistan, and Uzbekistan. At the same time, I draw particular attention to Kazakhstan and Uzbekistan, occasionally adding Azerbaijan into the mix.

The rationale for this focus is threefold. Firstly, on top of rich natural resources, Kazakhstan and Uzbekistan, as well as Azerbaijan, harbour their own regional leadership ambitions and pursue active foreign policies. It distinguishes them from Kyrgyzstan and Tajikistan, which experienced higher levels of domestic turmoil and at times have teetered on the brink of being failed states, as well as from Turkmenistan that has been maintaining strict non-aligning neutrality verging on isolationism. Secondly, the three selected countries are among the key geostrategic and economic partners of the United States in the region.[26] Thirdly, throughout Japanese involvement in CA, these countries attracted the highest amount of either cumulative Japanese aid (Kazakhstan and Uzbekistan represent circa 77 percent of all aid to CA) or Japanese investment (Inpex and Itochu's Caspian projects in Azerbaijan and Kazakhstan).[27]

Why Central Asia?

The geostrategic significance of Central Asia has been widely acknowledged throughout its history, including the post-Cold War period. Prominent United States (U.S.) foreign policy thinker Zbigniew Brzezinski referred to CA and the Caucasus as the 'Eurasian Balkans' in his oft-quoted work *The Grand Chessboard*.[28] Brzezinski made a historical parallel with the Balkan peninsula of the early twentieth century, an area in which conflict and resource potential did not only bring about the rivalry of major powers, but also sparked the global armed conflict of World War I. While this approach is an example of the New

10 *From New Great Games to New Silk Roads*

Great Game discourse and invites a critical reception, it nonetheless grasps the widespread external risk-averse perception of CA.

Countries of the region, namely, Kazakhstan, Kyrgyzstan, Tajikistan, Turkmenistan, and Uzbekistan, are characterised by authoritarian regimes, plentiful natural resources, and political risks.[29] The degree of instability varied from post-civil war failed state reconstruction (Tajikistan in the past) to minor Islamist threat (Uzbekistan, Kyrgyzstan). 'The Eurasian Balkans' are sandwiched between major regional powers (China, Iran, and Russia) and other turbulent countries (Afghanistan, Pakistan, and the People's Republic of China's (PRC's) Xinjiang-Uighur Autonomous Region), together with which they are sometimes referred to as 'Arc of Instability.'[30]

Internally, cooperation between these post-Soviet countries is hindered by intra-regional disputes, such as international borders in the Ferghana Valley and access to water resources. Externally, the power vacuum created by the Union of Soviet Socialist Republics (USSR) collapse in 1991 is viewed by a number of researchers as encouraging potential rivalry between China, Russia, and the United States in this strategic region, especially since the start of the 'war on terror' in 2001 and the rise of the Shanghai Cooperation Organisation.[31] Certain 'middle powers,' such as Turkey, Iran, Israel, and South Korea, have also been active in their CA diplomacy since 1991.[32]

Most recently, during his visit to Kazakhstan in September 2013, the PRC President Xi Jinping announced the initiative of the Silk Road Economic Belt, where CA would be a major piece.[33] As this research will show, Xi's grand design exhibited several commonalities, as well as differences, with Japan's earlier New Silk Road involvement. Moreover, Abe Shinzō's 2015 plans to compete with China for Asian infrastructure projects included CA as well, although Southeast Asia and South Asia were the main 'theatre' of infrastructure rivalry.

Initially, Japanese officials regarded CA as 'merely a backward part of Russia.'[34] Yet, the 'Silk Road Countries,' as categorised by Japanese official discourse, have gradually increased their weight in Japan's international agenda.[35] 'The Stans,' as they are also sometimes informally called, may not always appear a top priority for Japanese diplomacy, as at times the region warranted a mere two paragraphs in the MOFA's Diplomatic Bluebook. Nonetheless, its significance is conditioned by CA's paramount importance to Eurasian security and its abundant natural resources, Tokyo's increasingly proactive role in Asian affairs, and its profound involvement in financial aid programmes.[36] Japan's stable position among the top three official development assistance (ODA) donors of CA countries, held since 1998,[37] and especially Japan's proactive promotion of CA's eligibility to multi-lateral financing were among the major indicators of Tokyo's growing attentiveness to this emerging region in need of large-scale investment.

Nevertheless, Japan's security involvement in Afghanistan (2001–9) and to a lesser extent Tajikistan showed that the mercantile and aid facets of Japan's policy towards the region are not the only facets, despite their relative dominance.[38] Another indicator of the surging significance of relations between Japan and CA was the evolution of their institutionalisation. Over the past 16 years, it has developed from individual bilateral contacts in the 1990s via the 'Silk Road diplomacy' concept of 1997–9 fostered by Prime Ministers Hashimoto Ryūtarō and Obuchi Keizō, to the 'Central Asia Plus Japan' framework (2004–present). The latter was launched by Foreign Minister Kawaguchi Yoriko and featured regular multi-lateral meetings of senior officials as well as civil society representatives.[39]

Why Japanese Silk Road diplomacy?

Japan became one of the first states outside CA to use the concept of Silk Road in its formal diplomatic rhetoric in 1997–8, predating similar ideas in the United States and PRC. Ex-Soviet CA countries became a new frontier in Japan's Asian diplomacy.[40] One of the earliest post-Cold War era mentions of the New Great Game and the Silk Road in the context of CA politics includes a reference to Japan's commercial interests.[41] Following their independence from the USSR in 1991, Japan has gradually achieved the rank of their top donor and developed a unique relationship, very different to both Japan's ties with other Asian countries and to CA's interactions with other major powers, such as Russia, China, or the United States. Japan contributed greatly to the strengthening of the newly independent states' international status, acting de facto as a referee 'club member' for the several international institutions it was a member of. By the late 1990s, Japan was arguably the first country to introduce the now popular Silk Road cliché into its official diplomatic discourse. In 1997, Prime Minister – and former Finance Minister with past EBRD involvement – Hashimoto Ryūtarō called for 'a Eurasian diplomacy,' involving the 'Silk Road countries' of CA.[42] This initiative predated the 'Silk Road Strategy Act of 1999' of the United States and highlights the underappreciated proactivity of Japanese foreign policy.[43]

Furthermore, Japan applied its projected commonality with CA to the elaboration of a long-term vision for this region's development.[44] This vision manifested not only bilaterally, but also in such multi-lateral projects as CAREC launched by the Asian Development Bank simultaneously with Hashimoto's Eurasian diplomacy.[45]

In the meantime, while the first decade of the relationship's history (between the mid-1990s and mid-2000s) was marked by clear growth trends and achieved institutionalisation, its second decade showed symptoms of inertia and saturation. The special nature of this relationship, hailed as disinterested and non-conflictual, has been acknowledged both in Japan and in CA. However, its institutionalisation in the mid-2000s through the establishment of the Central Asia plus Japan framework occurred simultaneously with a certain plateau. This downward trend can be exemplified by lower aid disbursement in 2005–10, despite Japan's earlier top donor status, by stagnation in the attentiveness of Japanese senior officials, and by the absence of visits by Japanese prime ministers between 2006 and 2015.

According to some Japanese experts, the lows in Abe's attention to CA in 2012–15 resulted from frequent delays by the Japanese bureaucrats, despite the active push in favour of closer ties with the region made by individual Diet

12 *From New Great Games to New Silk Roads*

members since Abe's return to power in 2012.[46] Yet, in the mid-2000s and earlier, the situation was different. Moreover, arguments stating that CA lost its past allure for Japan may be countered with considerations that Japan is continuing routine cooperation with CA, including day-to-day running of the existing institutional frameworks, and perhaps the lack of strategy is intentional. Tokyo could thus be simply keeping a deliberately low-key profile in foreign affairs, as part of a 'Goldilocks consensus' grand strategy, described by Richard Samuels, that is 'not too hard but not too soft, not too Asian and not too Western.'[47] What merits a separate inquiry is therefore the question of whether there was indeed a change in Japan's approach to CA and an evaporation of enthusiasm in the relationship, or whether the absence of dramatic progress is optimal in a routine conduct of affairs – an equilibrium that can only be altered for the worse.

Methodology

One of the contributions this study makes is the introduction of findings based on a large corpus of interviews with more than 40 respondents including middle- and senior-level Japanese officials, as well as their CA counterparts. The ranking of respondents varied from line managers to former and incumbent ambassadors, ministers, senators, and vice presidents. The selection criterion for most of them, besides availability for interviewing, was the possession of first-hand ground experience of Japanese government or corporate activities in the region. One exception was a representative of the Ministry of Economy, Trade, and Industry, who did not have a specialised background relevant for CA, despite serving in the respective department. Whilst the interviews were in-depth and addressed a largely identical set of questions with slight variations depending on the field and background of each respondent, it was decided not to rely on a single questionnaire. This choice was made in order not to affect the respondents' willingness to participate, given the time pressure of one-hour slots allocated within their daily routines of incumbent officials.

I corroborate the interview results with secondary sources available on the matter in various languages, namely, English, French, Japanese, and Russian, including written first-person accounts and memoirs, as well as primary sources such as statistics, official speeches, and internal institutional documents kindly provided by some of the respondents.

Chapter outline

This research addresses five key topics in five respective chapters. Chapter one lays out an overview of Japanese foreign policy in post-Soviet Central Asia (especially, Kazakhstan and Uzbekistan) from the viewpoint of diplomatic history, identifying key policy constituencies and principal spheres of interaction. It concentrates on critical junctures for Japanese involvement throughout the past two decades with a particular emphasis on the Koizumi period and subsequent LDP premierships, contextualising Tokyo's CA diplomacy within relations with Washington, Beijing, and Moscow. Its objective is to trace the evolution of the link between Japan's CA involvement and other key relationships under the LDP cabinets. The overarching question this chapter poses is whether CA was an opportunity for the Japanese political elites to maximise their power abroad at low cost or not and whether these actors seized this opportunity. I also show here that strong autonomous agency, multi-vector manoeuvring, and rent-seeking dynamics of CA states shaped their ties with Japan, highlighting an evolution in their diplomatic priorities and challenging the recurrent misperception of them as objectified 'pawns' in the New Great Game.

Chapter two looks into the partisan dimension of Japanese foreign policy-making. Here, I examine the impact made by the cabinets of the Democratic Party of Japan in 2009–12 on the course of Japanese foreign policy vis-à-vis Central Asia as compared to their Liberal Democratic Party predecessors and successors. I discuss personal and factional factors and changes in foreign policy priorities, thus explaining Tokyo's inertia and Central Asia's lower priority on the DPJ governments' diplomatic agenda.

Chapter three on financial aid suggests that the contribution from Ministry of Finance officials to overall relationship development, especially in 1992–2005, has been greater than traditionally depicted by existing scholarship. Emphasising Japan's role as a concessional lender in the NSR, this chapter also analyses the geopolitical implications of several multi-lateral infrastructure projects in the region sponsored by Japan, arguing that they were highly likely to be among the key prototypes of China's Belt and Road. The third chapter looks in detail at Japanese development finance in CA and into the agency of non-diplomatic Japanese officials who served as drivers behind the relationship, most notably those affiliated with the MOF and other financial institutions, both Japanese (JICA, Japanese Bank for International Cooperation) and international (ADB, EBRD, the World Bank). Its aims are: (i) to demonstrate the strategic contributions that are overlooked when Japanese Silk Road diplomacy is analysed strictly from the perspective of the MOFA and (ii) to provide a partial explanation of the lull in the relationship in the late 2000s. In other words, this chapter answers the question: what role did Japanese financial bureaucrats play in Tokyo's CA policy, and how did they influence the evolution of the diplomacy as a whole? I argue that Japanese aid became a key factor in driving the overall relationship and rendering it partially inert in 2006–9. Japan's aid to CA started as proactive assistance in the early 1990s, largely driven by the MOF officials who provided developmental advice; became instrumentalised in the late 1990s as Japanese Eurasian diplomacy unfolded; and switched its rationale in the post-9/11 era as Japan's burden sharing with the United States increased, thus outweighing securing natural resources as the reason for Japanese involvement in the region. To engage in counterfactual history, one could provocatively claim that the absence of aid as a driver of this relationship would result in an overall lower profile of the latter for both sides. Furthermore, to the extent that the Japanese aid relationship with CA was modelled on its earlier involvement in Southeast Asia in terms of neutralising China's appeal in the region, this approach was sustainable for Japan only until the mid-2000s for financial, geopolitical, and personal reasons.

14 *From New Great Games to New Silk Roads*

Chapter four analyses the international political economy of natural resources relevant to Japanese interests in CA – oil and gas, rare metals, and uranium – and the overall commercial attractiveness of CA from the perspective of Japanese businesses with regional exposure. This chapter problematises CA's natural resources and economic attractiveness for the Japanese government and Japanese companies and examines the cyclical factors relevant to CA commodities. It unveils a divergence of strategic approaches among individual Japanese corporates choosing between forward-looking and risk aversion, anticipation and adaptation, and, in certain cases, a shift between those strategies. The first part of Chapter four focuses on the oil and gas sector, revealing the predominance of anticipatory behaviour. Its second part examines the uranium and rare earths mining sector, revealing the predominance of adaptation over anticipation.

This analysis places the Japanese resource strategy in the region against the background of critical junctures that occurred in the global commodity markets throughout the past two decades and shaped the policies of CA countries. I emphasise the role of the external economic environment in shaping Japan's relationship with CA. The objective of this chapter is also to add the perspectives of Japanese corporate officials and trade representatives with experience in CA to the academic database on the subject. This chapter debates the significance of CA natural resources for Japan, which, I believe, tends often to be exaggerated in the existing scholarship as rationale for Japanese regional involvement.[48] This exaggeration was pointed out in existing scholarship by Uyama Tomohiko, who highlighted the prevalence of the MOFA and MOF over the METI in the relationship with CA.[49] Nonetheless, since this criticism stemmed mostly from a MOFA-centred vision and lacked an international political economy perspective and deeper cross-checking with the METI officials, I further unpack and refine this view. In particular, I outline the roles of the METI and METI-related agencies, namely, Japan Oil, Gas and Metals National Corporation (JOGMEC) and its predecessor Japan National Oil Corporation (JNOC), which were more pronounced in Caspian energy projects and Kazakh uranium as opposed to wider CA affairs.

Chapter five examines the policy of mixed signals regarding the Belt and Road Initiative and the Asian Infrastructure Investment Bank that Japanese senior officials including Prime Minister Abe have been pursuing since 2015. The Japanese government frequently alternated readiness to cooperate with more confrontational stances, arguably rather by design than by miscalculation. This chapter explores whether Japan competes or cooperates with China in financing Asian infrastructure and promoting regional connectivity projects in the NSR – various transit sub-regions of Eurasia, Asia, and even Africa. It also addresses concepts that best describe Japan's behaviour in that field: balancing, engagement, hedging, mercantilism, reactivity, and proactivity.

Finally, I append a conclusion which reviews the findings of the book and explores contemporary and future policy implications, as well as areas for future research.

From New Great Games to New Silk Roads   15

Notes

1 Further scholarship on the discursive aspects of the New Silk Road and New Great Game: Timur Dadabaev, 'Discourses of Rivalry or Rivalry of Discourses: Discursive Strategies and Framing of Chinese and Japanese Foreign Policies in Central Asia,' *The Pacific Review* 2018: 1–35.

2 'Weighing Abe's Asian Diplomacy,' *The Japan Times*, 4 December 2014, http://www.japantimes.co.jp/opinion/2014/12/04/editorials/weighing-abes-asian-diplomacy (Accessed 1 February 2015). In 2014–15, Shingetsu News Agency reported August 2014 and August 2015 as planned dates for CA visit. '"Central Asia Plus Japan" meeting to be held in Kyrgyz in July; PM Abe mulling tour of Central Asia in August,' *Shingetsu News Agency*, 18 June 2014, https://www.facebook.com/permalink.php?story_fbid=671755912879233&id=118721134849383 (Accessed 10 May 2015) and 'PM Abe Planning Tour of Five Central Asian Countries in Late August: First Since Koizumi's 2006 Tour of Region,' *Shingetsu News Agency*, 12 April 2015, https://www.facebook.com/permalink.php?story_fbid=809864095735080&id=118721134849383 (Accessed 10 May 2015).

3 Abe's first premiership dates: September 2006–September 2007. Details on two-way official visits between Japan and Central Asia, https://www.mofa.go.jp/region/europe/index.html.

4 Private communication with former Japanese diplomat who quoted the cabinet's responses to regular questions about the visit from interested parties in the Diet and other segments of Japanese politics.

5 The Silk Road Fund is one of the financial vehicles established in 2014 for funding the BRI. Its initial announced capital was $40 billion with $16 billion penned for continental projects (Silk Road Economic Belt, as opposed to Maritime Silk Road). CAREC stands for Central Asian Regional Economic Cooperation and is a multi-lateral ADB program founded in 1996 and encompassing projects worth over $34.5 billion as of 2019.

6 Traditionally, Japan's key foreign policy priorities focused on its relations with the United States, PRC, ROK, Southeast Asia, the European Union, and Russia.

7 Interviews with former officials of the MOF and MOFA, Tokyo, January 2012.

8 Shingetsu News Agency, 5 May 2015 and 21 May 2015, https://www.facebook.com/permalink.php?story_fbid=826166017438221&id=118721134849383; https://www.facebook.com/permalink.php?story_fbid=820055578049265&id=118721134849383 (Accessed 10 June 2015).

9 Nikolay Murashkin, 'China, Russia and the New Great Game in Central Asia,' *Russia Direct*, 18 October 2013, http://www.russia-direct.org/content/china-russia-and-new-great-game-central-asia (Accessed 10 February 2014).

10 Yachi served as vice foreign minister in 2005–8, became Abe's diplomatic strategist during his first premiership, and resumed this quality as special advisor to the cabinet upon Abe's return to power in 2012. Moreover, Yachi went on to become national security advisor and the secretary general of the national security secretariat established on 7 January 2013. A career diplomat and former head of the MOFA's European affairs department, Kanehara was appointed assistant deputy chief cabinet secretary during Abe's second premiership and became one of two deputy secretary generals of the National Security Secretariat (NSS), the other one being Takamizawa Nobushige from the Ministry of Defense. A thorough account of the NSS structure and purpose is provided in Yuichi Hosoya, 'The Role of Japan's National Security Council,' *AJISS-Commentary* No. 199, 17 June 2013.

11 With the exception of the state visit of the Turkmen President Gurbanguly Berdymukhamedov to Japan in 2013.

12 Author's field interviews in Japan and CA with representatives from the MOF, MOFA, METI, and several Japanese companies. The involvement of each of these officials is

16   *From New Great Games to New Silk Roads*

detailed in relevant chapters of this book. While the posts of Kuroda (head of Bank of Japan) and Amari (minister in charge of economic revival) in the 2012 Abe cabinet are not directly related to CA affairs, both officials have had a notable involvement with the region. Kuroda served as head of the ADB, while Amari in his tenure as head of the METI led a Japanese mission to CA in 2007 with the focus on developing further cooperation in the field of rare earths and uranium. Yachi, alongside Kanehara Nobukatsu, is usually credited with the design of the Arc of Freedom and Prosperity (AFP), a Japanese foreign policy concept involving CA and publicised by Asō Tarō in Abe's premiership. Asō's relation to CA does not limit itself to the AFP, as he visited CA in the late 1990s while being a head of the Economic Planning Agency during the post-Hashimoto Eurasian diplomacy in the Silk Road region.

13 *Nemawashi* is a Japanese term of organisational culture, referring to a lengthy process of laying groundwork and preparatory activities prior to making major decisions and striking cooperative agreements. 'Japan's Silk Road Diplomacy: Paving the Road Ahead,' the title of the first edited volume on Japanese diplomacy in CA (Len et al. 2008), expresses a similar idea, albeit without expressly stated intention.

14 Reinhard Drifte, 'Japan's Eurasian Diplomacy: Power Politics, Resource Diplomacy or Romanticism?' In *The Caspian: Politics, Energy and Security*, ed. Shirin Akiner (London: RoutledgeCurzon, 2004), 252–68; Tomohiko Uyama, 'Japanese Policies in Relation to Kazakhstan: Is There a "Strategy"?' in *Thinking Strategically: The Major Powers, Kazakhstan, and the Central Asian Nexus*, ed. Robert Legvold (Cambridge, MA: American Academy of Arts and Sciences MIT Press, 2003), Esen Usubaliev, 'Politika Yaponii v Tsentralnoii Azii – geopoliticheskii aspekt' [Japanese policy in Central Asia – a geopolitical aspect]. *East Time*, 4 April 2007; http://easttime.ru/analitic/3/9/150. html (Accessed 27 April 2010); and Akio Kawato, 'Japan's Strategic Thinking toward Central Asia,' in *Japanese Strategic thought Toward Asia*. eds. Rozman, Gilbert, Tōgō Kazuhiko, and Joseph P. Ferguson (New York: Palgrave MacMillan, 2007).

15 The term 'on-and-off diplomacy' was used by Kawatō Akio in 2008, while that of 'colourless diplomacy' was used by Iwashita Akihiro of Hokkaido University (interview in February 2012).

16 Fumio Kishida, 'Kazakhstan, Japan mark 25 years of diplomatic relations,' *Kazinform*, 30 April 2017, http://lenta.inform.kz/en/kazakhstan-japan-mark-25-years-of-diplomatic-relations_a3021924 (Accessed 30 August 2019).

17 See 'Kajō na senryakuron ni ochiiru na. Chūō ajia wo meguru kokusai seiji to nihon gaikō' [Not falling for excessive strategising. International politics concerning Central Asia and Japan's diplomacy], *Gaikō Forum* (June 2009): 22–31.

18 This point is congenial with Kenneth Pyle's findings in *Japan Rising: The Resurgence of Japanese Power and Purpose* (New York: PublicAffairs, 2007) and those of Richard Samuels in *Securing Japan: Tokyo's Grand Strategy and the Future of East Asia* (Cornell, 2007). The influence of domestic political and structural constraints on foreign policy-making as well as the phenomenon of reactivity is explained by Kent Calder in 'Japanese Foreign Economic Policy Formation: Explaining the Reactive State,' *World Politics*, 40, no. 4 (1988): 517–41.

19 Murat Laumulin and Farkhod Tolipov, 'Uzbekistan i Kazakhstan: Bor'ba za liderstvo?' [Uzbekistan and Kazakhstan: a struggle for leadership?], *Security Index* 1 (2010): 105–28.

20 'Tomohiko Uyama: diplomatiyu Kazakhstana mozhno nazvat' mnogovektornoy tol'ko uslovno' [Tomohiko Uyama: Kazakhstan's diplomacy can be called multivectored only conditionally], *Sayasat*, 16 June 2016, http://sayasat.org/articles/1646-tomohiko-ujama-djiplomatiju-kazahstana-mozhno-nazvat-mnogovektornoj-tolko-uslovno (Accessed 16 June 2016).

21 'Independent Kazakhstan and the "black box" of decision-making: understanding Kazakhstan's foreign policy in the early independence period (1991–4)', University of St. Andrews (United Kingdom), ProQuest Dissertations Publishing, 2014. U640181.

22 Andrey Kazantsev, *Bol'shaya igra s neizvestnymi pravilami: mirovaya politika i Tsentralnaya Aziya* [The Great Game with unknown rules: world politics and Central Asia], Moscow: MGIMO University, 2008, 43.

23 Address by Prime Minister Hashimoto Ryūtarō to the Japan Association of Corporate Executives, 24 July 1997, http://japan.kantei.go.jp/0731douyukai.html (Accessed 28 March 2014); *9.11 jiken kara 1 nen. Chūō ajia kara sekai to rekishi wo yomitoku* [One year from 9/11. Figuring out the world and history from Central Asia]. Symposium proceedings. Tokyo: NPO Japan-Uzbekistan Society, 2002, 10.

24 Hokkaido Central Eurasia Research Association, http://src-h.slav.hokudai.ac.jp/casia/ (Accessed 28 May 2015).

25 Address by Vice Minister of Finance Ishii at the 13th Annual EBRD Session, 19 April 2004.

26 U.S. commercial interests have largely been focused on the Caspian hydrocarbons of Azerbaijan and Kazakhstan.

27 ODA white paper (2011); INPEX website, business in Eurasia (Europe & NIS), http://www.inpex.co.jp/english/business/nis.html (accessed 2 April 2014). Following Abe's 2015 visit, the investment distribution may change in favour of Turkmenistan if the financial commitments Abe announced during the trip become factual.

28 Zbigniew Brzezinski, *The Grand Chessboard: American Primacy and Its Geostrategic Imperatives* (New York: Basic Books, 1997).

29 Most notably, hydrocarbons in Caspian states – Azerbaijan, Kazakhstan, Turkmenistan – and, to a lesser extent, natural gas in Uzbekistan; uranium ores, precious and rare metals mostly in Kazakhstan and Uzbekistan.

30 The term 'Arc of Instability' was introduced in the 1970s in the United States, initially referring to Afghanistan and the Muslim republics of the Soviet Union, subsequently enlarged in the 2000s to a group of unstable countries or 'failed states' spanning from Africa through the Middle East to CA.

31 Kazantsev, *Bol'shaya igra s neizvestnymi pravilami: mirovaya politika i Tsentralnaya Aziya*; Shirin Akiner, ed., *The Caspian: Politics, Energy and Security* (London: RoutledgeCurzon, 2004); Mark Burles, 'Chinese Policy Toward Russia and the Central Asian Republics,' RAND, 1999, http://www.rand.org/content/dam/rand/pubs/monograph_reports/2007/MR1045.pdf (Accessed 25 March 2014).

32 By 'middle powers' the theory of international relations designates the countries that are not great powers, but can still wield moderate influence on the international scene and have an international recognition. In relation to Japan, the term was initially used by Soeya Yoshihide, who advocated a need for middle-power diplomacy as a new autonomous grand strategy for Japan. See Soeya Yoshihide, Tadokoro Masayuki, and David A. Welch, eds. *Japan as a 'Normal Country'? A Nation in Search of Its Place in the World* (Toronto: University of Toronto Press, 2011); William T. Tow, Mark J. Thomson, Yamamoto Yoshinobu, and Satu P. Limaye, eds., *Asia-Pacific Security. US, Australia and Japan and the New Security Triangle* (London: Routledge, 2007), Aihara Kiyoshi, 'Japan's Middle-Power Diplomacy,' The Tokyo Foundation, 13 January 2009, http://www.tokyofoundation.org/en/articles/2008/japans-middle-power-diplomacy (Accessed 30 April 2010). Numerous authors have examined the growing involvement of Middle Eastern and East Asian countries in CA, for instance, see monographs by Andrey Kazantsev (2008), Madeleine Laruelle and Sébastien Peyrouse (2010).

33 'Xi suggests China, C. Asia build Silk Road economic belt,' *Xinhua*, 7 September 2013, http://news.xinhuanet.com/english/china/2013-09/07/c_132700695.htm (Accessed 30 September 2013).

34 Kawatō Akio, 'Japan's strategic thinking toward Central Asia,' in *Japanese Strategic Thought toward Asia*, eds. Gilbert Rozman et al. (New York: Palgrave, 2007), 228, 233.

18   *From New Great Games to New Silk Roads*

35 By the 'Silk Road region' officially Tokyo (for instance, in Prime Minister Hashimoto Ryūtarō's Eurasian diplomacy speech) designated the Newly Independent States of Caucasus and CA, referring to their historic involvement in the Silk Road trade. Whilst this meaning of the term was retained in irregular usage by some Japanese officials, gradually, it was narrowed down to CA only, as the countries of South Caucasus strengthened ties with Europe.

36 Over $3.6 billion in 1993–2013, both on bilateral and multi-lateral bases. Source: JICA ODA White Papers.

37 The scale of the ODA provided followed the same year-on-year evolution as the overall Japanese ODA, with notable exception of a major increase in assistance to Kazakhstan and Uzbekistan in 2003–4, on the eve of the establishment of 'Central Asia Plus Japan' framework. Source: Japan's ODA data by country. Central Asia and Caucasus, http://www.mofa.go.jp/policy/oda/data/03ap_ca01.html (Accessed 25 April 2010).

38 Japan's Maritime Self-Defense Force has conducted refuelling support to vessels engaged in the Maritime Interdiction Operations of Operation 'Enduring Freedom' in the Indian Ocean. Besides, by 2009 Japan had committed assistance of $2 billion and had implemented $1.46 billion in humanitarian assistance, political process, security, human resource development, and economic infrastructure. The refuelling mission was ended in late 2009, following the DPJ's advent to the power. In return, Japan increased its aid to Afghanistan by $5 billion. In Tajikistan, Japan provided emergency assistance, employment creation and vocational training, and missions of election observers.

39 Central Asia Plus Japan dialogue, http://www.mofa.go.jp/region/europe/dialogue/index.html (Accessed 25/4/10).

40 Timur Dadabaev, 'Central Asia: Japan's New "Old" Frontier,' Asia Pacific Issues, No. 136, pp. 1–12, February 2019.

41 'The New Great Game in Asia.' *New York Times*, 2 January 1996, http://www.nytimes.com/1996/01/02/opinion/the-new-great-game-in-asia.html (Accessed 17 March 2014).

42 Address by Prime Minister Hashimoto Ryūtarō to the Japan Association of Corporate Executives, 24 July 1997, http://japan.kantei.go.jp/0731douyukai.html (accessed 28 March 2014).

43 An amendment to the U.S. Foreign Assistance Act of 1961. Quoted from: Shirin Akiner, Rovshan Ibrahimov and Ariz Huseynov, 'Interregional Cooperation in Eurasia,' *SAM Review*, Special Double Issue/Volume 9–10, September 2013: 11.

44 Address by Prime Minister Hashimoto Ryūtarō to the Japan Association of Corporate Executives, 24 July 1997, http://japan.kantei.go.jp/0731douyukai.html (Accessed 28 March 2014).

45 CAREC, From Landlocked to Linked in, ADB 2013.

46 Private communication with former Japanese Ambassador to one of the CA countries, 2012; Interview with a Japanese diplomatic official in one of the CA countries, 2013.

47 Richard Samuels, *Securing Japan: Tokyo's Grand Strategy and the Future of East Asia* (Ithaca, NY: Cornell, 2006), 9.

48 Kent E. Calder, 'Japan's Energy Angst and the Caspian Great Game,' *NBR Analysis*, 12, no. 1, 2001, http://www.nbr.org/publications/element.aspx?id=288 (Accessed 11 February 2014).

49 Uyama, 'Japanese Policies in Relation to Kazakhstan: Is There a 'Strategy'?', 172.

1 Central Asia on Japan's diplomatic agenda

Security, resources, and humanitarianism

Introduction

There has been little consensus among analysts on the aims of Japan's foreign and security policy in Central Asia and the drivers behind it. Certain scholars, as well as Japanese former and incumbent diplomatic officials, pointed out the 'developmental' focus of Japanese involvement. This focus is contrasted with 'geopolitical' interests, stressing that Japan is not in competition with Russia and China in any kind of 'New Great Game' between major powers for influence in post-Cold War Central Asia (CA).[1] According to this view, Japan's engagement is benign, since its aid is provided without excessive ambition or hope for reciprocation, unlike, for instance, in the case of official development assistance (ODA) provided to the Middle Eastern countries to secure energy supplies.[2]

Although these interpretations are consistent with the traditional Japanese post-1945 peaceful low-key diplomatic posture conceptualised by the so-called Yoshida and Fukuda doctrines, they are rather static and insufficiently nuanced.[3] Such positions are also much less widespread among the non-Japanese students of Japan's foreign policy or its Silk Road strategy, for instance, Michael Green, Essen Usubaliev, or Timur Dadabaev, as well as among Japanese ex-officials working in the fields other than diplomacy.[4] The discrepancy between the interpretations of the Japanese Silk Road diplomacy by Japanese scholars (who underline and, at times, advocate the absence of strategic vision or geopolitical motives) and non-Japanese scholars (who consider that Japan does have a pragmatic strategy as well as a realist approach in it) is also present in broader analyses of Japanese foreign policy and national strategy outside CA.

Argument

This chapter will test the hypothesis that Japan's CA diplomacy embodies clear geopolitical aspirations and strategic thinking, without necessarily characterising its relationship with CA as part of a wider conflict such as the 'Great Game,' if placed within a broader external security context for Japan. Consequently, this chapter retraces the milestones of Japan–CA relations (see Table 1.1) through

20 *Security, resources, and humanitarianism*

Table 1.1 Milestones of Japan–CA diplomatic relations

1992	Recognition, diplomatic relations established.
1993–4	Japan's Ministry of Finance officials strongly support aid mechanisms for the region through OECD DAC, EBRD, and ADB, facilitating CA's access to capital.
1997	PM Hashimoto announces Eurasian Diplomacy From The Pacific, including closer cooperation with Russia and the Silk Road Countries (CA and the Caucasus).
1998	PM Obuchi announces Silk Road Action Plan: supporting democracy and economic reforms, reconstruction of transport infrastructure, and mineral resources exploration.
2004	FM Kawaguchi introduces Central Asia plus Japan framework, inspired by Japan's multilateralism with Southeast Asia.
2006	FM Asō, MOFA officials Yachi and Kanehara come up with the concepts of Arc of Freedom and Prosperity, Transformation of CA Into A Corridor Of Peace And Stability. PM Koizumi visits Kazakhstan and Uzbekistan.
2007	METI head Amari Akira visits Kazakhstan and Uzbekistan with an emphasis on uranium and rare earths.
2009	PM Asō proposes the concept of Eurasian Crossroads: development of North-South and East-West corridors in Eurasia with focus on ports, rail, and road infrastructure and using Japan's technologies.
2009–12	Shift from value-oriented diplomacy to pragmatism and 'business as usual' approach under the DPJ legislatures.
2013–15	PM Abe revives the relationship, focusing on economic aspects and becomes the second ever Japanese PM to travel to the region and the first to visit all five states.

the prism of changing security perceptions. It focuses on the evolution of Japanese strategic perceptions of Asia and national security in the post-Cold War period focusing on the Liberal Democratic Party of Japan (LDP) cabinets from Hashimoto Ryūtarō (1996–8) to Asō Tarō (2008–9), as well as Abe Shinzō's second premiership (2012–present).

Such a timeline is chosen because it was under and by Hashimoto that the objectives of Japan's engagement in CA were initially formulated on the official level, while Asō, during his leadership of the Ministry of Foreign Affairs (MOFA) under Abe, came up with the latest to date conceptualisation of CA in Japanese diplomacy – namely, the Arc of Freedom and Prosperity (AFP) – devoting a separate chapter to this vast area in a conceptual book, which outlined his main policy views. Japan's relations with CA under the Democratic Party of Japan-led cabinets are examined in Chapter 2.

In particular, this chapter will assess to what extent Japan's CA diplomacy might be interpreted in relation to such key issues in Japanese foreign policy as adjusting to a changing international system in order to keep a leading position, addressing distant threats as part of the 'global security' concept, and dealing with a rising China. The timeline goes through Abe's second premiership, which, as I argue, avoided discursive grand design concepts in CA, prioritised mercantilist promotion of Japanese exports, and refocused regional rhetoric on the Indo-Pacific

Security, resources, and humanitarianism   21

rather than continental Eurasia, including the change of posture vis-à-vis Russia to proactively accommodating as opposed to the mild balancing and overbalancing of the mid-2000s.[5] Ultimately, this chapter shows that diplomatic history alone is insufficient in understanding the full extent of Japan's CA involvement and lays the groundwork for additional lines of inquiry expounded in subsequent chapters.

Theory defining security and strategy for Japan

The notion of national security is a core concept in the neo-realist paradigm of international relations theory.[6] According to this theoretical approach, states in the anarchic international structure behave in a self-help way and want to ensure their survival as a minimum requirement before achieving further objectives. Rather than ensuring the balance of power, as the predecessor realist paradigm would suggest, the states are seeking security.[7] Security in international relations was traditionally regarded as protection of a state from an armed aggression.[8]

However, during the post-Cold War period, various non-military dimensions of security have also come forward, such as resilience to economic shocks, protecting the environment, countering international terrorism and international crime, or fighting the international epidemics of diseases.[9] Ole Waever, a prominent scholar of security from the Copenhagen School of International Relations and a post-structural realist, gave the following definition of security: 'it is a capacity of a society to preserve its specific character despite changing conditions and real or virtual threats.'[10]

In order to maintain this capacity, the states, according to the neo-realist paradigm, adopt certain strategies. Whether Japan has a national strategy as an attribute of a 'normal state,' and whether Japan is such a normal state, especially in regard to its place in international politics, has been a subject of a long and still ongoing debate among the scholars of Japanese politics.[11] Little consensus has been reached on that matter, however, as already mentioned in the introduction. In general, many authors outside Japan (Michael Green, Kenneth Pyle, Gilbert Rozman, Richard Samuels) tend to attribute a possession of a strategic vision to Tokyo, whereas many Japanese scholars have portrayed Japan as lacking a national strategy (Hosoya Yūichi until 2013, Iriye Akira, Ozawa Ichirō, Tadokoro Masayuki, Tamamoto Masaru) and having a foreign policy that is 'ad hoc, reactive and equivocating' (Satō Seizaburō).[12]

A similar pattern can be observed in the scholarship concerning Japan's foreign policy in CA. Where Japan was considered to have some sort of international strategy, this strategy was characterised by scholars as stemming from its own vulnerability (*fuan*) perception, adaptive, and reactive.

In order to understand what political action or approach can be qualified as strategic, this chapter agrees with the approach taken in the volume *Japanese Strategic Thought toward Asia*. Before assessing the strategic quality of

22 *Security, resources, and humanitarianism*

contemporary Japanese Asian policy, the authors of this comprehensive work identify the following criteria as making a thought 'strategic:'

> We ask to what extent was thinking targeted at making Japan more secure, prosperous, and respectable. Also, we consider to what degree was it directed toward reassuring the Japanese public rather than rousing them, solving recognized problems instead of postponing or exacerbating them, and putting in place a process of careful deliberation at home and consultation abroad. These criteria stress the pursuit of long-term aims, balancing the expansion of Japan's influence with success in winning greater trust abroad, and avoidance of excessive dependency with recognition of the need for increased interdependence.[13]

What kind of security strategy options does Japan have in theory in its mixed bag of preferences? The neo-realist paradigm suggests that due to uncertainty regarding other states' intentions, there is a lack of trust in international relations that is called a 'security dilemma.' In the context of facing this dilemma, states' strategic responses to perceived threats may take diverse forms: engagement, balancing, hedging, bandwagoning, or a combination of any of them. Engagement can be characterised as 'efforts to enhance exchanges and contacts by way of positive and non-coercive means,' which 'often overlaps with soft options of appeasement or accommodation.'[14] Balancing can take explicit forms of 'demonstrated commitment to containing or frustrating the rise of a challenging power via force aggrandizement' (internal balancing) and 'alliance formation and/or preventive war' (external balancing).[15] Hedging can be seen as a form of internal balancing, being a choice of cautious behaviour by a state which does not opt to pre-empt daringly.[16] Bandwagoning is a form of hedging, which 'refers either to siding with the strongest power for profit-sharing and rent-seeking (offensive bandwagoning) or to joining the emerging challenger to counter dominance by the hegemonic power deemed more threatening (defensive bandwagoning).'[17]

Japan's foreign policy mix in the post-Cold War period has involved all of the mentioned elements, which can be a sign of normality for a rational state actor in the neo-realist paradigm, according to which the national strategies arise normally, being almost defined by the environment.[18] Japanese diplomacy has been interpreted as preferring hedging, as well as bandwagoning, by Richard Samuels, while its stance towards a rising China was characterised as a combination of balancing and engagement by Korean scholar Chung Jae-ho.

As Samuels pointed out, since the Tokugawa period and especially after Japan's entry into international politics under the Meiji emperor, the country was siding with what it has seen as the dominant power of the time (i.e. bandwagoning): the Netherlands, Great Britain, Germany, and the United States. If seen from a structural perspective (neo-realism is also called 'structural realism,' due to its emphasis on the determinist impact of international structure upon the behaviour of states), since the Meiji period, Japan sought to secure a high position in the international hierarchy topped by Western countries.

Security, resources, and humanitarianism   23

It continued doing so after World War II, but this time primarily with economic means, rather than traditional military ones, given the renunciation of the belligerency right in the constitution and 'free riding' on the security alliance with the United States.[19] Nonetheless, this integration and institutionalisation with the West, reflected, for instance, in Japan's membership in the Trilateral Commission, did not necessarily imply a full concert with the West in foreign policy. Japan has also hedged from European and American protectionism by promoting regional economic integration in East Asia, thus demonstrating the approach Samuels called a 'Goldilocks consensus.'[20] This chapter will further argue that Japan's approach towards CA in the 1990s included elements of both hedging and bandwagoning.

However, the aforementioned strategy choices primarily address the state's behaviour towards the threats perceived from other state actors. Meanwhile, in the post-Cold War period, international relations have seen a surge of non-state actors (for instance, transnational extremist groups, such as Al-Qaeda) and threats to international security stemming from such actors or from global issues, for instance, nuclear proliferation or unequal access to energy resources which are of crucial importance for the sustainability of growth in emerging economies.

Japan's behaviour in international relations should thus be assessed not only through the neo-realist prism in terms of strategies applied to ensure its security vis-à-vis other states, or, if looked at from the structural perspective of international political economy, through the country's aspiration to raise its status in the Western-dominated international system.[21] Neo-realist interpretations of Japan's diplomatic stance with a realist security policy and mercantilist economic policy (sometimes viewed as aggressive) increasingly gained attention in the post-Cold War period, challenging previously dominant liberal idealist views.[22] Liberal idealists viewed Japan as a democratic pacifist state and an elite-guided mercantile state self-constrained by pacifist norms, such as renunciation of the belligerency right in Article 9 of the Japanese constitution.[23] Chapter 4 examines the mercantile aspects of Japan's CA policy in greater detail applying it to natural resources.

Nevertheless, the Japanese post-World War II embrace of a liberal democratic developmental model, successfully expressed as 'Peace and Happiness through Economic Prosperity and Democracy' and its strong 'soft power' capacities still have a considerable influence over the formulation of the country's foreign policy.[24] This influence has been exercised by one of the powerful domestic stakeholder constituencies of middle-power internationalists in the 1990s, succeeded by mercantilists and Asianists after 9/11.[25] In accordance with the liberal viewpoint and its 'democratic peace theory' holding that democracies rarely go to war with one another, Japan can be viewed as a democratic market economy and a responsible 'global citizen' that aspires to promote democratisation, socio-economic development, and market reforms in the world in general, and in Asia in particular, including CA.

The early 1980s saw the development of a new concept of 'comprehensive security' (*sōgō anzen hoshō*). This approach implied greater emphasis

24 *Security, resources, and humanitarianism*

on economic and diplomatic means than on military ones to ensure national security.[26] The non-military facet of the strategy was further enhanced in 1988 through Prime Minister Takeshita's International Cooperation Initiative, which focused on strengthening Japan's contribution to international peace, expansion of the ODA, and promotion of international cultural exchange. This initiative was developed by Takeshita's successors Kaifu and Uno.[27] After the Union of Soviet Socialist Republics (USSR) collapsed in 1991 and Japan began to progressively build relations with the post-Soviet countries, the latter two pillars of this international cooperation approach were present in Japan's diplomacy towards the newly independent states, including CA.

Thus, Japanese contemporary perceptions of international security would not be reduced to preventing potential conflicts with other states by ensuring parity with their power, but would also involve contributing to democracy and prosperity in general as a foundation for a more peaceful world, in which Japan as a major exporter could secure and expand its trade. This chapter considers that Japanese post-Cold War involvement in CA should be interpreted from multiple perspectives – through neo-realist, liberal, and constructivist paradigms, due to their complementarities, as well as domestic power shifts in Japan. An exclusively neo-realist view would result in confining the relations between Japan and other state actors to a 'zero-sum game,' which would be reductionist, and limit understanding of the internal decision-making process inside both the Japanese and CA foreign policies, for instance, the inconsistencies resulting from reshuffles. A predominantly liberal view can be challenged by pragmatic and realistic interpretations of the Japanese foreign policy, particularly valid in the post-Cold War period. A combined approach can be regarded as similar to the notion of 'analytical eclecticism,' formulated by Peter Katzenstein and explained in the introduction. These epistemological approaches also share a common premise in the case of Japan: the self-perception of the country as relatively vulnerable within the international structure and fearing isolation.

Having said that, it is equally crucial to note that, when analysing Japan's foreign policy, one must avoid overreliance on the anthropomorphised view of Japan as a monolithic actor and also take into account the nature of internal decision-making in Japan which has often been handicapped by lack of interaction between various bureaucratic actors (e.g. MOFA, Ministry of Finance [MOF], and Ministry of Economy, Trade and Industry [METI]) and ministerial merry-go-rounds.

Early relations between Japan and Central Asia: bandwagoning with the West?

Conventional wisdom can explain CA's low priority in Tokyo's foreign agenda by such factors as the absence of territorial proximity as compared to Russia or China, lack of previous direct relations, and the region's comparatively modest role in the global security architecture. Indeed, such fundamental policy documents as the 2004, 2010, and 2014 editions of 'National Defense Program

Security, resources, and humanitarianism 25

Guidelines' bear no reference to Central Asia, except one passage in the 2004 NDPG which can be interpreted equivocally:

> In particular, stability in the region spreading from the Middle East to East Asia is critical to Japan. Japan traditionally has close economic ties with this region, its sea lines of communication run through the region, and Japan depends almost entirely on energy and natural resources from overseas. In this context, Japan will strive to stabilize the region by promoting various cooperative efforts in conjunction with other countries sharing common security challenges.[28]

By contrast, such issues as the nuclear status of the Democratic People's Republic of Korea, unresolved territorial disputes with China, Republic of Korea, and Russia, or uncertainty in the cross-Taiwan Strait relations, affecting the stability of maritime communications, are vital to Japan's security and lie within its immediate defence perimeter.[29] So what vital considerations drove Japan to CA?

In the post-Cold War era, Japanese security perception has gradually evolved from the concept of 'comprehensive security' formulated in the 1980s to beyond the scope of its foremost neighbours. It was particularly manifest after 9/11, when Prime Minister Koizumi visited the United States in order to express his support for the 'war on terror.' This backing materialised particularly in the refuelling mission for the International Security Assistance Force (ISAF) coalition ships in Afghanistan and later in the dispatch of a Self-Defence Forces humanitarian contingent to Iraq.

However, the roots of this trend became clear already during Hashimoto's premiership (1996–8). Hashimoto insisted on the 'situational' interpretation of security cooperation with the United States, rather than a 'geographical' one which would confine such cooperation to the Far East sensu stricto.[30]

After the end of the Cold War, the notion of 'national interest' gradually emerged in Japan's foreign policy debate, becoming increasingly realist, because of the change in the global security environment. Strategic geopolitical motives were present alongside cultural diplomacy and development assistance during the initial stages of relationship-building between Japan and Silk Road countries.

Reinhard Drifte argued that one of the drivers behind Japan's involvement in CA in the early 1990s was its fear of isolation entailed by the emerging rapprochement between the countries of the former Socialist Bloc and Western security structures.[31] The latter included such institutions as the Conference for Security and Cooperation in Europe, transformed in 1994 into an organisation (OSCE), and initiatives of the North Atlantic Treaty Organisation (NATO): North Atlantic Cooperation Council and Partnership for Peace. This cooperation was not limited strictly to the European part of the ex-USSR and former Warsaw Treaty Organisation: the countries of CA and Caucasus became members of the OSCE and partners of NATO (mid-1994, although Tajikistan joined only in 2002).

The global structure has evolved following the collapse of the USSR, Japan's main security threat during the Cold War, and a new *fuan* has loomed in the

26 Security, resources, and humanitarianism

Japanese political establishment, requiring an adaptation to the changed conjuncture. Japan responded by becoming *inter alia* an associate member of the OSCE, where it was regarded as a 'soft-security' provider in the OSCE region due to its leading position as net donor of the ODA, not only worldwide, but also in the Silk Road region. In quantitative terms, the comparative value of Tokyo's ODA in CA has drastically risen from 36 percent of Washington's ODA in 1994 to more than 108 percent in 1997.[32]

Furthermore, Japan also brokered the entry of the Silk Road countries into multi-lateral development banks. With Japanese help, CA states became members not only of the European Bank for Reconstruction and Development (EBRD), founded to support the transition in the post-Socialist states, but also in the Asian Development Bank (ADB); such cross-membership was unprecedented.[33] Japan has historically been the top contributor to the ADB, one of two largest shareholders alongside the United States, and has chaired the bank since its foundation in 1966.[34]

Japan's active role in promoting the ADB since its origins was aimed at rebuilding confidence with the neighbours that had suffered from Japanese imperialism, in particular Southeast Asian states.[35] Clearly, Japan did not face a similar issue in CA, and its catching up with the Western countries of the early 1990s can be interpreted as bandwagoning aimed at the reconfirmation of Japan's status on the top of the international hierarchy. Nonetheless, Japan's developmental contribution to CA and the early success in natural resources of the 1990s cannot be explained by the evolution of security perceptions alone, and should take into account the agency of MOF officials and Japanese corporations, which I examine in the respective empirical chapters.

In the case of Kazakhstan specifically, another motive for Japan's early cooperation boost was the denuclearisation of this CA country, which found itself an independent nuclear full-cycle state after the collapse of the USSR, albeit with nuclear stockpiles that were unguarded and unaccounted for.[36] Japan's historic commitment to nuclear non-proliferation as part of its diplomacy laid a foundation for broader cooperation in the future, namely, the stable supply of Kazakh uranium for Japan's own nuclear power which accounted for about a quarter of its electricity until 3/11.[37]

The grounds for closer relations with the CA states were not limited to politico-economic matters, but featured a cultural and, to a certain extent, romantic dimension. The global ideological conflict was over and a realignment of a new nature was taking place, this time including civilisational borders, as suggested by Samuel Huntington in his famous work on the 'Clash of Civilizations.'[38] According to this spatial concept, Eastern Europe and, initially, Russia became part of the New Europe, while CA countries managed to both join the Euro-Atlantic security structures and revive the sense of cultural proximity with the Asian countries. Similar to how Turkey started to seek new contacts with the Turkic peoples of CA (present in all ex-Soviet states of the region), Japan was also becoming aware of its cultural and ethnic proximity to CA nations which also shared Mongolian and Northeast Asian historic heritage.[39] Already throughout

Security, resources, and humanitarianism 27

the 1980s, the Japanese television channel NHK showed a series of 30 documentaries, devoted to the history of the Silk Road – shot in co-production with Chinese Central Television.

Limits of cooperation

Yet, in the immediate aftermath of the USSR collapse, the knowledge of CA countries in Japan was limited, as well as the number of diplomatic professionals with relevant competences. This situation originated in the Cold War (especially before Nixon's rapprochement with China), when the MOFA was mostly dominated by officials with expertise focused on the United States and, to a lesser extent, China. At the time, Asian countries westward of India were designated in diplomatic jargon as 'West of Burma,' and diplomats tried to avoid those destinations in their careers.[40] In the wake of the Cold War, CA received its own division (*shitsu*) inside the MOFA, and the staffing generally consisted of specialists in Russian and Soviet affairs. According to Kawatō Akio, CA's lower exposure to media and big politics actually facilitated practical policy implementation, while the *shitsu* status of the CA division made it a gateway to a quicker career rise.

The end of the Soviet empire was in general less 'visible' from the Japanese side, than from that of its Western allies in Europe: borders as well as the territorial dispute remained the same in the Far East of the USSR – the neighbour simply changed its name to the 'Russian Federation.'[41] In addition, MOFA officials displayed a tendency to be resolutely hard-lined in their attitudes towards Moscow. Perestroika arguably stimulated this attitude with new opportunities: Gorbachev recognised the territorial issue, previously unacknowledged by the Kremlin, whereas the first Yeltsin administration (1991–6) initially demonstrated a concession-prone stance. This can explain why Japan's pace of engaging with CA was still quite slow in the early 1990s and despite various development projects, the first official defining of CA in the Tokyo's foreign agenda only saw light in 1997 under Hashimoto.

Hashimoto's Eurasian diplomacy

In the mid-1990s, Japan's policy towards China started to take a cautious turn. Japan's official assessment of a potential China threat became more ostentatious, as the government-approved National Defence Program Outline 1995 contained an implicit reference to China and consequently stressed the need to strengthen the security alliance with the United States. The alliance was reinvigorated in 1996 and reinforced Japan's role. Subsequent Japanese defence white papers focused on the potentially adversarial role of China's ballistic missiles. In parallel, Japanese ODA to China came under tighter scrutiny, while its size was reduced.[42] Japan's MOF leadership and the community of developmental officials also noted the change of tide towards China and considered it in the aid policy towards CA.[43]

28 *Security, resources, and humanitarianism*

On 24 July 1997, Prime Minister Hashimoto made a speech to the Japan Association of Corporate Executives (*Keizai Dōyūkai*), where he placed Japan's foreign policy towards Russia, China, and former Soviet countries under a new umbrella concept of 'Eurasian diplomacy.' Although for the latter group, the MOFA's press conference used the term Commonwealth of Independent States which includes all former Soviet republics except the Baltic countries, Hashimoto in his speech explicitly referred to the 'Silk Road region, encompassing the CA republics of the former Soviet Union and the nations of the Caucasus region,' but not including Belarus, Moldova, or Ukraine.[44]

The full name of Hashimoto's new policy was 'Eurasian diplomacy viewed from the Pacific.' The Pacific dimension is important, because the context of the speech implied Japan's response to actions already taken by the West. Namely, Hashimoto acknowledged a prior 'careful watch' of the new security structure emerging in the transition countries and 'stemming from the U.S., across the Atlantic Ocean, through Europe and over the former Soviet Union, to reach the Pacific Ocean as a vast region which takes on the characteristics of a Eurasian diplomacy viewed from the Atlantic.'[45]

There are five important inferences to be made from this speech. Firstly, the choice of the term 'Eurasia' with its focus on Russia, China, and CA, was reminiscent of Halford Mackinder's concept of the 'Heartland.'[46] While I am not asserting direct links between Mackinder's idea and Hashimoto, the geostrategic and continentalist aspect of Hashimoto's speech was tangible, especially if contrasted to the concept of 'sea power' developed by maritime strategist Alfred Mahan and historically influential in Japan.

Secondly, Hashimoto acknowledged the linkage of his idea to the actions undertaken by Japan's Atlantic allies and juxtaposed these actions with his own initiative. In that regard, Eurasian Diplomacy (ED) echoed earlier Japanese bandwagoning with the United States and the European Union in the region and made it difficult to consider Hashimoto's initiative as simply dictated by disinterested charitable intentions.

Thirdly, Hashimoto addressed mutual cultural interest between Japan and CA:

> Fortunately, these countries have great expectations of Japan as an Asian country, and at the same time, Japan has deep-rooted nostalgia for this region stemming from the glory of the days of the Silk Road.[47]

Fourthly, Hashimoto has proposed three main directions for Japanese foreign policy in CA: (i) political dialogue, (ii) cooperation in the fields of economy and natural resources, and (iii) cooperation in peace-building through nuclear nonproliferation, democratisation, and the fostering of stability. The cooperation was thus widened beyond development assistance.[48]

Finally, Hashimoto demonstrated attention not only to the cooperation between the Western countries and Eurasian ones, but also to the growing partnership between Russia and China, which held 'the key to the formation of an international order.'[49] The prime minister then stressed the necessity of building

Security, resources, and humanitarianism   29

even more constructive relations with Russia and China. Such a stance can with considerable confidence be interpreted as strategic thinking, since not only does the head of state acknowledge the global significance of engaging its two large neighbours, but he also hints at the importance of a Sino-Russian partnership for regional balance in Asia.

This thinking can qualify as both realist and strategic, since the long-term option of being left out of the adjustments in the international system might have caused a situation where Japan would face an allied Russia and China. Both of these countries had unsettled territorial disputes with Japan, were permanent members of the United Nations Security Council, and therefore, also 'held the keys' to the Japanese entry in this institution. Engaging both states would therefore prevent a potential 'zero-sum game,' a realist concept in international relations theory according to which the improvement of the security position of one state is automatically detrimental to the security position of another state.

Moreover, the early post-Cold War record of Japan's relations with both countries was unsatisfactory. Hashimoto marked a turning point in improving the relations with Russia through Japan's support of Russia's engagement in the political discussions of the Group of Eight in 1997 and Asia-Pacific Economic Cooperation in 1998. During Hashimoto's bilateral meetings with Yeltsin, informally labelled 'Boris and Ryū,' the Japanese prime minister decided to discontinue the dogmatic line of his predecessors on the territorial issue.[50]

Conversely, China, as it was previously mentioned, was increasingly viewed as a threat by the Japanese defence establishment, following the People's Republic of China's (PRC's) assertive behaviour in the Third Taiwan Straits crisis and the reconfirmation of the Japanese–American Security Alliance in 1996.

The concept of Eurasian diplomacy was elaborated by Tōgō Kazuhiko, then deputy director general of the MOFA's Department of European and Oceanic Affairs and a representative of the MOFA's 'Russia school.'[51] The interaction between the prime minister and the MOFA on the launch of the new policy was remarkably thorough.[52] The organisation of a region tour by high-ranking Japanese officials followed the inauguration of the diplomacy.

However, further implementation of this policy was hindered by several factors. Among them were: the siphoning off of available resources for dealing with the Asian economic crisis in 1997–8 and such domestic constraints as regular rotation in the MOFA, Hashimoto's resignation following the LDP defeat in the 1998 Upper House elections, and lack of continuity with succeeding cabinets of Obuchi and Mori. As a result, the relations with CA have had an 'on-and-off' nature and progressed slower than envisaged by the 'Eurasian diplomacy' concept.[53] Furthermore, in 1998, the Japanese member of the United Nations (U.N.) observer mission in Tajikistan Akino Yutaka was killed by local assailants. Although Akino's death negatively affected CA's image as a dangerous area, it also drew attention to the regional problems of human security – a concept which emerged in 1999 from the efforts of LDP politicians, such as Takemi Keizō, and came to the forefront during the premiership of Koizumi Jun'ichirō (2001–6).[54]

30 *Security, resources, and humanitarianism*

Koizumi and 9/11: an 'Afghanisation' of Japan's Central Asian policy?

Koizumi's tenure featured a reinforced cooperation with the United States after the events of 9/11, which included 'burden sharing' in Afghanistan and related securing of the neighbour CA states. Japan's CA policy became a part of dealing with distant threats as one can infer from the report published by the Tokyo-based National Institute for Defense Studies, the Japanese Ministry of Defence's think-tank.[55] Ensuring 'global security' and combating terrorism had its 'human' dimension – necessity to stabilise potential or actual failed states that may harbour al-Qaeda's operatives. The key perception in such a 'global security' facet was that globalisation has made Japan vulnerable to threats and effects from even situations in 'distant regions,' and hence the country needs to be a global actor in order to protect its interests. For instance, a Japanese vessel refuelling mission was dispatched in 2001 to join the ISAF coalition.

Due to its fragility and potential of Islamist-led destabilisation, CA was interpreted by the Bush administrations (2001–9) within the concepts of Greater Middle East and the Arc of Instability. Helping to prevent potential conflicts in the region, therefore, became a task for Japan, in the context of its alliance with the United States and its assistance in the 'war on terror.'[56] In 2001, the Japanese government provided more than $20 million of urgent grants to Uzbekistan and Tajikistan in order to contribute to political stability and economic development of these countries with a fragile domestic situation.[57] In parallel, Japan sought to improve its resource procurement security by accessing CA's mineral riches – an aspect I examine in Chapter 4.

The logic of wider geopolitical alignments might also be traced in the Japanese approach towards CA in the early 2000s. As Kyrgyz analyst Essen Usubaliev argued, in 2002, Japan has contributed to the improvement of the relations between Uzbekistan and the United States, including the opening of an American military base at Karshi-Khanabad (K2), necessary for the support of the ISAF operations in Afghanistan.[58] Uzbekistan's foreign strategy since its independence involved both an aspiration towards regional leadership and constant manoeuvring among the great powers, such as Russia, the United States, and China.

Initially, the security aspirations of U.S.–Japan alliance were welcome in CA. According to former Japanese ambassador to Uzbekistan and Tajikistan Kawatō Akio, in 2002, the Uzbek President Islam Karimov had chosen to pursue a closer orientation towards the West in order to avoid potential colonialist subjugation by Russia.[59] He visited Washington DC in March 2002 and signed a 'Strategic Partnership' with the United States, proceeding then to Japan where he also proposed and signed a similar partnership together with a joint declaration on friendship, strategic partnership, and cooperation. Earlier, in 1999, Japan signed a strategic partnership with Kazakhstan, most likely stimulated by the entry of Japanese companies into the giant Kashagan oilfield development. In December 1999, Kazakhstani President Nazarbayev visited Tokyo.

Security, resources, and humanitarianism 31

Notwithstanding the validity of Kawatō's argument on Uzbekistan's intention to move closer to Washington and away from Moscow, its timeline should be widened as this drift had become manifest in 1999. The new Uzbek-American security cooperation was founded on shared concerns over the Taliban's advance in Afghanistan and growing Islamist presence in the Ferghana Valley. The 1998 bombings in East Africa put the spotlight on Afghanistan-based Osama bin Laden and drew Washington closer to post-Soviet countries bordering Afghanistan. In 1999, Tashkent experienced its own explosions and requested the assistance from the Moscow-led Collective Security Treaty Organisation (CSTO), but the Kremlin viewed the events as a domestic Uzbek affair not qualifying for the CSTO help. Moscow's response angered Karimov and contributed to his rapprochement with Washington.[60] In 1999, Uzbekistan went as far as joining the GUAM, a bloc of post-Soviet republics seeking to reduce Moscow's influence upon them.[61] Karimov's 'honeymoon' with the West lasted until the 2003 EBRD session in Uzbekistan, which marked the reverse trend towards a rapprochement with China and Russia. I analyse these events in greater detail later in this chapter and in Chapter 3.

Domestic impediments

The internal bureaucratic aspects of Japan's foreign policy decision-making have had their impact on the actual implementation of strategic partnerships. Firstly, although the Japanese diplomats on the spot were supportive of the format, their actions were hindered by lack of understanding and enthusiasm in the MOFA's Tokyo headquarters. Secondly, the ministry's weight in decision-making under Koizumi had decreased in comparison to the past due to greater powers endowed to the cabinet by the prime minister. Koizumi was generally more active in foreign affairs than his predecessors, due to the struggle for partisan support in the LDP, the enthusiasm of the Bush administration to upgrade the alliance with Japan, and the rising concern of the public over Chinese assertive behaviour.[62]

The particular reason for institutional change in the cabinet was the lack of leadership that Japanese politics experienced in the last decade of the twentieth century. The Japanese constitution traditionally vested executive power in the cabinet, not in the prime minister. In the process of decision-making, however, reaching unanimous consensus with the cabinet proved difficult due to factionalism in the Parliament and the political importance of bureaucrats, the public trust in which considerably deteriorated throughout the 1990s.[63] The administrative reform, designed by Hashimoto and finalised in early 2001 through the revised Cabinet Law, strengthened the policy initiative and decisive power of the prime minister, reinforced the role of the cabinet, especially in times of crises, and weakened the influence of certain ministries, among which was the MOFA, simultaneously increasing that of the MOF. Such reform allowed Koizumi to respond swiftly to the events 9/11 and propose support to the United States without delay, striking a contrast to the Kaifu administration's response to the 1990 Gulf War.[64]

32 *Security, resources, and humanitarianism*

Thirdly, a number of scandals happened to Japanese high-ranking diplomats in the early 2000s: in particular, involving the member of parliament (MP) Suzuki Muneo and Foreign Minister Tanaka Makiko. Tanaka became the MOFA's head in 2001 under Koizumi and was known for her tough stance on the territorial issue with Russia, which was heavily criticised by Suzuki – leading expert on Russia in the MOFA. In January 2002, Tanaka was replaced by Kawaguchi Yoriko because of her constant discord with the Diet members and diplomatic gaffes. Although Suzuki won this political battle, he himself soon came under scrutiny because of allegations he was accepting bribes in return for political favours and corruption in the ODA projects he was responsible for.[65] Suzuki's arrest and resignation in early 2002 had a detrimental effect since they entailed a loss of qualified specialists in the ex-USSR, including CA, from the MOFA and a closer control on the further ODA projects in the region.[66]

Finally, the lack of coordination between Japanese bureaucratic entities hindered the development of Japanese relations with Silk Road countries: Nakayama Kyōko, the Japanese ambassador in Uzbekistan and Tajikistan in 1999–2002 hailed from the MOF and had connections in the Japanese Bank of International Cooperation. Meanwhile, Kawatō Akio, who replaced her in 2002, was a career diplomat and did not have such a networking base in the financial bureaucracy.[67]

Central Asia plus Japan: seeds of balancing China?

Because of these obstacles, cooperation between Japan and the region progressed slower than expected in 2002–3. However, since the end of 2003, the MOFA CA direction underwent yet another reshuffle, and a new team was more welcoming of improving relations with the region. This bureaucratic change resulted in the first regular framework: 'Central Asia plus Japan' (CAJ) forum, established following the visit to Kazakhstan, Kyrgyzstan, Tajikistan, and Uzbekistan by the then Foreign Minister Kawaguchi Yoriko in August 2004.

It is worth noting that, according to Kawatō, it is the lack of high-rank interest in CA affairs that actually allowed the diplomats to establish a framework that could work without regular approval from the cabinet. In 2003, Japanese diplomats in the region started informally discussing the idea of an organisation similar to Association of Southeast Asian Nations (ASEAN) in CA with CA officials. What is also interesting, initially officials in Japan contemplated a possibility of joining the Shanghai Cooperation Organisation (SCO), but decided that Japan as the only 'Western capitalist' state might become used by other members and thus decided to proceed with the framework of CAJ.[68]

According to Kawaguchi, who was not a CA expert, CAJ was inspired by her communication with Tanaka Tetsuji, a Bank of Japan official and a consultant to then-president of Kyrgyzstan Askar Akayev. Kawaguchi maintained that CAJ was neither a continuation of Eurasian diplomacy nor MOF activities, but rather a standalone geopolitical project that, unlike Eurasian diplomacy, was less about Russia and more about China. CAJ was founded two years into the tenure of Hu Jintao, who was viewed as more assertive than his predecessor by both

Security, resources, and humanitarianism 33

MOFA and MOF bureaucrats. Koizumi-era U.S.–Japan alliance notwithstanding, Washington vetted CAJ as *fait accompli*, rather than in a prior consultation, which underscored Tokyo's autonomy in this field.[69]

During the above-mentioned visit, Kawaguchi strongly stressed the crucial nature of human rights and democracy, emphasising afterwards three principles in dealing with CA: 'respecting diversity, competition and coordination, and open cooperation.'[70] 'Open cooperation' hinted at Japan's disagreement with the vision of CA as exclusively Russia's or China's sphere of influence, which recurrently came up after 9/11 as the United States intensified their security cooperation with CA states. This rhetoric was later repeated by Asō and other conservatives in 2006 and Abe in 2015 as a call for 'open regionalism.' Such a combination of simultaneous appealing to the democratic values and respecting the local specificity of local countries was consistent with the Japanese approach towards CA in the 1990s, but the value aspect became the stumbling block in mid-2000s.

Critical juncture: Andijan-2005 and Japan's value-oriented diplomacy

Japan's involvement in CA has maintained a double nature regarding its Western allies. When dealing with 'hard' security threats, such as Afghanistan, Japan behaved cooperatively with the United States. However, in economy and 'softer' fields, such as human rights issues in the region or other problems related to the transition to democracy, Japan demonstrated its autonomy and even a competitive attitude vis-à-vis the West. The most illustrative example of this double nature and its limits was Japan's response to the events in the Uzbek city of Andijan, located in the Fergana Valley.

In 2005, an uprising in Andijan was severely suppressed by the authorities. The riots emerged as a protest to the court hearings during which a group of local businessmen was accused of cooperation with the leader of Islamist group Akramiya Akram Yuldashev, as well as of participation in banned organisations. Initially, the demonstrations were peaceful and allegedly financially supported by the suspects. However, after the Uzbek government arrested some demonstrators, on the night of 13 May, armed insurgents attacked a police outpost, a military one, and then the prison, resorting to murders and collecting weapons at each stage. Expecting a stern reaction from the authorities, the militants formed human shields with women and children. While the initiative of the final armed clash remains unclear, at the end, several hundred persons were killed, mostly by the government forces, but also by the insurgents themselves.[71]

The United States and the European Union heavily criticised Tashkent's crackdown, with sanctions being imposed on Uzbekistan by the European Union. In response, Uzbekistan continued to improve relations with Russia and China, since its ties with the West already started souring after the 2003 EBRD session in Tashkent (see Chapter 3).

The Japanese reaction towards Uzbekistan's handling of Andijan was mixed. On the one hand, prior to the Andijan events, Vice Foreign Minister Yachi Shōtarō had already started setting up Japan's closer cooperation with NATO

34 *Security, resources, and humanitarianism*

in 2005, which subsequently evolved into value-oriented diplomacy and the Arc of Freedom and Prosperity. In line with this unfolding policy, Koizumi-led Japan drastically reduced its bilateral aid to Uzbekistan after Andijan and joined the United Nations General Assembly resolution condemning Tashkent's crackdown.[72]

On the other hand, Japan did not seek to cut multi-lateral aid, and its official reaction did not include a public denunciation, even though the SCO members had taken a critical stance towards American military bases, while Uzbekistan ultimately achieved the withdrawal of the K2 base. Moreover, in the same time period (2005–8), Japan curtailed loan aid disbursements to other major recipients in the region unrelated to the Andijan events: Azerbaijan and Kazakhstan (see Figure 1.1). Meanwhile, in spring 2007, Abe's cabinet dispatched METI head Amari Akira on a resource diplomacy mission to Uzbekistan and Kazakhstan, but bilateral loan aid was restored only by the DPJ.

Was it a 'carrot and stick' approach or a vacillating policy? This bigger picture suggests that besides geopolitical factors and Japan's alignment with the United States, other drivers were at play, namely, a shift in the agency of Japanese financial bureaucracy and macroeconomic environment. Subsequent chapters examine these factors in greater detail.

In June 2006, Foreign Minister Asō delivered a speech on CA at the Japan National Press Club, and a few days later, Tokyo hosted CAJ dialogue with a notable U.S. involvement. According to the MOFA, both events were timed to 'draw attention' and 'deflect influence' from the China, Russia, and SCO meeting

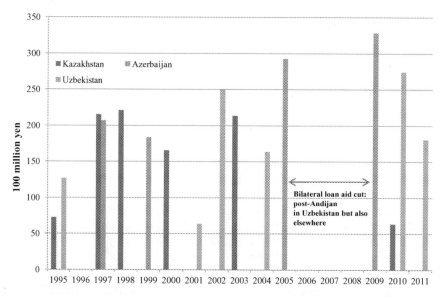

Figure 1.1 JICA loan aid to major Silk Road countries in 1995–2011 (from JICA).

Security, resources, and humanitarianism 35

in Shanghai scheduled for 15 June that year.[73] However, Tokyo may have erroneously interpreted the situation in 'zero-sum-game' terms and miscalculated Washington's motivations, which can be seen from later diplomatic cables involving American officials:

> ... U.S. policy is not 'anti-Russia' or, for that matter, anti-anyone. Rather, we offer an affirmative, not negative, vision to the countries of the region, and in this sense are simply 'anti-monopoly.' Our primary goal is to bolster their sovereignty and independence by broadening their range of choice. It is unclear whether *the Japanese, who still tend to view the region through a traditional 'Great Game' prism,* focused on both Russia and China, fully agree.[74]

Tokyo's above-described misunderstanding represents a case of so-called internalised *gaiatsu* or pressure resulting from Japan's expectations of itself.[75]

Furthermore, in August 2006, Prime Minister Koizumi Jun'ichirō even briefly visited Kazakhstan and Uzbekistan, becoming the first Japanese prime minister to do so and the first Western leader to visit Uzbekistan after Andijan.[76] What may appear as a 'good cop' role – the United States being the 'bad' one – can be better explained by the comfortable and risk-free context for the trip. Koizumi was already in the final month of his premiership, CA represented something new for the Japanese public, a farewell visit to the United States was in the near future, while a journey to East Asia would be difficult at the time due to the tensions over the Yasukuni shrine.

During the visit, Koizumi, whose active involvement in foreign affairs distinguished him from many predecessors, did not formulate any new policies besides stressing the need for energy cooperation, especially in uranium, but even there he encouraged private business to take the lead. In Kazakhstan, the prime minister signed a memorandum on cooperation in peaceful exploitation of nuclear energy and uranium mine development. According to Kawatō, Koizumi's visit coincided – although was not orchestrated with – with a minor détente in Uzbekistan's relations with the European Union and the United States.[77] This view, however, is disputable, as Japan fully restored the relations with Uzbekistan only in 2009. Moreover, Japan's contribution to the social and economic development and energy cooperation was reformulated reflecting changing alignments in the region.

All-in-all, although Koizumi was proactive in expanding the U.S.–Japan alliance after 9/11 and fostering relations with CA through partnerships and CAJ dialogue, Japan's hesitant 'half-measure' response to the Andijan events had a mixed record. Although Tokyo sent to Tashkent a strong message of unity with Brussels and Washington, it may have jumped the gun by overestimating the actual scale of Washington's 'anti-Russian' stance in CA. From the vantage point of pragmatism – a recurrent approach in Japan's CA diplomacy – it ultimately negatively affected Japan's credibility in Russia and CA, while less human rights-sensitive donors, for instance, People's Republic of China (PRC) and Republic of Korea (ROK), partially filled its aid niche.

36 *Security, resources, and humanitarianism*

The Great Game Plays Japan: the impact of CA politics and policies on the relationship

The section title follows a transpositional pun called 'Russian Reversal' in English-speaking popular culture. This discourse swaps what is traditionally perceived as the subject and the object in a given relationship.[78] While, according to several Japanese officials and scholars, Japan was not necessarily willing or capable to play any sort of Great Game in CA, this stance was not always taken for face value by the local elites. Consequently, the power game in which CA elites consider themselves being involved affected Japan's position in the region, nonetheless.

Clan rivalry and securitisation

While the pre-eminent role of executive power in CA governance corresponds with what is widely recognised as authoritarian and personalist regimes, such personalism is possible to the extent it maintains a balance between key factions of regional clans, ethnic groups, and relevant patron-client networks. In other words, it is a hybrid authoritarianism where the authoritarian leader is a skilled balancer walking a tightrope between clans rather than an almighty despot.[79] The brands of factionalism vary in different countries, for instance, Kazakhstan and Turkmenistan have a rather tribal division, in Uzbekistan and Tajikistan, affiliations are more region-based, whilst in Kyrgyzstan, it is a mixture of both with tribal base and clear north-south division. Uzbekistan, as I will show further in this section, is perhaps the most salient example of regular balancing of various groupings by the country's former President Karimov.

One instance that demonstrates the link between domestic clan rivalry in CA and the region's international politics is the phenomenon of 'securitisation' of the CA political agenda, observed in the 2000s. Securitisation in this specific case refers to the prominence gained by international cooperation on anti-terrorism between large external players, such as China, Russia, and the United States, and CA states. Further to the provision of training, hardware, software, and surveillance technologies to regional governments, anti-terrorist campaigns expanded into internal criminal law. As Alexander Cooley noted:

> The global war on terror provided an ideal opportunity for [CA] regimes to frame their internal security practices as part of a broader international coalition and to justify coercive practices as part of a 'permanent international state of emergency.'[80]

This 'securitisation' had its consequences for domestic politics impacting the balance between agencies. In Uzbekistan, for instance, it resulted in a strengthening of position of relevant domestic power groups who also oversaw international security cooperation (i.e. security and law enforcement services). *Siloviki*, as the representatives of these services are informally referred to in the

Russian-speaking countries, enhanced their influence vis-à-vis their financier and economist rivals for power and ultimately leadership succession. In addition to their traditional function of ensuring domestic safety and regime survival, *siloviki* also became an interface of international cooperation in their own right as key counterparts in security aid and training generously provided by China, Russia, and the United States. Thus, they gained a larger presence on the foreign assistance agenda of Uzbek and other CA governments, encroaching on the territory previously dominated by officials from financial and economic agencies.

Uzbekistan's 2005 pivot to Russia and China: a domestic power shift?

In Uzbekistan, the period of 2003–5 marked a power shift in local clan rivalry – which, as I examine below, negatively affected the relationship with Japan at the time. Firstly, the power shifted from relatively West-leaning liberals to relatively more conservative *siloviki*, who, on the one hand, supported growing security cooperation with Russia and China, but, on the other, remained involved in security cooperation with the United States as well. Secondly, this tug-of-war had a regional dimension, as it involved the redistribution of power between clans from Tashkent, Samarkand, and Fergana. During this period, the Samarkand clan and its affiliates temporarily sidelined the previously dominant Tashkent clan, which happened to include several key pro-Westerners at the time, and smaller Fergana clan. As the relationship between two historically dominant Tashkent and Samarkand clans is often characterised as both cooperative and competitive, this power struggle can also be viewed as internal rebalancing within the political class. As several key Uzbek statesmen handling the relationship with Japan happened to belong to the Tashkent clan and relatively Western-friendly wing at the time, their temporary defeat in domestic politics resulted in a lower profile Uzbekistan–Japan relationship.

Tashkent's 2005 rapprochement with Moscow was induced by the deterioration in Uzbekistan's ties with the United States and the European Union due in part to their reaction to two key 2005 events in CA: Kyrgyz 'Tulip Revolution' in March and suppression of the uprising in Uzbekistan's Andijan in May of the same year. However, the reshuffling of top Uzbek officials in favour of those from less pro-Western, relatively more pro-Russian factions and security services started in February 2005 (i.e. prior to the events in Kyrgyzstan and Andijan). This sequence suggests that the political tide in Tashkent started to turn before what was seen as attempted 'colour revolutions.' With the benefit of hindsight, one may suggest that an early recognition of these new developments in clan power struggle could have altered the policy response from external powers, including Japan.

Whilst Japan's main foreign policy acts in connection with the Andijan events included the curtailment of financial aid to Tashkent and Japanese support for the U.N. General Assembly resolution condemning Karimov's handling of the riots, these acts had several negative outcomes and demonstrated a certain lack of understanding of the Uzbek domestic politics by the Japanese decision-makers.

38 Security, resources, and humanitarianism

Firstly, although milder than sanctions imposed by the European Union and the United States, Japan's response unintentionally contributed to further weakening of the Uzbek factions considered comparatively more Western-friendly, as it reduced their 'resource' of foreign financing, including the Japanese one. Secondly, Japanese reaction affected the overall allocation of aid across the Uzbek patronage system, as the reduction of funds received by the country's financial and economic ministries implied an increase in Uzbekistan's dependence on more obscure, less publicly accountable aid in the form of international security cooperation. Thirdly, Japan's slashing of aid resulted in a vacuum that drew in alternative finance from Japan's competitors, for instance, the ROK and PRC. It was in the aftermath of the Andijan-related sanctions that the Korean Development Bank solidified its position in Uzbekistan and became one of the dominant lenders during Uzbekistan's isolation from the West (2005–9).[81]

Personalities matter in Uzbekistan: reformers and conservatives

Prior to 2003–5, Rustam Azimov, a state financier and a key point person in the Japanese–Uzbek relationship, was considered the most prominent candidate for presidential succession within the Tashkent clan, according to Russian expert Andrey Grozin. Ideologically, Azimov had been positioning himself as a young reformer and a pro-Western statesman. Azimov's career path brought him to regular interactions with Japan: at the dawn of Uzbek independence, he was appointed head of the National Bank of Uzbekistan, moving on to become finance minister in 1999 and deputy prime minister in 2000. His status of the Uzbek–Japanese 'relationship handler' was crystallised when Azimov became the co-chair of the Uzbek–Japanese economic cooperation committee on the Uzbek side.[82] Together with the then-Foreign Minister Sadykh Safayev, Azimov was branded as pro-reform and pro-American in the early 2000s.

Another 'handler' of the relationship with Japan, Economy and Foreign Trade Minister Elyor Ganiyev also reportedly belonged to the Tashkent clan and was considered a second option for successor at the time, but did not demonstrate autonomous foreign policy preferences, adjusting to the president's. In contrast to many similar bureaucratic players of the economic bloc, Ganiyev reportedly had good relations with the National Security Service. Initially, it arguably helped him during the strengthening of *siloviki* in 2005 and promotion to the post of foreign minister. Subsequently, however, it was also one of the reasons President Karimov moved Ganiyev from the Foreign Ministry back to External Economic Relations and Trade in 2006.[83] Although Ganiyev's back-and-forth appointments between the helms of Foreign Affairs (2005–6 and 2010–12) and External Economic Relations and Trade (1997–2005, 2006–10, 2012–present) were primarily driven by Karimov's intentions to maintain a balance of power in domestic politics, they incidentally affected the relationship with Japan, since Ganiyev was one of the prominent 'Japan hands' on the Uzbek side. In the record of 28 visits to Japan paid by top Uzbek officials between 1991 and 2016, Azimov (four visits) and Ganiyev (ten visits) became the most 'frequent flyers,' apart

Security, resources, and humanitarianism 39

from President Islam Karimov (three) and former Prime Minister Utkir Sultanov (four). The four-year absence of visits from Uzbekistan to Japan between June 2006 and April 2010 corresponds to the post-Andijan low in the relationship, although Japanese officials kept visiting Uzbekistan in the same period.[84] Former ambassador to Japan (1998–2001) and former Minister of External Economic Relations and Trade Alisher Shaykhov was another reportedly Western-friendly statesman with supposed ties to the Tashkent grouping at the time and an important cog in the Uzbek–Japanese relationship who saw his political status temporarily lower during the Uzbek power shift in the early 2000s.[85]

By extension, prior to the 2005 *siloviki* rise and Andijan events, Azimov, Safayev, and other relatively Western-friendly officials appeared as the most likely beneficiaries of a post-succession power shift. However, Andijan marked a watershed. Besides the narratives of domestic human rights violations and fighting Islamist extremists, the incident also had a clan dimension. Namely, certain experts viewed it as a revolt by the Fergana clan which was unhappy with the status quo of inter-clan rent allocations, subsequently suppressed by Tashkent and Samarkand clans.[86] But Andijan was also the culmination of the reformers' defeat by traditional power brokers and security services. S. Frederick Starr succinctly grasps this power shift in his 2006 work on clans in CA:

> It was the hope of his key advisors that the 'democracy promotion' clauses that they inserted prominently in the Strategic Partnership agreement signed after 9:11 could be used to exert pressure on the main power base of the regional networks and magnates, namely, the Ministry of Internal Affairs. However, the U.S., preoccupied with the operations in Afghanistan, did not exert the pressure that the reformers around Karimov (Safayev, Gulyamov, etc.) had hoped it would. This undercut the reformers and forced Karimov himself back into the hands of the power brokers. As this happened, Uzbekistan again embraced the Russian/Chinese authoritarian model, which posed no danger to the country's traditional power brokers.[87]

Andijan's consequences sealed Islam Karimov's ensuing drift away from Washington to Moscow and Beijing, as the Andijan uprising took place only a few months after the Tulip Revolution in neighbouring Kyrgyzstan and was thus interpreted by the Uzbek authorities as a Western-inspired 'colour revolution' attempt. As a result of both trends, the Tashkent clan apparently became sidelined in favour of restoring overall inter-clan balance. For instance, Sadykh Safayev's foreign minister portfolio was replaced by less important posts of senator and head of parliamentary foreign affairs committee. According to Grozin, Karimov also grew wary of Safayev's close relations with Western leaders, which made him appear to be the potential leader of a 'colour revolution.'[88]

The clan rivalry mattered for Japan on several levels. In the Uzbek case specifically, further to the 2003 EBRD scandal analysed in Chapter 3, Rustam Azimov, then Elyor Ganiyev stepped into the shade, giving way to another potential successor of the time, Shavkat Mirziyoyev, who went on to become the prime

40 *Security, resources, and humanitarianism*

minister (and ultimately, the president in 2016). These domestic political changes occurring in 2003–5 reduced, albeit temporarily, the overall political clout of Azimov and Ganiyev, two statesmen who incidentally were Japan's key point persons in financial and commercial matters.

According to U.S. diplomatic cables, Japan temporarily slashed its aid to Uzbekistan because of Tashkent's ruthless handling of Andijan. This aid conditionality, previously absent in the relationship between Japan and CA, can either be taken at face value or with a grain of salt, since it can also be interpreted as Tokyo officials saying what they believed their Washington counterparts wanted to hear – the rhetoric of burden sharing mixed with deflecting the influence of China and Russia.

On a counterfactual note, had the inter-clan rivalry and resulting clan rebalancing by President Karimov played out differently both for involved individuals and groups during Andijan, the Uzbek–Japanese relationship could have evolved differently in 2005–8. Similarly, as Chapter 4 examines in greater detail, the Kazakhstani domestic politics affected the Kazakh–Japanese nuclear cooperation, since the key stakeholder on the Kazakh side, nuclear power magnate Mukhtar Dzhakishev, underwent prosecution due to his political affiliations.

At the clan level, however, by dramatically reducing its aid to Uzbekistan in 2005, Japan indirectly and, most likely, unintentionally reduced the resources of Azimov, Ganiyev, and their fellow Tashkent clansmen considered more Western-friendly and reliant on external flows. Domestically, this ad hoc conditionality of Japanese aid, even if temporary, hurt their positions compared to *siloviki* rivals. In this light, the subsequent termination of the American lease for the Uzbek military base Karshi-Khanabad in summer 2005 may shed additional light on the role of clan rivalry and rent-seeking in the Japan–CA relationship.

U.S. eviction from the K2 base: clan and rent-seeking implications

Alexander Cooley makes an important distinction between foreign aid to ministries of finance or similar government bodies and assistance in the form of cooperation between security and defence establishments. In particular, he considers the second type less transparent, more corruption-prone, and having a weaker contribution to the recipient, as comparatively larger portions of security assistance were appropriated by the officials rather than trickling down to the population through patronage networks as would be the case of the first aid type.[89] The aid from Japan, both bilateral and multi-lateral, falls under the first type of assistance.

This aid peculiarity of CA is important in the assessment of the influence of key 2005 events in Uzbekistan upon the country's relationship with Japan: power rebalancing between rival factions and clans, the Andijan uprising, and subsequent ousting of the United States from the K2 military base. Due to the limited knowledge of intricate CA politics of inside Japanese elites, Japan's decision to cut aid to Uzbekistan in line with a tough stance taken by Washington and Brussels had two adverse effects. Firstly, it undermined Japan's image as

Security, resources, and humanitarianism 41

a disinterested player in the region and, secondly, in terms of domestic politics impact, the cut in aid may have come across as 'friendly fire' to the comparatively pro-Western and more reform-minded factions in Uzbekistan and, by extension, in CA. Nevertheless, Japan decided to reorient its new aid projects towards technical assistance directly impacting the Uzbek people during that period (2005–8), demonstrating an acknowledgement of the elite predation problem.[90]

As described earlier, the Uzbek security establishment tightened its power grip in early 2005, following the appointment of officials close to the security services. In July 2005, however, the conservative security faction lost a major source of income – the American tenancy of the K2 base, which was closed per the demand of the Uzbek Ministry of Foreign Affairs. In terms of international politics, the termination of the base lease by the United States reflected a landslide in the regional balance of power in favour of Russia- and China-led SCO. In July 2005, the SCO adopted a declaration urging the member states including Uzbekistan to 'set a final timeline' for the ISAF-used base leases.[91] Still, as far as Uzbek domestic politics are concerned, although the crucial importance of the K2 lease termination implied a top-level support from the Uzbek leadership for ending the lease, it also may reflect a certain inter-clan dimension, as the base closure can be seen as a loss for the security services.

There is too little evidence to establish the exact role of individual clans or the Ministry of Foreign Affairs in the decision-making on the K2. There are also facts contradicting this version: for instance, prior to issuing the eviction notice, the Uzbek authorities had contacted their American counterparts six times in order to discuss the terms of the lease, but received no response each time.[92] Nonetheless, whether intentionally or not, the rivals of security services were likely to benefit from the K2 eviction in the logic of a domestic power struggle.

The security services compensated the loss of rent from the K2 by more opaque security cooperation with the U.S. Department of Defense, as well as with increased support from the reinvigorated security cooperation with Russia and China. According to Cooley, the security aid in CA tends to be largely less transparent and more easily appropriated by local elites than foreign aid channelled through the Finance and Foreign Affairs Ministries, which is better reallocated through patronage networks. In this context, Japan's slashing of foreign aid to Uzbekistan in 2005–8 indirectly contributed to the deterioration of the Uzbek patronage system.

Meanwhile, although Japanese officials sought a penalising effect from their downsizing of aid to Uzbekistan, the impact was softened by the rising windfall income of commodity prices at the time. According to American diplomatic officials, Azimov and the Uzbek government were able to directly benefit from their stakes in natural resources companies.[93]

After the K2 eviction, Rustam Azimov had been restoring his top political positions since July 2005 – the time of the K2 decision. In July 2005, he became the minister of foreign economic ties, investment, and trade, in November 2005 – the finance minister again, in April 2006 – deputy prime minister, and, finally, in 2008, he again became the first deputy prime minister while keeping the finance ministry

42 *Security, resources, and humanitarianism*

portfolio. By the time Japan had restored the aid programmes to Uzbekistan and redressed the overall relationship in 2009, Azimov was again one of the country's key power brokers and remained at this position until the 2016 leadership change, when President Mirziyoyev moved him to less influential positions.[94]

Clientelism and rent-seeking at the international level?

One of key functions the above-described top leadership performs in CA political systems is the reconciliation of rent-seeking interests among patron-client groups and networks. Another characteristic of CA elites relevant for the purposes of this book and inferred from Cooley's work is their role of 'brokers and gatekeepers' between local constituencies and external patrons.[95]

Andrey Kazantsev made a similar observation in his 2008 volume, arguing that those elite brokerage practices have deep roots in CA history. In the late Tsarist and in the Soviet period, Russia became the only hegemonic 'external' patron by incorporating CA within its empire. The regional elites thus had to exercise their brokerage only with the imperial centre, namely, St. Petersburg for a short while, and, for most of the period of Soviet dominance, Moscow. The evolution of CA states' foreign policies after 1991 can thus be explained in structuralist terms as a return to a traditional pre-Russian multitude of external patrons, of which Japan *volens nolens* became one.

Kazantsev contends that the tradition of CA multi-vectorism has developed due to the centuries-long habitation of Turkic- and Persian-speaking tribes along the key transit and trade arteries between large powers such as the historical Silk Road. It is particularly relevant to nomadic peoples, from which many historical CA military elites originated and became brokers between local sedentary populations and outer players. The tribes, in particular, nomads, would often pledge nominal allegiance to various stronger sedentary powers, exchanging the public good of trade route security for tribute and vassal status from the player in question, for instance, Chinese, Ottoman, Persian, or Russian empires.[96] These alliances would, however, regularly alternate between rival great powers, thus linking their frequent bandwagoning rotation with clientelism. The Cold War era 'sealed' the region for external transactions and transit operations, except those authorised by Moscow.

On the contrary, the post-1991 independence period brought back on the international agenda the connectivity of the New Silk Road and, consequently, the security of Eurasian continental trade routes, including pipelines. One feature that remained constant in CA's relations with Russia after 1991, however, was the institutional handling of this relationship by Moscow.

While CA's independence brought about the sovereignty of regional elites, Moscow-CA links partially preserved the nature of ties between two post-Soviet *nomenklatura* bureaucrats, perpetuating Soviet-era patron-client ties, which explains why the overall relations remained close, in addition to the mere fact of a shared past. As I argue in Chapter 3, Japanese financial bureaucrats managed to create their own bureaucrat-to-bureaucrat ties with CA *nomenklatura* through aid and mechanisms of advice, especially in Uzbekistan.

Security, resources, and humanitarianism 43

Clientelism is also one element most narratives of cultural and social similitudes between Japan and CA somehow avoid. Although patronage networks and clans as subjects of political agency have been salient in modern Japan, exemplified, for instance, by post-war LDP pork-barrel policies, the CA version of comparable political structures remained a terra incognita for the Japanese. And yet, Japanese aid in a broad sense, that is, including access to the ADB, World Bank (WB), and other multi-lateral funding bodies, can and should be viewed as a potential source of external rent for CA elites, extending the domestic framework of CA clientelism to the international level and qualifying Japan as one of new international patrons that joined Moscow in this context after 1991.

According to an interviewed World Bank official from Japan, rent-seeking incentives create their own economic and political dynamics in CA. For instance, certain reforms and borrowing policies advocated for by a given government can be used to protect rent-seeking. The donors therefore need to be particularly discerning in exercising caution and distinguishing statements from reality.[97] Owing to post-Soviet flawed privatisation, demodernisation, deindustrialisation, and resulting reliance on natural resources, access to commodity assets and other sources of rent became the primary currency of patron-client relationships and influenced economic development.

Can foreign aid be considered a present-day equivalent of protection money? Although this formulation would be very provocative and far-fetched, I argue that it is at least partially valid from the standpoint of political realism. Post-9/11 'securitisation' of CA politics brought about their involvement in various Western assistance programmes as part of the Washington-led 'war on terror.' As security issues related to Afghanistan and the Middle East have been looming large on the international agenda, CA regimes exploited their vulnerabilities such as proximity to the region and local Islamist undergrounds as leverage to attract funding from large powers, such as the United States, Germany, Russia, and others. As a side effect, this focus on CA insecurities contributed to the dominance of public-sector donors at the expense of private interests, as it entrenched the external perception of the region as risk territory rather than a land of opportunities.

Japan's understanding of Central Asia

How aware were the Japanese officials of the repercussions of their aid decisions in CA? On a more general note, according to Japanese officials with CA experience, the aforementioned clan structure and corresponding power struggle beneath its surface remained uncharted territory, meriting a profound study similar to Ruth Benedict's seminal 1946 volume *The Chrysanthemum and the Sword*.[98] Interestingly enough, the Japanese language uses the same term *habatsu* for CA clans as for Japanese factions, cliques, and groupings.

Lack of Japanese expertise on CA factionalism is part of a larger narrative of a general shortage of knowledge of CA in Japan, regularly quoted in interviews with officials as one of the reasons for Japan's disadvantaged position in the region.[99] While academic scholarship of the region has developed in Japan

44 *Security, resources, and humanitarianism*

throughout the twentieth century, Japanese CA studies took its contemporary shape rather recently, in late 1990s–early 2000s.[100] For instance, the Japan Association for CA Studies was established in 2004.[101] Another likely reason for this knowledge shortage in the Cold War aftermath was the focus of Japanese political Sovietology on the decision-making in Moscow, rather than in CA, which attracted predominantly humanities.

Although the clan system predates CA's post-Soviet transition experience, during that experience, it strengthened its institutionalisation and merged into the post-Soviet patron-client governing system.[102] The dynamics of clan rivalry are more important than political rivalries within formal institutions, which serve rather as a façade than actual units of political organisation. Many institutional borrowings from modernity, such as nation state and representative republicanism, are still being developed in CA. Meanwhile, ad hoc, the informal and personalist nature of current political systems impedes long-term institutional development in the region and increases transaction costs.

In turn, these structural specifics of CA politics hardly resonate well with such features of Japanese post-war foreign policy identity as prioritising norms, rules, and compliance with international order.[103] Since 1991, CA countries have been struggling to establish any kind of autonomous regional order, not only due to the interference of external players, but also owing to acute internal differences, especially between the states bordering the Fergana Valley. Although Japan certainly has made attempts to facilitate regional cooperation, manifested, for instance, in the CAJ dialogue, it had neither the capacity nor the political will to create such regional order single-handedly.

However, one of Japan's post-Cold War diplomatic priorities remains the incorporation of China into the status quo international order as a responsible stakeholder and not a kind of challenger that Japan itself was before World War II.[104] In this regard, Tokyo's intentions were harmonised with Washington, and international order meant a U.S.-led order in the first place. The predicament of CA states, from that perspective, is that their close ties with Beijing and Moscow, at best, limit their abilities to fit into this kind of order. According to a World Bank interviewee, 'the region cannot survive without Russia whether they like it or not. There are a lot of very strong undercurrent relations [between Russia and CA] both ways. Japan's relationship [with the region] should also be put in this context.'[105] In turn, this predicament limited Japan's own foreign policy capacity to contribute to international norms and rules, when applied to CA.

The Chinese dimension of Japan–Central Asia relations

Japan and the Shanghai Cooperation Organisation

Historically, Japan has demonstrated instances of distinguishing itself from the Western states by its less demanding stance on democratisation and authoritarianism in developing countries, for instance, in Myanmar or Zimbabwe.[106] Yet in

Security, resources, and humanitarianism 45

the case of CA, this Japanese approach coincided with the slightly critical attitude towards the SCO and an inconsistent appeal to democratic values in 2005–7.

For instance, the criticism of the SCO was voiced by diplomat Kawatō Akio and by Saitō Tsutomu, the editor-in-chief of the right-wing newspaper *Sankei Shimbun*. During a meeting in Bishkek with participants of the Japan International Cooperation Agency (JICA) program for young leaders in CA, Saitō said the countries of the region should refuse cooperation with China within the SCO and maintain friendlier relations with the West.[107]

By contrast, Japanese scholar Iwashita Akihiro made the case for Japan's engagement with the SCO, although it did not gain traction in Tokyo's policy circles.[108] Indeed, outside the zero-sum-game paradigm, Japan and the SCO would both be interested in promoting regional peace, stability, and development in the shared security perimeter of Eurasia, and the SCO would have the 'hard' security capacity Japan lacked.[109] Nonetheless, although the SCO's goals declaratively include 'making joint efforts to maintain and ensure peace, security and stability in the region,' these aspirations were not taken for face value, being overshadowed by the larger ambitions of 'moving towards the establishment of a new, democratic, just and rational political and economic international order.'[110]

The SCO's primary objective involved combating the Islamist radicalism threat, present in Kyrgyzstan, Tajikistan, and Uzbekistan. SCO members – China, Kazakhstan, Kyrgyzstan, Uzbekistan, Tajikistan, and Russia – have expressed an apologetic and supportive position in regard to the Uzbek official reaction to the Andijan incident. According to the SCO, the unrest was inspired by radical Islamists.[111] While the official opinions in the West were quite unanimously criticising Uzbekistan, subsequent Western scholarship suggested that Muslim extremist groups, such as Akramiya, were indeed involved in the uprising. Furthermore, they intentionally resorted to armed violence, which distinguished them from casual civilians involved in the so-called 'colour revolutions' in Georgia (2003) and Ukraine (2004).[112] Such extremism is represented in CA by both the established presence of transnational groups (Hizb ut-Tahrir, Al-Qaeda), and local ones (Islamic Movement of Uzbekistan), many of which are based in the Ferghana Valley, close to Andijan. Their radicalisation was underpinned by complex intertwined factors: socio-economic crisis, political repression, post-Soviet identity crises, regional rivalries, and foreign proselytising.[113]

Nevertheless, the SCO has also been viewed quite accurately as the instrument of Russian and Chinese influence on CA.[114] In addition to Russia's traditional seeking of better stability in its 'near abroad' and closer cooperation in the field of natural resources, in 2005–6, Russia was also particularly wary of 'colour revolutions' in ex-USSR countries, which it perceived as American-inspired regime change. In terms of military involvement, Russia's presence in the region has been by far the most important: it stations troops in Kyrgyzstan and Tajikistan.[115] Most countries in the region, except Turkmenistan and, intermittently, Uzbekistan (1999–2006 and 2012–present), are members of the CSTO – another Russia-led security bloc in the former Soviet Union. After the attenuation of Sino-Soviet tensions in the 1980s and partial demilitarisation of the border, the Chinese

46 *Security, resources, and humanitarianism*

military presence in CA has been confined to security forces in Xinjiang.[116] Yet, officially, Beijing was very sensitive to the deployment of American troops at the K2 (Uzbekistan) and Manas (Kyrgyzstan) bases. This opposition culminated in the 2005 statement of the SCO urging the United States to withdraw its military bases from the region.[117] Subsequently, the K2 base was closed in 2005 at the request of the Uzbek government, while the one in Manas remained in operation until 2014 despite Russian and Chinese opposition.[118]

Conversely, the leaders in Beijing viewed the SCO as primarily a means of securing the neighbourhood of its separatist Xinjiang region, neighbouring Kazakhstan, Kyrgyzstan, and Tajikistan.[119] However, to Moscow's discomfort, officially, China has also strongly used the SCO to promote economic cooperation with CA where its economic presence has been increasing since the independence of these post-Soviet states. Was China's expansion in CA a source of concern for Japan?

Premises for balancing and engaging rising China by Japan

At the turn of the century and further into the early 2000s, China has actively developed its economic and political relationships in Asia, particularly focusing on Southeast Asia. China strengthened its ties with ASEAN through the ASEAN-China Free Trade Area, the Treaty of Amity and Cooperation in Southeast Asia (thus pledging to the 1967 ASEAN Charter core elements), and the Declaration of Conduct in the South China Sea. By virtue of signing the latter two documents, China renounced the use of force in the dispute settlement. China also came forward as a mediator between the Myanmar regime and other actors.[120]

These processes were simultaneous to the Chinese involvement in the SCO and were a part of its strategy of 'peaceful rise' via integration in the regional system and its platforms. This Chinese strategy has borne fruit and built confidence: all ASEAN member states had, at this stage, seemingly rejected the containment approach to China and acknowledged that the ASEAN Regional Forum was a means of socialising rather than containing China.[121]

In this context, it is worth inquiring whether parallels could be drawn between the aforementioned Andijan case and Hashimoto's assistance to Myanmar in 1997 or Abe's courting of Zimbabwe in 2016 despite the poor human rights record in both countries and respective U.S. criticism. In both instances, Japan's aid was deemed necessary to prevent the recipients' drift to China, as Beijing was progressively forging a partnership with Yangon and Harare, benefiting from the opportunities created by the Western sanctions.

Hashimoto's pro-engagement course towards Myanmar, using the ODA as a major means of pressure and competing with the Western approach, continued under his successors Obuchi, Mori, and Koizumi. Certain Japanese scholars labelled this policy as 'quiet diplomacy' and acknowledged its purpose of balancing China.[122] Going further, if Japanese Asian diplomacy was trying to match China's initiatives in Southeast Asia from the latter half of the 1990s through the Koizumi era, it seems reasonable to apply a similar logic towards CA.[123]

Security, resources, and humanitarianism 47

The countries of CA would be less likely than the countries of Southeast Asia to feel ambivalent towards Japanese Asian diplomacy, given that painful World War II memories and fear of a stronger Japan are issues in Japan's relations with many of its East Asian neighbours. Moreover, as I expound in Chapter 3, they were considering Japan as a developmental role model. While the Chinese experience of gradual transition from communism to capitalism is also often considered as a role model in the former USSR (especially Russia and CA), for CA, it appears to put their independence at stake through an increased reliance on both Chinese capital and economic presence.

CA leaders have demonstrated a strong sentiment for avoiding incorporation into a new Sino-centric system, which they have already experienced in the past history of Chinese imperial expansion.[124] The most notable example of this insecurity is the memory of the conquest of the Dzungar state by the Qing Dynasty in the eighteenth century. Furthermore, during the Great Cultural Revolution more than 70,000 refugees fled from Xinjiang to CA.[125]

The anxiety is weaker in the countries that do not have a common border with China, for example, Uzbekistan.[126] On the contrary, the neighbouring states, especially the smaller ones, like Kyrgyzstan and Tajikistan, have tangible concerns.[127] Even the attitude of Kazakhstan – arguably the regional leader so far – towards its increasing dependence on China has been a mix of alarmism and pragmatism. In 2009, China had overtaken Russia as the largest trading partner of Kazakhstan and gained control of almost one-third of the Kazakhstani oil production.[128] The Kazakhstani Prime Minister Karim Massimov – fluent in Mandarin and educated in Beijing and Hunan – expressed an optimistic and pragmatic view regarding relations with China, but this position was not always shared by other officials or the general public.[129] Loans provided by the PRC to Kazakhstan were regarded by its officials as benefiting mostly China and preserving the Kazakh economy's specialism in raw materials, as this sector benefited the most from the Chinese capital.[130] In winter 2009–10, Kazakh activists protested against the government's plan to lease to China one million hectares of Kazakh farmland adjacent to Chinese western borders. Members of the public saw such a lease as the beginning of a Chinese expansion.[131]

Although cautious views of China's rise in the post-Cold War Japan can be traced back to the 1990s, the official Tokyo perception of China as a major potential threat was initially publicly formulated in the above-mentioned National Defense Policy Guidelines (NDPG) of 2004.[132] Such visions were mostly disseminated in the academic community and among security experts, as well as various representatives on the right end of Japanese politics: anti-Communists, traditional right-wingers, or pro-Taiwan lobbyists.[133]

In the new post-Cold War international security environment, Japan gradually started facing its new key dichotomy: relations in a triangle with the United States and China. Dealing with a rising China became a centrepiece of Japan's security puzzle since the second half of the 1990s. As Tōgō Kazuhiko – the author of Hashimoto's Eurasian diplomacy concept and a representative of the MOFA's 'Russian school' – metaphorically described it, Japan wanted to avoid

48 *Security, resources, and humanitarianism*

two nightmares: U.S.–China conflict and U.S.–China bypassing of Japan, similar to the so-called Nixon-*shokku* of 1973 – Japan's shock regarding U.S.–China rapprochement which Japan became aware after the event and without adequate consultation from Washington.[134]

This spectre reappeared again during the first Obama presidency (2009–13) in the face of a possible U.S.–China 'G2' arrangement. This idea of China and the United States jointly steering global governance was initially raised in American academic circles in 2006, voiced again by Zbigniew Brzezinski in early 2009, and reflected in media discussions prior to the president Obama's visit to Asia in autumn 2009.[135]

Thus, finding a right combination of balancing and engaging China became one of the missions for Japanese diplomacy starting from the late 1990s, going throughout and apparently beyond the first decade of the twenty-first century. As formulated by Samuels, Japan in the vein of its 'Goldilocks consensus' had to find a 'strategic convergence,' acceptable to the United States and attractive to China.[136]

Potential natural partners for such hedging could be numerous in East, Southeast, and South Asia. Several scholars have mentioned in this regard Taiwan, Mongolia, Australia, and India.[137] The Koizumi administration was actively trying to prevent Russia's drift to China, that was stimulated by Tokyo's tough stance on the Kuril dispute.[138] Yet, although Koizumi used the carrot of lobbying a Russian oil pipeline project from Eastern Siberia to the Pacific Ocean as an alternative to a China-supported Angarsk-Daqing project (see Chapter 5 for details), he still opposed Russia over CA through CAJ dialogue, as I have shown earlier.

A pattern of greater rivalry in Sino-Japanese relations under Koizumi was reflected by various Japanese initiatives such as the prime minister's 2002 visit to Southeast Asia, as well as increased Japanese efforts to improve security and assistance ties with different nations on China's southern and western flanks, including India, Pakistan, Afghanistan, and CA.[139] The latter, considering its strategic geographic position and rich resources could thus serve as both an obstacle for Chinese expansion and a partner in engaging China, since stability, development, and democratisation in CA would have benefited vulnerable Xinjiang through the mitigation of a shared terrorist threat and regional economic cooperation helping poverty alleviation.

From Arc of Freedom and Prosperity to Eurasian Crossroads

Initially, the possibility of balancing against China in CA was not openly voiced by Japanese officials, except in the aforementioned opinions of Kawatō Akio, Saitō Tsutomu, and individual METI officials. Nevertheless, the 'points of attention' towards a rising China in Japan do coincide chronologically with activity in CA.

Japan's first attempt at engaging China took place under the Hashimoto administration following the Third Taiwan Straits Crisis of 1995–6. It is under Hashimoto that the Eurasian diplomacy focusing on Russia, China, and CA was formulated in early 1997. That said, Hashimoto belonged to the more

Security, resources, and humanitarianism   49

China-friendly LDP faction of Heiseiken (Heisei Research Council) and hardly harboured any intention of outright antagonism.

In 2004, under Koizumi, China was designated as a potential threat in the NDPG, and it is in 2004–6 that 'Central Asia plus Japan' was established by Foreign Minister Kawaguchi with China in mind and subsequently used to deflect the SCO's influence.

Abe Shinzō, a member of a conservative, nationalist, and neo-revisionist policy constituency succeeded Koizumi as prime minister in September 2006. While his stance towards China was regarded by many scholars as tough during both of his premierships (2006–7, 2012–present), it also involved elements of engagement and détentes.[140] Abe mentioned the importance of cooperation with CA, albeit marginally, in his 2006 manifesto book *Utsukushii kuni-e* in the same chapter where he stressed the need for Japan's partnership with India and Australia.[141] By forging partnerships with Canberra and Delhi, Abe activated new lines of external balancing vis-a-vis China – what later became known as Democratic Security Diamond or the Indo-Pacific Quad was initially called the 'Asian-Oceanic G3 Plus America.'

After Abe's resignation in 2007, Fukuda Yasuo assumed the post of prime minister. Fukuda had a 'dovish' position and China-friendlier views, despite hailing from the same Seiwaken faction as Abe, which was otherwise considered pro-Taiwan and adverse to Beijing. Consequently, Fukuda's foreign policy did not include any notable measures on balancing China, let alone doing so via CA.

It is Asō Tarō, Abe's foreign minister and Fukuda's successor, who combined both close attention towards CA and the desire to confront China's rise. Asō, his vice-minister Yachi Shotarō (2005–8), and MOFA officials Kanehara Nobukatsu and Taniguchi Tomohiko developed the strategic concept of AFP – the third large-scale initiative of Tokyo vis-à-vis CA after Eurasian diplomacy and Central Asia plus Japan. AFP constituted a part of value-oriented diplomacy (*kachikan gaikō*) that, according to Yachi, originated from his 2005 meetings with NATO colleagues.[142]

In both his 2006 speech inaugurating AFP and homonymous book published in 2007, Asō made a tacit parallel to the 'Arc of Instability' going through vulnerable countries mostly situated in Asia where Japan's contribution towards further democratic reforms and stability (value-oriented diplomacy) is necessary.[143] The volume dedicates a separate chapter to the Silk Road countries that are situated in this vulnerable zone. Besides CA countries, the arc included Cambodia, Laos, Vietnam (together referred as CLV), Georgia, Azerbaijan, and Ukraine. While all of these countries share a Socialist past and some of them have abundant rich energy resources (CA, Azerbaijan), most of them (CA and CLV) also share concerns over a rising China, which they perceive as challenge.

The fragility of CA countries was metaphorically portrayed by Asō as 'interior continental magma.' He suggested three pillars for Japanese policy in CA: security and development to 'cool' the 'magma,' open regional cooperation, and universal values, closing the chapter with the ideas of integrating Afghanistan in the CAJ framework.[144]

50 *Security, resources, and humanitarianism*

This approach can thus be regarded as consistent with the past Japanese involvement in CA, all the more that Asō was also seeing it as part of Japan's engagement with the West and linkage with NATO in particular, echoing Hashimoto's reasoning for Eurasian diplomacy. Besides that, Asō was director general of the Economic Planning Agency under Hashimoto, shared Hashimoto's views on the relations with CA, and actually was a member of the high-ranking delegation sent to the region following Hashimoto's speech. In 2002, Asō had become the head of the LDP Parliamentary Friendship League with Uzbekistan (*giinrenmei*) and remained in that position for several years. I examine Asō's involvement in Uzbekistan as finance official and LDP politician in Chapters 3 and 4.

AFP proposed closer cooperation with NATO and active promotion of democratisation in unstable Eurasian countries, including CA. In addition to CAJ, in June 2007, the Asō-led MOFA established the GUAM Plus Japan framework involving the grouping of Georgia, Ukraine, Azerbaijan, and Moldova supported by the United States and viewed officially by Moscow as anti-Russian.[145] Although the replication of CAJ into GUAM may appear consistent from the standpoint of value-oriented diplomacy aiding democracy promotion in post-Soviet countries, the consistency is rather artificial. By the mid-2000s, GUAM was an inert and inconsistent grouping (despite claiming democracy promotion in member states, it included Azerbaijan, known for its poor democratic record), negatively viewed by Russia. Japan was likely to have achieved the same results with individual GUAM members without antagonising Russia. The maintenance of the GUAM Plus Japan framework showed a tolerance for inertia and 'template' thinking in Japanese foreign policy.

The AFP project and Japanese diplomacy in CA under Abe raised significant suspicions in Beijing and Moscow, who at the time continued to actively foster cooperation via the SCO.[146] Although Japanese experts with first-hand knowledge of the situation argued in 2008 that 'Japan is not in competition with Russia and China in its engagement drive with the Central Asian republics,' diplomatic cables involving MOFA officials show otherwise.[147] This evidence shows that in the mid-2000s, the SCO was a matter of concern not only among the Japanese conservatives, but also in diplomatic circles.[148] Subsequently, one of the authors of the AFP concept, Taniguchi Tomohiko, claimed that this vision was not aimed at antagonising Russia, but rather at getting it to the negotiation table over the territorial issue and boosting Japan's profile in Japan's relations with the United States and European countries.[149]

Meanwhile, internal discontinuities and tensions within the Japanese government again blocked the initiative from consistent implementation as it was the case with Eurasian diplomacy after Hashimoto. During Abe's premiership, both NATO's Global Partnership initiative began to wane and the prime minister's views on diplomacy were different from Asō's, since they placed an important emphasis on relations with India and Australia. In 2007, Asō was replaced by Machimura Nobutaka at the helm of the MOFA and was later defeated by Fukuda in the election for the LDP chairmanship. Neither

Security, resources, and humanitarianism 51

Machimura nor Kōmura Masahiko who headed the MOFA under Fukuda attempted to pursue the AFP project. Although the scheduled CAJ meeting of senior officials took place in 2007, CAJ foreign minister meetings were not convened between 2006 and 2010.

Although the AFP concept was interpreted as a policy for balancing China, it remained a 'paper tiger' without practical implementation during Abe, Fukuda, or Asō's premierships.[150] Primary reasons for its non-fulfilment include the change of priorities, Fukuda's friendly stance towards China, and the urgent need to deal domestically and internationally with the financial crisis of 2008–9.[151] It is hard to grasp CA's reaction to AFP due to the lack of evidence. Japan's inability to deliver was unlikely to receive a positive assessment due to the dominance of realist thinking in CA capitals and apprehension towards externally devised concepts such as the Greater Middle East and concepts seeking to integrate CA closer with Afghanistan – an idea perceived in CA rather as a risk than of an opportunity.

Two months before the 2009 election, which turned out to be a landslide victory for the rival DPJ, Asō came up with a connectivity infrastructure initiative dubbed Eurasian Crossroads. Although the concept did not materialise, it clearly indicated the importance the LDP continued attaching to trans-Eurasian infrastructural projects – four years before the Belt and Road Initiative (BRI). Another notable highlight is how Asō viewed the roles of China and Russia, this time indicated as potential partners alongside India – possibly, to soften the effect from AFP, which was directly mentioned in Asō's speech. It is worth citing a large part of the speech (abbreviations and italics are mine):

I would like to draw your attention to CA and the Caucasus region, which lie at the very center of the AFP and enjoy abundant energy and other resources. Japan will engage in cooperation to bring the Eurasian continent together *both north to south and east to west* via this region. I call this the initiative for a Eurasian Crossroads. Running vertically will be the 'North-South Logistics and Distribution Route,' a route that will run *from CA through Afghanistan to the Arabian Sea*. I envision the development of both *roads and railways*. Horizontally there will be an 'East-West Corridor,' a route running *from CA through the Caucasus to Europe*. I envision developing *ports* on the coast of the Caspian Sea, among other ideas. The development of such regional infrastructure will unite resource-rich CA and the Caucasus in one whole region that includes Afghanistan and Pakistan which needs a foundation for the economy. I have in the past spoken of Asia's subregion-wide development such as the concept of the Delhi-Mumbai Industrial Corridor in India and the Mekong Economic Corridors in Indochina. Through these projects, it will be possible for example to shorten the travel time from Ho Chi Minh City in Vietnam to Chennai, India from the current roughly two weeks by sea to only eight days by developing infrastructure and making use of Japanese technology such as 'one stop' services at border crossings. We can envision a future in which we connect this series of initiatives to

52 *Security, resources, and humanitarianism*

develop a route by which people, goods, and capital flow freely, traversing the entirety of the Eurasian continent beginning at the Pacific Ocean and ending in Europe. This could also be called *a modern-day version of the Silk Road* and today I have shared with you this major initiative that contains just such a vision.[152]

Asō continued stressing natural resources as CA's main attraction and offered a Silk Road vision based on building infrastructural corridors, both meridional and latitudinal, doing so four years before Xi Jinping's announcement of the BRI. While extending a formal welcome to Beijing and Moscow, the vectors of corridors proposed by Asō were, in fact, heading away from China and Russia. Although this is not anti-thetical to export flows of these countries, it may also be indirectly construed as continued encouragement of diversification of CA's routes away from the region's two giant neighbours. Unlike ADB's Central Asian Regional Economic Cooperation (CAREC), the Eurasian Crossroads involved Japan directly, although not to the extent that the BRI is Sino-centric. One can only counterfactually wonder what could have become of this vision if the LDP stayed in power in August 2009 and if the Japanese government's financial resources were not committed to battling the global financial crisis and domestic fiscal issues.

Abe II: proactivity, pragmatism, and strategic use of infrastructure

Abe's second premiership (2012–present) marked both a continuity and sharp contrast with his previous term. As I mentioned earlier, Abe showcased an unprecedented diplomatic proactivity, visiting a record number of foreign countries as part of raising Japan's international profile and promoting Japanese exports, including infrastructure. Abe's new foreign policy concept was labelled 'a diplomacy that takes a panoramic perspective of the world map' (*chikyūgi wo fukan suru gaikō*).[153]

Abe avoided discursive grand design concepts in CA, prioritised mercantilist promotion of Japanese exports, and ultimately refocused regional rhetoric on the Indo-Pacific rather than continental Eurasia. His administration preserved both the eagerness to compete with China and the readiness to engage with it, evidenced by Abe's meetings with Chinese leaders and the trips of his key advisor Yachi Shōtarō to Beijing. As early as June 2014, Abe has been mulling a visit to CA, which ultimately materialised in October 2015. Abe's visit became the second ever by a Japanese prime minister since Koizumi's 2006 trip and included all five countries, while more Japanese officials have visited CA in the first three years of Abe's premiership than in the decade preceding Abe's return to power. Three of four METI heads who visited CA (Amari Akira, Edano Yukio, Motegi Toshimitsu, and Sekō Hiroshige) were members of Abe cabinets: Amari in 2007, Motegi in 2014, and Sekō in 2017. Abe's 2015 trip resulted in $27 billion worth of contracts stressing both the promotion of Japan's exports and the pan-Asian span of Sino-Japanese infrastructure rivalry. Abe reiterated his call for 'open regionalism' in CA, similar to synonymous appeals made by Foreign Ministers Kawaguchi and Asō a decade earlier, this time clearly eyeing China, but despite this rhetoric, the main angle was commercial rather than geopolitical. Abe's visit coincided with a similar tour of the region made by Secretary of State John Kerry. Although some Russian experts interpreted these two visits as synchronised, this conclusion appears far-fetched, given the long preparation of Abe's visit.[154] Moreover, Kerry inaugurated the C5 + 1 meeting format (five CA states plus the United States), in all likelihood inspired by CAJ and showing Washington's diplomacy in CA can follow Tokyo and not only lead.

By contrast, despite declarative adherence to democracy principles and policy favouring Japan's alliances with democratic states announced in 2012 as the Democratic Security Diamond, Abe's second premiership de-emphasised the value component from his diplomacy towards Russia and CA, where during Koizumi's rule and Abe's first premiership, Tokyo had previously advocated democracy promotion or encouragement.[155] In 2013, Abe declared that building a strong country was a value he shared with President Vladimir Putin and continued courting Moscow even in the aftermath of the 2014 Ukrainian crisis.[156] Moreover, Abe offered to Putin a potential cooperation in CA to strengthen the region's borders, confirming a departure from antagonising Russia.[157] While paying lip service to the openness of CA in his rhetoric and promoting quality infrastructure in the region, on balance, Abe II's CA policy dampened previous oscillations between value-oriented diplomacy and pragmatism in favour of the latter. This damping was in line with the increased role of the METI at the expense of the MOFA during Abe's second premiership.[158] As a result, during most of Abe's second administration, Tokyo's diplomacy in CA remained predominantly mercantilist, materialising in the Top Sales approach – sealing large-scale international commercial deals through agreements by top executives or national leaders.[159] The appointment of former METI chief Motegi Toshimitsu as the new head of the MOFA during the September 2019 cabinet reshuffle is likely to further crystallise these neo-mercantilist trends.

President Mirziyoyev's December 2019 visit to Japan highlighted the pragmatic aspect of the relationship by focusing on resources and energy infrastructure. JICA and the Uzbekistani government agreed on a new major long-term cooperation programme of sizeable value of over US$3.5 billion, involving energy, industrial modernisation, agriculture, infrastructure, environment, and healthcare.[160] In particular, Japan pledged 187.9 billion yen, or US$1.7 billion, in loans for power generation technologies and exports of horticulture.[161] Uzbekistan's Navoi Mining and Metallurgy Combine signed major agreements on the supply of uranium to Japan: a US$636.4 million contract with Itochu and a US$510.1 million contract with Marubeni to cover between 2023 and 2030.[162] JOGMEC and the Uzbekistani government signed an agreement on surveying gold and tungsten resources.[163]

At the same time, this neo-mercantilism of the Abe premiership is likely to be affected by the securitisation of economic issues, although its implications for CA are unclear at this stage. This securitisation is evidenced by LDP heavyweight Amari Akira's 2019 proposal to establish Japan's version of the

54 *Security, resources, and humanitarianism*

U.S. National Economic Council and by plans to establish a new policy group under the National Security Secretariat of the Cabinet Secretariat in 2019–20.[164] This institutional design was aimed at increasing the prime minister office's powers over guiding economic security policy and at providing policy response to perceived challenges stemming from China, such as the BRI and Huawei's 5G development.

In 2014, Japan regained the rank of Uzbekistan's top donor, despite the country's continued low performance in democratisation indices. These developments marked a contrast with the 2005–8 post-Andijan policy of roughly the same foreign policy team, but were in line with Abe II's strategic use of aid. Furthermore, during Abe II, Defence Minister Nakatani Gen became the chairman of the Japan–Kyrgyz Parliamentary League of Friendship and announced the first ever visit to Kyrgyzstan by a head of Japan's Defence Ministry.[165]

Besides pragmatism, this changed position reflected Abe's readiness to subordinate various foreign policy elements to the goal of balancing China, but also to prioritise the areas of competition with greater selectivity. While under Koizumi and Abe I value-oriented diplomacy was instrumental in strengthening the alliance with the Bush administration, its unsustainability, low benefits, and hostile reception in Eurasia arguably contributed to this policy's reassessment under Abe II. During Abe's second premiership, his foreign policy team also had more experience and appeared set on a more long-term vision enabled by the cabinet's comparative longevity.

Conclusion

This chapter has assessed Japan's post-Cold War cooperation with CA under the LDP rule through the lens of dominant security and foreign policy imperatives. The Japanese officials formulated a number of comprehensive diplomatic approaches towards CA, both reactive and proactive. These approaches were consistent whenever they materialised and were not disruptively affected and rendered 'on-and-off' by the structural problems of Japanese domestic decision-making: frequent leadership changes, rotations inside the MOFA, and power balance shifts between bureaucrats and the cabinet.

Furthermore, Japanese diplomacy towards CA evolved in accordance with the perceived imperatives of the political elite's security thinking in relevant periods, such as adjusting to the post-Cold War international structure, addressing post-9/11 international terrorism, and dealing with China's rise. In their CA policy, the LDP-led cabinets have shown a regular alignment with the United States, which at times was affected by 'zero-sum-game' thinking. In the LDP reign of the 2000s, Japan's CA policy became influenced by rhetorical grand designs, such as the Energy Silk Road, Arc of Freedom and Prosperity, Corridor of Peace and Stability, and the 2009 Eurasian Crossroads. The latter concept was relatively the closest to the BRI in terms of vision. By contrast, the grand visions of Abe's second premiership – the Indo-Pacific, Asia–Africa Growth Corridor,

Security, resources, and humanitarianism 55

and Partnership for Quality Infrastructure, rarely targeted CA specifically as a region due to the shifted focus of Sino-Japanese competition to Southeast and South Asia.

Nevertheless, the conclusions based purely on diplomatic history, classic theories of international relations, and security considerations, provide only a limited insight into the factors that shaped Japan's policies in CA. They do not fully account for the oscillations in Japan's aid and energy policy in CA and require the incorporation of additional dimensions: partisan politics in Japan, domestic politics and foreign policies in CA, the promotion of development and financial assistance, and natural resources.

Notes

1 Akio Kawatō, 'What is Japan up to in Central Asia?' in *Japan's Silk Road Diplomacy: Paving the Road Ahead*, eds. Christopher Len, Tomohiko Uyama, and Tetsuya Hirose (Washington, DC: Central Asia-Caucasus Institute & Silk Road Studies Program, 2008), 15–30; Round table 'East Asian Perspectives on the Architecture of the Global Community' at Chatham House with the presence of high-ranking Japanese officials, 16 March 2010. The geopolitical rivalry over post-Cold War CA is often compared to the 'Great Game' played between British and Russian empires in the same region in the late nineteenth century.
2 Uyama Tomohiko, 'Japan's Diplomacy towards Central Asia in the Context of Japan's Asian Diplomacy and Japan-U.S. Relations' in *Japan's Silk Road Diplomacy: Paving the Road Ahead*, eds. Len et al., 101–20.
3 According to Japan's first post-World War II Prime Minister Yoshida Shigeru, Japan had to prioritise its economic development and maintain a low diplomatic profile, thus entrusting the military defence matters to the United States. The 'Fukuda doctrine' was a set of principles for Japanese foreign policy expressed by Prime Minister Takeo Fukuda in 1977, when he declared that Japan should not become a military power and should engage in cooperation with ASEAN and other Southeast Asian countries as an equal partner. However, after the outbreak of the war between Kampuchea and Vietnam, Japan decided to support ASEAN and demonstrate coolness officially towards Hanoi. See Nishihara, *East Asian Security and the Trilateral Countries*, 16.
4 Interview with former METI official Mitsuhiro Maeda, March 2010.
5 Parts of this chapter were published in Nikolay Murashkin, 'Japan's Value-Oriented and Resource Diplomacy in Central Asia: Before and After Belt and Road' in *Japan's Foreign Policy in the 21st Century: Continuity and Change*, Lam Peng Er and Purnendra Jain (eds.), Lexington (forthcoming).
6 Most notably, Kenneth Waltz, *Theory of International Politics* (Boston: McGraw-Hill 1979); John Mearsheimer, *The Tragedy of Great Power Politics* (New York: W. W. Norton & Company, 2001); Stephen Walt, *The Origins of Alliances* (Ithaca: Cornell University Press, 1987).
7 Most notably, Hans Morgenthau and Kenneth Thompson, *Politics Among Nations*, 6th edition (New York: McGraw-Hill, 1985); Edward H. Carr, *The Twenty Years' Crisis* (New York: Harper Perennial, 1939); and Reinhold Niebuhr, *Christian Realism and Political Problems* (New York: Scribner, 1953).
8 Thierry de Montbrial, *L'action et le système du monde* [Action and the World System]. (Paris: Presses Universitaires de France-Quadrige, 2002), 218.
9 Ibid., 219.
10 Ole Waever et al., *Identity, Migration and the New Security Agenda in Europe*. (London: Pinter. 1993), 17–40.

56 Security, resources, and humanitarianism

11 Although important progress on this matter was achieved by Nakasone Yasuhiro and Koizumi Jun'ichirō, it was Hatoyama Yukio who formed a dedicated government body explicitly for national strategy (*Kokka Senryaku Kyoku*, or National Policy Unit) in 2009. Abe Shinzō in the beginning of his first premiership had an aspiration of setting up a National Security Council, however, this plan was not fulfilled until his second term in 2012. Press conference by PM Hatoyama Yukio, 16 September 2009. http://www.kantei.go.jp/foreign/hatoyama/statement/200909/16kaiken_e.html (Accessed 25 April 2010).

12 There are some exceptions to this division, for instance, Nishihara Masashi. He has continuously advocated the strategic nature of Japanese foreign policy in relation to Southeast Asian states, albeit with a focus on economic means. See Nishihara Masashi, *East Asian Security and the Trilateral Countries. A Report to the Trilateral Commission* (New York: New York University Press, 1985), 16–18; Nishihara Masashi, *Senryaku kenkyū no shikaku. Anzen hoshō senryaku dokuhon: Heiwa to anzen no tame no 12shō* [Strategic Studies Perspective. A Reader on Security Policy: Twelve Chapters on Peace and Security]. (Tokyo: Ningen-no kagakusha, 1988), 186–87.

13 Gilbert Rozman, Kazuhiko Tōgō, and Joseph P. Ferguson, eds. *Japanese Strategic Thought toward Asia* (New York: Palgrave MacMillan, 2007), 2.

14 Chung, Jae Ho. 'East Asia Responds to the Rise of China: Patterns and Variations,' *Pacific Affairs* 82, no. 4 Winter (2009–2010): 660.

15 Ibid.

16 Richard Samuels, *Securing Japan: Tokyo's Grand Strategy and the Future of East Asia* (Ithaca: Cornell University Press, 2007), 7.

17 Chung, *East Asia Responds to the Rise of China*, 660–1.

18 David Welch, 'Embracing normalcy: Toward a Japanese "National Strategy,"' in *Japan as a 'Normal Country'? A Nation in Search of its Place in the World*, eds. Yoshihide Soeya, Masayuki Tadokoro, and David A. Welch (Toronto: University of Toronto Press, 2011), 19.

19 David Arase, *Buying Power. The Political Economy of Japan's Foreign Aid* (London: Lynne Rienner Publishers, 1995), 204–5.

20 Samuels, *Securing Japan*, 8–9.

21 Ibid.

22 Satō Yoichirō and Hirata Keiko, eds. *Norms, Interests, and Power in Japanese Foreign Policy* (New York: Palgrave MacMillan, 2008), 11; Robert O. Keohane and Joseph S. Nye, '*Power and Interdependence: World Politics in Transition*,' 1977.

23 Satō and Hirata, *Norms, Interests, and Power*, 9–11. The term 'mercantile state' was introduced by Kōsaka Masataka, a political scientist and a biographer of Prime Minister Yoshida Shigeru, in order to devise an optimal posture for Japan – similar to that of thirteenth-century Venice and seventeenth-century Holland, which prospered while the peace was maintained by other states, and argued that while they had navies to protect their sea lanes of communication, they were not excessively aggressive. Kōsaka, 1996. Quoted from Richard Samuels, 'Securing Japan: The Current Discourse,' *The Journal of Japanese Studies* 33, no. 1 (2007): 125–52.

24 Asō Tarō, *Jiyū to han'ei no ko* [The Arc of Freedom and Prosperity], (Tokyo: Gentōsha, 2007), 225.

25 Samuels, *Securing Japan*, 14.

26 Akaha Tsuneo, 'Japan's Comprehensive Security Policy: A New East Asian Environment,' *Asian Survey* 31, no. 4 (1991): 324.

27 Ibid., 328.

28 National Defense Program Guidelines for FY2005. Ministry of Defence. http://www.mod.go.jp/e/d_policy/pdf/national_guideline.pdf (Accessed 27 April 2010).

29 Ibid.

Security, resources, and humanitarianism   57

30 Tōgō Kazuhiko, 'Japan's Strategic Thinking in the Second Half of the 1990s,' in *Japanese Strategic Thought Toward Asia*, eds. Rozman et al., 85.

31 Reinhard Drifte, 'Japan's Eurasian Diplomacy: Power Politics, Resource Diplomacy or Romanticism?' in *The Caspian: Politics, Energy and Security*, ed. Shirin Akiner (London: Routledge Curzon, 2004), 279.

32 Michael Robert Hickok, 'The Other End of the Silk Road: Japan's Eurasian Initiative,' *Central Asian Survey* 19, no. 1 (2000): 24.

33 'With Oil and West's Appeals in Mind, Tokyo Plans for Central Asia,' *International Herald Tribune*, 16 December 1992. Quoted from Drifte 'Japan's Eurasian diplomacy: Power politics, resource diplomacy or romanticism?' 280.

34 Asian Development Bank and Japan, Fact Sheet, 1–6: http://www.adb.org/Documents/Fact_Sheets/JPN.pdf (Accessed 28 April 2010).

35 Funabashi Yōichi, *Asia Pacific Fusion. Japan's Role in APEC* (Washington DC: Institute for International Economics, 1995), 228.

36 Interview with Prof. Siddharth Saxena, chairman of Cambridge Central Asia Forum, February 2010; David Hoffman, 'Half a Ton of Uranium – and a Long Flight.' *Washington Post*, 21 September 2009.

37 'Japan Signs Nuclear Pact with Kazakhstan,' *Reuters*, 2 March 2010, http://uk.reuters.com/article/idUKTOE62107120100302 (Accessed 27 April 2010). Japan's non-nuclear and anti-proliferation stance originated in the early post-war period. Its non-nuclear status was reaffirmed by several Japanese leaders, such as Ikeda Hayato, Hatoyama Ichirō, and Kishi Nobusuke, and became a condition of the alliance with the United States. In 1967, Prime Minister Satō Eisaku officially introduced the Three Non-Nuclear Principles of Japan: Non-possession, non-production, and non-introduction, subsequently expanding them with the promotion of nuclear power for peaceful purposes and global nuclear disarmament. In 1970, Japan signed the Non-Proliferation Treaty, but did not ratify it until 1976.

38 Huntington's thesis appeared valid in the first half of the 1990s, however, subsequent history challenged his theory on numerous occasions, for instance, the drift of Ukraine, Georgia, and Serbia towards the European Union and NATO in the mid-2000s.

39 Hickok, The Other End of the Silk Road, 25.

40 Robert A. Scalapino, ed. *The Foreign Policy of Modern Japan* (Berkeley, CA: University of California Press, 1977), 27, 33.

41 Hasegawa Tsuyoshi, 'Japan's Strategic Thinking Toward Asia in the First Half of the 1990s,' in *Japanese Strategic Thought Toward Asia*, ed. Rozman et al., 62.

42 Jiang Wenrang, 'The Japanese Assessment of the "China Threat,"' in *The China Threat: Perceptions, Myths and Reality*, eds. Herbert Yee and Ian Storey (London: RoutledgeCurzon, 2002), 159.

43 Interview with former MOF official, December 2011.

44 Address by Prime Minister Hashimoto Ryūtarō to the Japan Association of Corporate Executives, 24 July 1997, http://japan.kantei.go.jp/0731douyukai.html (Accessed 28 March 2014).

45 Ibid.

46 Halford Mackinder's argument was one of the early geopolitical approaches and took place in the context of rivalry between the British and Russian empires over CA (i.e., The Great Game), supported by the British alliance with Japan that was in conflict with Russia.

47 Address by PM Hashimoto.

48 Akio Kawatō, 'Japanese Strategic Thought Toward Central Asia,' in *Japanese Strategic Thought Toward Asia*, ed. Rozman et al., 231.

49 Address by PM Hashimoto.

50 Tōgō, 'Japan's strategic thinking in the second half of the 1990s,' 90. Prior to Hashimoto, the Japanese leaders have reiterated a non-compromising position

58 Security, resources, and humanitarianism

demanding the transfer of all four disputed islands as a condition to the signing of a peace treaty. Conversely, Moscow's position alternated the non-recognition of the territorial issue and the adherence to the 1956 Joint Declaration, implying the transfer of two islands, Habomai and Shikotan, after the signing of a peace treaty.

51 MOFA's 'Russia school' did not imply sympathy toward Russia, rather an area of specialism of diplomats, although the MOFA's post-war history included instances of rivalry between 'America school' and 'Russia school.'

52 Kawatō, *Japan's Strategic Thinking Toward Central Asia*, 231.

53 Ibid.

54 MOFA: Address by State Secretary for Foreign Affairs Takemi Keizō, Lecture Meeting 'Capacity Building for Human Dignity: The Essence of the International Order in the 21st Century,' 1 September 1999, Asia Society, New York, http://www.mofa.go.jp/policy/human_secu/speech9909.html (Accessed 25 April 2010).

55 East Asian Strategic Review 2009, National Institute for Defense Studies. http://www.nids.go.jp/english/publication/east-asian/pdf/2009/east-asian_e2009_08.pdf (Accessed 20 April 2010).

56 *9.11 jiken kara 1 nen. Chūō ajia kara sekai to rekishi wo yomitoku* [One Year from 9/11. Figuring Out the World and History from Central Asia]. Symposium proceedings. Tokyo: NPO Japan-Uzbekistan Society, 2002.

57 Kawatō, 'Japanese Strategic Thinking Toward Central Asia', 232.

58 Essen Usubaliev, 'Politika Yaponii v Tsentralnoii Azii – geopoliticheskii aspekt' [Japanese Policy in Central Asia – A Geopolitical Aspect]. *East Time*, 4 April 2007. http://easttime.ru/analitic/3/9/150.html (Accessed 27 April 2010).

59 Kawatō, 'Japanese Strategic Thinking Toward Central Asia', 232.

60 Dilip Hiro, *Inside Central Asia* (Noida: HarperCollins Publishers, 2009), 164–71.

61 The GUAM Bloc consists of Georgia, Ukraine, Azerbaijan, and Moldova, since Tashkent suspended its membership in following with a new rapprochement with Moscow in the mid-2000s. Despite low and irregular activity of this forum, the Japanese MOFA established a relationship with it in the form of 'GUAM plus Japan' meetings in 2007, which have been maintained to date, albeit with low frequency and ultimate prioritisation of functional agenda, such as agriculture or medicine. *GUAM purasu Nippon iryō wākushoppu no kaisai* [GUAM Plus Japan. Medicine Workshop Opening], http://www.mofa.go.jp/mofaj/press/release/press4_000602.html (Accessed 14 February 2014).

62 Rozman et al. eds., *Japanese Strategic Thought Toward Asia*, 23.

63 Tomohito Shinoda, *Leading Japan: The Role of the Prime Minister* (Westport, CT: Praeger, 2000), 197, 201.

64 Ibid., 26–9.

65 Ferguson 'Japanese Strategic Thinking Toward Russia,' in *Japanese Strategic Thought Toward Asia*, ed. Rozman et al., 214–15.

66 Drifte, 'Japan's Eurasian Diplomacy: Power Politics, Resource Diplomacy or Romanticism?' 290.

67 Ibid., 233.

68 Ibid., 234–5.

69 Interview with Kawaguchi Yoriko, November 2013.

70 Policy Speech by Kawaguchi Yoriko, minister for foreign affairs of Japan, at the University of World Economy and Diplomacy, Tashkent, Uzbekistan, 26 August 2004, *Adding a New Dimension: Central Asia plus Japan*, http://www.mofa.go.jp/region/europe/uzbekistan/speech0408.html (Accessed 20 April 2010).

71 Zeyno Baran, S. Frederick Starr, and Svante E. Cornell. *Islamic Radicalism in Central Asia and the Caucasus: Implications for the EU* (Central Asia-Caucasus Institute & Silk Road Studies Program, 2006). https://www.silkroadstudies.org/new/docs/Silkroadpapers/0607Islam.pdf (Accessed 29 April 2010).

Security, resources, and humanitarianism 59

72 06TOKYO2992, A/S Boucher's May 30 Meeting With European Ddg Yagi on Central Asia, 31 May 2006, http://cables.mrkva.eu/cable.php?id=66130 (Accessed 15 April 2014).

73 06TOKYO3193. Foreign Ministers Release 'Action Plan' at Central Asia Plus Japan Dialogue, U.S. Embassy in Tokyo, http://cables.mrkva.eu/cable.php?id=67325 (Accessed 31 March 2014).

74 06TOKYO7164. U.S.-Japan Central Asia Dialogue: Part Two, Foreign Assistance and Project Finance, U.S. Embassy in Tokyo, http://cables.mrkva.eu/cable.php?id=91030, (Accessed 30 October 2015).

75 Daniel M. Kliman, *Japan's Security Strategy in the Post-9/11 World: Embracing a New Realpolitik* (The Washington Papers), Washington, DC: Praeger, 2006, 77, quoted in Dadabaev, 2016, 161.

76 Kawatō, 'Japanese Strategic Thinking Toward Central Asia,' 241.

77 Ibid.

78 'Russian Reversal' refers to a transpositional pun popularised by the Soviet immigrant comedian Yakov Smirnoff and playing on the exaggerated perceived polar differences between the United States and USSR in the Cold War era. The pattern reverses what is traditionally perceived as subject and object, for instance: 'in America you can always find a party, in Soviet Russia the party can always find you.' See 'In Soviet Russia, snowclones overuse you', *Language Log*, 29 January 2004, http://itre.cis.upenn.edu/~myl/languagelog/archives/000402.html (Accessed 9 November 2015).

79 Turkmenistan is an exception, as its first President Niyazov was able to completely dominate by sidelining rival clans, while his successor Berdymukhamedov inherited and preserved this system. Japanese media and government-affiliated think tanks debated the Japanese aid policy in supporting reactionary regimes, demonstrating both criticism and its countering by the examples of authoritarian regimes turned into democracies, such as ROK. Hirose Tetsuya, 'Chūō Ajia wo meguru kokusai josei no henka', *JIIA Column*, 24 January 2006, https://www2.jiia.or.jp/RESR/column_page.php?id=69 (Accessed 23 April 2015); Aikyō Masanori, 'Kaihatsu ni okeru hō no yakuwari – Hō to kaihatsu: sono riron to tenbō' [The Role of Law in Development – Development of Law: Its Theory and Prospects], *Ajia Keizai*, XLVI 4 (2005): 78–88; 'Keitai wo mōchikomenai! "Akarui dokusaikoku" Turkmenistan' [No mobile phones! 'Enlightened authoritarian state' of Turkmenistan], *Sankei Shimbun*, 23 October 2015, http://www.sankei.com/politics/news/151023/plt1510230036-n1.html (Accessed 30 October 2015).

80 Cooley, *Great Games, Local Rules*, 99. Former UK Prime Minister Tony Blair served as highly paid adviser to the government of Kazakhstan, helping it to legitimise its policies in the West.

81 'UzKDB bank plans to become leader in Central Asia, CIS,' *UzReport*, 10 May 2006, http://news.uzreport.uz/news_5_e_11922.html (Accessed 10 March 2016).

82 Japanese co-chair was Mitsui representative Mr Oohashi. Interview with Mitsui officials, June 2011.

83 US embassy cable – 06TASHKENT1358_a, Fm Ganiev Out, Norov In, https://wikileaks.org/plusd/cables/06TASHKENT1358_a.html (Accessed 19 April 2016).

84 MOFA: Uzbekistan Kyōwakoku – Kiso dēta [Republic of Uzbekistan – Basic data]. http://www.mofa.go.jp/mofaj/area/uzbekistan/data.html#section1 (Accessed 20 June 2016).

85 Alisher Taksanov, 'Regional'naya elita i bor'ba za vlast' v Uzbekistane' [Regional elite and power struggle in Uzbekistan], *Proza.ru*, https://www.proza.ru/2009/08/12/54 (Accessed 31 August 2019).

86 Private communication with a UK-based expert on Central Asia.

87 S. Frederick Starr, 'Clans, Authoritarian Rulers, and Parliaments in Central Asia,' *Silk Road Papers* (Central Asia-Caucasus Institute & Silk Road Studies Program, 2006), 12.

60 *Security, resources, and humanitarianism*

88 Andrey Grozin, 'Kto pridet na smenu Islamu Karimovu?' [Who will replace Islam Karimov?], *GlobalRus.ru*, http://arabeski.globalrus.ru/opinions/152692/ (Accessed 5 March 2016). During Shavkat Mirziyoyev's presidency (2016–present), Safayev came back to prominence as the deputy speaker of the Uzbek Senate and chairman of its foreign affairs commission – an appointment fitting with Mirziyoyev's logic of improving ties with foreign partners, including the United States.

89 Cooley, 2012: 118.

90 U.S. embassy cable. 06TASHKENT730. Ganiev And Azimov To Visit Japan, http://cables.mrkva.eu/cable.php?id=60582 (Accessed 24 February 2016).

91 Declaration of Heads of Member States of SCO, Astana, 5 July 2005, http://www.china-daily.com.cn/china/2006-06/12/content_6020345.htm (Accessed 14 August 2013).

92 Private communication with Dr Shirin Akiner of SOAS, October 2013.

93 U.S. embassy cable. 07TASHKENT2029_a. Resource Nationalism: Grab What You Can, https://wikileaks.org/plusd/cables/07TASHKENT2029_a.html (Accessed 24 February 2016).

94 Gul'nara Karimova obvinila vitse-premiera Azimova v korruptsii [Gulnara Karimova accused Vice Prime Minister Azimov of corruption], *CA-News*, 27 March 2013. http://ca-news.org/news:1061157 (Accessed 27 February 2015).

95 Cooley, *Great Games, Local Rules*, 27.

96 Kazantsev, *Bol'shaya igra s neizvestnymi pravilami*, 118–25.

97 Interview with a Japanese World Bank official, April 2013.

98 Kitamura Toshiharu 'Reisen no hōkai kara 20 nen wo heta ikokoku keizai.' [Transition Economies: Twenty Years after the End of the Cold War]. *Journal of Asia-Pacific Studies* 15 (2010): 105.

99 Interview with a MOFA official in charge of Central Asia and Caucasus, March 2012.

100 Some notable examples include the *Classified Catalogue of Books. Section VIII. Central Asia in the Tōyō Bunko*, Tokyo, 1969; Kazutoshi Nagasawa, 'Silk Road Studies in Japan: Its history and Present Situation', *International Seminar for UNESCO Integral Study of the Silk Roads: Roads of Dialogue*, Osaka, 1988. http://en.unesco.org/silkroad/sites/silkroad/files/knowledge-bank-article/silk_road_studies_in_japan_its_history_and_present_situation.pdf (Accessed 27 March 2016); and Tomohiko Uyama, 'The Contribution of Central Eurasian Studies to Russian and (Post-)Soviet Studies and Beyond', *Kritika: Explorations in Russian and Eurasian History* 16, no. 2 (2015): 331–44.

101 Ibid., 334.

102 Nikolay Murashkin, 'Japanese Involvement in Central Asia: An Early Inter-Asian Post-Neoliberal Case?' *Asian Journal of Social Science* 43 (2015): 59.

103 For a detailed examination of norms in Japanese foreign policy, cf. Satō and Hirata, eds. *Norms, Interests, and Power*, 2008.

104 Yachi Shōtarō and Abe Shinzō voiced arguably the most crystallised expression of this approach.

105 Interview with a Japanese World Bank official, April 2013.

106 Rozman et al., *Japanese Strategic Thought Toward Asia.*

107 Nargiza Yuldasheva. 'Kyrgyzstan should leave SCO, Tsutomu Saito says.' *News Agency 24.kg*, http://eng.24.kg/politic/2008/03/04/4781.html (Accessed 20 May 2010).

108 Iwashita Akihiro (ed.), *Toward a New Dialogue on Eurasia: The Shanghai Cooperation Organization and Its Partner* (Sapporo: Slavic Research Center, 2007).

109 MOFA (2005): Press Release of 'Central Asia plus Japan' Dialogue/Senior Officials Meeting, 4 March 2005. http://www.mofa.go.jp/announce/announce/2005/3/0304-2.html (Accessed 11 April 2010).

110 Shanghai Cooperation Organisation, official website: http://www.sectsco.org/EN/brief.asp (Accessed 23 April 2010).

111 'Human Rights Overview: China,' *Human Rights Watch*, 18 January 2006. http://www.hrw.org/english/docs/2006/01/18/china12270.htm (Accessed 25 April 2010).

Security, resources, and humanitarianism 61

112 Baran et al., *Islamic Radicalism in Central Asia and the Caucasus*, 35–8.
113 Ibid., 7.
114 Kazantsev, *Bol'shaya igra s neizvestnymi pravilami: mirovaya politika i Tsentralnaya Aziya*, 216–20.
115 The Military Balance 2010 (London: International Institute for Strategic Studies, 2010), 364–73.
116 The SCO originated from the international negotiations on the border demarcation between CA, China, and Russia.
117 'China, Russia-led alliance wants date for U.S. pullout.' *USA Today*, 5 July 2005. http://www.usatoday.com/news/world/2005-07-05-asia-summit_x.htm (Accessed 15 April 2010).
118 In 2009–14, the base was called Transit Centre at Manas.
119 Christopher M. Clarke, 'Xinjiang – Where China's Worry Intersects the World.' *YaleGlobal*, 19 March 2010. http://yaleglobal.yale.edu/content/xinjiang-where-chinas-worry-intersects-world (Accessed 29 April 2010).
120 Zhang Yunling and Tang Shiping, 'China's Regional Strategy,' in *Power Shift. China and Asia's New Dynamics*, ed. David Shambaugh (Berkeley, CA: University of California Press, 2005), 32–3.
121 Ibid., 54.
122 Isami Takeda, 'Nihon no tai Myanmar gaiko no yon gensoku to wa' [Japan's Myanmar Policy: Four Principles], *Gaikō Forum* 1, no. 154 (2001).
123 Rozman et al., *Japanese Strategic Thought toward Asia*; Shambaugh, *Power Shift*, 52–3.
124 Kazantsev, *Bol'shaya igra s neizvestnymi pravilami: mirovaya politika i Tsentralnaya Aziya*, 347.
125 In the 1750s, the Qing army conquered the Dzungar Khanate and exterminated circa 500,000 Dzungar, thus almost completely annihilating this ethnic group. For more details: Michael Edmund Clarke. *In the Eye of Power* (doctoral thesis), Brisbane 2004, 37; Peter Perdue. *China Marches West: The Qing Conquest of Central Eurasia*, 283–87. Mark Levene in A. Dirk Moses. *Empire, Colony, Genocide: Conquest, Occupation, and Subaltern Resistance in World History*, 2008, 188.
126 Burles, Mark. 'Chinese Policy Toward Russia and the Central Asian Republics,' RAND, 1999, http://www.rand.org/content/dam/rand/pubs/monograph_reports/2007/MR1045.pdf, (Accessed 25 March 2014).
127 Ibid., 52.
128 Isabel Gorst, 'Kazakh PM Defends Growing Links with China,' *Financial Times*, 28 December 2009. http://www.ft.com/cms/s/0/d8dee514-f3d9-11de-ac55-00144feab49a.html (Accessed 27 April 2010).
129 Ibid.
130 Nikolay Kuzmin, 'O, divnyi kitaiskiy mir. Kredity iz KNR usilivayut zavisimost kazahstanskoi ekonomiki ot gosudarstva [Brave Chinese World. Loans from PRC reinforce the dependence of Kazakhstani economy on the state],' *Expert-Kazakhstan*, 16 November 2009. http://www.centrasia.ru/newsA.php?st=1258387080 (Accessed 21 April 2010).
131 Rayhan Demytrie, 'Kazakhs Protest against China Farmland Lease,' *BBC News*, 30 January 2010. http://news.bbc.co.uk/1/hi/8489024.stm (Accessed 29 April 2010).
132 Yoshihide Soeya, 'Trilateralism in Northeast Asia,' in *Asia-Pacific Security. US, Australia and Japan and the New Security Triangle*, ed. Tow et al. 95; Jiang Wenrang, 'The Japanese Assessment of the "China Threat,"' 151.
133 For instance, Hiramatsu Shigeo. *Chūgoku no Senryakuteki Kaiyō shinshutsu* [*China's Strategic Advance into the Ocean*], Keisō Shobō, 2002; Amako Satoshi. *Chūgoku wa kyōi ka* [Is China a Threat?], Keisō Shobō, 1997. Quoted from Seiichirō Takagi, 'Studies of China's Foreign and Security Policies in Japan,' in *China Watching.*

62   *Security, resources, and humanitarianism*

Perspectives from Europe, Japan and the United States, ed. Ash et al. (Oxon: RoutledgeCurzon, 2007), 189–212; Jiang, 'The Japanese Assessment of the "China Threat,"' 153.

134 Tōgō, *'Japan's Strategic Thinking in the Second Half of the 1990s'*, 85–90.
135 Personal communication with former METI official, March 2010.
136 Samuels, *Securing Japan*, 201.
137 Chung, East Asia Responds to the Rise of China, 660; Soeya, 'Trilateralism in Northeast Asia,' 92; Abe, *Utsukushii kuni-he*, 159–60.
138 Rozman et al., *Japanese Strategic Thought Toward Asia*, 30.
139 Robert G. Sutter, *China's Rise in Asia: Promises and Perils* (Lanham, MD: Rowman & Littlefield Publishers, 2005), 125–26.
140 Samuels, *Securing Japan*, 15.
141 Shinzō Abe, *Utsukushii kuni-he* [Towards a Beautiful Country] (Tokyo: Bungeishunjū, 2006), 161.
142 Interview with Yachi Shōtarō, professor at Waseda University, March 2012.
143 Speech by Asō Tarō, minister for foreign affairs on the Occasion of the Japan Institute of International Affairs Seminar. *'Arc of Freedom and Prosperity: Japan's Expanding Diplomatic Horizons:'* http://www.mofa.go.jp/announce/fm/aso/ speech0611.html (Accessed 25 April 2010).
144 Asō, *Jiyū to han'ei no ko*, 220–34.
145 MOFA: GUAM purasu Nihon kaigō [GUAM Plus Japan Meeting] http://www.mofa. go.jp/mofaj/area/europe/guam/ (Accessed 15 April 2010).
146 MOFA (2008), Kōmura gaimudaijin no Roshia hōmon (Kekka gaiyō) [Visit of Foreign Minister Kōmura to Russia (overview of results)], http://www.mofa. go.jp/mofaj/kaidan/g_komura/russia_08/kg.html (Accessed 9 March 2016); Zhao Qinghai, 'Japan's Diplomacy in Central Asia,' *China International Studies* 17, July/ August (2009): 157–70.
147 Len et al., eds., *Japan's Silk Road Diplomacy*, 11; 06TOKYO3193. Foreign Ministers Release 'Action Plan' At Central Asia Plus Japan Dialogue, U.S. Embassy in Tokyo, http://cables.mrkva.eu/cable.php?id=67325 (Accessed 31 March 2014).
148 Stefan Blank, 'Strany Vostochnoy Azii stremyatsya ukrepit' svoi ekonomiches-kiye pozitsii V Tsentral'noy Azii' [East Asian Countries Look to Strengthen Their Economic Positions in Central Asia], *Eurasia.net*, 5 June 2008, http://russian. eurasianet.org/departments/insight/articles/eav060508ru.shtml (Accessed 20 May 2010); Yuldasheva, 'Kyrgyzstan Should Leave SCO, Tsutomu Saito says.'
149 Tomohiko Taniguchi, Beyond 'The Arc of Freedom and Prosperity': Debating Universal Values in Japanese Grand Strategy, Asia Paper Series 2010 (Washington, DC: The German Marshall Fund of the United States, 2010).
150 Zhao, 'Japan's Diplomacy in Central Asia'; Lee Cheng-hung. 'Japan's "Arc of Freedom" Shifting the Balance,' *Taipei Times*, 30 August 2007; Personal communication with former METI official Mitsuhiro Maeda, 2010.
151 Takeshi Yuasa, 'Consolidating "Value-Oriented Diplomacy" Towards Eurasia? The "Arc of Freedom and Prosperity" and Beyond,' in *Japan's Silk Road Diplomacy*, ed. Len et al., 47.
152 Japan's Diplomacy: Ensuring Security and Prosperity, Speech by Tarō Asō, Prime Minister of Japan, https://japan.kantei.go.jp/asospeech/2009/06/30speech_e.html (Accessed 31 August 2019).
153 MOFA: A powerful partner in 'diplomacy that takes a panoramic perspective of the world map,' 9 May 2014, http://www.mofa.go.jp/erp/ep/page22e_000373.html (Accessed 13 July 2015).
154 Alexander Knyazev, 'Bols'haya igra v Tsentral'noy Azii idet s peremennym uspe-khom' [The Great Game in Central Asia takes place with intermittent success], *Nezavisimaya gazeta*, 16 November 2015, http://www.ng.ru/courier/2015-11-16/11_ game.html (Accessed 20 November 2015).

Security, resources, and humanitarianism 63

155 Abe Shinzō, 'Asia's Democratic Security Diamond,' *Project Syndicate*, 27 December 2012. https://www.project-syndicate.org/commentary/a-strategic-alliance-for-japan-and-india-by-shinzo-abe?barrier=true (Accessed 3 July 2013).

156 Prem'er-ministr Yaponii Sindzo Abe: U vlasti – gor'kii vkus [Japan's Prime Minister Shinzo Abe: Power Has A Bitter Flavour], *Rossiyskaya Gazeta*, 29 April 2013, quoted from https://topwar.ru/27424-premer-ministr-yaponii-sindzo-abe-u-vlasti-gorkiy-vkus.html (Accessed 30 August 2019).

157 'Japan, Russia to help tighten Central Asian borders,' *Nikkei Asian Review*, 12 February 2016. http://asia.nikkei.com/Politics-Economy/International-Relations/Japan-Russia-to-help-tighten-Central-Asian-borders (Accessed 15 April 2014).

158 Markus Winter, 'Abe and the Bureacracy: Tightening the Reins,' *The Diplomat*, 16 June 2016, http://thediplomat.com/2016/06/abe-and-the-bureacracy-tightening-the-reins/ (Accessed 16 June 2016); private communication with a MOFA official, November 2018.

159 Nikolay Murashkin, Japan and Central Asia: Do Diplomacy and Business Go Hand-in-Hand? Etudes de l'Ifri, Ifri, April 2019. 25. Communication with a Japanese expert, August 2018.

160 'Soglasovany prioritety dolgosrochnogo partnerstva s JICA' ('The priorities of long-term partnership with JICA were agreed on'), President of Uzbekistan's official website, December 19, 2019, https://president.uz/ru/lists/view/3161 (Accessed 19 December 2019).

161 'Japan to provide $1.7 bil. in loans to improve Uzbek infrastructure', *The Mainichi*, 20 December 2019.

162 'Uzbekistan postavit v Yaponiyu uran na bolee chem 1 mlrd dollarov' ('Uzbekistan to provide uranium worth over US$1 billion to Japan'), Kun.kz, January 7, 2020, https://kun.uz/ru/news/2020/01/07/uzbekistan-postavit-v-yaponiyu-uran-na-boleye-chem-1-mlrd-dollarov (Accessed 8 January 2020).

163 'Uzubekisutankyōwakoku seifu kikan to kin tangusuten shigen chōsa ni kakaru kyōtei-sho o teiketsu. Yūbō chiku de no kyōdō chōsa o tsūjite, kankei kyōka to tōshi kikai sōshutsu o suishin' (Signing of Agreement on Gold and Tungsten Resource Survey with Government of the Republic of Uzbekistan. Promoting the Strengthening of Relations and Creating Investment Opportunities through Joint Surveys in Prospective Areas), JOGMEC, December 19, 2019. http://www.jogmec.go.jp/news/release/news_08_000075.html?fbclid=IwAR3Q0-_KZXtkXOpHy9UCkN_tRT-gLElwY_F72qd2APKWpzjXRhw-MsVEnMeQ (Accessed 19 December 2019).

164 Keizai-gaikō-anpo, Kantei de ichigenka seifu kokka anpo-kyoku ni senmon busho [Economy, diplomacy, security centralised in a specialised department under the Cabinet's National Security Secretariat], *Nikkei*, 19 September 2019; Jimin Amari shi 'keizai teko ni kakoikomi, kōmyō' taiō e nipponban NEC teigen [LDP's Amari suggests a Japanese version of the NEC as response for clever enclosure of economic leverage], *Mainichi*, 20 March 2019.

165 'Ministr oborony Yaponii nameren posetit' Kyrgyzstan' [Japan's Defence Minister intends to visit Kyrgyzstan], *CA-NEWS*, 12 July 2016, http://ca-news.org/news:1192988 (Accessed 12 July 2016).

2 Silk Road diplomacy of the DPJ cabinets

Continuity, inertia, and change

Introduction

Three governments formed by the Democratic Party of Japan (DPJ) ruled the country for three years, following a landslide victory at parliamentary elections in August 2009 and until a reverse landslide in December 2012. Before and after its electoral victory, the DPJ's main domestic objective was to differentiate itself from the Liberal Democratic Party (LDP), and to do so while facing the tough challenge of reviving the national economy and tackling the consequences of the 2008 financial crisis. In these harsh conditions, the role of Central Asia (CA) in Tokyo's diplomatic agenda was bound to be sidelined even further than during Fukuda and Asō's premierships or, at least, to reflect the difference in the new government's foreign policy priorities.

The relative decline in CA's importance in Japan's foreign policy can be illustrated by a decrease in the frequency of visits paid by Japanese officials to CA. For instance, despite the normalisation of Uzbekistan's foreign relations with the United States (U.S.), the European Union (E.U.), and Japan in 2009, only three senior DPJ officials went on a trip to the country – half the amount of visits in the preceding three years and one-fourth of the trips during the first three years of Prime Minister Abe Shinzō's second premiership.[1] In the same period, Japanese officials visited the more commercially lucrative Kazakhstan six times, demonstrating the prevalence of economic considerations over political ones. Besides domestic economic problems, the DPJ's priorities included a rapprochement with China, an attempted normalisation with Russia, and the changing Japanese contribution to the International Security Assistance Force (ISAF) operations in Afghanistan as part of the alliance with Washington.

According to former Uzbek ambassador to Japan Alisher Shaykhov, the DPJ distinguished itself by taking a less 'sentimental' approach to CA than the LDP, but was adversely impacted by domestic politics, lack of resources, and its own attempts to differentiate itself from the LDP by fostering ties with different countries, in particular, focusing on East Asia.[2]

This chapter chronologically examines both the changes and continuities that Japanese policy-making in general and towards CA in particular underwent during the premierships of Hatoyama Yukio, Kan Naoto, and Noda Yoshihiko. Three

The DPJ era: continuity, inertia, and change   65

DPJ prime ministers and four foreign ministers brought about three distinct foreign policy courses, highlighting the significance of individuals and internal divisions in Japanese foreign policy towards CA. This analysis provides a useful illustration of the role of such factors in Japanese foreign policy-making as partisan politics, factionalism, institutional continuity and the role of bureaucrats who remained prominent despite the DPJ's efforts to reduce it. Did domestic constraints hinder decision-making in the DPJ's foreign policy, similarly to the LDP? Or was the situation different – and was Japan less reactive – with a different party in power? In other words, which factors, relevant to Japanese diplomacy, maintained their continuity under a different party and which factors changed?

Argument

I argue that under the DPJ rule, Japanese foreign policy in Eurasia in general and CA in particular had three notable characteristics. Firstly, it suffered from the usual structural constraints: frequent government rotations up to the prime minister level, short-lived incomplete reforms, and lack of relevant experience, although the latter criticism of the DPJ is limited by the absence of prior governance track record *ipso facto*. Secondly, foreign policy became sidelined to the periphery by bigger agenda items and, on balance, displayed more reactivity than proactivity in terms of following the changes in U.S. foreign policy towards Uzbekistan. Thirdly, some niche fields of cooperation with the region inherited from the LDP – or rather, continued by bureaucrats – remained 'business as usual,' namely, the Central Asia plus Japan dialogue (CAJ) and rare earths and uranium mining, especially until the Fukushima accident. Nevertheless, the DPJ's avoidance of grand designs towards CA and preference for pre-established routine is not necessarily negative. Rather, sticking to existing mechanisms helped render interaction with CA more institutionalised inside Japanese bureaucracies.

In explaining these developments, I posit that among the driving forces behind the DPJ's foreign policy towards CA, the adaptation to Japan's changing international environment weighed more than the interplay between domestic constituencies. Structural forces influencing the DPJ's policy course remained broadly the same as under the LDP. Domestically, factionalism and partisan politics maintained their inhibiting effect through frequent bureaucratic rotations and the display of personal factors. Although Hatoyama Yukio became the first post-World War II prime minister to successfully set up a dedicated government entity in charge of national strategy (*kokka senryaku kyoku*, or National Strategy Unit), it has not gained much traction.[3] The DPJ prime ministers preserved the weakness of their LDP predecessors, whose cabinets had been understaffed with temporarily seconded bureaucrats.[4]

As far as the domestic equation of the DPJ politics was concerned, the slogans and promises of Hatoyama's electoral platform were reflecting the demand of Japanese society for changes in the political system. The leitmotif of the DPJ's rhetoric stylistically and, to an extent, ideologically echoed the internationally acclaimed presidential campaign of Barack Obama that highlighted the

66 *The DPJ era: continuity, inertia, and change*

possibility of reforms. In the meantime, Ozawa Ichirō and other DPJ leaders were also aspiring to enact a fully fledged Westminster model of a two-party parliamentary regime instead of the current system still favouring the LDP's dominance.[5] Yet either despite the significance of the DPJ's 2009 landslide victory or due to unrealistic voters' expectations caused by ensuing euphoria, the said demand for systemic change ultimately was not met by the Hatoyama cabinet.[6]

An alternative to the LDP being one of cornerstones of the DPJ's electoral campaign, the rhetoric strongly emphasised a differentiation between the two parties.[7] Essentially, the 2009 vote was rather a protest against the LDP's domestic failures than in support of Hatoyama's foreign policy. However, according to Nomura Shunsuke, despite the attempts to put this alternative into practice, the DPJ continued the tradition of the so-called 'quasi-change of regime' of its rivals and predecessors.[8] This term was originally coined by Japanese political scientist Kitaoka Shin'ichi, who argued that the history of the LDP cabinets essentially boiled down to the change of flag between the wings inside the party, rather than actual change of policy.[9]

As I will demonstrate in this chapter, quasi-change of regime is a concept applicable to minor agenda items, such as CA policy, which either remained unchanged from within or underwent cosmetic changes and was mostly affected by the external events, such as the 3/11 Fukushima disaster. The majority of the DPJ's leadership was represented by former LDP politicians with similar experience and shared worldview.[10] The DPJ backbenchers were distinguished by internal heterogeneity and strong factionalism, less traceable than in the case of the LDP, however, due to the absence of official publications caused by the DPJ's intention to maintain a positive image.[11] Riding the criticism of Asō's cabinet (2008–9) and contrasting the DPJ platform with the outcomes of the LDP's rule in its ascent to power, Hatoyama's team continued to act like an opposition rather than the majority party due to lack of experience. In particular, many DPJ Diet members lacked experience in foreign policy, especially when it came to CA. Ultimately the DPJ failed to deliver on the promises of an alternative policy and could not achieve intra-party consolidation.

In the foreign policy field, the DPJ rule was arguably influenced by the legacy of Hatoyama Ichirō and generational politics, as it started with a pledge to gain more autonomy from the U.S. and mend relations with Japan's East Asian neighbours and Russia. To avoid animosity, Tokyo scrapped the LDP's diplomatic concepts viewed as potentially unwelcome in Beijing or Moscow, namely, Asō's Arc of Freedom and Prosperity (AFP, thus stepping away from the narratives of promoting democratic values and challenging resource nationalism). In addition, DPJ-era Ministry of Foreign Affairs (MOFA) officials occasionally 'cosmetically' altered the term, referring to the concept as Arc of *Peace* and Prosperity (*heiwa to han'ei no ko*), demonstrating a departure from value diplomacy (*kachikan gaikō*) and merger with the related concept of Corridor of Peace and Stability.[12] The DPJ's China-friendly posture thus conditioned its greater pragmatism towards CA. Nonetheless, the intra-party vision of foreign affairs in general and attitudes to China and other major powers in particular was not uniform, varying across factions and constituencies, as I examine in the next section.

Partisan politics, ideological currents, and factions

'Inventory of fixtures:' what did the DPJ inherit from the LDP?

In order to analyse the subject topic from the perspective of Japan's adaptation to the external environment, it is worth recalling the geopolitical context in which the DPJ took the reins and started to draft its diplomatic agenda along the main vectors of its bilateral relations – the U.S., China, Republic of Korea (ROK), and Russia. As indicated previously, scholars of post-World War II Japanese foreign policy often characterised Japan as a 'reactive state,' expanding the concept proposed by Kent Calder.[13]

During the Cold War, Japan's 'free riding' on American security guarantees partially conditioned and compensated its reactivity. However, the aftermath of 1991 brought a 'rediscovery of geopolitics' to the Japanese elites, as described by scholar Yuasa Takeshi, as well as an incentive for greater autonomy in foreign policy.[14] This change was due to the Union of Soviet Socialist Republics (USSR) implosion, changes in the geostrategic rationale for the alliance with Washington, and the rise of China, all of which drastically affected the East Asian balance of power and stimulated Japanese policy elites to be more active, but also changed its sources of external pressure.

As I demonstrated in the previous chapter, from the mid-1990s onwards, the main stratagem in the Japanese government was the necessity of finding a new position in Tokyo's triangular relations with Washington and Beijing. More specifically, this complex task consisted of establishing an optimal combination of three elements: Tokyo's greater diplomatic autonomy, a mix of engaging and balancing China in East Asia, and simultaneous prevention of both a Sino-American clash and avoiding the recidivism of the modern-day equivalent 'Nixon shock.'[15]

The DPJ inherited from their predecessors the aforementioned stratagem, together with such long-standing issues as the Democratic People's Republic of Korea (DPRK) nuclear programme and unsettled territorial disputes over the island territories of the Kurils (Northern Territories), Senkaku (Diaoyu), and Liancourt Rocks (Dokdo, Takeshima) with Russia, People's Republic of China (PRC), and ROK, respectively.

While the changing geopolitical landscape and the rise of China were gaining traction as challenges necessitating a corresponding long-term strategy from Japan, the assessment of this strategy was mixed among the scholars of Japanese foreign policy in general and with regards to its CA vector in particular. The scholars differed as to whether Japan had such a strategy or not, and if it did, whether it was consistent or not. This mixed assessment persisted during the tenure of DPJ cabinets.[16]

This problem can be exemplified in the question of the so-called 'normal status' of the Japanese post-war foreign and defence policy.[17] The incongruence between Japanese diplomacy and the country's 'weight category' in international politics would thus be viewed as abnormal, as if the country were punching below its weight, if one resorts to anthropomorphising Japan as a 'player.'

68 *The DPJ era: continuity, inertia, and change*

The idea of Japan's return to 'normal status' was popularised in the early 1990s by Ozawa Ichirō, the DPJ's once-'shadow shogun,' or behind-the-scenes leader, and a former LDP heavyweight.[18]

Since the 1990s and into the DPJ era, the main dilemma of Japanese external security reflected two constants – U.S. as 'insurer' and China as both a challenge to be balanced and a prospective partner, with narrow room for manoeuvre left for Japan in between those two powers. As I demonstrate further, Japan's relations with the U.S. and China set the framework coordinates for the foreign policy preferences of various Japanese political constituencies in general and strongly influenced DPJ-era Japan's relations with CA, albeit rather in specific instances than on a regular basis.

Parties and factions

Whilst political realism can be viewed as dominant in the strategic thinking of the Chinese or Russian establishment throughout most of the post-Cold War era, the scholars of Japanese political elites made the case for equilibrium between several groups.[19] Namely, Richard Samuels highlighted such denominations as 'mercantilists' (Miyazawa Kiichi), 'Asian internationalists' (Terashima Jitsurō), and various proponents of 'normal nationalism:' from neo-revisionists (Abe Shinzō) to 'globalists' (Ozawa Ichirō).[20]

Although those groups were not formally distinguished inside the DPJ according to their foreign policy positions, experts highlighted four currents: 'neo-autonomists,' favouring a significant revision of relations with the U.S. and a rapprochement with the PRC (Hatoyama Yukio, and to a lesser extent Okada Katsuya), 'realists' – conservative wing of the party (Maehara Seiji, Noda Yoshihiko, Nagashima Akihisa), 'pacifists' from the old party guard and former Socialists (Hiraoka Hideo) and, finally, pragmatic 'centrists,' leaning to realism, but without clear-cut ideological preferences in diplomacy (Kan Naoto, Sengoku Yoshito, Matsumoto Takeaki, Edano Yukio).[21]

The role of factions in Japan–CA relations prior to the DPJ rule is ambiguous. Officials with ties to the Japanese financial community have admitted the LDP's *Seiwa Seisaku Kenkyūkai* faction (Seiwa Policy Research Council, or Seiwaken) was a factor and a driver of the overall relationship, as I explain in greater detail in Chapter 4.[22] In particular, the faction's contribution would be evoked in relation to its period as *Mori-ha* (1998–2006), when it was led by ex-Prime Minister Mori Yoshirō. Mori was known for his involvement in Russo-Japanese relations, including the period after departure from the post of prime minister.[23] Mori, his fellow Seiwaken member Fukuda Yasuo, and Asō Tarō joined the LDP Parliamentary League of Friendship (*giinrenmei*, or *giren*) with Uzbekistan, which shows the level of senior politicians this CA country potentially had access to. Asō went on to become the league's chair.

However, Prime Ministers Hashimoto and Obuchi who spearheaded such landmark initiatives as Eurasian diplomacy and the Silk Road Action Plan belonged to the second-largest LDP faction and a rival of Seiwaken – Heisei

The DPJ era: continuity, inertia, and change 69

Kenkyūkai faction (Heisei Research Council, informally known as Heiseiken). And Hashimoto's track record at Ministry of Finance (MOF) was likely to weigh more in the practical implementation of his Eurasian diplomacy than factional affiliation. It is during Hashimoto's tenure as finance minister (1989–91) that Chino Tadao, a key CA proponent in the Japanese financial bureaucracy, became first the head of MOF's international finance division (*kokusaikyoku*) and then a vice minister of international affairs. Moreover, according to former Foreign Minister Kawaguchi Yoriko, her 2004 initiative of Central Asia plus Japan was neither a continuation of Hashimoto's and Obuchi's initiatives, nor had a notable relationship with either factions or MOF.[24]

Furthermore, according to Councillor Nakayama Kyōko, a former ambassador to Uzbekistan and the spouse of Seiwaken's former Secretary General Nakayama Nariaki, the role of partisan politics should not be exaggerated in the case of policy-making towards CA.[25] Although the Diet operates two parliamentary leagues of Uzbek–Japanese friendship convened by the LDP and the DPJ, both parties demonstrated bipartisanship regarding CA. For instance, when Uzbekistan's President Karimov visited Tokyo in February 2011, Diet members held a supra-partisan gathering (*chōtōha*).

Nevertheless, while Nakayama confirmed the importance of Mori as individual and then-faction leader during the LDP era, she highlighted the DPJ's lack of diplomatic experience as the main factor in its CA policy rather than bipartisanship per se.[26] Interviewed MOFA officials also quoted the DPJ's lack of experience in foreign affairs as the reason for continuity in Japanese policy towards CA in 2009–12.[27]

In terms of internal politics and private interests, the DPJ has not demonstrated less 'pork-barrel' politics domestically, according to German scholar Chris Winkler.[28] After Koizumi limited welfare spending and reduced election campaigning costs, the LDP under Abe I returned to clientelism, and the DPJ demonstrated continuity. If the logic of a patron-client relationship is applied to the Japan–CA aid relationship, underpinned by catering to the interests of Japanese businesses, its domestic premises did not markedly change under the DPJ, especially given its tug-of-war with bureaucrats.

Interviewees representing various Japanese corporations, predominantly from the natural resources divisions, extended the lack of diplomatic experience to both parties and echoed the view that partisan politics had little to zero impact on relations with CA. Finally, respondents inside the MOFA emphasised the continuingly preponderant weight of bureaucrats in Japanese decision-making as the reason for the relatively smaller role of elected politicians.[29] Section three examines in greater detail the role of the MOFA bureaucrats under the DPJ.

In particular, when comparing the LDP and DPJ rule, the differences between the China policies of Seiwaken and Heiseiken (the former faction of several DPJ politicians) may actually have impacted Tokyo's vision of CA as far as the policy towards China is concerned. Heiseiken members leaned towards engagement with Beijing rather than balancing, which was reflected in the 1997–8 Eurasian diplomacy of Prime Ministers Hashimoto and Obuchi, both hailing

70 *The DPJ era: continuity, inertia, and change*

from this faction.[30] The chair of Heiseiken (then known as the Takeshita faction) in 1987–93 was the future DPJ leader Ozawa Ichirō before his splitting from the LDP. The DPJ's first Foreign Minister Okada Katsuya was also a member of Heiseiken in the early 1990s before he left the LDP together with Ozawa to join the Japan Renewal Party. Although Ozawa and the first DPJ Prime Minister Hatoyama Yukio headed different DPJ factions, Ozawa's background and influence over foreign policy towards China was significant during Hatoyama's premiership and Okada's tenure at the helm of the MOFA. In this context, the DPJ's scrapping of the AFP concept was in line with Heiseiken's traditional China-friendly posture and resulting engagement policy.

Hatoyama's 'Tokyo drift' keeps Central Asia's profile low, but steady

In this section, I examine four factors that limited Hatoyama's cabinet involvement in CA affairs. Firstly, Hatoyama's philosophy of fraternity (*yūai*) in East Asia, inherited from his grandfather Prime Minister Hatoyama Ichirō, implied mending ties with Beijing – strongly lobbied by the DPJ heavyweight Ozawa.[31] As a result, the MOFA abandoned AFP, even entirely removing the concept's map from its website.[32] Secondly, this move was in line with Hatoyama's broader policy of rapprochement with Moscow, where AFP also sparked criticism.[33] Thirdly, in line with his 'neo-autonomist' labelling, Hatoyama sought greater autonomy in relations with Washington, the most CA-relevant materialisation of which manifested in the changed nature of Japanese contribution to the ISAF mission in favour of financial 'burden sharing.' Tokyo replaced the Maritime Self-Defense Force (MSDF) refuelling mission in the Indian Ocean with an enhanced $5 billion aid package to Afghanistan. Finally, Hatoyama's Foreign Minister Okada pushed for a reform of Official Development Assistance (ODA) administration, which received mixed reviews among Japanese ODA practitioners and, according to some of them, hindered aid provision to CA.[34]

Domestically, the policy-making of Hatoyama and other DPJ prime ministers was affected by their drive to shift the balance of power in Japanese governance away from bureaucrats and towards politicians. As part of that push, the DPJ government established a National Strategy Unit with Kan Naoto in charge. Among other measures, the DPJ increased the share of appointments of non-career diplomats (up to the ambassador level) stationed in Japanese embassies, including those in CA.[35]

The DPJ's attempt at a politician-led government and resulting redistribution of power created a source of tension with bureaucrats, viewed in the post-war politics as the part of an 'iron triangle' with the LDP and big business. The bureaucrats opposed the DPJ's policy using the lack of foreign policy experience among the DPJ members of parliament (MPs) as a counterargument. As a result of the DPJ's own inconsistencies and bureaucratic resistance, Hatoyama's version of the National Strategy Unit did not gain traction, losing its influence to rival institutions and became mostly decorative.[36]

The sources of Hatoyama's conduct were not only partisan, but also personal, highlighting the importance of individuals and family ties in Japanese policy-making. In his campaign rhetoric and subsequent statements, the new DPJ leader drew parallels between his diplomatic approach and that of his grandfather Hatoyama Ichirō, the author of post-war Japanese–Soviet normalisation.

Hatoyama's Central Asian policy: avoid antagonising China and stick to pragmatism

The idea of fraternity devised by Hatoyama Sr. and known as *yūai* became the foundation of his grandson's diplomacy, in particular, the East Asian Community project (EAC). Both Hatoyama Sr. and Hatoyama Jr. advocated a greater autonomy for Japan in its relationship with the U.S., which stimulated Washington's support to their domestic opponents. Both the EAC project and a more equal partnership with the U.S. were reflected in the DPJ's pre-election manifesto.[37] The main ideological input on Hatoyama's foreign policy was provided by his advisor Terashima Jitsurō, a representative of the so-called 'Asian international-ists.' Terashima's works criticised contemporary Japan for an U.S.-centric world-view and contended that Tokyo should reduce mutual distrust in East Asia, while reaching certain equidistance between Beijing and Washington.[38] Hatoyama's *yūai* policy of pursuing fraternal ties with PRC and ROK did not directly address CA, maintaining the region's perception in Tokyo as a peripheral agenda item. However, as part of an attempt to mend ties with neighbours, the DPJ abandoned the AFP concept to avoid the antagonisation of China and Russia. At the same time, it is under Hatoyama that Japan preserved and, at some instances, strength-ened economic and financial cooperation with CA, namely by, firstly, promoting the exports of infrastructure in general, and for CA's benefit in particular, sec-ondly, by building nuclear cooperation with Kazakhstan, and, thirdly, by restor-ing ODA ties with Uzbekistan after the post-Andijan distancing (2005–9).[39]

The DPJ governments raised the profile of infrastructure in Japanese eco-nomic diplomacy. This is reflected in the respective wording of Japanese doctri-nal documents, such as the MOFA's Diplomatic Bluebook. From 2010 onward, infrastructure has had a dedicated detailed section in the document, consistently earning about two dozen mentions in contrast to one, two, or zero hitherto.[40] The Hatoyama cabinet stressed the importance of promoting infrastructure exports – three years before Xi Jinping's 2013 announcement of the Belt and Road Initiative (BRI) – as Japanese companies started losing bids to interna-tional competitors.[41] In retrospect, the DPJ's policy mix of promoting of infra-structure exports and mending ties with Beijing shows that the interpretations of Japan's post-Belt and Road infrastructural policies should not be reduced to competing with China.

The promotion of infrastructure by the Hatoyama cabinet was visible in Japan's relationship with Central Asia. Namely, the 2010 session of the CAJ dialogue's Fourth Tokyo Dialogue was *Future Improvements to Logistics Infrastructure in the Central Asia Region*. Japanese State Secretary for Foreign Affairs Fukuyama

72   *The DPJ era: continuity, inertia, and change*

Tetsurō devoted to this topic, and to infrastructure in general, nearly a half of his speech. Although the term connectivity had a narrower usage at the time, the emphasis on logistics infrastructure indicates the continuity with connectivity infrastructure, which saw broader usage in public discourses after the BRI-related rhetoric gained traction worldwide. Fukuyama's speech made references to the 2006 CAJ Action Plan, which was adopted at the heyday of Koizumi's and Asō's policies of checking Russia's and China's influence in CA.[42] However, the DPJ's rationale for this reference was rather driven by mercantilism and needs to build ties with domestic business groups, than by a diplomatic continuity with its China-averse predecessor government.

In March 2010, Foreign Minister Okada signed the Agreement for Cooperation in the Peaceful Use of Nuclear Energy with the Kazakhstani ambassador in Japan Akylbek Kamaldinov. As a basic document for nuclear cooperation, the agreement enabled a stable uranium supply to Japan and was the culmination of the LDP-era Japanese–Kazakhstani nuclear cooperation, building on the agreements signed during President Nazarbayev's visit to Tokyo in 2008.[43]

Furthermore, Hatoyama met Nazarbayev on the margins of the 2010 Nuclear Security Summit in Washington, DC, where the latter was seeking American help to host a nuclear fuel bank in Kazakhstan. Subsequently, Hatoyama went on to chair the DPJ Japanese Parliamentary League of Friendship with Kazakhstan and visited Kazakhstan in May 2011, after his tenure.

Under Hatoyama, Suzuki Muneo, a politician with strong ties in Russia and post-Soviet states, was appointed the chairman of the Committee on Foreign Affairs in the House of Representatives. He led a parliamentary delegation to Tajikistan in September 2010, a few days before the Supreme Court of Japan upheld his conviction for bribery.[44] The DPJ's choice for Suzuki, notwithstanding his compromised reputation, was likely to be based on his ground knowledge of CA: Suzuki visited Tajikistan three times in 2000–2002.

Although Hatoyama changed Japan's contribution to ISAF in favour of financial assistance and recalled the MSDF refuelling mission, Japan's resumption of full-scale cooperation with Uzbekistan had a propitious external context. European and American sanctions were lifted in October 2009, and Tashkent gradually replaced Islamabad as Washington's prime security partner in Afghanistan-bound continental transit.[45] Japan's re-upgrade of relations with Uzbekistan was already palpable in 2008 under the LDP, which can be evidenced by the signing of the 2008 investment agreement, contacts between senior officials and continuing grant aid in absence of loan aid. Nonetheless, at the very top level, Tokyo's decision to synchronise with the E.U. and the U.S. showed that external interests again acted as a brake on dramatic change in Japanese foreign policy.[46]

Okada's ODA reform

Perhaps the key action of the Hatoyama cabinet that affected CA as much as the abandonment of the AFP and nuclear cooperation agreement with Kazakhstan was the reform of ODA spearheaded by Foreign Minister Okada and ultimately

The DPJ era: continuity, inertia, and change   73

harmonised with the DPJ's New Growth Strategy (*shinseichōsenryaku*).[47] Okada was intent on rendering the assistance mechanisms more efficient, especially given financial constraints in the aftermath of the 2008 global financial crisis.[48] The ODA review did not address any of the CA countries specifically, but mentioned Afghanistan.

The reception of the ODA reform differs among aid practitioners depending on their organisational perspective. Firstly, according to Japan International Cooperation Agency (JICA) officials stationed in CA countries, the reform complicated aid provision, as it increased parliamentary scrutiny and, as a result, slowed the approval process.[49] According to JICA officials in Tokyo, however, Okada's reform was rather an internal plan concerning the technical system of aid implementation (*jisshi taisei*) on the Japanese side and did not have or intend to have a particular impact on CA specifically.[50] Secondly, JICA respondents in Tokyo considered the DPJ rule to be of no particular consequence for Japanese assistance in CA. As already mentioned in the previous section, JICA respondents stationed in the region suggested that the China engagement stance brought into the DPJ by Ozawa and other former Heiseiken members was arguably the main general difference between the DPJ and LDP that impacted the DPJ's CA policy, apart from Okada's reform.

Okada carried out the ODA reform in the wake of Hatoyama's decision to replace the MSDF refuelling mission in the Indian Ocean with a \$5 billion aid package to Afghanistan. This 'financialisation' of Japan's contribution to Afghanistan's securitisation further enhanced the factor of proximity to Afghanistan in Japanese decision-making on aid to CA. That is, the fact of sharing borders with Afghanistan would weigh in favour of a recipient CA country during a respective budget approval process.[51]

Hatoyama-Kan transition and violence in Kyrgyzstan

The DPJ's shift from idealism to pragmatism in CA policy and its decrease in priority can be illustrated by Tokyo's cautious and low-profile reaction to the second Kyrgyz coup d'état and ensuing civil unrest in April–June 2010, which came in contrast to a more involved response from Tokyo to the first Kyrgyz coup d'état in 2005. Following the ouster of President Bakiyev in May 2010, the southern part of the country, including the city of Osh, suffered from interethnic violence. In particular, clashes broke out between the Kyrgyz and Uzbeks living in the Kyrgyz part of the Fergana Valley. The change in the MOFA's respective 2005 and 2010 statements marked Japan's overall distancing from 'hard security' problems in CA.[52]

The first Kyrgyz coup d'état took place in March 2005 at the peak of the Koizumi Jun'ichirō's premiership and affected President Akayev, a long-time partner of Tokyo. Meanwhile, the April–June 2010 events in Kyrgyzstan started with the ouster of President Bakiyev, much less favoured in Tokyo due to his corruption, which exceeded that of his predecessor. The Kyrgyz events also coincided with a succession from Hatoyama to Kan, triggered by domestic political

74 *The DPJ era: continuity, inertia, and change*

scandals and Hatoyama's mishandling of the Futenma relocation, that is, when Japanese leaders clearly had other priorities. Nevertheless, from the viewpoint of human and grassroots security favoured by Tokyo, the 2010 situation in Kyrgyzstan was graver than in 2005 due to greater violence – the Kyrgyz interim government even called for the assistance of the CSTO forces, but the request was declined by Moscow.

The fact that Tokyo opted for more of a wait-and-see approach in 2010 than in 2005 underlined Kyrgyzstan's reduced importance for the DPJ government, and a change of Japan's political priorities and circumstances. Commercially, Kyrgyzstan is less lucrative than its larger neighbours; its former credentials as the least authoritarian country in the region were tainted by Bakiyev's rule (2005–10) and interethnic violence, while the DPJ opted out of the LDP's value-oriented diplomacy and democracy promotion. The DPJ-era chairman of the Japan–Kyrgyz Parliamentary League of Friendship was Sutō Nobuhiko, a crisis resolution expert and a member of the Committee on Foreign Affairs in the House of Representatives. However, available evidence on his involvement in Kyrgyzstan only concerns his post-conflict missions at the Kyrgyz elections in 2010 and 2011.[53] The DPJ's position on Kyrgyzstan – despite the latter's previous informal status of favoured CA recipient – reflected the party's inflexibility in juggling multiple priorities, prudential reluctance to interfere, and the preoccupation with domestic politics and personnel rotations.

To sum up, Hatoyama's foreign policy de-emphasised the value-based element from its CA vector set by the LDP predecessors and upped the pragmatism. While Hatoyama's attempts at rapprochement with Moscow were unsuccessful in terms of practical progress, the improvement of hydrocarbon supplies from the Russian Far East reduced CA's attractiveness as a potential alternative.

Although Hatoyama was considered as belonging to a neo-autonomist DPJ faction, his CA policy reflected not so much his affiliation with domestic constituencies, as an adaptation to a changing environment. While Hatoyama financialised Japan's contribution to ISAF burden sharing with the U.S., he also followed suit with the U.S. and the E.U. to continue Fukuda's policy of restoring political dialogue and cooperation with Uzbekistan, downgraded after the 2005 Andijan event. Although this policy can be interpreted as alignment with Washington and Brussels during both the imposition and lifting of sanctions on Uzbekistan, it also reflected the emphasis on pragmatism. Hatoyama's grand design of *yūai* targeted primarily East Asia, keeping CA business as usual. Six years after his resignation, during Abe's second premiership, Hatoyama joined the advisory panel of the Beijing-led Asian Infrastructure Investment Bank, which many initially viewed as a rival to Japan-led Asian Development Bank (ADB).[54] The continuation of nuclear cooperation with Kazakhstan and the reassessment of ODA in favour of more restrictive policies, reflected Japan's energy strategies and dealing with the consequences of the global financial crisis. The next section examines how the DPJ's CA policy evolved under the Kan cabinet (2010–11).

The DPJ era: continuity, inertia, and change   75

Force majeure oscillations: external shocks dampen Kan's foreign policy

In June 2010, Hatoyama was succeeded by his Finance Minister Kan Naoto, as Ozawa temporarily took a back seat in order to preserve the party's rating before the upcoming House of Councillors election. Despite his family ties to the ancient Sugawara clan, Kan stood out as an exception in the aforementioned range of political dynasties.[55] His *alma mater* was Tokyo Institute of Technology, rather than the prestigious University of Tokyo (and its Department of Law) or other Japanese establishment factories, where most of his predecessors graduated from.[56] Kan entered mainstream politics from an environmental grassroots movement and reached commanding heights at the DPJ by the late 1990s. His rhetoric during the elections to the upper chamber primarily focused on domestic politics, while his distancing himself from Ozawa cemented his support. According to Weston Konishi, Kan belonged to centrists without clear-cut ideological preferences, albeit leaning towards realism.[57] Kan's first notable diplomatic move was an apology for colonial rule offered to Seoul in August 2010 on the centenary of Korean annexation by Japan, showing the continuation of DPJ's engagement with East Asian neighbours.

Kan was the only DPJ prime minister to have some first-hand knowledge of CA. In his tenure as vice prime minister and minister of finance, Kan visited Tashkent in May 2010 to attend the 43rd ADB Annual Meeting, on the margins of which he met the Uzbek President Islam Karimov.[58] The meeting was the first annual ADB gathering held in CA and, according to then-ADB head Kuroda Haruhiko, 'Tashkent had been chosen for the role Uzbekistan played in the region and its transport and hotel infrastructure.'[59] By contrast, Hatoyama Yukio visited CA (Kazakhstan) only in 2011, only after his premiership. Furthermore, although Kan was in charge of devising a national strategy under Hatoyama, it is during Kan's premiership that long-term strategy planning became particularly complicated, owing to heightened tensions with Japan's neighbours and the shock of 3/11, which required quick policy responses bound to reinforce reactivity.

The 2010 Senkaku incident and its implications for Central Asia

Initially, Kan kept Okada Katsuya as foreign minister. In August 2010, Okada visited Tashkent for a scheduled meeting of the CAJ dialogue. It was the first visit of a Japanese foreign minister to CA since Kawaguchi Yoriko's 2004 trip and the first foreign minister meeting of CAJ since 2006. This hiatus demonstrated that despite the initiatives of CAJ (2004) and AFP (2006), Japan assumed a rather low profile in practical diplomacy towards CA in the second half of the 2010s during the region's tilt towards China and Russia, shifting the focus from political dialogue towards resource cooperation. Parliamentary Senior Vice-Minister for Foreign Affairs Banno Yutaka visited Turkmenistan in November 2010 and Kazakhstan in December 2010 to attend the Organisation for Security and Cooperation in Europe (OSCE) Summit in Astana, although these trips were primarily a formality.

76 *The DPJ era: continuity, inertia, and change*

A month after his visit to Uzbekistan, however, Okada was replaced by Maehara Seiji following the internal elections for the DPJs presidency, where Kan defeated Ozawa and during the climax of the 2010 tensions with China over the Senkakus. Similarly to Kan, Maehara had his background in grassroots politics. He had a friendly attitude to Washington and was charged with mending the rift in the alliance made under Hatoyama. Despite some initial resistance from Maehara, the new DPJ cabinet confirmed the Futenma agreement with Washington. Another prominent figure in Kan's foreign affairs team was Cabinet Secretary General Sengoku Yoshito, a longtime ally of Kan's, also a former activist and a proponent of rapprochement with the PRC and ROK.[60] And yet it is the second DPJ cabinet that experienced the most turbulence in Japan's relations with its Northeast Asian neighbours, both positively and negatively affecting CA's place on Tokyo's foreign agenda.

The sequence of international scandals was kicked off by the incident involving a Chinese trawler near the Senkaku/Diaoyu Islands disputed by Japan, China, and Taiwan. On 7 September 2010, a fishing ship under the PRC flag collided with the Japanese coast guard in the territorial waters around the islands, which resulted in the fishermen's arrest by Japan. During the custody of the trawler's captain, Beijing put pressure on Japan, exposing the Kan government to an endurance test. As anti-Japanese demonstrations took place in China, the Chinese media frequently broadcast stern statements made by the People's Liberation Army (PLA) representatives, while Chinese companies *de facto* blocked their Japan-bound exports of rare metals, essential for Japanese industry.[61]

An inconsistent response by the Kan cabinet created an impression of the absence of an action plan for such emergency situations. Although Tokyo's initial reaction was harsh, the trawler's captain was released ultimately as a result of Beijing's pressure and Sengoku's desire to appease their East Asian neighbour.[62] The Kan cabinet's inconsistent response measures and proneness to external pressure attracted criticism both from other factions and from the parliamentary opposition.[63]

Most importantly, the 2010 Senkaku incident stimulated Japan to speed up its policy of diversifying the sources of rare metal imports at the expense of China's share, including CA as major source of relief, although PRC's dominance in this market and its propensity to unilateral measures had been causing importers concern for a while. The role of CA in the Japanese government's drive to ensure its resource supply, in particular, that of rare earths, can be illustrated by the examination of Uzbekistan's President Karimov's visit to Japan in February 2011, only a month before the disaster, and by the activities of the Japanese Parliamentary League of Friendship with Kazakhstan before and after 3/11.[64]

Karimov's 2011 visit and Gemba's creativity

Karimov's visit was his third to Japan following the trips in 1994 and 2002. It had the rank of an official working visit, involving a state call on the Emperor and Empress of Japan, also for the third time, which is a rare case in Japanese protocol and demonstrated the symbolic importance attached to Karimov's trip trumpeted by the Uzbek state media.

The DPJ era: continuity, inertia, and change 77

During his meeting with Karimov, Kan made uranium and rare earths the focal point of bilateral economic cooperation, as the Japan Oil, Gas, and Metals Corporation signed a related memorandum of cooperation with its Uzbekistani counterpart Goscomgeology (State Committee on Geology and Mineral Resources) during Karimov's visit.[65] Furthermore, Kan announced the decision to extend ODA loans for the electrification of the Karshi-Termez Railway, strategically important for Afghanistan-bound transport links.[66] Uranium and ODA were the highlights of Karimov's meeting with Foreign Minister Maehara Seiji.[67] On both occasions, Karimov reiterated his country's longstanding support of Japan's United Nations Security Council bid, revoked only once – following Japan's criticism of the Andijan unrest suppression by the Uzbekistani government in 2005.

Besides cooperation in uranium and rare earths mining and development assistance, Karimov's visit was preceded by the first ever interparliamentary Uzbekistan–Japan forum, held in Fukushima in January 2011 and showing the DPJ's creativity in reinventing bilateral relations with Uzbekistan beyond the LDP legacy. The choice of location can be explained by two factors. Firstly, it was based on the legacy of Soviet-era interregional ties twinning the Fukushima Prefecture and the Soviet Socialist Republic of Uzbekistan as partner provinces, not least because many of the Japanese prisoners of war (POWs) who worked in Uzbekistan were originally from Fukushima. These interregional ties are currently institutionalised via the Uzbekistan house in the town of Shimogamachi, visited by the Uzbek delegation, and via the Association for Cultural and Economic Cooperation Fukushima-Uzbekistan.[68] Secondly and most importantly, Fukushima is the home province (and contained the electoral district) of Gemba Kōichirō, who later went on to become foreign minister in the Noda cabinet and held a number of key posts at the time of the subject forum: state minister in charge of national strategy, chairman of the DPJ, secretary general of Parliament League (*giinrenmei*) DPJ-Uzbekistan.[69] The interparliamentary forum involved the suprapartisan (*chōtōha*) gathering of both the DPJ and LDP demonstrating not only creativity, but also bipartisanship in dealing with Uzbekistan and, by extension, with CA. The LDP was represented by former Prime Minister Asō Tarō, chairman of the LDP *giinrenmei*.

The DPJ's willingness to use interparliamentary ties, even if routinely, was also demonstrated through the events held by the Japanese Parliamentary League of Friendship with Kazakhstan. On 9 March 2011, two days before the Fukushima incident, the league held a protocol roundtable involving Kazakh Ambassador to Tokyo Akylbek Kamaldinov and former Prime Minister Hatoyama, chairman of the League.[70] In May 2011, Hatoyama attended the Astana Economic Forum and met with Kazakh officials. His meeting with the Foreign Minister Yerzhan Kazykhanov confirmed the continuation of Japanese–Kazakh joint ventures in the field of atomic energy and rare earths mining.[71] As I explain in Chapter 4, the joint venture (JVs) had been set up in the late 2000s between the Kazakh state-run nuclear corporation Kazatomprom and its Japanese partners Toshiba and Sumitomo. The continuity of Japanese–Kazakh nuclear cooperation after Fukushima showed pragmatism in Kan's

78 *The DPJ era: continuity, inertia, and change*

foreign policy and the limitation essentially to domestic politics of criticism directed at the 'nuclear village' (*genpatsu mura*), meaning a highly organised lobby for the nuclear industry.

Another DPJ-era trend was an increase in the appointments of officials with MOF, Ministry of Economy, Trade and Industry (METI), and METI-affiliated Japan Oil, Gas and Metals National Corporation (JOGMEC) backgrounds to Japanese embassies in CA, in particular at the junior and middle level or as a secondment.[72] Most likely, CA's low priority in the ranking of the MOFA careers facilitated the diversification of the talent pool required by the rising importance of economic and financial matters in the resource-rich region, especially prior to the 2011 Fukushima accident. As I point out in Chapter 4, such appointments were scarce at the very top level: only one Japanese ambassador to Kazakhstan (MOF-affiliated Harada Yūzō, 2010–13) and only two ambassadors to Uzbekistan and Tajikistan (MOF-affiliated Nakayama Kyōko, 1999–2002, METI-affiliated Katō Fumihiko, 2013–16) did not have a MOFA background. When asked about the Japan–Kazakhstan relationship in a private communication in 2011, Ambassador Harada said 'there isn't much going on,' referring to the low level of activity in the relationship.[73]

When it rains it pours: post-Fukushima sensitisation of nuclear policy, energy mix rebalancing, and revival diplomacy

The triple shock of the March 2011 events – earthquake, tsunami, and Fukushima-1 nuclear accident reverberated on the Japanese policy towards CA in several ways. Firstly, the balance between domestic and foreign issues in the Japanese leadership and Japanese society tilted further towards domestic matters. Meanwhile, Kan's approval rating fluctuated between the lows of 20–28 percent. Secondly, the national energy mix started being revised at the expense of the nuclear power share and in favour of larger hydrocarbon consumption, in particular natural gas, due to its better conformity with Japan's environmental undertakings. This was a reverse trend in the Japanese nuclear power sector compared to the 'nuclear renaissance' in the second half of the 2000s, as based on the 2006 National Energy Plan, the government's policy was to support the construction of new reactors, increase the volumes, diversify the sources of uranium supply, and export Japanese nuclear technologies overseas.

While 2010 tensions with China pushed Japan to step up its purveyance of rare earths and, therefore, uranium ores overseas, Fukushima's political fallout put a damper on those procurement expansion plans six months later. It greatly increased the political sensitivity of all of METI's nuclear-related policies, increasing reluctance in decision-making.[74] The alarmist discourse criticising the *genpatsu mura* (atomic village) dominated the Japanese public field.[75]

After Fukushima, all nuclear reactors were suspended for maintenance and audit. Although Japanese corporations did not scrap their plans for uranium mining and purchase abroad, further expansion was given a temporary standstill.[76] Notwithstanding the obvious reputational damage incurred by the Japanese energy industry from the Fukushima incident, the Japanese companies did not scale down their participation in foreign tenders on nuclear reactor construction.[77]

The DPJ era: continuity, inertia, and change 79

Halfway through the 3/11 tragedy, Japanese diplomacy received a new leader. Maehara's deputy Matsumoto Takeaki was appointed as the new head of the MOFA, known for his pro-American position and solid experience in key parliament committees (as well as direct lineage to the historic nineteenth-century Prime Minister Itō Hirobumi).[78] Maehara was forced to resign against the backdrop of a campaign financing scandal: he reportedly received donations from a ROK citizen resident in Japan while the Japanese legislation prohibits financial support to politicians from foreign nationals.[79]

The new minister made it his priority to improve Japan's foreign relations after Fukushima. In spring 2011, the so-called 'revival diplomacy' (*fukkō gaikō*) went beyond Matsumoto's foreign trips to secure natural resources and support for Japanese contractors necessary to rebuild infrastructure.[80] Maehara's successor was explaining the situation to foreign partners, expressing gratitude for assistance, and exploring the opportunities for cooperation in reconstruction through attracting tourists, investment, and an overall image boost.

Fukushima's emergence on the agenda and a need for reinforcing international cooperation on post-disaster reconstruction gave an additional impulse to the trilateral summit between Japan, China, and South Korea in May 2011. The meeting was neither tarnished by another instance of Senkaku tensions, albeit of smaller scale this time, nor by minor verbal skirmishes with ROK over a Korean history textbook supporting Seoul's claims over Takeshima/Dokdo.

All-in-all, Kan's foreign policy arguably returned the Japanese polity to the pre-election status quo. Firstly, in relations with Washington, the Japanese leadership was 'once bitten, twice shy.' Bilateral cooperation was reinforced after the Senkaku incident and by Operation Tomodachi, providing disaster relief after 3/11. Meanwhile, tensions were decreased despite ongoing hard talks on Futenma. Secondly, the Kan cabinet had to mobilise all its resources for emergency management: from territorial disputes, which revealed the party's insufficient diplomatic experience, to the natural disasters of March 2011, which became not only an unprecedented challenge for post-war Japan, but also a seismic shock for the country's diplomacy. Karimov's visit and Gemba's interparliamentary Japan–Uzbek forum at Fukushima prior to 3/11 were notable high points demonstrating both continuity and originality of the Japanese foreign policy. However, the 3/11 disaster reversed the table, dampening the uranium cooperation, and reinforced the significance of Japanese natural gas imports, amply available from neighbour Russia, but not from CA. It is this state of affairs that Kan handed over to the third DPJ Prime Minister Noda Yoshihiko in September 2011.

Noda's pragmatism: post-Fukushima resource diplomacy, Trans-Pacific Partnership, new hopes on the Russian front

Noda became prime minister after Kan had to resign following the criticism of his leadership on the handling of various aspects of 3/11 and Ozawa refused to back Maehara because of the latter's hawkish stance on China.[81] Similarly to Kan, Noda ascended to the premiership from the position of finance minister,

80 *The DPJ era: continuity, inertia, and change*

and domestic problems predictably became his main concern: the continuation of post-3/11 reconstruction, reforms in the power sector, and economic revival. The third DPJ prime minister stayed the unpopular course on financial improvement, reiterating Kan's intention to raise the consumption tax from 5 to 10 percent. This measure has been discussed in Japan since the Koizumi premiership and seen necessary to reduce Japan's world-largest public debt and support the welfare system. Kan's support of the tax hike made his ratings plummet, as it was a departure from the DPJ's election promise.

Affiliation with a particular constituency appears to have weighed more than family background in Noda's policy-making. In terms of biography, Noda had several things in common with his immediate predecessors. Not a hereditary politician, he graduated from the same young leader school as Maehara – Matsushita Konosuke Management Institute.[82] The institute also was the *alma mater* of new Foreign Minister Gemba Koichiro and a few other members of the small Kaseikai faction, led by Noda and opposed to Ozawa Ichiro, similarly to the Maehara-Edano faction.[83] Noda's foreign policy advisor office was assumed by Nagashima Akihisa, a 'realist' like the third DPJ prime minister himself, a proponent of strengthening the U.S.–Japan alliance, and a key defence expert in the Kan cabinet. Noda's policy towards CA was conditioned by the above agenda and focused on pragmatism.

Resource diplomacy: the post-Fukushima version

Noda made resource diplomacy (*shigen gaikō*) his priority, as resource-poor Japan needed an urgent re-adjustment of its energy mix following the suspension of all nuclear reactors, while an appreciating yen facilitated the purchasing power of Japanese companies for the acquisition of overseas assets. Noda reflected these priorities in his policy speeches and made organisational adjustments accordingly.[84] Namely, he set up a cabinet-based task force dubbed 'Strategic Council on Resource Diplomacy' (*shigen gaikō senryaku kaigi*), headed by Chief Cabinet Secretary Fujimura Osamu and involving bureaucrats from the MOFA, METI, and JOGMEC, as well as the representatives of the private sector.[85] This vision of resource diplomacy assigned CA with the rare earths niche, alongside South America, Southeast Asia, and Africa. The niches for hydrocarbons were taken by the Middle East and Russia (both oil and gas), Southeast Asia (oil), and Africa (oil and coal).[86] The Council was supposed to lift the priority of resource producers and devise an ODA and infrastructure export strategy targeting the new priority partners. News about the Council's establishment, however, appears to be the only information available in the public domain on its activity, which may suggest that it was another short-lived initiative which did not gain traction, although subsequently, the essence of these ideas was taken on board by Prime Minister Abe Shinzō upon his return to power in December 2012.

Japan's CA policy during the Noda premiership continued the predecessors' pragmatism and mostly revolved around strengthening the routine cooperation rather than making bold announcements. Although Gemba Kōichirō became

The DPJ era: continuity, inertia, and change 81

the head of the MOFA, the 3/11 image consequences limited the soft power allure of the Uzbekistan-Fukushima connection, which did not gain further traction either.

Nevertheless, Noda's spurred CA-related activities with a flurry of official visits to the region, especially to Kazakhstan, reflecting the country's importance for Japan's rare earths procurement. In fact, it is during Noda's tenure that Japanese officials most actively visited CA, accounting for seven of fourteen overall DPJ-era trips: three of six to Kazakhstan (all in 2012), two of three to Tajikistan, one to Kyrgyzstan (the only DPJ visit there), and one of three to Uzbekistan.[87] Two of those instances were noteworthy, both taking place in May 2012: the visit to Kazakhstan by METI head Edano Yukio and a concomitant visit to Uzbekistan by Parliamentary Senior Vice-Minister for Foreign Affairs Yamane Ryūji and the MOFA's Special Representative on CA Kōzuki Toyohisa.[88]

Due to its focus on the business of natural resources – rare earths in this instance – I provide the analysis of Edano's visit in Chapter 4. The main takeaway for the DPJ was that the leadership spill from Kan to Noda was not detrimental to the continuity of pragmatic cooperation with Kazakhstan. Edano's visit to Kazakhstan was followed up by the trips of Parliamentary Vice-Minister for Foreign Affairs Hamada Kazuyuki in September 2012 and State Minister of Economy, Trade, and Industry Kondō Yōsuke in October 2012.

More importantly, Edano's trip to Kazakhstan on 3 May was synchronised with a trip to Uzbekistan by Yamane Ryūji and Kōzuki Toyohisa on 4 May. The material results of Yamane's trip appear modest, focusing on routine formalities and the acknowledgement of Japan's financing for Afghanistan-bound railway projects in Uzbekistan. In addition, Yamane announced a ¥202 million grant as development assistance for Uzbek young statesmen to study at Nagoya University, Uzbekistan's long-established provider of legal education.[89] More important, perhaps was the timing – most likely a signal to Tashkent that it had not been abandoned in favour of Astana, and political ties with Uzbekistan were still important for Japan.

Noda's resource diplomacy towards Russia

Finally, the Russian front of Noda's diplomacy also experienced a mini-détente, along the lines of Noda's above-described resource diplomacy eyeing Russian natural gas, which reinforced CA's rare earths 'niche' for Japan. In December 2011, the Diet ratified a bilateral Russo-Japanese agreement on nuclear cooperation. The growing share of hydrocarbons in the Japanese energy mix boosted Russia's attractiveness as an economic partner that was confirmed, for instance, by the participation of Japanese companies in the construction of an LNG terminal in Vladivostok.

Noda's activities demonstrated his readiness to proactively approach Russia in his resource diplomacy. Noda managed to reduce tensions both in all three territorial disputes and in relations with the U.S. and boost the regional economic integration in multiple ways. The Japanese corporations preserved their positions

82 *The DPJ era: continuity, inertia, and change*

in the global export of nuclear technologies.[90] The softening of the export arms regime and readiness to review participation in peace-keeping operations marked a more decisive security policy. Although there is insufficient evidence to characterise Noda's series of well-executed tactical moves as 'grand strategy,' his diplomacy demonstrated a rather successful evolution towards the optimal foreign policy formula in the spirit of the 'Goldilocks Consensus' formulated by Samuels.[91]

Furthermore, Noda's policies confirmed Kitaoka's theory of quasi-change of regime, since, compared to predecessors, they demonstrated significant continuity with the LDP, despite the theoretical requirement of differentiation from rivals and delivery on the DPJ's promises. Noda's diplomacy was similar to Abe's – especially Abe II (2012–present), which also de-emphasised the value element of foreign policy.

Conclusion

In this chapter, I have sought to demonstrate that despite the change of ruling party, Japanese foreign policy towards CA experienced its traditional structural constraints, became sidelined to periphery by larger agenda items, and, on balance, displayed more reactivity than proactivity in terms of following the changes in U.S. foreign policy towards CA, especially Uzbekistan. Still, some pre-DPJ era niche projects of cooperation were continued by bureaucrats and remained 'business as usual,' namely, the CAJ dialogue and the partnership on rare earths and uranium, especially until 3/11.

The DPJ's years in power showed that the independent variable of oscillations between proactivity and reactivity in Japanese foreign policy did not particularly vary depending on partisan politics and, instead, followed the pattern of adaptation to the wider, external environment.

Together with the inconsistencies, diplomatic inexperience and errors made by the Hatoyama and Kan cabinets, the DPJ's security policy, and return to LDP-style realism under Noda were also in line with Nomura's application of Kitaoka's theory of quasi-change of regime to the DPJ rule and suggested the continuity of Japan's search for 'normal status' in international affairs.

In the case of CA specifically, although partisan politics historically contributed at the level of individual factions, such as Seiwaken under Mori's leadership, its overall impact was limited and secondary to the importance of ideological preferences across various elite constituencies: neo-autonomists like Hatoyama, pragmatic realists like Noda, and centrists like Kan. Pragmatism was the most prominent feature all three DPJ cabinets demonstrated towards CA after Hatoyama had removed value-based elements of his LDP predecessors from diplomacy. Intra-DPJ ideological preferences alone also have had limited influence. For instance, Hatoyama's neo-autonomism was limited by reactivity: Japan synchronised the restoration of its Uzbekistan ties to the pre-2005 level with similar policies pursued by the U.S. and the E.U., even though the Japanese leadership was already mulling this action in 2008, but awaiting a change of tide in the West.

The DPJ era: continuity, inertia, and change 83

The most important implications for the DPJ's CA policy came from the external environment, namely, the 2010 disputes with China, the foreign policies and domestic politics of CA countries, and from unforeseen *force majeure* events, such as the 'black swan' event of 3/11.[92] While the Fukushima disaster stymied the publicity of Japan's nuclear cooperation with CA, together with the 2010 Senkaku tensions, it spurred Japan's interest in CA's rare earths and Russian natural gas, fixing those niches more permanently. The DPJ laid solid groundwork for subsequent improvement in Japanese ties with CA under Abe II.

Notes

1 MOFA: Uzubekistan Kyōwakoku – Kiso dēta [Republic of Uzbekistan – Basic data]. http://www.mofa.go.jp/mofaj/area/uzbekistan/data.html#section1 (Accessed 20 June 16).
2 Interview with Alisher Shaykhov, former ambassador of Uzbekistan to Japan and chairman of chamber of commerce and industry of Uzbekistan, June 2011. The DPJ's focus on East Asia as distraction from Central Asia was also corroborated in interviews with Japanese private sector officials.
3 Abe attempted to set up a National Security Council during his first term (2006–7), but did not manage to finalise it before his resignation. Notable precedents also included Koizumi Jun'ichirō's usage of the Situation Center and *Kantei* during 9/11 and administrative environments created during Hashimoto's premiership. See Shinoda Tomohito, *Koizumi Diplomacy: Japan's Kantei Approach to Foreign and Defense Affairs* (Seattle, WA: University of Washington Press, 2011).
4 Hosoya Yuichi, 'The Role of Japan's National Security Council,' *AJISS-Commentary* no. 199 (2013): 4.
5 Kotani Tetsuo, 'Zigzag Neudachi' [Zigzag of no luck], *Russia in Global Affairs*, 20 December 2010, http://www.globalaffairs.ru/number/Zigzag-neudachi-15065 (Accessed 10 May 2012). The electoral system established by the 1994 reforms involved parallel voting with first-past-the-post (FPTP) single-member electoral districts and proportional representation.
6 The distortionary effect of the FPTP voting system should also be considered in the interpretation of both 2009 and 2012 'landslides.'
7 John Swenson-Wright, 'East Asia: Searching for Consistency,' in *America and a Changed World: A Question of Leadership*, ed. Robin Niblett (Malden, MA: Wiley-Blackwell, 2010), 7–8.
8 Nomura Shunsuke, *Japan's Search for Autonomous Diplomacy: A Comparison of the Foreign Policies of the Hatoyama Administrations*. Thesis (Cambridge, UK: University of Cambridge, 2011), 40–41.
9 Kitaoka Shin'ichi, *Jimintō* [Liberal-Democratic Party] (Tokyo: Yomiuri Shimbunsha, 1995).
10 Elgena Molodiakova, 'Prikhod demokratov vo vlast': politicheskoye zemletryaseniye' [DPJ's Advent to Power: A Political Earthquake]. *Japan* 2010. Yearbook (Moscow: AIRO–XXI, 2010), 7.
11 Carmen Schmidt, 'The DPJ and Its Factions: Benefit or Threat?,' *Hitotsubashi Journal of Social Studies* 43, no. 1 (2011): 1–21.
12 Interview with a MOFA official in charge of Central Asian affairs, March 2012; MOFA: 'Central Asia as a Corridor of Peace and Stability,' speech by Asō Tarō, Japan National Press Club, 1 June 2006, http://www.mofa.go.jp/region/europe/speech0606.html (Accessed 19 April 2016).
13 Kent Calder, 'Japanese Foreign Economic Policy Formation: Explaining the Reactive State,' *World Politics* 40, no. 4 (1988), doi:doi.org/10.2307/2010317.

84 The DPJ era: continuity, inertia, and change

14 Yuasa Takeshi, 'Central Asia in the Context of Japanese-Russian Relations,' *China and Eurasia Forum Quarterly* 8, no. 2 (2010), 134.

15 By the term 'Nixon shock,' in this case I refer to the rapid normalisation of Washington's relations with Beijing exercised by the Nixon administration in the early 1970s without prior consultations with Japanese leadership as ally in security treaty.

16 Uyama Tomohiko, 'Japanese Policies in Relation to Kazakhstan: Is There a "Strategy"?' in *Thinking Strategically: The Major Powers, Kazakhstan, and the Central Asian Nexus*, ed. Robert Legvold (Cambridge, MA: American Academy of Arts and Sciences MIT Press, 2003); Dmitry Streltsov, 'Moskva i Tokyo: vyiti iz spyachki' [Moscow and Tokyo: Exit the hibernation], *Russia in Global Affairs*, 22 October 2011, http://www.globalaffairs.ru/number/Moskva-i-Tokio-vyiti-iz-spyachki-15365 (Accessed 25 May 14).

17 Soeya Yoshihide, Tadokoro Masayuki, and David A. Welch, eds., *Japan as a 'Normal Country'? A Nation in Search of its Place in the World* (Toronto: University of Toronto Press, 2011), 3–5.

18 In 1993, Ozawa published his manifesto book *Nippon kaizō keikaku* [Blueprint for a new Japan: The rethinking of a nation]. During the DPJ reign, Ozawa headed the largest faction of the party until leaving DPJ in 2012. Schmidt, 'The DPJ and Its Factions: Benefit or Threat?:' 3; Onishi Norimitsu, 'For Japan's Insider-Turned-Rebel, Decade-Old Revolution Is Still a Work in Progress,' *New York Times*, 18 January 2004, http://www.nytimes.com/2004/01/18/world/for-japan-s-insider-turned-rebel-decade-old-revolution-still-work-progress.html (Accessed 25 May 14).

19 On the role of realism in Chinese and Russian strategic thoughts, see: Tang Shiping, From Offensive Realism to Defensive Realism: 'A Social Evolutionary Interpretation of China's Security Strategy,' *State of Security and International Studies*, S. Rajaratnam School of International Studies, 2007; Li Xiaoting, 'Applying offensive realism to the rise of China: Structural incentives and Chinese diplomacy toward the neighboring states,' *International Relations of the Asia-Pacific* (2015) doi:10.1093/irap/lcv019; Tatyana Romanova, 'Neoclassical Realism and Today's Russia,' *Russia in Global Affairs*, 7 October 2012, http://eng.globalaffairs.ru/number/Neoclassical-Realism-and-Todays-Russia-15681 (Accessed 26 May 2014).

20 Richard J. Samuels, *Securing Japan: Tokyo's Grand Strategy and the Future of East Asia* (Ithaca, NY: Cornell University Press, 2007), 124–130.

21 Weston S. Konishi, *From Rhetoric to Reality: Foreign-Policy Making under the Democratic Party of Japan.* April 2012, http://www.ifpa.org/pdf/fromRhetoricToReality.pdf (Accessed 10 June 12), 51.

22 Interview with the European Bank for Reconstruction and Development (EBRD) official, May 2011, interview with Councillor and former Ambassador to Uzbekistan and Tajikistan Nakayama Kyōko, March 2012.

23 Mori served as the Japanese co-chair of the so-called 'Wise Men Council' – a joint Russo-Japanese track-two body for informal policy discussion.

24 Interview with former Foreign Minister Kawaguchi Yoriko, November 2013.

25 The Nakayamas have left the LDP in 2010, as of 2016, Nakayama Kyōko represented the Party of Hope. Nakayama Kyōko's page on National Diet of Japan website, http://www.sangiin.go.jp/japanese/joho1/kousei/eng/members/profile/7007043.htm (Accessed 5 June 2018).

26 Interview with Nakayama Kyōko, March 2012. The importance of Mori's individual role was confirmed by Uzbek respondents with knowledge of the matter, for instance, former Ambassador to Japan Alisher Shaykhov.

27 Interview with a MOFA official in charge of Central Asian affairs, March 2012.

28 Chris Winkler, A comparative perspective on Japan's 'turn to the right,' presentation at the Japanese Studies Association of Australia conference, 1 July 2015.

29 Interview with a middle-level MOFA official stationed in one of CA countries, May 2011.

The DPJ era: continuity, inertia, and change   85

30 Interview with JICA official, April 2013.
31 Hatoyama's conscious efforts to distinguish himself from the previous LDP adminis-tration, by explicitly tilting towards Asia and away from Japan's traditional reliance on the United States demonstrate continuity with the diplomatic debates of the 1950s during his grandfather Hatoyama Ichirō's premiership. They also have deeper roots in the Japanese political debates dating back to the end of nineteenth century when Fukuzawa Yukichi, on the contrary, argued in favour of Japan's 'De-Asianisation' (*datsu-a ron*).
32 Yuasa Takeshi, Lecture at International University of Japan, 5 June 2013.
33 MOFA (2008), Kōmura gaimudaijin no Roshia hōmon (Kekka gaiyō) [Visit of Foreign Minister Kōmura to Russia (overview of results)], http://www.mofa.go.jp/mofaj/kaidan/g_komura/russia_08/kg.html (Accessed 9 March 2016).
34 Murashkin, 'Japanese Involvement...,' 74.
35 'Kan Picked as Japan's National Strategy Minister,' *Reuters*, 5 September 2009, http://www.reuters.com/article/2009/09/05/us-japan-politics-cabinet-idUS-TRE5840JL20090905 (Accessed 10 May 2012).
36 Detailed accounts of DPJ's attempted decision-making reforms can be found in Karol Zakowski, *Decision-Making Reform in Japan: The DPJ's Failed Attempt at a Politician-Led Government*, Routledge, 2015, Masahiro Horie, 'Budgeting in Japan after the global financial crisis: Postponing decisions on crucial issues,' *The Global Financial Crisis and its Budget Impacts in OECD Nations: Fiscal Responses and Future Challenges*, eds. John Wanna, Evert A. Lindquist, Jouke de Vries (Cheltenham, UK: Edward Elgar Publishing, 2015), 129–30.
37 *Minshutō no seiken seisaku* [DPJ's government policy] Manifesto 2009, http://www.dpj.or.jp/policies/manifesto2009 (Accessed 24 March 2016).
38 Terashima Jitsurō, *Sekai-wo shiru chikara* [Power of knowing the world] (Tokyo: PHP, 2010), 20.
39 Address by H. E. Dr. Yukio Hatoyama Prime Minister of Japan. *Japan's New Commitment to Asia – Toward the Realization of an East Asian Community*, http://japan.kantei.go.jp/hatoyama/statement/200911/15singapore_e.html (Accessed 24 March 2012).
40 MOFA Diplomatic Bluebooks 2007–17.
41 Interview with former METI official; 'Abe's "new mercantilism" bears fruit for Japan.' *Nikkei Asian Review*, 4 January 2016, http://asia.nikkei.com/Politics-Economy/Policy-Politics/Abe-s-new-mercantilism-bears-fruit-for-Japan.
42 MOFA: 'Central Asia plus Japan' Dialogue, The Fourth Tokyo Dialogue: Keynote Speech by Mr. Tetsuro Fukuyama, state secretary for foreign affairs of Japan, 25 February 2010, https://www.mofa.go.jp/region/europe/dialogue/speech1002.html.
43 Kazakhstan signs cooperation deal with Japan, 3 March 2010, http://www.world-nuclear-news.org/NP-Kazakhstan_signs_cooperation_deal_with_Japan-0303104.html (Accessed 29 April 2015).
44 Vstrecha s parlamentskoi delegatsiei Yaponii [Meeting with the Japanese parliamen-tary delegation], President of Tajikistan, 3 September 2010, http://www.president.tj/ru/node/2360 (Accessed 15 May 2012).
45 Viktoriya Panfilova, 'Uzbekskii ryvok na Zapad,' [Uzbekistan drives towards the West], *Nezavisimaya gazeta*, 11 November 2009.
46 Uzbekistan: Japanese Officials Comment on Bilateral Cooperation, Uzbek Officials, diplomatic cable ID: 09TASHKENT105_a, 27 January 2009, https://wikileaks.org/plusd/cables/09TASHKENT105_a.html (Accessed 30 March 2014).
47 Interviews with JICA officials April 2012. Shinseichōsenryaku. Genkinanihon fuk-katsu no sinario [New Growth Strategy. Scenario for the revival of a healthy Japan], prime minister's cabinet 18 June 2010, www.kantei.go.jp/jp/sinseichousenryaku/sinseichou01.pdf (Accessed 20 April 2015).

86 *The DPJ era: continuity, inertia, and change*

48 Enhancing Enlightened National Interest: Living in harmony with the world and promoting peace and prosperity– ODA Review Final Report June 2010, Ministry of Foreign Affairs of Japan, http://www.mofa.go.jp/policy/oda/reform/pdfs/review1006_report.pdf (Accessed 20 April 15).

49 Interview with a JICA official based in one of the Central Asian countries, March 2013.

50 Interview with a JICA official, April 2012.

51 Interview with a JICA official based in one of the Central Asian countries, March 2013.

52 MOFA (2005) Statement by the Press Secretary/Director-General for Press and Public Relations, Ministry of Foreign Affairs, on the Situation in the Kyrgyz Republic 25 March 2005, http://www.mofa.go.jp/announce/announce/2005/3/0325-2.html (Accessed 15 April 2010); MOFA (2010) Statement by Press Secretary/Director-General for Press and Public Relations, Ministry of Foreign Affairs, on the Destabilization of the Situation in the Kyrgyz Republic, 8 April 2010, http://www.mofa.go.jp/announce/announce/2010/4/0408_01.html (Accessed 15 April 2010).

53 'Japanese parliamentarians say they did not notice serious violations able to impact voting results in Kyrgyzstan,' *AKIpress*, 31 October 11, http://akipress.com/news:411921/ (Accessed 17 May 2012).

54 'Former Japanese leader Hatoyama to buck precedent, join advisory panel of China-Led AIIB,' *The Japan Times*, 26 June 2016, http://www.japantimes.co.jp/news/2016/06/26/business/economy-business/former-japanese-leader-hatoyama-to-buck-precedent-join-advisory-panel-of-china-led-aiib/#.V3BYBPmLTIV (Accessed 26 June 2016).

55 The families of many Japanese politicians trace their lineage to ancient clans, the most salient example being, arguably, Prime Minister Abe Shinzō, who descends from the Chōshū clan known for its support to the cause of restoration of Imperial rule in Japan in the 1860s. While the Sugawara clan is ancient, the only known modern politicians among its famous descendants include Taishō-era Prime Minister Ōkuma Shigenobu and Kan Naoto.

56 The notable exceptions include three of Kan's closest predecessors: Asō Tarō graduated from Gakushūin, Fukuda Yasuo studied at Waseda, while Abe Shinzō earned his degree from Seikei University.

57 Weston S. Konishi, *From Rhetoric to Reality: Foreign-Policy Making under the Democratic Party of Japan* (Boston: Institute for Foreign Policy Analysis, 2012), v–vi and 15–22.

58 Information digest, Embassy of the Republic of Uzbekistan to the United Kingdom of Great Britain and Northern Ireland, 3–4 January 2011, http://www.uzbekembassy.org/e/press_releases/17020/ (Accessed 27 April 2016).

59 ADB president visits Tashkent ahead of annual meeting, 18 February 2010, *UzNews.net*, http://www.uznews.net/en/world/12474-adb-president-visits-tashkent-ahead-of-annual-meeting (Accessed 8 May 2014).

60 Kanako Takahara, 'Sengoku's growing influence causes a stir,' *Japan Times*, 23 October 2010, http://www.japantimes.co.jp/text/nn20101023f1.html (Accessed 17 May 2012).

61 While Tokyo viewed the ban as calculated retaliation, the Chinese authorities denied the existence of a formally documented prohibition. 'China denies rare earth export quota report,' *Reuters*, 20 October 2010, http://www.reuters.com/article/us-china-rareearth-idUSTRE69J30Y20101020 (Accessed 14 May 2012).

62 Kotani, Tetsuo, 'Zigzag neudachi.'

63 Novym generalnym sekretarem kabineta ministrov Yaponii naznachen demokrat Yukio Edano [Yukio Edano appointed as new cabinet secretary general], http://www.itartass.ur.ru/lentanews/155779.html (Accessed 27 April 2012).

The DPJ era: continuity, inertia, and change 87

64 Visit to Japan of His Excellency Mr. Islam Karimov, President of the Republic of Uzbekistan and Mrs. Tatyana Karimova, MOFA, 14 January 2011, http://www.mofa.go.jp/announce/event/2011/1/0114_01.html (Accessed 27 April 2012).

65 Japan–Uzbekistan Summit Meeting, MOFA, 9 February 11, http://www.mofa.go.jp/announce/announce/2011/2/0209_01.html (Accessed 12 May 2012).

66 Memorandum on Economic Cooperation between the Ministry of Foreign Affairs of Japan and the Ministry of Foreign Affairs of The Republic of Uzbekistan, MOFA, 9 February 2011, http://www.mofa.go.jp/region/europe/uzbekistan/visit1102/memo.html (Accessed 12 May 2012).

67 Courtesy Call from Minister for Foreign Affairs Seiji Maehara on President Karimov of the Republic of Uzbekistan, MOFA, 9 February 2011, http://www.mofa.go.jp/announce/announce/2011/2/0209_02.html (Accessed 12 May 2012).

68 Information digest, Embassy of the Republic of Uzbekistan to the United Kingdom of Great Britain and Northern Ireland, 3–4 January 2011, http://www.uzbekembassy.org/e/press_releases/17020/ (Accessed 27 April 2016).

69 Purofīru [Profile], http://www.kgemba.com/profile/ (Accessed 27 April 2016); First Uzbek–Japanese interparliamentary forum held, UzReport Information Agency, 4 January 2011, http://mir.uzreport.uz/news_e_83923.html (Accessed 12 May 2012).

70 'Tokyo holds roundtable on Kazakh-Japanese relations prospects,' *Kazinform*, 10 March 2011, http://www.inform.kz/eng/article/2359093 (Accessed 6 May 2012).

71 'V Astane sostoyalas' vstrecha glavy MID RK s eks-prem'er-ministrom Yaponii Yu. Hatoyamoi' [Astana hosts the meeting between the head of the Kazakh Foreign Ministry and ex-Prime Minister of Japan Yukio Hatoyama], *Kazinform*, 4 May 2011, http://www.inform.kz/rus/article/2377044 (Accessed 6 May 2012).

72 Interview with a Japanese diplomat stationed in one of the CA countries, May 2011.

73 Private communication with Ambassador Harada Yūzō, June 2011.

74 Interview with METI official, May 2012.

75 Richard R. Samuels, *3.11: Disaster and Change in Japan* (New York: Cornell University Press, 2013), 110–50.

76 Interview with a Sumitomo employee, June 2011.

77 Sekiguchi Toko, 'Japan, Vietnam to Move Forward on Nuclear Deal,' *Wall Street Journal*, http://online.wsj.com/article/SB10001424052970204528204577009401285976844.html (Accessed 14 May 2012).

78 'Japan appoints Takeaki Matsumoto as Foreign Minister.' *BBC News*, 9 March 2011, http://www.bbc.co.uk/news/world-asia-pacific-12684614 (Accessed 10 May 2012).

79 Maehara's hawkish position on relations with China following the 2010 collision incident – before his MOFA tenure – drew additional criticism.

80 Fukkō gaikō gutaika wo shiji – Matsumoto gaishō [Revival diplomacy: Foreign Minister Matsumoto explains the details] http://jp.wsj.com/Japan/Politics/node_224303 (Accessed 10 May 2012).

81 'Naoto Kan Resigns as Japan's Prime Minister,' *The Guardian*, 26 August 2011, https://www.theguardian.com/world/2011/aug/26/naoto-kan-resigns-japan-pm (Accessed 29 May 2012).

82 The institute was established by the founder of Panasonic, Matsushita Konosuke.

83 Schmidt, 'The DPJ and Its Factions: Benefit or Threat?': 9–10.

84 Policy Speech by Prime Minister Yoshihiko Noda to the 178th Session of the Diet, 13 September 2011, http://japan.kantei.go.jp/noda/statement/201109/13syosin_e.html; Policy Speech by Prime Minister Yoshihiko Noda to the 180th Session of the Diet, 24 January 2012, http://japan.kantei.go.jp/noda/statement/201201/24siseihousin_e.html (Accessed 16 May 2012).

85 'Shigen gaikō senryaku kaigi secchi he Noda Seiken, minkan kigyō mo kuwae' [Noda government, private sector join the establishment], *Asahi*, 14 October 2011, http://www.asahi.com/special/minshu/TKY201110130666.html (Accessed 30 May 2012).

88 *The DPJ era: continuity, inertia, and change*

86 Ibid.
87 Japan–Kazakhstan Relations (Basic Data), http://www.mofa.go.jp/region/europe/kazakhstan/data.html; Japan–Kyrgyz Republic Relations (Basic Data), http://www.mofa.go.jp/region/europe/kyrgyz/data.html; Japan–Tajikistan Relations (Basic Data), http://www.mofa.go.jp/region/europe/tajikistan/data.html; Japan–Turkmenistan Relations (Basic Data), http://www.mofa.go.jp/region/europe/turkmenistan/data.html; Japan–Uzbekistan Relations (Basic Data), http://www.mofa.go.jp/region/europe/uzbekistan/data.html (Accessed 29 April 2016).
88 Official Trip of Yukio Edano, Minister of Economy, Trade, and Industry, to India and Kazakhstan, METI, http://www.meti.go.jp/english/press/2012/0510_01.html (Accessed 30 May 2012).
89 'Uzbekistan, Japan hold ministerial consultations,' *Trend*, 5 May 2012, http://en.trend.az/casia/uzbekistan/2022459.html (Accessed 30 May 2012).
90 'Turkey expecting nuclear bids from China, Japan, S Korea: Minister.' *Platts*, http://www.platts.com/RSSFeedDetailedNews/RSSFeed/ElectricPower/8154276; PM Noda looks to promote nuclear exports, *Yomiuri*, 6 December 2011, http://www.yomiuri.co.jp/dy/national/T111205005819.htm (Accessed 17 May 2012).
91 Richard J. Samuels, *Securing Japan. Tokyo's Grand Strategy and the Future of East Asia*, 9.
92 'Black swan' is a term coined by economist Nassim Taleb in his monograph *The Black Swan: The Impact of the Highly Improbable* (Random House, 2007).

3 Japan's aid in the New Silk Road

Developmentalism, securitisation,
and likely prototype for Belt and Road?

Introduction

This chapter examines in detail Japanese financial assistance in Central Asia (CA) and the agency of non-diplomatic Japanese officials who served as drivers behind the relationship, most notably those affiliated with the Ministry of Finance (MOF) and other financial institutions, both Japanese (Japan International Cooperation Agency [JICA], Japan Bank for International Cooperation [JBIC]) and international (Asian Development Bank [ADB], European Bank for Reconstruction and Development [EBRD], the World Bank). Its aims are: (i) to demonstrate the strategic contributions that are overlooked when Japanese diplomacy in the region is analysed strictly from the perspective of the Ministry of Foreign Affairs (MOFA) and (ii) to provide a partial explanation of the lull observed in Japan–CA relations in the late 2000s.

The main question this chapter addresses is: what role did Japanese financial bureaucrats play in Tokyo's CA policy, and how did they influence the evolution of this diplomacy as a whole? I argue that Japanese aid became a key factor in shaping the overall relationship between Japan and the region, and had consequences beyond Japan and individual CA countries, but it also had its stages of 'euphoria' (1990s) and 'fatigue' (2000s). What made Japanese development aid so important was the critical impact of key Japanese bureaucratic personalities and the specific tailored advice they provided as well as Japan's ability to provide financing with less political conditionality than Western donors.

Japanese assistance to CA was launched proactively in the early 1990s and initially largely driven by the MOF officials who also provided developmental advice on specific reforms. It further became instrumentalised in the late 1990s as Japanese Eurasian diplomacy unfolded and became part of Japan's 'burden sharing' with the United States in the post-9/11 era, thus outweighing the drive to secure access to natural resources as the primary reason for Japanese involvement in the region. If one were to resort to counterfactual history, it could be provocatively argued that the absence of aid as a driver would have resulted in a lower profile for the overall relationship.

I begin by stressing the macroeconomic environment affecting both the MOF and CA in the 1990s and 2000s and trace the changing rationale for development

90 *Aid: development, security and connectivity*

assistance and the evolution of the global donor landscape from one of Western hegemony to the rise of Asian donors. Furthermore, I provide an account of mutual cultural perceptions between Japan and CA, linking them to the development philosophy on both sides. I illustrate the unique traits and challenges of CA as a recipient of Japanese aid by comparing it to the similar role of Southeast Asia. After contextual examination, I analyse the roles of specific Japanese officials and aid practitioners in the relationship, considering the role of idealism, individual impact, and generational change in shaping policy. Finally, I focus on the case study of Central Asian Regional Economic Cooperation (CAREC), a multi-lateral infrastructure program of the ADB, demonstrating Japan's under-researched contribution to the regional political economy, subsequently partially emulated by China in its Belt and Road project.

Definitions and detailed argument

The Organisation for Economic Cooperation and Development (OECD) defines overseas development assistance (ODA) as flows that are: (i) provided by state and local governments or their executive agencies; (ii) administered with the promotion of the economic development and welfare of developing countries as the main objective; and (iii) concessional in character and convey a grant element of at least 25 percent. For the purposes of this chapter, I resort to a general term 'development assistance,' which includes both the ODA as disbursement of funds per se, including multi-lateral financing, and the contribution of the MOF officials in their capacity as financial advisors. For instance, the 'ODA' typically refers to loans, grants, or technical cooperation provided to a specific CA country, whilst developmental financial advice I take to be consultations provided to CA governments by Japanese officials from the MOF, JICA, and other organisations. In Japanese terms, the latter aspect is also known as 'intellectual assistance' (*chiteki shien*) or 'soft assistance' (*sofuto shien*) and is illustrated by events such as seminars for ministers from the Central Asian countries that Japan held in Tokyo under the auspices of the EBRD.[1] Whilst the ODA and financial assistance in the larger sense have been closely associated with post-war Japanese foreign policy in general, they have also gained a paramount role in the relationship between Japan and CA. Since existing scholarship provides compelling accounts of the humanitarian facet of Japanese ODA to CA, I focus predominantly on strategic infrastructure finance including loan aid and development advice provided by the MOF officials.[2]

Both the way Japan achieved certain long-term tangible results from its engagement (via, for instance, the contribution to the ADB's CAREC project), and the limits of a Japanese regional presence warrant close examination. In particular, the evolution of Japanese foreign aid to CA in the 1990s and 2000s through three separate stages of euphoria, fatigue, and stabilisation, demonstrates the reasons for the stagnation (2005–9) in the overall multi-lateral relationship between Japan and the region, as well as Japan's motivation behind its developmental contribution in CA.

Aid: development, security and connectivity 91

As set out in the preceding chapters, Japanese foreign policy is no stranger to the discourses of New Silk Road or the New Great Game in Eurasian affairs. As one of the earliest and largest donors to the region since its independence, Japan was also, arguably, the first major power to officially employ the term 'Silk Road' in its political and diplomatic language.

Similarly, Japanese officials were actively involved in first large-scale trans-CA infrastructure projects. Existing scholarly accounts of Japanese foreign infrastructure policy have demonstrated that post-war Japan adapted its pre-war and wartime 'techno-imperialism,' or active politicised construction of infrastructure objects in Asia, to boost its economic growth and foreign development assistance after World War II.[3] Yet it would be reductionist to either interpret Tokyo's aid motivation as a mere self-interested craving for CA raw materials or to exaggerate its willingness to join any sort of New Great Game with larger powers, especially considering the perspective of Japanese former diplomats and scholars critical of such engagements.[4] The contrast between China's Belt and Road and the ADB's CAREC that can arguably be seen as its Japan-inspired predecessor shows that geopolitics with immediate and direct self-oriented benefit is only one part of the Japanese aid equation.[5]

The Japanese experience in CA, in particular, that of financial assistance, provides useful inferences about Tokyo's own foreign policy-making. Firstly, instead of anthropomorphizing Japan as a single monolithic entity, one observes the interplay between several constituencies, most notably the contribution of the MOF. Secondly, Japan's alliance with the United States does not always come up as the determinant of Tokyo's own diplomatic agenda, and the importance of Washington's pressure on Tokyo should not be overemphasised in CA affairs. In other words, Japan's subservience to the United States (U.S.) foreign policy decisions, often pointed out in the literature on post-war Japanese diplomacy, was limited in the case of CA. Finally, the Japanese aid to Silk Road projects effectively exhibits the dichotomy between disinterested and pragmatic foreign policy approaches, separately analysed in existing scholarship.[6]

Whilst remaining forthright about their pragmatic intentions in CA, Japanese officials nevertheless attempted to rule out Japan's great power ambitions, stressing their unwillingness to participate in any kind of 'Great Game.' Examining the way Japan shaped its financial aid policy to the region helps to analyse such a strategic, but not strictly 'zero-sum-game' approach, because, on balance, Tokyo did not 'weaponise' its financial assistance in CA, except one notable instance in Uzbekistan, and demonstrated a considerable degree of idealism and romanticism.[7] Whilst the ODA and natural resources have been at the heart of Japan's relations with the region, in my view, the former has outweighed the latter in shaping the overall relationship.

In addition, reflecting CA states' autonomous agency in international affairs, the Japanese aid experience not only reconfirmed the multi-vectored orientation of CA diplomacy, but also demonstrated the influence of the CA domestic patron-client relations and the priority need of regime survival in shaping the foreign policies of individual CA states. This perspective prevents the observer from

92 *Aid: development, security and connectivity*

falling into the trap of objectifying the region as a mere receptacle of great powers' actions or as monolithic entities. This issue is mainly treated in my third chapter dealing with CA policies towards Tokyo, but certain illustrations of the impact of the role of recipient countries are highlighted here.

Theory

In this chapter, I revisit the historical narrative of the relationship in the field of finance and aid, looking into the role of policy-making carried out by Japanese financial officials indirectly involved in 'Eurasian Diplomacy' over the past two decades. I stress the importance of interpersonal ties and personalities in shaping the political economy of Japan–CA development finance. In particular, I place this case into the broad context of international finance throughout the 1990s and 2000s, keeping an eye on the simultaneous evolution of both Tokyo and CA's relationships with Moscow, Beijing, and Washington.

While I highlight the MOF's role in overall geopolitical Japanese engagement in CA, in this chapter, I discuss not only the MOF's activity as unitary monolithic actor, but also the role of specific Japanese aid officials involved in CA matters, some of whom became proactive in shaping the Japan–CA relationship and served as policy entrepreneurs. Structurally, the MOF has not had a dedicated CA unit, apart from ad hoc assignments at the Financial Policy Institute (*zaiseik in'yūkenkyūjo*) and at the International Organisations Bureau dealing with multilateral aid.[8] Although most of these officials had a MOF background or affiliation, they typically worked in a variety of national and international institutions, such as the ADB, the EBRD, JBIC, JICA, the World Bank, or Japan's diplomatic missions in CA. Although I am not implying the existence of a distinct, organised community with a single and conscious purpose, especially given the frequent pattern of informal rotations within the Japanese bureaucracy, one cannot help observing a shared experience among the Japanese finance and aid professionals working with CA. In Japanese, this is referred to as *Ōkurashō kankeisha nettowāku* or the 'network of MOF affiliates.'

A notable manifestation of this network is the informal Japanese patronage of CA within the EBRD, where Japan also contributes 8.5 percent of the bank's capital; the Japanese paramount position at the ADB; and the recurrent assignment of Japanese officials to CA matters at the World Bank. Importantly, this wide representation of Japan in the bureaucracies of international financial institutions (IFIs) improved the availability of quality information on CA that would otherwise have been less accessible for Tokyo decision-makers.[9] By extension and as a suggestion for further sociologic research, a case could be made for analysing the Japanese developmental community and their recipient counterparts through the lens of Bruno Latour's actor-network theory, although this is outside the scope of this chapter.[10]

The MOF's centrepiece role in the Japanese political system and foreign policy has been extensively covered in existing scholarship, as well as the role of Japanese foreign aid as an instrument of power.[11] For instance, Kent Calder in his

Aid: development, security and connectivity 93

article on the reactivity of Japanese foreign policy made a forecast about Japan's future activism which can be considered relevant and almost visionary when applied to Japan's CA involvement:

> The strongest prospects for Japanese activism will most likely appear in energy and finance, where sharp global price fluctuations and Japan's dependence on world markets create an overwhelming interest in shaping future international regimes.[12]

Such activism was seen early into the post-Socialist transition of the 1990s, as Japan welcomed the EBRD's vigorous capital-raising in yen: in 1992, some 31 percent of the EBRD's total borrowing was yen-denominated.[13] Japan has also rapidly become the EBRD's largest counterpart for co-financing, reflecting the Japanese preference for risk-sharing and multi-lateralism in finance.[14] In addition, the Japanese government particularly relied on multi-lateral institutions, such as the EBRD or ADB, in matters pertaining to CA, for it considered its own expertise in the region significantly limited.[15]

Michael Green, another authoritative scholar of Japanese foreign policy-making, characterises the MOF's political weight in the 1990s as follows:

> As the 'ministry within the ministries,' Japan's MOF has traditionally exerted unparalleled influence over all aspects of Japan's public policy, including foreign affairs. The core of MOF's influence lies in two of its functions: the budget bureau that holds the carrot of expenditures and the tax bureau ... which hold the sticks of revenue collections and audits. ... In addition, there are usually more than two dozen former MOF officials in the Diet, a number twice as high as former Ministry of International Trade and Industry (MITI) officials and the negligible numbers of former MOFA officials ... MOF's direct role in foreign affairs is managed by the International Bureau. ... The bureau is responsible for exchange rate policy, liaison with international financial institutions such as the IMF and World Bank, and financial policy toward developing countries. In fact, MOF officials dominate the Japanese representation in many of these international financial institutions. ... One area where MOF is clearly energetic and ambitious ... is in its push for a larger Japanese role in the management of the international financial system.[16]

I show below that the above characteristics of Japanese financial power and MOF as the key cog in Japanese foreign policy-making were relevant in understanding Japan's developmental engagement with CA starting from the latter's independence and until the mid-2000s. As I mentioned earlier, during Hashimoto Ryūtarō's tenure as finance minister (1989–91), Chino Tadao – who later went on to become a key CA's 'chaperon' in the Japanese financial bureaucracy – was appointed the head of the MOF's international bureau (*kokusaikyoku*) and vice minister of international affairs.

94   *Aid: development, security and connectivity*

The role of development models in financial assistance

At the crossroads of development models

In the mid-1990s, Magosaki Ukeru, the first Japanese ambassador to Uzbekistan and a proponent of assisting CA countries in their transition from planned to market economies, supported this policy by quoting the statements of the Uzbek President Islam Karimov, according to which 'Asian approaches are suitable for Asians' and 'Japan would be the best model [for Central Asia].'[17] According to political economist and International Relations (IR) scholar Robert Gilpin, the theory of East Asian developmental state was notably salient at the time, attributing the outstanding economic success of Japan and other East Asian countries to 'their adoption of the developmental state model in which the state had to play the central role in guiding economic development and had to lead rather than follow the market.'[18]

Japan was a particularly comfortable partner for the states in the region: it was seen by the local authoritarian leaders as neutral (unlike Russia or Turkey, which were seen as harbouring expansionist intentions) and less demanding on the issues of democratisation and human rights (unlike Western countries) – a stance demonstrated by the much less politically conditional nature of Japanese economic assistance to the region. By adopting the Japanese model of political, social, and economic development from the 1950–70s, CA countries hoped to secure a greater degree of independence from Europe and the United States, which by contrast were much stricter in the implementation of reform plans and policy concepts. The bursting of the Japanese bubble in 1991 and resulting 'lost decade' of domestic economic problems for Japan were probably considered by the CA leaders as the price of progress and an avoidable long-term scenario, rather than the inevitable dead-end stage of the 'Japan Way.' It is no surprise that the heads of states that had ambitions for regional leadership in CA – Kazakhstan and Uzbekistan – declared their orientation towards the Japanese developmental model in order to maintain equilibrium between various powers dealing with the region. A look at the media-discourse of the leaders of CA states when commenting on relations with the European Union, the United States, and Japan highlights the local preference for Asian values over European ones.[19] Such values and the developmental model based thereupon imply that democratisation follows the establishment of a market economy, as was the case in Republic of Korea (ROK), while the Western model of development epitomised by the Washington Consensus and 'big bang' approach demanded the simultaneous pursuit of economic and political liberalisation.[20] In Eastern European transition countries – Czechoslovakia, Hungary, and Poland – democratisation and market reforms were simultaneous. Although Japan was not necessarily trying to outmatch the Western countries in CA, the competitive nature of its developmental involvement could not be ignored by its officials.

Ultimately, however, despite the rhetoric of individual CA leaders praising Japanese-style capitalism, as well as strong cooperation with other Asian countries, the CA republics have pursued their own *sui generis* economic model,

Aid: development, security and connectivity 95

equally distinct from neo-liberalism and the 'flying geese' model associated with the East Asian economic miracle.[21] Although this model involves a strong government dirigisme comparable to the Asian developmental state model, unlike in East and Southeast Asia, it primarily relies on the exports of local commodities rather than those of finished goods produced through the hosting of manufacturing and assembly lines of delocalising multi-national corporations. By advocating gradualist policies, individual CA leaders may have been motivated by rent-seeking dynamics, very strong in the region.[22] Nonetheless, the Japanese contribution in the field of development, including the development model choice, had significant consequences for the foreign policy-making of both Japan and CA. Understanding the role and evolution of Japanese developmental diplomacy towards the region sheds light on the broader Japanese role in CA.

According to my hypothesis, the Japanese early contribution to CA's market transition, itself an important part of Japan's overall regional involvement, could be viewed in the context of Japan's and the MOF's financial challenges in the 1990s. CA's independence in 1991, following the dissolution of the Soviet Union and quest for a new development model, coincided with the period of tests for the MOF, which resulted from both the international finance environment of that era and domestic problems.

Firstly, it was in this period that Japan actively promoted its development model and East Asian economic miracle as an alternative to the so-called Washington Consensus (WC).[23] The 1997 Asian financial crisis reignited those debates with new intensity, especially given its impact on the 1998 Russian financial crisis, and in turn had further consequences for the CA transition economies.[24] Secondly, whilst many Western donor countries entered the so-called 'aid fatigue' in the early 1990s, Japan, on the contrary, raised its donor profile and adopted an ODA charter in 1992 in order to counter criticisms of excessive mercantilism and pragmatism in its aid philosophy.[25] Thirdly, the 1990s was the period of turbulence for the MOF itself, as the powerful ministry came under tighter scrutiny amidst the failure of deregulation reforms in the aftermath of the bursting of the real estate bubble.[26,27]

In this context, Tokyo and, more specifically, its diplomats and finance officials acting as advisors strongly encouraged gradualist (*zenshinshugi*) transition policies in the region, as opposed to radical shock therapy. In addition, as Michael Green noted, the 1990s saw a strengthening of Japan's identity as an Asian actor 'allied with America but serving as Asia's breakwater against the chaos of Anglo-American capitalism and culture.'[28] Through endorsing transition policies in CA countries, in particular, gradualism in Uzbekistan, Japan solidified its foreign partner profile as a broadly disinterested development sponsor and unique role model. For instance, according to the Uzbekistan's Vice Prime Minister Azimov, the Japanese model was preferred in 1996 to the British or American model when the Uzbek President Islam Karimov decided to establish a banking and financing academy for in-house education of the future Uzbek financiers.[29] By contrast, it took the World Bank almost 15 years to figure out a way to deal with Uzbekistan, which was partly induced by this organisation's

96 *Aid: development, security and connectivity*

preference for Washington Consensus-type policies.[30] Meanwhile, Japan's low-profile approach and established alliance relations with the United States helped to avoid antagonising Washington: for instance, thanks to Tokyo's lobbying in the field of foreign trade, Washington granted most favoured nation treatment to CA states.[31]

The first decade of the relationship between Japan and the Silk Road countries was thus largely driven by development mentoring, which included not only reform advice per se, but also the provision of aid. Japan's ability to provide infrastructure financing was of particular importance in this context, as CA countries needed investments in dilapidated Soviet infrastructure, but were short of funds in the immediate aftermath of their independence. This deficiency was due to a number of factors: low commodity prices in the 1990s; privatisations in CA had reduced state income from assets; and the tax base had not yet become a sufficiently solid and stable source of public finance.

The penchant towards gradualism in CA was underpinned by witnessing the harsh effects of neo-liberal transition policies in neighbouring post-Soviet countries. Gradual economic liberalisation instead of the acceptance of WC conditionality provided an eventual insulation effect for certain CA countries (for instance, Uzbekistan) during the 1997 and 2008 financial crises, but it also had its limits and produced a number of adverse effects, highlighted below. Incidentally, the Asian crisis of 1997 and the 2008 global financial crisis happened to roughly match, respectively, the time boundaries of Tokyo's maximum and minimum developmental interest towards the region.

The policy-making carried out by various government officials in the Japanese financial community contributed to the formulation and implementation of Japanese 'Silk Road diplomacy' (as this policy is discursively described within the official Tokyo diplomatic agenda) in the 1990s and 2000s. I further examine to what extent the MOF was influential in the overall geopolitical engagement of Japan in CA, as compared to remaining key ministries of the *sanshōchō* (three-ministry) system – as the MOFA and the Ministry of Economy, Trade, and Industry (METI), whose roles are covered in respective chapters of this book.

Shades of gradualism: foreign policy pragmatism and the evolution of Japan's ideological posture

There are two common misperceptions about the motivation behind Japan's contemporary involvement in CA. In terms of geopolitics, it may be overemphasised that Tokyo was providing financial aid in exchange for access to raw materials and to accommodate American interests as part of burden-sharing within its alliance with the United States. Secondly, from the viewpoint of political economy, Japanese cooperation with CA may appear as the expansion of capitalist practices to post-Communist newly independent states. Japan is a part of Western-dominated IFIs, a key element in the world economy, and a key American ally in Asia. From this perspective, Japan's behaviour could be interpreted as providing CA with incentives to transition to a capitalist Western-dominated social

Aid: development, security and connectivity 97

and economic model. By contrast, the European Union (E.U.) and especially the United States deployed both incentives and disincentives (sanctions, tougher reform requirements in exchange for foreign aid).

However, such perspectives are oversimplified and reductionist. Contextualising the history of the actions by Japanese finance officials, a key constituency shaping Tokyo's CA policy, within CA's economic history reveals counter-intuitive ideational and human dimensions behind this policy. This evidence suggests a strong element of idealism in Japan's assistance to CA during the 1990s.

Japanese developmental involvement in post-Soviet CA emerged and evolved as a precursor and early variant of post-neo-liberalism. I use the definition of neo-liberalism provided by social anthropologist Bob Jessop, who views it as 'a political project that is justified on philosophical grounds and seeks to extend competitive market forces, consolidate a market-friendly constitution and promote individual freedom.'[32] Post-neo-liberalism could thus be viewed as a form of governance, retaining some features of neo-liberalism, adjusting to particular failures and shortcomings of the neo-liberal model, in particular in the field of welfare policies.[33]

The Japanese gradualist transition philosophy, with a focus on investment in the public sector and the criticism of the WC, can be viewed as a form of post-neo-liberalism promoted by Japanese government officials and Japanese representatives of IFIs.[34] As already mentioned, these individuals combined a positive attitude towards the region with several important powers: advice on reforms, provision of bilateral financial aid, and supporting CA's access to diversified capital sources by promoting CA's assistance eligibility in various international clubs of which Japan was already a member. In the case of regional development banks, however, the lending was not strictly Japanese and predominantly came from a variety of international sources. The Japanese involvement was thus not as Foreign Direct Investment (FDI)-intensive as in Southeast Asia and relied more on developmental guidance and institutional power.

The policy originated in the immediate aftermath of the Washington Consensus' inception and was reinforced by the subsequent criticisms of the WC by certain economists in the late 1990s.[35] The 1997 Asian and the 1998 Russian financial crises, as well as the development of the 'Third Way' in the United Kingdom, coincided with the first official formulation of Japan's Eurasian diplomacy by Prime Minister Hashimoto and 'Silk Road Action Plan' pursued by Hashimoto's successor Obuchi.[36] The downsides of 'shock therapy' reforms in neighbouring Russia and Eastern Europe provided an additional justification for economic gradualism in the minds of CA elites, who were also moving towards more authoritarian control at home.

Nonetheless, the degree of gradualism varied from republic to republic. Uzbekistan, which is the region's most populous and arguably the most industrialised country, embraced gradualism more firmly than Kazakhstan and Kyrgyzstan, which followed the International Monetary Fund (IMF) and World Bank (WB) policy courses. Turkmenistan's gradualism was part of the

98 *Aid: development, security and connectivity*

country's generally isolationist policy under President Saparmurat Niyazov, while Tajikistan's gradualist posture was preconditioned by its raging civil war (1992–7) and its consequences.

Paradoxically, the choice in favour of gradualism made by CA countries and the resulting slower pace of reforms ensured that they would be eligible for development finance almost indefinitely. As can be seen in the records of the EBRD annual statements by Japanese officials, CA and the Caucasus have been repeatedly placed under the Early Transition Countries (ETCs) category. This category included the countries where transition lagged in comparison to more advanced peers. The Japanese EBRD officials urged a redistribution of support from the more advanced transition recipients in favour of the ETCs, citing as a rationale the ETCs's slow reform pace. For instance, in 1998 the EBRD Governor for Japan Nakajima Mahito said in his speech:

> ... the operations of the bank should not be excessively concentrated in countries that are at an advanced stage of transition. In certain respects, it may be easier to process projects in countries that have already made substantial progress. However, a *proactive approach* [my italics] in regions where a greater need exists for transition support – for example in Central Asia and in the Caucasus region – will enhance our overall contribution in promoting transition, even if the bank finds it more challenging in terms of project structuring.[37]

The peak development of Japanese diplomacy in CA took place under Prime Minister Koizumi, branded as a proponent of neo-liberal reforms inside Japan to spur growth, including the reduction of state paternalism and the welfare state and the privatisation of the postal service. By the time Koizumi came to power, Japanese developmental involvement in CA had already gained full traction. Koizumi's neo-liberalism, however, did not have any direct ideological repercussions on Japan's CA policy – except in the key sense that Koizumi-era MOF officials became more dissatisfied with the slow pace of CA reforms and less enthusiastic about gradualism. Koizumi's primary impact on CA-destined aid was in shifting its focus towards 'burden sharing' with the United States and ISAF operations in Afghanistan, as the prime minister was keen to reinforce the U.S.–Japan alliance and mulled a revision of the Japanese Constitution.

Although Koizumi's successors Abe Shinzō and Asō Tarō maintained a degree of pragmatism towards the region by placing economic prosperity before political liberalisation and stressing the importance of CA's natural resources, they also emphasised the promotion of democracy in a value-based diplomacy and criticised resource nationalism. The internal contradictions of this stance, characterised by the Uzbek scholar Timur Dadabaev as reflecting Japan's uncertainty whether to pursue the policies of idealism or pragmatism, had a rather adverse impact on Japan's relations with CA, as I demonstrate in Chapter 4.[38]

Aid: development, security and connectivity 99

The 2008 global financial crisis unfolded simultaneously with the maturing stabilisation of Japanese involvement. It affected Kazakhstan – considered less gradualist than Uzbekistan, Tajikistan, or Turkmenistan – quite strongly due to its reliance on commodity exports and imprudent operations with exotic commodity-related derivative securities. The country, however, demonstrated resilience and did not take long to rebound. Meanwhile, Uzbekistan, Kazakhstan's more 'gradualist' rival for regional leadership, was internationally less exposed financially and operated a less liberalised business environment.

Gradualism had the benefit of insulating countries from the crisis and preventing them from falling into recession. Nevertheless, Uzbekistan's economic firewalls cushioned the state not only against the crisis' adverse effects, but also hindered the country's post-crisis development, which had boasted solid growth rates in the previous decade. Kazakhstan was not only more exposed, but also more agile in securing an economic turnaround than its regional neighbours, as demonstrated by its long-standing position as a regional investment leader. According to United Nations Conference on Trade and Development, in post-crisis years (2010–12), Kazakhstan attracted foreign investment triple the size of all the other CA countries combined. Turkmenistan's performance in this index is one-fifth of Kazakhstan's, despite Turkmenistan's second position. Uzbekistan's accumulated investment ranked third in CA – 13 times less than that of Kazakhstan. Kazakhstan also ranked better in corruption perception indexes and in indicators of statehood strength.[39] For CA states opting for a gradualist approach, the results were therefore mixed. In the 1990s, gradualist Uzbekistan was widely seen as the region's business and investment hub, only to be replaced by a less gradualist-minded Kazakhstan in the 2000s.

External environment: a basis for donor-recipient relationship?

In order to illustrate the complex nature of the relationship between Japan and CA and, most notably, its human dimension, I include in my narrative several examples of cultural memories and mutual perceptions prior to placing the argument in the macroeconomic context. Given the significant weight of the personal factor in this relationship involving high-ranking officials, such inferences should not be disregarded.

Ideational aspect: cultural perceptions and stereotypes

The cultural memories related to Japanese prisoners of war (POWs) in CA, examined in the previous chapter, constituted an important foundation for further development of bilateral relations, according to the accounts by former Japanese diplomats and MOF officials.[40] Furthermore, on the Japanese side, in the late 1980s, the television channel NHK broadcast a documentary series dedicated to the history of the Great Silk Road, which sparked an interest among the Japanese public towards CA as an exotic destination with a shared cultural heritage. Most notably, academics from Soka University (Tokyo) and Silk Road Studies

100 *Aid: development, security and connectivity*

Centre (Kamakura) were engaged in archaeological excavations in Uzbekistan's Surkhandarya region, which together with northern Afghan provinces, was a part of the historic Kushan Empire that helped spread Buddhism to the Far East.[41]

The search for the common origins of the Japanese and Central Asians became itself both a cooperation objective and driver, creating various stereotypes, reinforcing Orientalist, and self-Orientalist perceptions.[42] For instance, certain Japanese corporate officials paid particular attention to the dichotomy between the nomadic and sedentary inhabitants of CA and the region's role as rather a more commercial nexus, than a production locus. Such perceptions varied between countries, with Kazakhstan initially seen as more nomadic, influenced by Russia, and lacking its own cultural tradition, as opposed to Uzbekistan, considered more 'Asian,' sedentary, and autonomous from Moscow, with nomadic and 'Asian' Kyrgyzstan situated somewhere in between.[43]

A similar attitude existed in Japanese government circles.[44] Uzbekistan's 'Asian' image was stimulated by declarations made by the Uzbek leadership in favour of the Asian economic model and gradual development in the 1990s.[45] The MOF-affiliated expert Kashiwagi Shigeo, a Keio University professor and first vice-rector of the Uzbek Banking and Finance Academy, associated this perception with Uzbekistan's gradualist approach to economic policy-making:

> … From the Japanese people standpoint, Uzbekistan is a country toward which a particular closeness [*shitashimi*] is felt. Uzbeks' looks, behaviour, mentality resemble extremely those of the Japanese people, while the gradualism adopted by Uzbekistan since its independence in some aspects closely resembles the Japanese post-war way of thinking.[46]

This projected commonality between post-Socialist countries in transition and post-war Japan was used by MOF officials as early as 1991, when Japan started supporting the EBRD lending operations.[47] Hashimoto Ryūtarō represented Japan as head of the MOF at the second EBRD meeting.

The Kazakh leadership, on the contrary, has consistently promoted the country as Eurasian rather than solely Asian, deliberately differentiating itself from the rest of CA.[48] These diverging approaches can be explained by geographic, demographic, and economic differences. In contrast to Uzbekistan, Kazakhstan's legacy from the Union of Soviet Socialist Republics (USSR) included a long border with Russia, Soviet nuclear weapons, and a 48 percent Russian population, which left its leadership less leeway in its relations with the Kremlin and the West. Kyrgyzstan differed from Kazakhstan and Uzbekistan in having less power measured in terms of population, land, and resources, resulting in a more muted and non-exclusive Eurasian rhetoric used by its first President Askar Akayev to avoid the antagonisation of Russia. Under Akayev, Kyrgyzstan became *manadeshi* (a 'favourite disciple') of the Japanese developmentalists, as, in comparison to its neighbours, the country was less affected by the 'resource curse' and demonstrated a relatively milder authoritarianism.[49] During their initial reforms, both Kazakhstan and Kyrgyzstan accepted the

Aid: development, security and connectivity 101

conditionalities of Bretton Woods institutions and attempted to attract investments from the Western countries via liberalised legislation.[50] Uzbekistan, on the contrary, opted for gradual reform without political strings attached, while initially maintaining an investor-friendly legislation, and placed a closer focus on investments from Asia, especially South Korea.

Yet, declaratory pro-Asian and pro-Eurasian rhetoric – that is, equally friendly towards Europe, Russia, and Asia – translated differently into practical modernisation when it came to picking an appropriate model of foreign education to foster development and growth. The Kazakh academics recognised the necessity for a Kazakh version of nineteenth-century Japan's historic Iwakura mission, and the Kazakh government introduced a Rhodes Scholarship-style approach when it created the Bolashak programme in 1993.[51] The scheme encouraged young Kazakhs to travel abroad in order to obtain education and best practices. By contrast, although Uzbek academics made a case for a similar national programme in their country and also drew parallels with the Iwakura mission, this thinking didn't bear practical results due to the lack of support from the Uzbek government.[52]

The 'student-teacher' pattern can be observed in the relationship between Japan and CA not only through the examples of official support for specific economic models or modernisation programmes, but also in cultural representations. Ultimately, this pattern resonated well with the 'patron-client' relations widespread among the CA elites, albeit only partially functional in their relationship with Japan. For instance, soon after the CA republics of the USSR had gained independence and started tackling the harsh realities of the new post-Cold War world, a Japanese film *O-Shin* was shown on local television and became popular among the region's inhabitants.[53] Although it is impossible to provide a quantitative assessment of its impact in the region, the film provided the role model of an Asian person making a success story through hard work and overcoming obstacles. This representation corresponded with Japan's post-war comeback economic miracle and was particularly popular amid the hardships faced by CA in the aftermath of the USSR implosion.

Although independence from Moscow offered a chance for autonomous nation-building, it came largely as a surprise to CA, where local populations voted strongly in favour of preservation of the USSR at the 1991 referendum and subsequently were among the strongest proponents of the Commonwealth of Independent States.[54] Certain Japanese experts with experience in the region agree on the unexpectedness of independence for CA, referring to it as *tana-bota* ('godsend' or a 'windfall').[55] In Russian scholarship, CA was viewed as 'kicked out' from the Soviet Union despite its opinion and thus as having its fate decided by forces external to the region.[56] The tension between Soviet-era republican leaders and the Kremlin was based mainly on two factors: the former were dissatisfied with CA's role as raw material supplier within the Soviet economy, while the latter perceived CA as a liability and an aid recipient. Independence provided a huge shock to the region's economies, since commercial ties were stronger between the republics, rather than within each of them domestically,

102 *Aid: development, security and connectivity*

making the region internally export-oriented towards other Soviet republics.[57] Ultimately, it resulted in reliance on Russia wielding a significant impact over CA's main export routes and finances.

In this context, Japan initially appeared as a 'perfect match' for CA. Firstly, in return for CA's backing of Tokyo's nuclear non-proliferation policies and its bid for a permanent seat in the United Nations Security Council, Japan provided financial aid, reform advice, and support for CA's eligibility to assistance from the ADB, the EBRD and the OECD Development Assistance Committee (DAC). Secondly, throughout the millennia of its turbulent history, the region has historically been a crossroads of civilisations and arena of conquests. Together with the CA ethnic and cultural tapestry, this history brought about its tradition of multi-vector foreign policies adopted by local peoples in order to balance between great powers.[58]

When explaining the Uzbek government's preference for Japan as a disinterested donor rather than the United States, the E.U., Russia, or China, Uzbek Vice Prime Minister Azimov made an explicit reference to Zbigniew Brzezinski's *Grand Chessboard* concept, which portrayed Eurasia and particularly CA as the locus of great power competition.[59] CA's self-perception as an object of external rivalry is valid today, even if a comprehensive vision of self is still uncertain in a region finding its feet in international affairs.[60] The relationship with Tokyo was thus convenient in that it would hardly be viewed both inside and outside the region as a zero-sum game in regard to relationships with other powers.[61] The opposite was in fact true, as in the early 1990s, many economic ties were severed between Russia and CA, both struggling with economic transition, so Japanese aid and advice neatly fit the 'patron' niche without repercussions on Russia-CA security cooperation.

When the five CA republics of the USSR became independent in 1991, they soon encountered a benign and proactive Japanese diplomatic engagement towards them. Besides boosting bilateral assistance and economic ties, officially Tokyo has vigorously promoted CA states in many international institutions, in particular the ADB, the EBRD, and the OECD's DAC. The simultaneous membership in two regional banks was unprecedented, thus providing CA with double access to international finance to sponsor the transition of individual states while highlighting Tokyo's contribution.[62]

Nevertheless, Japanese aid remained demand-based (*yōseishugi*), thus being subject to the changing foreign policy orientations of CA countries. For instance, the typical process for a yen loan would have the MOFA as the primary point of contact, with the applicant government placing a request via the Japanese embassy with JICA involved (and local authorities prioritising contacts with aid officials over others). The MOFA would then seek consultations with the MOF and METI as part of the *sanshōchō* system of tri-ministerial coordination.

Furthermore, when in 2004 Japan created the 'Central Asia plus Japan' diplomatic framework, it was based on such multi-lateral structures as the Association of Southeast Asian Nations (ASEAN) Regional Forum. The ASEAN Regional Forum was intended for Japan's interaction with Southeast Asian states, whose

Aid: development, security and connectivity 103

role as Japanese ODA recipients became a frequent template in the making of Tokyo's CA diplomacy by analogy.[63] Japanese officials viewed Japan as a catalyst for promoting intra-regional cooperation in CA and considered the ability of Southeast Asian states to promote regionalism via ASEAN despite their political and cultural diversity as a model for CA.[64]

Encouraging joint agenda-setting by five CA states became the MOFA's key goal, whereas financial aid was the key leverage Japan had over CA governments. While JICA's assistance was provided on a bilateral basis, the Central Asia plus Japan network sought to foster multi-lateralism in Japan's relationship with the region and inside the region itself. Although the above-mentioned Central Asia plus Japan framework originated from a discussion between Foreign Minister Kawaguchi Yoriko and Tanaka Tetsuji, a Bank of Japan (BOJ) official and a key point person in Japan's relationship with Kyrgyzstan, it neither directly stemmed from Hashimoto's Eurasian diplomacy, nor was it closely related to factional, parliamentary, or ministerial constituencies outside the MOFA.[65]

Officials and politicians related to the Japanese MOF have been key in shaping the Japanese approach towards CA states since the start of this relationship in the early 1990s. Their motivations were not only economic, but also geopolitical, embodying Japan's claim of responsible Asian leadership and global citizenship, and addressing their growing insecurity vis-à-vis China's rise, which also implied developing a relationship with countries at the Chinese border. Meanwhile, in the early 1990s, Chinese influence in CA was considerably weaker than at present, as the settlement of border disputes inherited from the Soviet era took five years ending in 1996.

Furthermore, in 1997–2001, such proactivity by the MOF alongside official diplomacy underpinned the Eurasian focus of three subsequent cabinets headed by Hashimoto, Obuchi, and Mori, who each carried out a consistent strategy of regional engagement. Although the main focal points of this 'Eurasian diplomacy viewed from the Pacific' were Russia and China in the wake of the Third Taiwan Strait crisis, the security context for Silk Road countries gained further importance, particularly in the case of Uzbekistan.[66]

At the time, Uzbekistan, together with the Kyrgyz Republic and unlike Kazakhstan, was a preferred partner of Japanese developmentalists for the reasons outlined above, namely, a friendlier attitude towards Japanese proactivity. Yet, although autonomous, Japanese Eurasian diplomacy has also developed in the context of Karimov's pro-American drift during the late 1990s, thus indirectly benefiting from a coincidence of interests with Washington, as I have explained in previous chapters.

Economic conditions for financial assistance: Central Asian
'demand' and Japanese 'supply'

This section links CA's needs for financial aid to the global and regional situation concerning their natural resources. A more detailed analysis of Japan's involvement in CA natural resources is provided in Chapter 4.

104 *Aid: development, security and connectivity*

In the 1990s, CA's propensity to deliberately involve multiple external players in regional affairs worked in Japan's favour for economic and political reasons. An opportune commercial context for Japanese companies in the region was created by macroeconomic trends and geopolitical tectonics, as well as a hiatus in the expansion of competitors from the PRC and ROK. Although American investment in Caspian energy in the early 1990s was to a large extent driven by Kazakhstan in return for its nuclear disarmament, further years placed geopolitics at the forefront, as the U.S. State Department pushed for pipelines bypassing Arab countries and Iran, whilst the post-Soviet Caspian republics sought to reduce their dependency on Moscow. Meanwhile, affected by the 1997 Asian financial crisis, many Chinese and Korean companies temporarily curtailed their CA operations, thus indirectly rendering the Japanese presence more marked in the absence of its East Asian rivals.[67]

Moreover, in the wake of the 1998 Russian financial crisis and subsequent rouble meltdown, the demand of rouble-reliant CA for foreign finance and investment significantly increased. Albeit more declarative than factual, Karimov's Asianist posture was reinforced and legitimated by the country's insulation from both crises due to stringent currency controls and protectionism. The Russian default was decried in Uzbekistan as a negative outcome of shock therapy and liberalisation imposed by the acceptance of conditionality of the Bretton Woods institutions.[68]

Whilst the financing from the JBIC and JICA accompanying Japanese business was one of the most affordable, the commodity prices were particularly low in the 1990s, thus reducing CA's bargaining power and purely commercial attractiveness.[69] This is, for instance, when the Kazakh treatment of the Japanese officials and business improved from previously somewhat 'intractable' to more favourable.[70] One noteworthy example was the 1998 International Petroleum Exploration-Teikoku Oil stock company (INPEX) entry in the international oil consortium developing the Kashagan field, welcomed by the Kazakh state that was aiming to diversify its foreign investor portfolio in favour of East Asia and, in particular, Japan.[71]

The global 'commodities boom' of the 2000s and 'nuclear renaissance' inside Japan (2004–11) maintained Japan's interest in the region's riches, refocusing it on uranium and rare earths in Kazakhstan and Uzbekistan.[72] This interest was, however, restricted to a few risk-taking Japanese companies and subsequently hindered by the difficulties encountered by some of them both at home and inside CA, as well as the post-Fukushima shift from nuclear energy to gas and renewables inside Japan.[73]

Conversely, the windfall income from the hike in commodities prices improved CA's own finances and increased the already high share of loan aid in Azerbaijan, Kazakhstan, and Uzbekistan. In parallel, all three countries improved their creditworthiness through securing their foreign borrowings by the pledge of their commodity exports. This lending, called structured commodity finance and popular during the 2000s commodity boom, granted resource-rich states access to a wider pool of commercial banks, and, in turn, a decreasing

Aid: development, security and connectivity 105

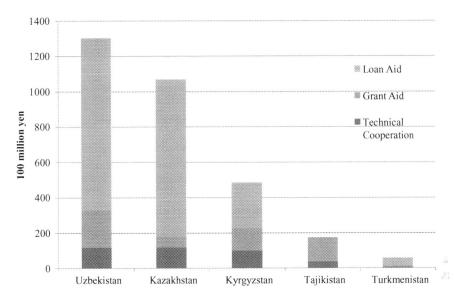

Figure 3.1 Japan's bilateral ODA in Central Asia (FY1993–2009), 100 million yen (from JICA).

reliance on ODA loans.[74] This trend can be seen in the virtual absence of new JICA loan disbursement to Azerbaijan, Kazakhstan, and Uzbekistan in the late 2000s (Figure 3.1), although in the case of Uzbekistan, Japan's aid reduction was linked to the 2005 Andijan incident.[75]

The Japanese role as CA's top donor started to slightly diminish, as the region's governments increased their own cushion of foreign reserves. In addition, the commodities supercycle spurred the construction and services boom in Russia, which, in its turn, contributed to a larger influx of migrant workers from CA (primarily, Kyrgyzstan, Tajikistan, and Uzbekistan) and, respectively, increased the share of their remittances in the Gross Domestic Product (GDP) of countries of origin.[76] According to Japanese sources, it is this larger self-reliance of resource-rich CA republics and Japan's overall ODA reduction that contributed to a more modest Japanese development assistance.[77]

In parallel, new non-Western countries, such as China (bilaterally) and Russia (bilaterally and via Eurasianist integration structures), gained prominence as donors in the 2000s. This greater risk appetite from China was underpinned by, firstly, CA's willingness to allow Chinese participation in equity, as opposed to Russia, and, secondly, by Beijing's capacity to secure its property rights in CA.[78] Japanese companies did not have capacities to match their Chinese competitors, in addition to the above-mentioned decrease in importance of CA hydrocarbons for official Tokyo and constantly delayed start of production at the Kashagan field.[79] The gradual lowering of CA's priority in the Japanese business community

106   *Aid: development, security and connectivity*

further rendered the regional presence mostly reduced to ODA-related projects and coincided with changes inside the MOF.

Following a generational change among the MOF bureaucrats in the mid-2000s, the enthusiasm about CA gradually decreased due to the sluggish pace of reforms, internal turbulence, and stagnant Japanese commercial presence, undermining the case for a preferential and proactive treatment of the region similar to Southeast Asia.[80] This 'fatigue,' however, was gradual and diluted by a macroeconomic and geopolitical context, which gave a new spur to the relations between Japan and CA. Within the JICA, for instance, CA's slowing reforms solidified the focus of the regional ODA on the creation of basic conditions and laying the groundwork for long-term changes, rather than aiming at quick fixes.[81]

As for geopolitics, the burden-sharing commitments within the U.S.–Japanese alliance related to the ISAF operations in Afghanistan and rising tensions between the new leaders in Japan and China gave CA a more strategic place on Tokyo's diplomatic and aid agenda. For instance, within the JICA's internal decision-making, it has become easier for regional departments to receive budget approval from the agency's top management for projects in case they were related to Afghanistan, as would be particularly the case in Uzbekistan and Tajikistan.[82] The link with Afghanistan also highlights the distinction between almost entirely 'humanitarian' Japanese ODA provided to the Caucasus and more 'strategic' assistance destined for CA.[83]

At the other end, the dynamics of CA's foreign orientations, together with their complex domestic power politics, often dependent on clan rivalry, shifted the ranks of Asia and Japan as foreign partners. In addition, numerous Japanese businesses, especially those listed in the U.S. stock exchanges tightened their compliance and reporting procedures, which made these companies more risk-averse towards CA.[84] This let Chinese and South Korean companies rise to prominence in the region, indirectly forcing Japan's retreat to secondary positions.

In other words, if we view CA countries as 'development clients' on the demand-side of the development sponsorship market and outside powers as 'suppliers' of development sponsorship, then in the 2000s, the supply side became more competitive and also politicised in terms of hard economic 'power projection' required, which ultimately led to a decrease in Japan's political and commercial appetite for new projects in CA.

In the light of foregoing circumstances, the impact of the Japan–ISAF 'burden sharing' on the Japanese ODA is arguably the only instance of Japanese reactivity to external pressure (*gaiatsu*), although not so much directly from another actor as from the circumstances of alliance with it. For avoidance of doubt, I do not claim to establish a specific decision-making example of actual pressure from Washington on Tokyo to provide aid against its interest, although it would be in line with the findings of Miyashita Akitoshi.[85] Although Japan cut its bilateral aid to Uzbekistan in 2005–8, it may have been an instance of Tokyo's internalised *gaiatsu*, that is, meeting what it then perceived as external expectations in the logic of strengthening the Koizumi-era U.S.–Japan alliance, rather than actual external pressure from Washington.

Aid: development, security and connectivity 107

Nonetheless, one cannot ignore the decreasing economic and increasing political rationale for Japan's grant and multi-lateral aid provision to Uzbekistan in the post-Andijan period. The country's commercial attractiveness for Japanese companies was decreasing, as was its reform pace and motivation, whilst the 2000s commodity boom boosted resource-rich Uzbekistan's own revenues. Thus, in my view and in the logic of counterfactual history, were it not for its location of strategic importance for the ISAF operations, Uzbekistan would have been more likely to graduate from the Japanese aid programmes in the late 2000s (see also Section 'Policy entrepreneurs and institutional continuities in the Japanese financial diplomacy').

Central Asia and Southeast Asia: differences for Japan

The context of Japanese assistance to CA is also special in its juxtaposition to and its difference from such a well-researched aid recipient region as Southeast Asia. Firstly, as already described above, the purely mercantile dimension of Japanese foreign aid appears less prominent in the case of CA, which in comparison with Southeast Asia represents a much less lucrative market given its size (the difference between the two is one order of magnitude), more complex regime for investment and trade, and much less accessible (at least by sea) landlocked geographical location. For many Japanese companies, CA ODA projects were not so much foot-in-the-door pathways for further business origination, as was often the case with economic aid in many countries – they were the bulk of their CA business operations and sometimes the only raison d'être for regional presence. Such CA specificity increases the rationale for extractive natural resources projects vis-à-vis other commercial operations. The model of the East Asian Miracle was thus impossible to adopt due to CA's low export capacity besides natural resources, smaller domestic markets, and a labour force which is neither much cheaper nor more productive than in Southeast Asia.[86]

Secondly, geopolitically, CA is less vital for Japanese national security than Southeast Asia. Although Japanese involvement in both regions has often been interpreted as a way of balancing or containing China via its neighbours, a consensus has not been reached on this matter. Southeast Asian sea lanes host Japan's oil imports (90 percent), natural gas (60 percent), and a transnational production network. By contrast, CA's transit and production value is marginal for Japan, which highlights the non-geopolitical aspect of its aid to CA.[87]

Infrastructure projects supported by Japan directly or via multi-lateral agencies such as the ADB (in particular, CAREC and Turkmenistan–Afghanistan–Pakistan–India Natural Gas Pipeline Project or TAPI) are aimed at diversifying the export routes of the landlocked region. CA economists named regional and global diversification of trade as key to the region's further transition from autarchy to interdependence.[88] CA was a newly independent post-Communist region on the path of transition to a market economy and nation-building following more than a century of being incorporated as provinces in the Russian Empire and the USSR. Not only is the region sandwiched between larger powers, but its pipeline

108   *Aid: development, security and connectivity*

and road networks were inherited from the Soviet era and thus mainly connected to the outer world via Russia. In the 2000s, China succeeded in improving its road and pipeline access to CA, but the link with southern routes towards the ports of the Indian Ocean remained unstable, creating an opportunity for Japan's involvement.

Japanese cooperation with Southeast Asia and CA has also had different historical origins. East and Southeast Asian states benefited from Japanese reparations as a result of the Second World War and in the context of the Cold War. The ADB was initially created as a vehicle for channelling these funds. The ADB was founded as part of settling post-war reparations to the Asian states that suffered from Japanese aggression. The reparations particularly concerned Southeast Asian states with which Japan had a rapprochement in the 1970s, in particular within the so-called Fukuda doctrine. Throughout the entire history of the ADB, Japan has been a key stakeholder, while all its directors have been Japanese and, as a rule, from the MOF.

The phenomenon of development in its post-Second World War shape was significantly shaped by U.S. President Harry Truman as a counterbalance against international Communist expansion, including Asia. Japan, further to entering into the 1960 security alliance with the United States, heavily engaged in international development. For instance, archival materials show that in the 1960s, the provision of Japanese financial aid to Indonesia sparked an internal debate inside the Japanese government: the MOF was reluctant to provide assistance, while the MOFA was strongly advocating such aid for foregoing political reasons and ultimately succeeded.[89] In the 1970s, the Japanese government stepped up its commitment to cooperation with Southeast Asia with the Fukuda doctrine.

CA was a different case altogether, because Japanese financial assistance started coming to this region after the end of the Cold War as part of a bilateral and international effort to help the transition of post-Soviet and post-Socialist countries to capitalism. Another difference was that when viewed from CA, the East Asian economic miracle was not only a proven concept, but also an attractive brand alternative to neo-liberalism. However, the geographical location of the newly independent states was quite the opposite of Southeast Asia. Although the historical Silk Road was a crossroads of civilisations and merchant routes, in the immediate aftermath of the USSR collapse, it was nothing more than a romantic past: CA's export competitiveness was severely hindered by its remoteness from major international communications and transport networks, thus enhancing its 'resource curse.'

Furthermore, newly independent CA did not need primary industrialisation when the advisors from the West and Japan started their activity: it had already been carried out during the Soviet period, while the population had a 98 percent literacy rate, with 20 percent having a university or college degree. The main development challenges in CA were not the creation of an industrial base in transition from agriculture or the prevention of subversion to Socialism like in Cold War Southeast Asia. It was to modernise the dilapidated infrastructure, to convert and diversify the economy from planned military-oriented autarchy into a market one, and to re-shape manually created regional division of labour inherited from the Soviet era and favouring monocultures, such as cotton. The progressive increase of Japanese ODA to CA, in line with Japan's position among its top ODA donors (varying from first to third spot) kept since 1998, was Tokyo's response to this emerging region's needs in large-scale investment.

Despite the differences, Southeast Asia often served Japan as a benchmark for engaging with CA: the Central Asia plus Japan framework was modelled on ASEAN Plus Three, while CA and Southeast Asia constitute key areas for the ADB's activities, and, as I show later, the bank's Greater Mekong Subregion project was a likely prototype for its CAREC project.[90] JICA's dedicated Japan Centres consolidating humanitarian projects operate in CA, Mongolia, Cambodia, Laos, and Vietnam, thus covering all former Socialist economies in Asia.

Another similarity between Japan's assistance to CA and Southeast Asia was in the maintenance of its traditional focus on loans and infrastructure.[91] In aggregate, the region's two large countries with regional leadership ambitions (Kazakhstan and Uzbekistan) have benefited from the bulk of the total Japanese CA aid. More specifically, this is reflected in a high proportion of loans made possible by their creditworthiness underpinned by natural resource endowment and resulting political weight. Another reason for a comparatively larger profile of Uzbekistan as recipient was its close relationship with Mitsui inherited from the company's Soviet operations and their relevance for the ODA with this country.[92] By contrast, financial assistance to Kyrgyzstan and Tajikistan that rank among the world's poorest nations was of a much smaller scale, especially in terms of loans, but stable and often incommensurate with their low creditworthiness, indicating a preferential treatment from the creditors. The foregoing contrasting records of Japanese assistance to CA and Southeast Asia and the peculiarities of intra-regional assistance distribution are explained not only by the different history of both regions, but also by the impact of individual Japanese financial officials.

Policy entrepreneurs and institutional continuities in the Japanese financial diplomacy

As previously mentioned, the strategic motivation of the MOF officials in the relationship with CA was driven, firstly, by considerations of Japan acting as a responsible Asian and global citizen, and, secondly, by dealing with a rising China.[93] Developing strong personal ties with the regional elites was thus an advantage for the early stage of the relationship. Nevertheless, it also made the relationship hostage to frequent fluctuations at both ends. In Japan, the MOF underwent internal restructuring in the early 2000s, scheduled rotations and generational shifts, which somewhat dispersed the core of ministerial specialists with CA experience.[94] Meanwhile, in CA, the *terra incognita* of clan interests inside the elites sometimes adversely affected Japan's presence or prevented it from further development due to their non-transparency.

110   *Aid: development, security and connectivity*

*Personalities matter in Japan: MOF officials proactively
establish bureaucrat-to-bureaucrat ties*

The MOF officials acted as policy entrepreneurs by shaping initial approaches in the philosophy and practice of financial aid towards the transition economies of ex-Soviet CA. Compared to their colleagues at the MOFA, they were less constrained in their activity towards the region. Since both Russia and CA belonged to the same European Affairs Bureau inside the MOFA, its officials often prioritised Russo-Japanese relations and were constantly considering Russia's potential 'allergic' reaction to what it viewed as interference in its 'backyard.'[95] Many of those MOF professionals would have a strong background in – and concomitant developmental ethos of – IFIs, such as the IMF, the WB, or the ADB. Nonetheless, this sub-community, albeit having its internal differences, would on average tend towards stronger gradualism in economic reforms than the adherents of the Washington Consensus.

The overseas developmentalist posture of the MOF decision-makers was consistent with their domestic strategic behaviour in Japan. The MOF's gradualist penchant and wariness of radical liberalisation at the time were underpinned *inter alia* by strong public scrutiny inside Japan that both MOF officials and the LDP came under in the mid-1990s. This pressure was due to painful failures in earlier deregulation reforms that abolished firewalls between financial institutions in order to liberalise the Japanese money market.[96]

The extent of actual gradualism would differ, however, not only from country to country in CA, as it was shown previously, but also from official to official inside the MOF, which had an 'old-boy' group and a *wakai* (junior) group. The old-boy group did not specialise uniquely in CA, but became a community of interests, including after leaving the ministry.[97] This group included, in particular, the late ADB director Chino Tadao, who can be viewed as a major promoter of CA in the Japanese financial establishment and who favoured a step-by-step approach. So did his former MOF colleague Nakayama Kyōko, who went on to serve as ambassador to Uzbekistan. Their comparatively junior peers, such as World Bank and later JICA top official Kodera Kiyoshi, supported a more radical transition.[98] Chino's philosophy of Asian development aid resonated well within CA's above-mentioned quest for particularism in values and economic reforms, as can be inferred from his interview with the *Japan Times*:

> Asia is not like Europe,' says Chino. 'Asia's most important characteristic is diversity. The political setup differs. Languages are very much diverse. The levels of development are very wide, ranging from about $200 a year (in Cambodia and Laos) to $30,000 (in Hong Kong and Singapore).[99]

Chino was a key figure in the Japanese ODA and other assistance projects addressing CA, including counselling on economic reforms, from the early 1990s up to mid-2000s. His contribution was paramount because the first contacts between Japan and post-Soviet republics of the region, especially Uzbekistan,

Aid: development, security and connectivity 111

in the immediate aftermath of the USSR collapse were taking place with his participation. It is in many regards thanks to his activity at the MOF that Japan has become a key donor of the Silk Road countries, whilst many of his like-minded colleagues with MOF background have taken over positions related to the region. While personal aspects are important in understanding Chino's role in Japan's CA policies, it is important to bear in mind that, above all, he was a professional technocrat, driven in his actions by the responsibilities of the posts he was appointed to throughout his career.

Inside Japanese financial bureaucracy, Chino held two top offices: he was the director of the MOF's International Bureau in 1989–91, and then, in 1991–3, served as vice-minister of finance for international affairs (*zaimukan*), a key policy-making position in Japan's MOF, prior to moving onto other important posts. The finance minister at the time was Hashimoto Ryūtarō, Japan's representative at the second EBRD session, the future prime minister and proponent of Japan's Eurasian diplomacy.

During his tenure as *zaimukan* (1991–3), Chino told the *New York Times* in 1991 that 'Japan wanted to transform its substantial foreign aid into a magnet for private capital (...) [and] will increasingly use its aid (...) as seed money to attract Japanese manufacturers or other industrial concerns with an attractive investment environment.' Asia, according to Chino, would be the primary focus for Japan, given its industrial strategy and dominant positions of Japanese companies in the region. Another notable stance that Chino expressed in 1991 was that Japan should refrain from providing any financial aid to the USSR until the latter clarified the relationship between the central government and the republics, reformed its economy, transferred Southern Kurils to Japan, and reduced its military presence in Asia.[100]

In 1992, Chino was temporary alternate governor for Japan at the EBRD, and presided over the ADB for two terms in 1999–2005. When Uzbek President Karimov and Vice Prime Minister Azimov were set on establishing Uzbekistan's Banking and Finance Academy in 1996, they addressed Chino and subsequently received assistance from the MOF.[101] Chino chaired the ADB when the bank supported such crucial projects for CA as CAREC, the infrastructure and connectivity initiative, and the TAPI gas pipeline, in which Chino was personally strongly involved.[102]

Chino's colleague and ally Nakayama Kyōko served as Japan's ambassador to Uzbekistan from 1999 to 2002. Her background in finance, institutional affiliation with financial technocracy, strong advocacy in favour of fostering links with CA and Uzbekistan, and personal ties with the Diet members significantly contributed to the relationship's evolution. Nakayama was a member of the LDP faction Seiwaken, noted for its relatively high-profile stance in relations with Eurasian countries since the Soviet era. She maintained close personal ties with the leadership of this key faction that regained the LDP leadership upon Mori Yoshirō's premiership in 2000. In particular, her spouse Nakayama Nariaki was the secretary general of Seiwaken. According to some interviewees, these ties were helpful in the implementation of Japanese projects with Uzbekistan.

112 *Aid: development, security and connectivity*

For comparison, Nakayama's colleague in Kazakhstan at the time was Mori Toshimitsu, a career diplomat affiliated with the MOFA's 'Russian school,' subsequently affected by the repercussions of the Suzuki affair on the ministry.[103]

Nakayama's ambassadorial appointment to Tashkent strengthened the confidential relationship that Chino managed to build with the Uzbek officials during his visits in the early 1990s. In March 2014, during the second Abe premiership, the Nakayama spouses were among numerous Japanese dignitaries who visited Uzbekistan as part of more proactive Tokyo's diplomacy; both were members of parliament (MPs) at the time, although neither held a senior government post.[104]

This highlight is important for several reasons. Firstly, Chino was regularly received by the Uzbek President Karimov, although he formally held the rank of vice-minister for international affairs – a key MOF position, but several levels lower in the hierarchy than Karimov's. This treatment was a virtual pre-requisite for exercising influence in post-Soviet states, many of which developed strong personalist regimes. Secondly, this level of trust and access certainly helped Chino later in furthering the ADB's projects once he assumed the bank's leadership. Moreover, Karimov was also a relevant counterpart for Chino not only by virtue of his position, but also by background. In the Soviet times, he spent 17 years in the Uzbek Republican Ministry of Finance, eventually making it to the top post and later serving as head of republican The State Planning Committee (Gosplan), the bureaucratic cornerstone of planned economy.

Given Tashkent's ambitions for regional leadership and its cornerstone location, Chino's personal connection with the Uzbek leader was essential for securing the commitment of a centrepiece country in a trans-border puzzle that the Japanese multi-lateral diplomatic approach was facing. Once Chino became the ADB chairman, his relationship with the Uzbek leadership persisted, partially thanks to the MOF-related ambassador Nakayama, although it shifted from strictly Kasumigaseki and the MOF's domain to Manila where the ADB is headquartered.

The downside of this interpersonal relationship, just like with any other one, was the absence of institutionalisation and dependency on political turbulence involving the specific personalities in question. On a similar note, as far as Kyrgyzstan is concerned, Chino developed a friendly relationship with the first Kyrgyz President Askar Akayev, who was in power from 1991 until 2005. After Akayev was overthrown following the 2005 Tulip Revolution, however, his successor Kurmanbek Bakiyev did not benefit from a similarly close relationship with the ADB head during the remainder of his tenure and after resignation.

Quicksands of Central Asian domestic politics and multi-vectorism

The scholarship of other countries' diplomacy in CA often overlooks the importance of neo-patrimonialism and patron-client structures in the region, which influence the formulation of CA's national interests and enhance the personal factor. Patron-client structures, in turn, are related to such long-established characteristics of CA countries as multi-vector diplomacies. These foreign policy

Aid: development, security and connectivity 113

courses varied between Kazakhstan's, Kyrgyzstan's, and, to a certain extent, Tajikistan's multi-lateralism, Uzbekistan's repeated alternation of pro-Western and pro-Russian postures, and Turkmenistan's neutrality and non-alignment bordering with isolationism.

The two foregoing features of CA politics help to better understand the limits of Japan's regional involvement. Despite establishing a solid personal relationship with CA elites, the Japanese officials struggled to handle the clan and kinship factors, in particular in Uzbekistan, although factionalism is a widespread phenomenon in Japanese politics.[105]

Central Asian, Western, and Russian scholarship of the region's domestic and intra-regional politics has consistently highlighted such features of local governance as personalist neo-patrimonialist regimes based on patron-client networks.[106] The informal rivalry of clans with regional and/or tribal identity prevails over formal institutions and national-level facades. In such circumstances, the national interest tends to be equated with the interests of a specific elite group's or clan's grip on power. The overlap between domestic and foreign affairs, highlighted by James Rosenau, is particularly enhanced in the case of CA elites by their post-Soviet Marxist heritage of perceiving foreign policy as a continuation of domestic policy.[107]

Whilst Japanese policy benefited from personal ties between Japanese officials and some representatives of CA *nomenklatura*, the relative gain for Japan can be considered smaller than for CA. As a part of the overall formulation of national interest, this relationship was affected by clan rivalry, particularly in the case of Uzbekistan, where the leadership sought to maximise its ability to say 'no' to external powers. When the latter category referred back to Russia in the late 1990s, the situation was more opportune for Japan. As Karimov relations with Washington became tense in the mid-2000s, however, Japan's special relationship with Uzbekistan was stabilised by Tokyo's alliance with Washington and Abe's 'value-oriented diplomacy.'

Besides establishing stable links with the Uzbek leader, Japanese officials benefited from working relationships with key figures in the Uzbek government. For more than a decade, Minister of Finance Rustam Azimov and Minister of Foreign Economic Relations, Industry, and Trade Elyor Ganiyev have been in charge of financial and economic matters and, therefore, points of contact for the Japanese ODA matters.[108] Azimov has known Asō Tarō since the latter's first trip to CA in 1997 in his quality as director of the Economic Planning Agency (EPA). Asō's position at the top of the EPA was important, as the EPA has traditionally been a part, albeit a minor one, of *yonshōchō*, a four-ministry decision-making system regarding foreign aid.[109] Both Ganiyev and especially Azimov, who was considered affiliated to the Tashkent clan, have been viewed as main potential successors of President Karimov, as confirmed in the cables of Tashkent-based American diplomats, informed by their Japanese counterparts.[110]

Azimov, who had held the position of first vice prime minister and had a reputation of a potential successor favoured by the West, had a long track-record of involvement in banking and finance. This included a close cooperation with

114 *Aid: development, security and connectivity*

the ADB, where Uzbekistan became the third-largest borrower.[111] Furthermore, Azimov's clout in the financial sector, including international finance, is considered one of the key power bases of the Tashkent clan.[112] His involvement with the ADB was used against Azimov by President Karimov's daughter and then-power broker Gulnara Karimova among other allegations to support charges of corruption, which were interpreted as part of the clan war.[113]

The reliance on personal ties demonstrated an exemplary downside when Azimov temporarily fell out of favour around 2003–5 following an EBRD session in Tashkent. During the event, Islam Karimov's policy was harshly criticised by Western officials, despite his desire to make the session a showcase event of his reforms in Uzbekistan. The officials in question were Clare Short, British secretary of state for overseas development and Jean Lemierre, French president of the EBRD.[114] On the contrary, the Japanese EBRD Governor Shiokawa Masajurō's address did not contain criticism vis-à-vis Uzbekistan – he singled out the country's strong growth performance among the rest of the Silk Road region.[115] Nonetheless, it was Uzbekistan's overall relationship with the EBRD that took a hit. Although technically the problems between the Uzbek government and the EBRD have nothing to do with the Japanese government, it is Japanese officials still who handle the bank's CA matters. Azimov's role was crucial in organizing the session intended to be a promotion of then-Western-friendly Uzbekistan, but EBRD's criticism infuriated Karimov, who took it as public humiliation on a live broadcast heavily advertised to the Uzbek audience.[116] Consequently, Azimov, who was also a long-term key relationship for the Japanese financiers, had to assume a lower political profile for a certain period of time in favour of Ganiyev. Once Azimov regained Karimov's favour, however, things were back to business as usual. Conversely, as Shavkat Mirziyoyev became president in 2016, he retained Ganiyev, but sidelined Azimov. Furthermore, while Karimov visited Japan three times during his presidency (1994, 2002, and 2011), Mirziyoyev's visit to Japan has been delayed until as late as December 2019, despite his otherwise active foreign travel, including the United States. This delay raised concerns among Japanese business circles, as it went contrary to the image of warm personal ties, established over two past decades. Hypothetically, had the Uzbek regime in question been less personalist and more institutionalised, there would perhaps be less rationale for external actors to rely on personal ties and be affected by internal dynamics of the regime.

Nonetheless, the ADB's presence in the overall equation of multi-lateral aid to Uzbekistan arguably worked in both Azimov's favour and, to an extent, in favour of the relationship with Japan. The EBRD exceptionally holds a political mandate, whilst the mandate of most multi-lateral development banks is strictly a development one, which is also the case of the ADB.[117] Thus, both Azimov and Japan had their risks stemming from the aid relationship with Karimov's regime diversified through an involvement with both development banks, albeit for different reasons and with an unknown level of intent in each case. If Japan or Azimov had had 'all their eggs in one basket,' the EBRD in this occurrence, the overall relationship would have been more vulnerable.

Aid: development, security and connectivity 115

2005–8: change of tide and back to business as usual

The EBRD event also marked the beginning of Tashkent's drift toward Moscow and Beijing, finalised after the 2005 Andijan events. Already in 2002–4, the World Bank officials noticed changes in the Uzbek government's attitude. While, in the 1990s they were able to get more statistical data and cooperation on sector-wide strategy work, around 2002–3, the government became less willing to share data and engage in policy-level dialogue. Around 2006, the World Bank decided to suspend all new lending programs to Uzbekistan; this situation lasted until the decade's end.[118] This change in Uzbek policy on data disclosure would have an indirect effect on the Japanese financial assistance to the country, as the MOF's analysis of recipient's repayment ability heavily relies on the assessments done by the IMF and WB.

As already mentioned, Uzbekistan did not receive JICA loans after Andijan (2005–8). Within this research, it was not possible to corroborate the possible causal link between this fact and the Uzbek government's change in policy of information disclosure to the WB, though the hypothetical existence of this link warrants separate examination. The main rationale for aid reduction was, in all likelihood, political and can be found in the concept of 'value-oriented diplomacy' developed under Koizumi, Abe, and Asō, as analysed in Chapter 1.

A leaked U.S. diplomatic cable linked Japan's ODA reduction to Uzbekistan after the 2005 Andijan event to the country's worsened human rights record:

> [MOFA Deputy Director General for Europe] Yagi said that Japanese Foreign Minister Asō told Uzbeki [sic!] Deputy Prime Minister Azimov during his Tokyo visit in May that *the Japanese government wants more efforts towards democratization and respect for human rights. The Japanese government slashed ODA to Uzbekistan dramatically last year to the two million USD level.* Japan hopes that Uzbekistan will better resist efforts to be pushed further into the Russian camp. DDG Yagi noted that Japan, the U.S. and the EU are limited in their Central Asian participation compared to Russia and called for close coordination of Western efforts.[119]

A later cable evidenced the Japanese knowledge of Uzbekistan's intention and request to receive more aid from Japan in that period, as well as the country's growing development gap with Kazakhstan. The cable in question pertains to the 2007 visit of the METI head Amari Akira to the region:

> [METI Trade Policy Bureau Director General Masakazu] Toyoda commented on the economic differences between Kazakhstan and Uzbekistan, saying that both countries have had the continuous rule of one president for the past 16 years but that Kazakhstan has enjoyed far greater economic growth. Toyoda noted the absence of development in Uzbekistan in contrast to big, new flashy buildings in Almaty, Kazakhstan. He asserted that Uzbekistan has now realized the disparity and is seeking Japanese overseas

116 *Aid: development, security and connectivity*

development assistance (ODA) to address it. Toyoda reported that Amari told the Uzbekistan government it must look for ways to improve economic growth and Toyoda believes Tashkent got the message. Toyoda also commented that Uzbekistan's regions are in even worse shape than its capital.[120]

Nevertheless, despite the value-tinted rhetoric covering pragmatism, Asō, like his predecessors, was also in favour of promoting the Japanese economic model in the region, conceptualising it as 'Peace and Happiness through Economic Prosperity and Democracy.'[121] Asō has been presiding over the Diet's Japan–Uzbekistan Friendship Association since 2002 and was one of few Japanese top officials with first-hand knowledge of the region. Although this knowledge allowed him to attenuate the democratisation rhetoric and criticism of resource nationalism with pragmatism, its reception inside the regional regimes was still mixed in the aftermath of 'colour revolutions' in Georgia, Ukraine, and Kyrgyz Republic. Certain CA experts interpreted such an approach as muted backing for Washington's diplomacy.[122] Other Uzbek government-related academics expressed a view that Uzbek–Japanese relations could be improved via, inter alia, furthering of democratic reforms in Uzbekistan and rapprochement between Tashkent and the Bretton Woods institutions.[123]

When in 2009 the Beijing-friendly DPJ took over the power from the Beijing-wary LDP, the new cabinet scrapped Arc of Freedom and Prosperity and rendered the diplomatic language less ideologically charged by shifting the focus from freedom to peace. In addition, in 2008, Uzbekistan started exercising yet another swing in its multi-vectorism and improved relations with the United States and the European Union. Japan followed suit by offering a new ODA package, which was in line with Hatoyama's shift in Tokyo's Afghanistan-bound 'burden sharing' from the Maritime Self-Defense Force, refuelling support to larger financial assistance.

Domestically, Hatoyama's DPJ cabinet and his Foreign Minister Okada introduced a reform plan for the ODA. It rendered the ODA parliamentary approval process much more difficult and spurred criticism of the party's lack of vision by ODA professionals, who considered their practice jeopardised by the new policy.[124] Okada's successor Gemba Koichirō attempted to maintain the relationship via placing more focus on inter-parliament and inter-regional ties. Nonetheless, the effect was limited, since in CA, like in many other Commonwealth of Independent States countries, the executive power and *nomenklatura* exercise greater influence than legislative bodies. Although Koizumi's reforms reduced bureaucratic clout and the DPJ struggled to counterbalance the long-established cooperation between the LDP and bureaucrats, Japanese politics were still considered to be dominated by bureaucrats as opposed to politicians, although Abe's second premiership may challenge this trend.[125]

Thus, the bureaucrat-to-bureaucrat link forged by the Japanese officials with CA in the 1990s turned out to be only partially effective to date, and more so for the CA elites, who took advantage of the relationship to secure their home position. Furthermore according to experts, the Tashkent clan gradually consolidated its position in rivalry over the Samarkand one, and one of the instruments

Aid: development, security and connectivity 117

in the struggle was the Tashkent clan's 'control of the Uzbek foreign policy, which was indirectly confirmed by continuing loans from the ADB, South Korea, and China, as well as weakening pressure from Europe.'[126]

Is it possible to equate the behaviour of specific officials to formal furthering of Japan's national interests, considering it as paradiplomacy by non-diplomatic actors? Formally speaking, Chino and his colleagues from the government's financial circles did not have a formal diplomatic mission. Japanese foreign policy is the eminent domain of the MOFA, whose control over the JICA's activities in the 1990s was tighter than at present, while the ADB is a multi-lateral institution fighting poverty. Is it possible in this case to consider Chino and his like-minded allies from the MOF as foreign policymakers, often sharing an alma mater, a certain professional ethos of development economist, as well as career track in international financial organisations (the Bretton Woods institutions, the ADB, the EBRD)?

It would be far-fetched to view the MOF activities as a mere extension or instrumentalization of the MOFA policy, especially in the ADB's case. Nonetheless, financial aid matters have traditionally served Tokyo as overt pragmatic instruments, spelling of foreign policy and fostering commercial interests of the Japanese companies overseas. Such an attitude was even heavily criticised by many Western donors in the late 1980s and early 1990s, although the moral side of such criticism could also be disputed given the pragmatism of the critiques.[127]

Furthermore, the MOF's role was fundamental since it has the last say in budget allocation, and inter-agency conflicts over aid issues have been occurring since the very beginning of the Japanese 'chequebook diplomacy' – starting from aid decisions regarding Indonesia and other Southeast Asian countries in the 1960s. For instance, Chino had spoken in favour of assisting Russia during the 1993 G7 summit in Tokyo, despite the MOFA's disapproval caused by the Northern Territories dispute, ultimately retracted after the American pressure in favour of Russia.[128] In addition, the political nature of Japan's assistance to CA could be exemplified by the cases of providing or renewing loan aid in the interests of relationship building despite negative implications of the borrower's low creditworthiness.[129]

There is evidence to confirm the signs of irregular coordination between a wider group of actors within the Japanese government. For instance, former ambassador to Uzbekistan Kawatō Akio, who replaced Nakayama Kyōko, admitted that the Diet and MOF ties of his predecessor had greatly facilitated her ambassadorial activity, in particular, in terms of budget approvals, whilst his background as a career diplomat required supplementary efforts.[130]

Nonetheless, 'Chino's group' motivation for promoting relations with CA proactively went beyond strictly institutional interests.[131] As his colleagues note, Chino was in many ways driven by personal sympathies towards a charming region that kept the memory of Japanese POWs and appeared to be a 'distant cousin' for the Japanese civilisation due to shared Silk Road and Buddhist heritage.[132] These sympathies transformed into a benevolent patronage if not lobbying (in the positive sense of the term), becoming a cornerstone for long-term stability of aid channels for CA.

118   *Aid: development, security and connectivity*

Chino left the ADB in 2005, but his successor Kuroda Haruhiko and his junior colleagues have maintained a positive view of the region and a personal cultural interest towards it.[133] Yet, after Chino's decease in 2008, CA has certainly lost one of its devout mentors and proactive supporters in Japan. The younger generation of government financiers that emerged in the neo-liberal tilt of Koizumi's cabinet was less enthusiastic towards most of CA, except Kazakhstan, due to the sluggish reform pace and marred investor environment, discrediting the countries' declaratory openness to Japanese investments.[134]

Meanwhile, the attitude of the Uzbek side became increasingly pragmatic and less 'romantic.' Uzbek top decision-makers related to the ODA projects prioritised them at the expense of other aspects of the relationship. For instance, a Japanese ODA official had a better chance of being granted an audience at the Uzbek government than a higher-ranked Japanese diplomat.[135]

Nonetheless, arguably the most lasting legacy of Chino and Japanese developmentalists to CA's development and geopolitics was the ADB-led project of CAREC, which is the subject of this chapter's final section.

CAREC: Japan's disinterested role in improving Central Asia's connectivity or indirect 'burden sharing' with the United States?

Dennis Yasutomo demonstrated Japan's weight in the ADB by showing that although the bank is a multi-lateral institution, it has been criticised as 'Japan's international development bank.' Furthermore, Tokyo had repeatedly used the ADB as a 'buffer in Japan's Asian diplomacy.' Yasutomo also characterised the ADB policy in the late 1980s and early 1990s as 'almost schizophrenic, a mixture of two different personalities, one passive and reticent and the other active and assertive.'[136] The Chino-era ADB (1999–2005) was certainly the incarnation of the latter 'personality.' In this section, I examine the CAREC project, which, I argue, was an example of Japan's pragmatic, strategic, proactive, and partly idealist involvement, while CAREC's evolution reflected the changes in the Chinese and American postures in CA in the mid-2000s.

CAREC origins (1996–2001)

CAREC was institutionalised at the turn of the twenty-first century, which was a crucial and challenging time for CA's security. In general and in terms of Japan's involvement, it can be viewed as the key multi-lateral infrastructure project for CA and Afghanistan. CAREC originated in the Asian Development Bank with a goal of improving trade and communications in the region, in order to 'unlock' it for the outer world, in particular via diversifying export routes for the landlocked region.[137] The ADB is considered the leading institution of financing transport infrastructure in CA, and CAREC can be viewed as its main vehicle.[138] CAREC is not the only ADB's functionalist project aimed at improving regional connectivity: the bank supported similar infrastructure revamps in the Greater Mekong Subregion and in South Asia.[139]

Whilst considering CAREC as part of the renewed Silk Road, neither Japan's official rhetoric, nor Japanese developmentalists directly claimed its 'ownership,' which stood in contrast to the New Silk Road projects furthered by Washington or Beijing.[140] And yet, both diplomatically and financially, CAREC reflected a 'win-win' approach. For Japan as a key player behind the ADB and CAREC, it struck an optimal balance between the idealist and pragmatic postures of Tokyo's diplomacy. The diversification of transport via CAREC is aimed at reducing CA's dependence on great powers, as the project included the development of southbound routes connecting the region with the Indian Ocean to provide an additional outlet to Russia- and China-dominated itineraries. In parallel, it engaged China and, indirectly, Russia, as stakeholders without entailing their backlash, thus avoiding a 'zero-sum-game' animosity. Nonetheless, China's Asian Infrastructure Investment Bank (AIIB) and Belt and Road Initiatives in the mid-2010s were more inclusive of Russia in terms of welcoming its membership as lender, although less so as borrower.[141]

In addition, although Japanese officials played a crucial role in forming CAREC by virtue of their predominance and activity in the ADB, the funds used for the project came from various and not solely Japanese sources – the pool included participant governments and international institutions.[142] Such diversification of capital sources resulted in a much more affordable risk profile for lenders including Japan, than in the case of purely bilateral assistance, the budget for which was cut several times by Tokyo throughout the 2000s. CAREC's scale is significant: throughout the past 18 years, the funding has grown more than 100-fold, from six projects worth $247 million in 2001 to 196 projects worth about cumulative $34.5 billion in 2017.[143] By 2016, its membership has grown to 11 countries: five post-Soviet CA states (Kazakhstan, Kyrgyzstan, Tajikistan, Turkmenistan, and Uzbekistan), China, Azerbaijan, Mongolia, Afghanistan, Pakistan, and Georgia.

CAREC's roots date back to 1996 when the ADB approved technical assistance for CA's economic development, namely, between Kazakhstan, Kyrgyzstan, Uzbekistan, and the culturally Turkic Xinjiang-Uighur Autonomous District of China. Xinjiang also had economic complementarities with Kazakhstan, in particular in the oil and gas sector.[144] Tajikistan joined in 1998, thus extending the organisation's geography to almost an entire coverage of the post-Soviet CA, as Turkmenistan in the time of Saparmurat Niyazov's rule was maintaining a strict neutrality and non-alignment principle that verged on isolationism. However, it was in 2000 that CAREC received its permanent institutional shape when its secretariat was created. In 2001, Manila, where the ADB is headquartered, hosted the first senior official meeting of the member states. In 2002, it was the turn of ministers to meet in the Philippine capital, thus continuing vertical institutionalisation.[145] Chino's tenure as ADB director (1999–2005) encompassed most of the project's foundation stage.

The maps below show an impressive progress made between the initial vision of regional connectivity in 1998 and 2008 (Figures 3.2 and 3.3):

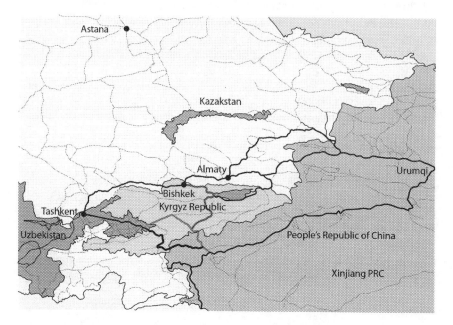

Figure 3.2 A vision of Central Asia's regional connectivity and cooperation, 1998 (from ADB).

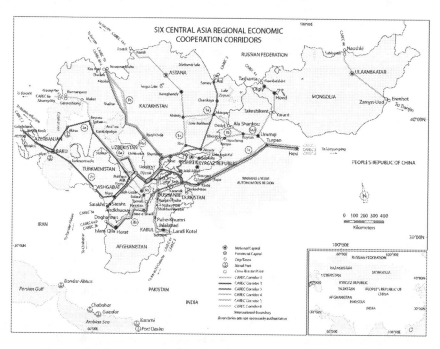

Figure 3.3 CAREC corridors in 2008 (from ADB).

Aid: development, security and connectivity   121

The project's inception occurred at an important juncture of Japan–CA relations. It only slightly pre-dated the first Japanese diplomatic formulation of its Eurasian diplomacy suggested by the Prime Minister Hashimoto in 1997.[146] As a reminder, Hashimoto wanted Japan to give a response to the Eurasian diplomacy of the Western countries, and have its own such diplomacy from the Pacific, implying a better engagement with Russia, China, and the Silk Road countries.[147]

CAREC's beginning also coincided with the popularisation of the term 'New Great Game,' referring to renewed geopolitical competition for control of pipelines and natural resources in newly independent CA. The cliché initially appeared in mass media around 1996 and mentioned Japan as one of the players, although subsequently, Japanese diplomats and academics denied Japanese intentions to be such a player.[148]

For CA states, whose export infrastructure was inherited from the USSR and dependent on Russia, transport projects, such as CAREC and pipelines, had a fundamental political and economic value, especially as they were neutral both vis-à-vis larger powers and within the region. Infrastructure projects were not only a way to regain the balance in relations with Moscow, but also a promising source of rent benefits from transit increased by the revival of historical Silk Road and sponsored externally. Around the time of CAREC's foundation and the beginning of the Japanese Eurasian diplomacy in the late 1990s, influential government-related experts from the region had promoted the idea of CA as a land bridge with a corresponding investor-friendly climate.[149]

Although Japan's basic self-interest in CA's freight transit potential for its export-import operations was not the main driver for CAREC and infrastructure financing, especially at the early stage, it was of notable significance as well. After the USSR collapse, China has been gradually taking over from Russia the role of functioning as the Eurasian Land Bridge, which implied both concerns and opportunities for Japan.[150] Japanese transportation professionals described the Japanese rationale in the way that remains relevant to the present date:

> Freight carried on the Silk Railway from China is generally bound for Central Asia. From there, freight can be sent by rail via Russia to Western Europe. This is relevant when considering Europe-bound freight from Japan. The route from Japan to Rotterdam via Central Asia is about 1000 km shorter than the route via Vladivostok and the Trans-Siberian Railway. But the longer Trans-Siberian railway involves only one time-consuming transshipment or bogie change to cope with different track gauges ..., while the shorter Central Asian route involves two. Furthermore, freight transported over the shorter route must undergo burdensome formalities at three or four border crossings (depending on the line taken), while the longer route involves only one. There would be advantages to using the existing shorter Silk Railway route and avoiding the Trans-Siberian's uncertain scheduling and high crime rate. But the Silk Railway will not be a viable option unless fees are reduced and customs and inspection formalities are simplified at international borders, and unless the time for transshipping and bogie changes is shortened.[151]

122 *Aid: development, security and connectivity*

Otsuka also pointed out the potential offered by the rail connection from Turkmenistan across the Iranian border to the Persian Gulf. According to him, such a route would be of benefit not only for CA, but also for Japan, provided the bottleneck at the Turkmenistan–Iran border was improved. While the Kazakhstan–Turkmenistan–Iran railway was launched in 2014, some Kazakhstani MPs considered its success very limited as of 2018.[152]

Japanese attention to CA infrastructure came directly not only from the government and government-affiliated corporations, which are viewed as principal risk-takers in Japanese overseas commercial ventures, but other sectors as well. The private sector was acting in line with the government's proactivity, attempting to anticipate and enjoy early-bird benefits: in spring 1998, Sumitomo proposed to create centres of integrated logistics in all main CA cities to manage the entire regional transport infrastructure.[153]

Afghanistan and the development of southbound corridors

Although CAREC is neither the first nor the only transport integration project involving CA, its advantage lies in its functionalist, non-politicised, and multi-lateral approach, while similar projects led by big players tend to raise wariness inside the region. Such suspicion concerned the concepts of Greater Central Asia (GCA) and Greater Middle East.[154] GCA was introduced in the second term of President George W. Bush, when CA countries drifted toward Beijing and Moscow and away from Washington, which they viewed as encouraging regime change and colour revolutions.

Afghanistan joined CAREC only in 2005, a year after the 'Central Asia plus Japan' forum was founded and Kabul began to participate in the Shanghai Cooperation Organisation (SCO) meetings. Initially, the ADB's treatment of Afghanistan paralleled the approach with Southeast Asia, similarly to CAREC's partial inspiration with the ADB's Greater Mekong Subregion project. At a 2004 Afghanistan conference in Berlin, Chino cited Cambodia, Tajikistan, and East Timor as successful cases of ADB's post-conflict reconstruction experience and highlighted the role of financial donors: 'Afghanistan is not a special or a worst case. There have been many similar cases, but we have made many successful countries. It does though depend on donors.'[155]

More important, however, is the fact that Kabul's CAREC accession took place around the same time with the increasing emphasis of the Japanese CA-bound ODA on connecting the region with South Asia. This prioritisation resonated with Washington's similar strategy for the region.

Although the United States devised their 'Silk Road Strategy Act' in 1999, it initially focused on developing the East-West infrastructure connections of the region. As the ISAF operations progressed from 2001 onward, however, Washington's vision of priorities in regional infrastructure shifted to linking CA with South Asia:

> The tendency to couple these two regions began with the US-led intervention in Afghanistan in 2001, but became more pronounced after Secretary

Aid: development, security and connectivity   123

of State Rice's visit to Central and South Asia in October 2005. In 2006, responsibility for the Central Asian republics within the US Department of State was moved from the Europe and Eurasia Bureau to the South Asia Bureau, thereby formally bracketing the two regions together.[156]

The idea of improving regional trade and removing custom barriers as part of pacifying Afghanistan was strongly popularized in the American establishment by the author of the GCA concept S. Frederick Starr.[157] It can be argued that the United States drew inspiration from Japan and in fact continued benefiting from the groundwork (*nemawashi*) laid by Tokyo via the ADB in the region wary of Washington's grand designs. Such an argument can also be supported by a U.S. diplomatic cable concerning the 2006 interaction between Deputy Assistant Secretary Chris Moore and the MOF Senior Deputy Director General Tamaki Rintarō in Tokyo:

> Moore noted the successful roundtable discussions the United States hosted … with Pakistan and Kazakhstan, and encouraged Japan to play a vital role in international efforts to promote development in the western border region of Pakistan and to foster regional integration in Central Asia. Tamaki expressed particular interest in Central Asia, noting … Koizumi's visit there. He asked about the State Department-Treasury Department balance of responsibility on both Afghanistan reconstruction and Central Asian economic integration. Moore confirmed the administration's strong interest in both areas and high-lighted State's cooperative work with Treasury and other agencies.[158]

Both CAREC's early success and its subsequent alignment with the U.S.-led New Silk Road initiative were stressed in 2011 by Chino's successor at the ADB's helm Kuroda Haruhiko, who also showed continuity with his predecessor in his support of the TAPI pipeline:

> Afghanistan is a means by which landlocked Central Asia can be integrated with markets in South Asia and beyond–an accomplishment that would have global benefits. … Regional cooperation and investments in infrastructure will ensure Afghanistan's position as a pivotal transit route. ADB is already working in all these areas. [infrastructure and regional cooperation] … are, in fact, at the heart of … CAREC …. The CAREC program works exclu-sively on transport, energy and trade facilitation. Through CAREC, we are investing in six major road and rail corridors, several of which are either in Afghanistan or Afghanistan bound. … On energy, we are assisting the Turkmenistan–Afghanistan–Pakistan–India Natural Gas Pipeline Project (or TAPI). We are financing regional transmission lines, including the one that now supplies electricity to Kabul from Uzbekistan …. In short, *ADB is already fully aligned to the Silk Road Initiative.* We have a clear strategy, a business plan that matches priorities to finances, and an effective and effi-cient platform to do more.[159]

124 *Aid: development, security and connectivity*

In the post-BRI years, the United States have stepped up their interaction with CAREC. For instance, in November 2014, a representative of the Department of State described Washington's position in the following way:

> The U.S. works closely with the ADB and its partners and has been a strong supporter of CAREC as part of our New Silk Road initiative to expand economic connectivity between Central and South Asia. The U.S. has prioritized four areas from 2014–16 under the New Silk Road initiative which align with CAREC's programs: (1) creating a regional energy market connecting Central to South Asia through electricity projects like CASA-1000 and TUTAP; (2) facilitating trade and transit through stronger investment frameworks, enforceable trade transit agreements and WTO membership; (3) streamlining customs and border operations to support open, but secure borders; and (4) connecting businesses and people across regional markets through trade fairs and entrepreneurship networks.[160]

The time of the speech (2014) and the context of 'pivot to Asia' pursued by the Obama administration since 2009 indicate that this American rhetoric can be viewed as a response to Beijing's Belt and Road Initiative. Nonetheless, given the foregoing context, Washington started building its current position profiting from the groundwork previously laid through Japanese efforts. Moreover, while the ADB – and Japan – kept supporting CAREC, given its strong functionalist value, it gradually distanced itself from less commercially viable and more geopolitical projects promoted by Washington, such as aforementioned CASA-1000, and kept a predominantly nominal involvement in TAPI, as Chapter 4 demonstrates.[161]

Furthermore, CAREC's goals could not be achieved without considering the Afghan issue in terms of building south-bound transport routes toward the Persian Gulf and in terms of security, Afghanistan shares its northern borders with Turkmenistan, Uzbekistan, Tajikistan, and China. Firstly, an improved commercial route bound for CA via Afghanistan would drastically reduce the transportation timing and therefore costs of goods, which is an idea originating in the mid-1990s.[162] Secondly, key transport and infrastructure projects carried out on the territory of CA republics became a part of the Northern Distribution network, supplying the ISAF troops in Afghanistan, once this dimension appeared after 9/11 and the beginning of operation 'Enduring Freedom.' Outside Afghanistan, the contribution from Japan and the ADB was provided to all three CA republics sharing the Afghan border: Uzbekistan, Tajikistan, and Turkmenistan.[163]

In Uzbekistan, the Japanese contribution to strategic railroad linkages can be exemplified by the sections of high-mountain railroad in Tashkent-Termez (in particular, sections Marakand-Karshi, Karshi-Tashguzar-Boysun-Kumkurgan-Termez, parts of CAREC Corridor 6), financed by the JBIC, JICA, and the ADB.[164] The railroad construction works were conducted by Mitsui, the flagship of Japanese companies in Uzbekistan and a main contractor of local Japanese ODA-related projects since the country's independence until the late 2000s.[165] The Japanese ambassador to Tashkent in 2007–10, Hiraoka Tsutomu, singled out the progress on the rail project as key achievement in his term.[166] The part of railroad connecting the frontier city of Termez with Afghan Mazar-e-Sharif was built by Uzbekistan with funding from the U.S.[167]

As a reminder, Uzbekistan is the only CA country to border all other regional states and is thus a natural centrepiece hub. The Termez railway is important because the Uzbek section of the Afghan border it connects to is the most secure and therefore transit-friendly of all CA countries bordering Afghanistan, namely, Turkmenistan and Tajikistan. By sponsoring the Karshi-Termez route since 2004, including its electricity support via the Talimarjan power project (also financed by Japan and the ADB), Japan increased the security of north-south freight communications and solidified the transit power of Uzbekistan (Figure 3.4).[168]

Border communications linking Tajikistan and Afghanistan are the product of multi-party cooperation. Up to the present date, five bridges have been built on the Panj River which forms most of the Tajik-Afghan border. Four of them are located in the Gorno-Badakhshan region and were constructed by the Aga Khan Foundation which is closely cooperating with the JICA.[169] The fifth bridge was funded by the United States, while Japan sponsored the motorway connecting this bridge to the town of Dusti. Addressing the bridge construction, the Afghan leader Hamid Karzai declared an intention to reduce the cargo transportation time from Tashkent to Iranian and Pakistani ports by improving Afghan infrastructure.[170]

In addition to Uzbekistan and Tajikistan, Turkmenistan is the third post-Soviet republic bordering Afghanistan, although trans-border infrastructure projects involving Turkmenistan are currently at the inception stage. In 1997,

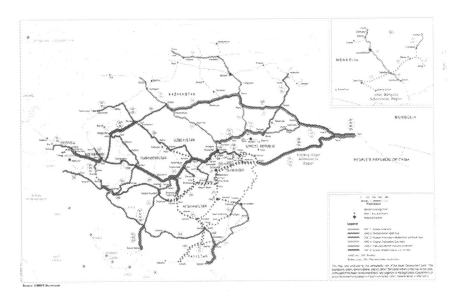

Figure 3.4 Central Asia Regional Economic Cooperation, designated rail corridors (from ADB).

126 *Aid: development, security and connectivity*

the JICA disbursed circa $45 million for overall modernisation of Turkmen railroads. However, the country's neutrality and non-alignment to alliances and coalitions under Turkmen President Niyazov excluded participation in the Afghan operations. Nevertheless, in his late rule and especially under his successor Gurbanguly Berdymukhamedov, the situation gradually started to change. Since 2007, Turkmenistan has become involved in the CAREC's North-South corridor.[171] In April 2011, the country received a $125 million grant from the ADB for a road improving its connectivity with Persian Gulf states, South Asia, and Kazakhstan.[172] In spring 2013, President Berdymukhamedov together with Afghan and Tajik leaders has announced the construction of a Tajikistan-Afghanistan–Turkmenistan road (connecting Turkmen Akmurad and Afghan Andhoi), the sponsors of which included both Japan and the ADB, as well as the Islamic Development Bank.[173]

From CAREC to BRI

Initially, similar unilateral infrastructure projects led by the United States and China in the region from the second half of the 2000s were facing both a cold shoulder from the local partners and a lack of financial resources. However, China's position started changing dramatically in 2013, when Beijing unveiled its Silk Road Economic Belt project.[174] Subsequently, Silk Road Economic Belt has become the continental segment of an even larger initiative called Belt and Road.

Belt and Road is still in the making; the scale of its finances remains imprecise ranging between $40 and $900 billion, and, therefore, merits a separate inquiry lying outside of the scope of this analysis. Nevertheless, it can be viewed as a competitor to CAREC and as its China-centred derivative, especially given Silk Road Economic Belt's current predominant focus on latitudinal East-West routes rather than the North-South ones, promoted by the United States.[175] Japan promoted both latitudinal and meridional corridors for functionalist and geopolitical reasons.

Although, according to Japanese ADB and EBRD officials, and certain scholars, China has been increasing its influence in CAREC in the late 2000s–early 2010s, Chinese officials have nonetheless been dissatisfied with Japanese domination inside the ADB.[176] According to certain Chinese scholars, this discomfort was part of Beijing's rationale behind establishing the AIIB:

> Although China is the largest economy in Asia, Japan dominates the ADB. Japan's voting share is more than twice that of China's, and the bank's president has always been Japanese. Looking at the landscape from Beijing's point of view, this is unquestionably a biased situation.[177]

The AIIB's founding figure and President Jin Liqun served as vice president of the ADB in charge of programs for South, Central, and West Asia in 2003–8, which shows his first-hand involvement in CAREC and confirms the likelihood of the Silk Road Economic Belt being inspired by CAREC. It was during

Chino's ADB presidency that Chinese officials – starting with Jin Liqun – became the ADB's vice presidents for the first time and started covering West, Central, and South Asia, including the CAREC programme. Appointments at the ADB's vice-presidential level suggest that the ADB's Japanese leadership accommodated China's increasing participation in Central and South Asian projects, rather than opposing it. Since the 2003 establishment of the office of vice president in charge of West, Central, and South Asia, it has been continuously held by Chinese officials for over 16 years. Jin Liqun, the first vice president (2003–8), subsequently became the first AIIB president. Jin's successor was Zhao Xiaoyu (2008–13), who subsequently headed the China Development Bank. Zhang Wencai has held the ADB vice presidency from 2013 until 2018, when he was succeeded by Chen Shixin. Chen has served as a board director for China in the New Development Bank and the AIIB.[178] Prior to 2003, the ADB had no Chinese vice presidents – a different vice president post was at times held by a South Korean national.

It would be hard to imagine this appointment policy without top-level support of Japanese officials, in particular ADB presidents Chino, Kuroda, and Takehiko Nakao. In parallel, the number of Chinese officials covering CAREC has been growing in the 2010s.[179] This consistent approval granted by the three aforementioned ADB presidents (all senior officials of Japan's MOF) for the appointment of Chinese senior officials in charge of the bank's Central, South, and Western Asian operations shows an accommodative and cooperative dimension of Japan's policy vis-à-vis China in CA.

Whether the Chinese own New Silk Road (NSR) project spurs further great power rivalry in CA with Japan remains to be seen, although some signs of such competition were tangible early into the BRI's existence. A senior Chinese official involved in CA affairs claimed during a private interview in October 2014 that China was the only country with sufficient financial capacity and willingness to support its Silk Road project, unlike other large powers.[180] Although partially valid and demonstrating that Beijing might have the resolve and risk appetite that other lenders are lacking, this view may nonetheless reflect a misinterpretation of Japan's financial imprint in CA. I touch upon the risk appetites and their perceptions of Japan and China as concessional lenders in Chapter 5.

In May 2015, the Japanese Prime Minister Abe Shinzō reacted to the Chinese AIIB initiative by promising to boost the Japanese funding of Asian infrastructure by $110 billion. The commitment involved both bilateral aid and Japanese contributions to the ADB, which may in turn further increase the ADB's funding for CA, whether via multi-lateral funding schemes such as CAREC or alternatives ones. A year later, in May 2016, the Japanese government raised the promise to $200 billion.[181] In August 2016, Abe pledged US$30 billion in public and private support for infrastructure development, education, and healthcare expansion in Africa, in addition to US$32 billion already pledged by Japan for 2013–18.[182] In June 2018, Abe announced plans to establish a $50 billion fund to boost infrastructure investment in Asia over the next three years.[183] I analyse

128 *Aid: development, security and connectivity*

these dynamics separately and in greater detail in a dedicated chapter on Sino-Japanese infrastructure competition and cooperation.

In October 2015, Abe visited CA, becoming only the second Japanese head of government in history to do so, the first one being Koizumi in July 2006. Abe's visit was preceded by the appointment of political scientist Kitaoka Shin'ichi as head of the JICA, indicating the emphasis on strategic aspects of Japanese aid.[184] Abe's visit to CA confirmed the importance of the region by the value of infrastructure and natural resource funds from Japan announced during the trip. Namely, out of aggregate $27 billion, $18 billion were slated for Turkmenistan, covering mostly gas production and the related TAPI pipeline project. Another $9 billion were announced in Uzbekistan, also including a hydrocarbon project, but mostly aimed at further improvement of infrastructure in this strategically centrepiece country of the region. Although some of $27 billion represented memorandums of understanding rather than tangible disbursements, the scale of transactions was nonetheless comparable with Japanese cumulative investment in the region and China's Silk Road Fund.

CA regimes appear to be clear beneficiaries of intensifying competition in development and infrastructure finance, as it is in the interests of their multi-vector diplomacies to further diversify the pool of sponsors and play external contenders against one another. This diversification may, however, come at the cost of decreasing transparency of funding schemes and their greater pragmatism, as China is not bound by the principles and ethical guidelines of the OECD DAC committee. Another dilemma is the response to China's expansive overseas lending from Western concessional lenders and Japan: ultimately, providing alternative debt to borrowers to supplant or pre-empt Chinese debt will still result in the growing indebtedness of the borrowers.

In this light, such CAREC's features as functionalism and low politicisation would be of particular value. However, those features may be subject to change as a result of Abe's policy of strategic use of the ODA, or to put it more critically, 'weaponisation of finance.' Nonetheless, as of August 2019, Sino-Japanese interactions in this field have included not only rivalry, but also cooperation in the form of co-financing. Over the course of CAREC's development and despite the temporary anti-Western posture of CA in the mid-2000s, Japan's regional involvement via the ADB and CAREC has not incurred major financial or political costs. CAREC can be arguably considered a great unsung 'asset' in Tokyo's diplomatic balance sheet, as it is usually attributed to the ADB and the participant governments, but Japan's important role of initial promoter and 'pacemaker' is unjustly overlooked. CAREC is not only the earliest multi-lateral international infrastructure project for the new Silk Road and a highly likely prototype for Belt and Road, but by far the most successful in terms of achievements and funds invested. Although CAREC formally includes several organisations besides the ADB and JICA, including other multi-lateral ones (World Bank, Islamic Development Bank (IsDB)), its design, inception and early development can be traced to the ADB, where Japan remained dominant, and specific Japanese government financiers, such as Chino Tadao.[185]

Conclusion

The analysis of Japan's development assistance to CA makes the case for a closer consideration of the political economy of developmental finance, of the agency of non-diplomatic officials on both sides, and external economic environment in the analysis of Japan's foreign aid policy. Both decades of Japanese engagement with post-Soviet CA were marked by the proactivity of Japanese MOF-affiliated officials. Their motivations included not only strictly financial professionalism or developmental ethos, but also politics, pursuing, in particular, the promotion of the East Asian developmental state model in the 1990s and, to an extent, a balancing of external powers vis-à-vis the region's nations. The contribution of these officials was crucial for CA's development in times of vulnerability, such as early post-Soviet market transition or recovery from the financial crises of 1997–8 in East Asia and Russia. This contribution can be considered, on the one hand, pragmatic, due to its consistency with Japan's adaptive response to a changing macroeconomic and geopolitical environment, and, on the other hand, idealistic due to the considerations of cultural proximity between Japan and CA and preferential lending conditions.

Notwithstanding the geopolitical reasoning behind the developmentalist aspect of the Japanese Silk Road diplomacy, Tokyo did not intend to join any kind of Great Game. Nonetheless, at some instances, Tokyo's alliance with Washington caused both indirect entanglement with the U.S. position and mis-interpretations of it. Still, Tokyo's policies contributed to defuse the game's potential tensions for CA by engaging both smaller and bigger countries in the functionalist 'win-win' project of CAREC, led by the ADB, where the international role of Japanese developmentalists is most pronounced. CAREC reduced CA's reliance on transit communications and financial resources controlled by larger powers.

CA countries, in line with their multi-vector foreign policies and propensity to maximise the number of external powers involved in the region, actively shaped Japanese financial and commercial involvement. However, Japan's role diminished as China and other non-Western countries gained prominence as donors, while the windfall income from the 2000s commodities rally improved CA's own funds.[186]

The continuity of the developmentalist relationship suffered once the 'Chino generation' with its approach of benevolent economic trusteeship of CA decreased its presence in policy-making and reforms stalled in the previously well-courted Uzbekistan. Concomitantly, the vigour in Japanese proactivity plateaued as a result of the above macro-trends, as well as government shifts in Tokyo, reforms, frequent rotations, and natural generational change in the MOF. Strong personal ties forged by the MOF officials with key figures in the CA establishment, were instrumental in furthering the overall bilateral ties, but partially exposed them to uncertainty related to clan rivalry. This was confirmed by President Mirziyoyev's side-lining of some politicians who played a key role and by delays in organising a visit to Japan for over three years.

130 *Aid: development, security and connectivity*

The return of low commodity prices in the mid-2010s is likely to bring about a decrease in the bargaining power of CA commodity producers. Nevertheless, the current situation is different from the 1990s in at least two ways. Firstly, the development landscape now involves a larger amount of competing donors. Secondly, infrastructure and finance rivalry is already unfolding between two of them, China and Japan, where Abe Shinzō extended his diplomatic proactivity to CA. Under Abe's second premiership, Japan has provided a considerably greater assistance to Kazakhstan and Uzbekistan than South Korea, and temporarily regained the status of Uzbekistan's top donor in 2014.[187] The strategic use of financial assistance has become a consistent key feature of Abe's foreign policy, although specifically in CA mercantilism became the dominant approach, as I show in Chapters 1 and 4. Chapter 5 examines the contemporary dynamics of Sino-Japanese co-opetition in Asian infrastructure.

Notes

1 Shigeo Kashiwagi, 'Chiteki shien to ha nani ka,' *Fainansu*, July 2014: 16–25; Interview with JICA official, November 2011; Statement by Nakahira Kōsuke, Special Adviser to the Minister of Finance, Temporary Alternate Governor for Japan at the fifth EBRD meeting (1996).
2 See Timur Dadabaev, *Japan in Central Asia. Strategies, Initiatives, and Neighbouring Powers* (Basingstoke & New York: Palgrave Macmillan, 2016), 35–86.
3 Aaron Stephen Moore, *Constructing East Asia: Technology, Ideology, and Empire in Japan's Wartime Era, 1931–1945* (Palo Alto, CA: Stanford University Press, 2013).
4 Uyama Tomohiko, 'Japanese Policies in Relation to Kazakhstan: Is There a "Strategy?"' in *Thinking Strategically: The Major Powers, Kazakhstan, and the Central Asian Nexus*, ed. Robert Legvold (Cambridge, MA: American Academy of Arts and Sciences MIT Press, 2003); Kawatō Akio, 'What is Japan up to in Central Asia,' in *Japan's Silk Road Diplomacy: Paving the Road Ahead*, eds. Christopher Len et al. (Washington, DC: Central Asia-Caucasus Institute, 2008).
5 In 2013, PRC President Xi Jinping unveiled a landmark China-led infrastructure investment initiative for the region, calling it the Silk Road Economic Belt, which would improve China's connection with Europe via CA. Subsequently, in 2014, the PRC government announced the setup of the Silk Road Fund to finance the infrastructure projects, as well as the establishment of the Asian Infrastructure Investment Bank. The latter has been initially viewed as an alternative to the ADB, the World Bank, and the International Monetary Fund. Subsequently its external threat perception has somewhat subsided due to the AIIB's modest scale and narrow mandate and because the bulk of concerns shifted to the BRI and relevant Chinese banks (CDB, Exim Bank).
6 For approaches of that kind, please consult Timur Dadabaev, 'Japan's Search for Its Central Asian Policy. Between Idealism and Pragmatism.' *Asian Survey* 53 (2013): 3; Nargis Kassenova, 'Japan's Hesitant Embrace of Central Asia: Will There be a Strategy?' in *Great Powers and Regional Integration in Central Asia: A Local Perspective*, eds. Mario Esteban and Nicolas de Pedro (Madrid: Exlibris Ediciones, 2009); Christopher Len, Tomohiko Uyama, and Tetsuya Hirose, eds., *Japan's Silk Road Diplomacy: Paving the Road Ahead* (Washington, DC: Central Asia-Caucasus Institute, 2008).
7 Here, I use the term 'romanticism' with regards to the shared Silk Road heritage between Japan and CA. It is therefore different from nineteenth-century romanticism, in particular from the imperialist romanticism of the Great Game discourse.

8 Interview with Councillor Nakayama Kyōko, March 2012.

9 Interview with a former MOF official, March 2012.

10 Bruno Latour, *Reassembling the Social: An Introduction to Actor-Network-Theory* (Oxford: Oxford University Press, 2005).

11 See the relevant sections in Calder (1988), Orr (1991), Green (2001), Arase (1993), Rix (1993), Söderberg (1996), Miyashita (2003), etc.

12 Kent E. Calder, 'Japanese Foreign Economic Policy Formation: Explaining the Reactive State.' *World Politics* 40 (1988): 541. doi:10.2307/2010317.

13 Statement by Katō Takatoshi, the temporary alternate governor for Japan at the second EBRD meeting (1992).

14 Statement by Nakahira Kōsuke, special adviser to the minister of finance, temporary alternate governor for Japan at the Sixth Annual EBRD Meeting (1997).

15 Interview with MOF official, January 2012.

16 Michael J. Green, *Japan's Reluctant Realism* (New York: Palgrave, 2001), 59–61.

17 Ukeru Magosaki, 'Chūō Ajia de nani ga okotte iru ka: Uzubekisutan to Nihon gaikō' [What is going on in Central Asia? Uzbekistan and Japanese diplomacy]. *Chūōkōron* May 1994: 160. Quoted from Uyama Tomohiko, 'Japan's Diplomacy towards Central Asia in the Context of Japan's Asian Diplomacy and Japan-U.S. Relations,' in *Japan's Silk Road Diplomacy: Paving the Road Ahead*, eds. Len et al. (Washington, DC: Central Asia-Caucasus Institute & Silk Road Studies Program), 109.

18 Robert Gilpin, *Global Political Economy: Understanding the International Economic Order* (Princeton, NJ: Princeton University Press, 2001), 316.

19 Markus Kaiser, 'Eurasien: "Neo-imperialistischer Diskurs oder gesellschaftliche Realität?"' [Neo-imperialistic discourse or societal reality?]. *Working Paper No 337* (Bielefeld, Germany: Sociology of Development Research Centre, University of Bielefeld), 2001.

20 Kent Calder and Viktoriya Kim, 'Korea, the United States, and Central Asia: Far-Flung Partners in a Globalizing World.' *Korea Economic Institute Academic Paper Series* 3, no. 9 (December 2008), http://www.keia.org/Publications/AcademicPaperSeries/2008/APS-CalderKim.pdf (Accessed 20 April 2010).

21 According to scholar Rafis Abazov, Kazakh President Nursultan Nazarbayev 'mentioned Japan, South Korea and Singapore as the models, in one of the first comprehensive outlooks for the post-independence 'strategy of rapid development.' See Nusultan Nazarbaev, 'Strategiya stanovleniya i razvitiya Kazakhstana kak suverennogo gosudarstva,' *Kazakhstanskaia Pravda*, 16 May 1992: 8–9. Quoted from Rafis Abazov, *Practice of Foreign Policy Making: Formation of Post-Soviet Politics of Kazakhstan, Kyrgyzstan, and Uzbekistan* (Washington, DC: NATO Research Fellowship Final Report), 1998.

22 Interview with a World Bank official, March 2013.

23 Gilpin, *Global Political Economy: Understanding the International Economic Order*, 321–2; interview with Professor Fukagawa Yukiko, June 2014.

24 The 1997 Asian financial crisis affected several emerging East Asian economies through the volatility of currency rates and speculative foreign portfolio investments and entailed a wave of criticism of the IMF. 1998 Russian sovereign debt crisis started after the government's default on its treasury bonds. It resulted in a significant drop in the rouble exchange value and dramatically affected the quality of living in Russia and post-Soviet countries with close ties to the Russian economy, including CA.

25 Evgeny Kovrigin, 'Kitaisko-yaponskiye otnosheniya cherez prizmu ofitsialnoy pomoshchi razvitiyu (OPR) v 1980–2000-h godah' [Sino-Japanese relations viewed through the lens of official development assistance (ODA) in 1980–2000], in *Japan* Yearbook, ed. Elgena Molodiakova (Moscow: Russian Academy of Sciences, 2012), 97–122.

26 Masato Kamikubo, *Bureaucratic Behaviour and Policy Change: A Case of Japan's Financial Market Reform in the 1990s as an Implication for the Study of Asian*

132　*Aid: development, security and connectivity*

Financial Integration, GIARI Working Papers, 5, 2007: 14–16, http://www.isn.ethz.ch/Digital-Library/Publications/Detail/?ots591=0c54e3b3-1e9c-be1e-2c24-a6a8c7060233&lng=en&id=137508 (Accessed 11 March 2014).

27　Green, *Japan's Reluctant Realism*, 60–61.

28　Ibid., 27.

29　Kashiwagi, 'Chiteki shien to ha nani ka? Uzubekisutan BFA muke shien no rei wo miru,' (Tokyo: Ministry of Finance, 2014), 17.

30　Interview with a World Bank official, March 2013.

31　Andrey Kazantsev, *Bol'shaya igra s neizvestnymi pravilami: mirovaya politika i Tsentralnaya Aziya*, 364–5.

32　Bob Jessop, 'Putting Neoliberalism in Its Time and Place: A Response to the Debate,' *Social Anthropology* 21, no. 1 (2013): 65–74.

33　Murashkin, 'Japanese Involvement...'.

34　MOF official Sakakibara Eisuke is a notable example here, as he emphasised the importance of Confucian work ethics in the economic growth achieved by Japan in the 1970s and 1980s and subsequently by many other East Asian countries.

35　Notable examples of the Washington Consensus' critics include such economists as Joseph Stiglitz, Gobind Nankani, and Dani Rodrik.

36　The 'Third Way' was the British incarnation of the cross-European trend of convergence between social democratic and liberal democratic ideologies in the aftermath of the Cold War, Thatcherism and Reaganomics.

37　Statement by Mahito Nakajima, governor for Japan, *EBRD Eighth Annual Meeting*, Kiev, 1998.

38　Timur Dadabaev, 'Japan's Search for Its Central Asian Policy. Between Idealism and Pragmatism.' *Asian Survey* 53, no. 3 (2013): 506–32.

39　*Investitsionnyi potentsial Uzbekistana* [Uzbekistan's investment potential]. Report by the International Institute for Political Expertise, July 2013, http://www.minchenko.ru/netcat_files/File/Uzbekistan%20issledovanie%2015_07_full.pdf (Accessed 3 October 13), 3–4.

40　Nakayama Kyōko. *Uzubekisutan no sakura* (Tokyo: Chuoh Publishing Co, 2005), 206; Kitamura Toshiharu, 'Fukuzatsu na kao wo motsu Chūō Ajia, soshite hito to hito to no tsunagari' [The complex figure of Central Asia and inter-personal ties], *Sōchōwa* 164 (2011): 38–46.

41　Dalverzin Tepe is an ancient settlement located on the territory of historic regional states, Sogdiana and Kushan kingdom. The research on the Silk Route's role in forming the origins of Japanese Buddhist heritage is a subject of Uzbekistan and Afghanistan's humanitarian cooperation with Soka Gakkai and, to a lesser extent, the New Komeitō Party affiliated with it. Soka Gakkai is a Japanese lay Nichiren Buddhist movement. Ikeda Daisaku, head of Soka Gakkai International, has become an honorary citizen of the Uzbek city of Navoi, whilst President Islam Karimov was made honorary doctor of the Soka University. 'Uzbekistan na Velikom Shelkovom Puti' [Uzbekistan on the great silk road] http://www.silkway.uz/religii (Accessed 10 February 2014), Soka Gakkai International website, http://www.sgi.org/news/events/events2007/events070922.html (Accessed 10 February 2014).

42　Interview with a Kazakh-Kyrgyz Japanologist, June 2011.

43　Interview with an official from INPEX, February 2012.

44　In the Japanese academic terminology the term 'Eurasia' is often used for the post-Socialist space (splitting it in Slavic Eurasia, Central Eurasia, and Turkic Eurasia) more frequently than in the West. Yet the Japanese government's internal classification of the CA republics varies with the agency: They are part of Europe in the MOFA's typology, but the JICA places them in Central Asia and Caucasus, thus distinguishing them from Eastern European transition countries that are aid recipients. The EBRD officials have demonstrated an infrequent usage of the term 'Silk Road.'

Aid: development, security and connectivity   133

45 Tomohiko, 'Japanese Policies in Relation to Kazakhstan,' 168.
46 Kashiwagi, 'Chiteki shien to ha nani ka? Uzubekisutan BFA muke shien no rei wo miru,' 17.
47 Address by Hashimoto Ryūtarō, minister of finance of Japan at the first EBRD meeting (1991), Statement by Katō Takatoshi, temporary alternate governor for Japan at the second EBRD meeting (1992).
48 Bulat Sultanov, 'Kazakhstansko-germanskoe sotrudnichestvo: sostoyanie i perspektivy' [Kazakhstani-German cooperation: Current situation and prospectives], in *Politicheskie i Ekonomicheskie Interesy Germanii v Kazahstane i Tsentral'noi Azii* [Political and economic interests of Germany in Kazakhstan and Cetnral Asia], ed. Bulat Sultanov (Almaty: Kazakhstani Institute for Strategic Studies, 2010), 19.
49 Interview with a former MOF official, March 2012.
50 Leyla Muzaparova, 'Energeticheskoe sotrudnichestvo Kazakhstana i Evropeiskogo Soyuza: problemy i perspektivy' [Kazakhstan-EU Energy Cooperation: Problems and prospects], in *Politicheskie i ekonomicheskie interesy Germanii v Kazahstane i Tsentral'noi Azii* (Almaty: Kazakhstani Institute of Strategic Studies, 2010), 108.
51 Nargis Kassenova, 'Mezhdu Evropoi i Aziei' [Between Europe and Asia], 16 May 2008, http://wew.kub.info/article.php?sid=21574 (Accessed 10 March 2014). In 1871, Prince Iwakura Tomomi led a mission of Japanese officials who embarked on a two-year journey abroad in order to visit advanced Western countries of the time and understand their sources of power.
52 Private communication with a former professor of the Tashkent State Institute of Oriental Studies, December 2011.
53 Interview with a JICA official previously posted to Uzbekistan, March 2012.
54 Kazantsev, *Bolshaya igra s neizvestnymi pravilami: mirovaya politika i Tsentralnaya Aziya* [The Great Game with unknown rules: World politics and Central Asia] (Moscow: MGIMO University, 2008), 194–5; 'Referendum o sokhranenii SSSR 17 marta 1991 goda. Spravka' [Referendum on the preservation of USSR 17 March 1991. Reference]. *RIA Novosti*, 15 March 2011, http://ria.ru/history_spravki/20110315/354060265.html (Accessed 22 May 2013). NB: in the Kazakh SSR the referendum wording differed from the rest of the country, describing the USSR future as 'a Union of equal sovereign states' instead of the general formula 'a renewed federation of equal sovereign republics.'
55 Tetsuji Tanaka, 'Dokuritsu nijūnen wo mukaeru chūōajiade okotteiru koto,' *Ajia jihō* 12 (2011): 56.
56 Kazantsev, *Bolshaya igra s neizvestnymi pravilami: mirovaya politika i Tsentralnaya Aziya*, 7.
57 Murat Laumulin, Farkhod Tolipov, 'Uzbekistan i Kazakhstan: Bor'ba za liderstvo?' [Uzbekistan and Kazakhstan: A struggle for leadership?], *Security Index* 1 (2010): 105–28.
58 Kazantsev, *Bol'shaya igra s neizvestnymi pravilami: mirovaya politika i Tsentralnaya Aziya*, 118. The term 'tapestry' as a conceptualisation of CA and processes inside it was coined by Dr Anise Waljee and her colleagues from the Cambridge Central Asia forum. It is used in a broader sense than designating mere ethnic diversity of the region.
59 Kashiwagi, 'Chiteki shien to ha nani ka? Uzubekisutan BFA muke shien no rei wo miru,' 18.
60 *Tsentral'naya Aziya-2020: vzglyad iznutri* [Central Asia-2020: A view from within]. Analytic report. Alatau Intellectual Club/Strategy Centre for social and political studies (Kazakhstan), http://www.iarex.ru/articles/29104.html (Accessed 26 March 2014).
61 In the early 1990s, the Kyrgyz President Askar Akayev offered help with solving the Northern Territories issue, but the seriousness of such an offer was disputable due to the low level of leverages that Bishkek had over Moscow, especially in such sensitive matters as territorial disputes.

134 *Aid: development, security and connectivity*

62 'With Oil and West's Appeals in Mind, Tokyo Plans for Central Asia,' *International Herald Tribune*, 16 December 1992. Quoted from Reinhard Drifte, 'Japan's Eurasian Diplomacy: Power Politics, Resource Diplomacy or Romanticism?' in *The Caspian: Politics, Energy and Security*, ed. Shirin Akiner (London: RoutledgeCurzon, 2004), 280.

63 Interview with a JICA official, February 2012; Interview with Kawaguchi Yoriko, former minister of foreign affairs, November 2013.

64 Interview with a MOFA official in charge of Central Asian affairs, March 2012.

65 Interview with former Foreign Minister Kawaguchi Yoriko, November 2013. Mr Tanaka served as special adviser to the first Kyrgyz President Askar Akayev.

66 Tōgō Kazuhiko, 'Eurasian Diplomacy in Japan, 1997–2001,' *Nippon.com*, 13 March 2014, http://www.nippon.com/en/features/c00205/ (Accessed 28 March 2014).

67 Paik Keun-Wook. *Sino-Russian Oil and Gas Cooperation: The Reality and Implications* (Oxford: Oxford University Press, 2012), 381; Kazantsev, *Bol'shaya igra s neizvestnymi pravilami: mirovaya politika i Tsentralnaya Aziya*, 363–4. Another reason for a greater risk appetite for CA displayed by Korean companies, as compared to the Japanese ones, was the difference in the size of respective domestic markets. The Korean market is tighter than the Japanese one, thus more actively pushing Korean companies for an overseas expansion. Besides, the ROK corporate presence in the Asia-Pacific was historically less established than that of Japan, which prevented the chaebol from contenting themselves with Southeast Asian markets and actively pursuing business in CA and elsewhere. Interview with ADB official, January 2012.

68 Dilip Hiro, *Inside Central Asia: A Political and Cultural History of Uzbekistan, Turkmenistan, Kazakhstan, Kyrgyzstan, Tajikistan, Turkey, and Iran* (London: Overlook Press Duckworth, 2009), 163–64.

69 Paik Keun-Wook, 'Sino-Russian Gas Cooperation: Regional and Global Implications,' *Paper Presented at the Seminar* (Cambridge: University of Cambridge, 28 February 2013); Interview with a JOGMEC official, March 2012.

70 Kawatō Akio, 'Japan's Strategic Thinking toward Central Asia,' in *Japanese Strategic Thought toward Asia*, eds. Gilbert Rozman, Kazuhiko Togo, and Joseph P. Ferguson (Palgrave Macmillan, 2007), 225–42; Uyama, 'Japanese Policies in Relation to Kazakhstan,' 168.

71 The consortium's initial name was OKIOC (Offshore Kazakhstan International Oil Consortium), currently it is known as NCOC (North Caspian Oil Consortium). Whilst Itochu's success in the Azeri sector of the Caspian can be attributed both to the company's private actions and state support from the JNOC and METI, extended to the INPEX as well, the INPEX participation in Kashagan involved a more considerable interaction between governments. Interview with a JOGMEC official, March 2012.

72 Nuclear renaissance (*genshiryoku runessansu*) refers to the Japanese energy policy in the 2000s favouring the development of nuclear power generation inside the country and a strong international presence in the reactor technology market.

73 Interview with a former MOF official, March 2012.

74 Observations based on the author's past professional experience in the banking sector. Azerbaijan was another country benefiting from secured loans of structured commodity finance and similar schemes. International commercial banks used this type of financing to generate new business opportunities with high-risk borrowers, as the assignment of the borrower's export contracts to the banks allowed them to mitigate the default risk – in the event of non-payment the lenders would have easily recovered the debt as the assigned commodities were of much higher liquidity than other assets the borrowers could pledge (buildings, equipment located in countries with weak systems of judiciary and property rights protection).

75 Kazafusutan kyōwakoku ni okeru JICA jigyō no gaiyō (2010) [Summary of the JICA's activities in Kazakhstan], Uzubekisutan kyōwakoku ni okeru JICA jigyō no gaiyō (2010) [Summary of the JICA's activities in Uzbekistan].

Aid: development, security and connectivity   135

76 According to the IMF estimates, in 2014, remittances accounted for more than 52 percent of Tajikistan's GDP.

77 Interview with Nakayama Kyōko, March 2012.

78 'Investitsionnyi potentsial Uzbekistana,' International Institute for Political Expertise, July 2013, http://www.minchenko.ru/netcat_files/File/Uzbekistan%20issledovanie%2015_07_full.pdf (Accessed 10 March 2013). CA's main commodities by country include: oil, gas, and ores, including uranium, for Kazakhstan; cotton, gold, and uranium for Uzbekistan; gold for Kyrgyzstan; and aluminium for Tajikistan. For details on the commodity aspect, please refer to Chapter 4.

79 Jacob Townsend and Amy King, 'Sino-Japanese Competition for Central Asian Energy: China's Game to Win,' *China and Eurasia Forum Quarterly*, 5, no. 4 (2007): 23–45.

80 Tanaka Fukuichirō, 'Chūō Ajia-Shiruku rōdo chiiki keizaiken no shijōkeizai ikō purosesu no tokushoku to kadai' [Characteristics and problems of market transition processes in the economy of Central Asia and Silk Road], *JBIC Report* #23, March 2005, http://jica-ri.jica.go.jp/IFIC_and_JBICI-Studies/jica-ri/publication/archives/jbic/report/review/pdf/23_05.pdf (Accessed 10 March 2014).

81 Interview with JICA official, April 2012.

82 Interview with JICA official, March 2013.

83 Interview with JICA official, April 2012.

84 Tighter compliance procedures were caused by the exposure of Japanese companies listed overseas, especially in the United States, to the requirements set by American security regulation, which have become stricter in the late 2000s, especially after the 2008 crisis.

85 Miyashita demonstrated five case studies in which Tokyo ended up changing its initial decision on provision or non-provision of foreign aid following the pressure from Washington. Miyashita Akitoshi, *Limits to Power: Asymmetric Dependence and Japanese Foreign aid Policy* (Langham, MD: Lexington Books, 2003).

86 In this sense, the 1997 consequences of the East Asian crisis not only reinforced an already reluctant attitude towards neo-liberal policies, further strengthened by the 1998 Russian debt crisis, but also brought about doubts in the resilience of the East Asian model per se. These doubts may have potentially resulted in the acceptance of reliance on natural resources as a source of economic growth to the detriment of re-industrialisation in sectors with higher added value. Although such a deliberate drift towards the over-reliance on natural resources, which coincided with an FDI influx in the Caspian oil, may have been viewed as a temporary measure, the 2000s commodities boom further entrenched the raw material specialisation of CA states in the global economy.

87 'Japan's Maritime Interests: View on Regional Maritime Situation,' Presentation at Griffith University, 29 June 2016 (Chatham House rule).

88 Bakhtiyor Islamov, 'Central Asian States: On the Way from Autarchic Dependence to Regional and Global Interdependence,' *Hitotsubashi Journal of Economics* 40, no. 2 (1999): 94.

89 National Archives of Australia. Indonesia Relations with Japan 3107/40/106 Part 18.

90 MOFA, Summary of Central Asia Plus Japan Tokyo Dialogue, http://www.mofa.go.jp/region/europe/dialogue/index.html (Accessed 25 April 2015).

91 This focus is highlighted in some analyses of Japanese foreign aid, for instance, Alan Rix, *Japan's Foreign Aid Challenge: Policy Reform and Aid Leadership* (London: Routledge, 1993) and Marie Söderberg ed., *The Business of Japanese Foreign Aid: Five Case Studies from Asia* (London: Routledge, 1996).

92 Marie Söderberg, ed., *The Business of Japanese Foreign Aid: Five Case Studies from Asia* (London: Routledge, 1996), 85. Mitsui opened its first office in the USSR in 1967. In 1987, Mitsui started the negotiations with the Soviet government on what would become in 2009 the first Russian Liquefied Natural Gas (LNG) plant on Sakhalin. Source: Mitsui's website https://www.mitsui.com/ru/en/company/message/index.html (Accessed 1 June 2016).

136 *Aid: development, security and connectivity*

93 Interview with a former MOF official, March 2012.
94 For instance, some of them were transferred to the government's watchdog for financial markets. Personal communication with an EBRD official. March 2013. Interview with an EBRD official, January 2012; Interview with an ADB official, January 2012.
95 Interview with Nakayama Kyōko, March 2012.
96 Kamikubo, *Bureaucratic Behaviour and Policy Change: A Case of Japan's Financial Market Reform in the 1990s as an Implication for the Study of Asian Financial Integration*, 14–16.
97 Interview with Nakayama Kyōko, March 2012.
98 Interview with a former MOF official, December 2011.
99 Rafferty, Kevin, 'Chino Cements Image as ADB's Best Chief Ever,' *Japan Times*, 21 February 2002.
100 Sterngold, James (1991) 'Japan's New Finance Official Plots an Independent Course,' *New York Times*, 5 August 1991. As Miyashita suggested, Japan subsequently changed its reluctance to provide aid to Russia in the early 1990s in favour of a positive stance following pressure from the United States.
101 Kashiwagi, 'Chiteki shien to ha nani ka? Uzubekisutan BFA muke shien no rei wo miru,' 17.
102 Interview with a Japanese EBRD official, March 2011, Keynote Speech by Tadao Chino at the CAREC Second Ministerial Conference, Tashkent, Uzbekistan, 12 November 2003; Opening Speech by Tadao Chino at the First CAREC Ministerial Conference, Manila, Philippines, 25 March 2002.
103 Vassily Golovnin, 'Razgrom "russkoy gruppy" zavershen' [The demise of Russian Group is finalised], *Kommersant*, 29 April 2002.
104 Posol'stvo Yaponii v Uzbekistane – Politicheskiye otnosheniya [Embassy of Japan in Uzbekistan – political relations], http://www.uz.embjapan.go.jp/relations/political/ (Accessed 6 August 2015).
105 The Japanese language even employs the same term (*habatsu*) to designate both CA clans and Japanese factions.
106 Specific works applying Max Weber's and Shmuel Eisenstadt's theories in CA include: Houchang E. Chehabi and Juan J. Linz, eds. *Sultanistic Regimes* (Baltimore: The John Hopkins University Press, 1998); Kathleen Collins, *Clans, Pacts, and Politics in Central Asia* (Cambridge, 2005); Farid Guliyev, 'Post-Soviet Azerbaijan: Transition to Sultanistic Semiauthoritarianism? An Attempt at Conceptualization' in *Demokratizatsiya: The Journal of Post-Soviet Democratization*, 13, no. 3 (2005): 393–435; Nicholas Kunysz, 'From Sultanism to Neopatrimonialism? Regionalism within Turkmenistan,' *Central Asian Survey*, 31:1 (2012): 1–16.
107 James N. Rosenau. *Along the Domestic-Foreign Frontier: Exploring Governance in a Turbulent World* (Cambridge: Cambridge University Press, 1997).
108 Interview with a former MOF official, January 2012.
109 Robert Orr, *The Emergence of Japan's Foreign Aid Power* (New York: Columbia University Press, 1990), 44–45.
110 US embassy cable. 09TASHKENT105_a. Uzbekistan: Japanese Officials Comment on Bilateral Cooperation, Uzbek Officials, https://wikileaks.org/plusd/ cables/09TASHKENT105_a.html (Accessed 24 February 2016).
111 Both during and after Chino's ADB presidency.
112 'Investitsionnyi potentsial Uzbekistana,' International Institute for Political Expertise, July 2013, http://www.minchenko.ru/netcat_files/File/Uzbekistan%20is sledovanie%2015_07_full.pdf (Accessed 10 March 2013).
113 'Doch' Karimova zapodozrila v korruptsii preemnika svoego ottsa' [Karimov's daughter suspects her father's successor of corruption], http://www.rosbalt.ru/ exussr/2013/03/27/1110844.html (Accessed 27 March 2014).

Aid: development, security and connectivity   137

114 Hiro, *Inside Central Asia*, 405.
115 Dai-12-kai EBRD sōkai Shiokawa zaimudaijin sōmu ensetsu [Statement by finance minister Masajurō Shiokawa at the Twelfth EBRD meeting] (4 May 2003).
116 Hiro, *Inside Central Asia*, 183–4.
117 Political aspects of the mandate of the EBRD, http://www.ebrd.com/news/publications/instituational-documents/political-aspects-of-the-mandate-of-the-ebrd.html (Accessed 10 June 2014); ADB's Work to Support Regional Cooperation in Asia and the Pacific, http://www.adb.org/themes/regional-cooperation/overview (10 June 2014).
118 Interview with a World Bank official, 2013.
119 US embassy cable – 06TOKYO2992, A/S BOUCHER'S MAY 30 MEETING WITH EUROPEAN DDG YAGI ON CENTRAL ASIA, 31 May 2006, http://cables.mrkva.eu/cable.php?id=66130 (Accessed 15 April 2014).
120 US Tokyo embassy cable – 07TOKYO2306, METI MINISTER'S VISIT TO CENTRAL ASIA, MIDDLE EAST ENERGY-FOCUSED, identifier: 07TOKYO2306, created: 23 May 2007 07:53:00, http://cables.mrkva.eu/cable.php?id=109365.
121 Asō Tarō, *Jiyū to han'ei no ko* [The arc of freedom and prosperity] (Tokyo: Gentōsha, 2007), 225.
122 Interview with an Uzbek political scientist Farkhod Tolipov, June 2011.
123 Ibrokhim Mavlonov, *Japan's Economic Diplomacy in Investment and Foreign Trade Policy, Including Economic Cooperation with Central Asian Countries* (Tokyo: The Japan Foundation, 2006), 7–8.
124 ODA Reform: Five Recommendations – Moving into the 21st century – Development Cooperation (DC) – Multi-sectoral Task Force for the Reform of Japanese ODA, June 2010, http://www.grips.ac.jp/forum-e/pdf_e10/ODA5E.pdf (Accessed 20 May 2014); Interview with JICA official in one of Central Asian countries, March 2013; Interview with former MOF official, March 2012.
125 Interview with a MOFA official, June 2011.
126 'Uzbekistan: naznachen novyi ministr vnutrennih del' [Uzbekistan: New minister of interior appointed], *Fergana News*, http://www.fergananews.com/news/21598 (Accessed 25 March 2014).
127 Emma Mawdsley, *From Recipients to Donors. Emerging Powers and the Changing Development Landscape* (Zed Books, 2012), 38.
128 'Chino Tadao ga shikyo – mae Ajia kaihatsu ginkō sōsai' [Chino Tadao passes away, former president of Asia Development Bank], http://www.47news.jp/CN/200807/CN2008071701000969.html (Accessed 27 March 2014); Miyashita, Akitoshi. *Limits to Power: Asymmetric Dependence and Japanese Foreign Aid Policy* (Lanham, MD: Lexington Books, c2003), 27.
129 This was, for instance, the case of Kyrgyzstan in the early 2000s – the country benefited from financial aid despite unattractive repayment capability. Private communication with former ADB employee (May 2012) and former Japanese Ambassador to Kazakhstan Mori Toshimitsu (April 2012).
130 Kawatō, 'Japanese strategic thinking toward Central Asia.'
131 'Chino group' is a term used only by the author for the purposes of this research and not used in the existing scholarship or media. I do not imply an organised community with formalised ties and central subordination (given the absence of data suggesting such institutionalisation), but rather an ad hoc community of MOF-affiliated professionals, with a past or present record of work in various governmental or intergovernmental organisations (ADB, EBRD, JICA, JBIC, World Bank, IMF) and not only related to CA by virtue of a respective charge assigned, but actively promoting the cooperation with the region.
132 Personal communication with a former MOF official, March 2012.
133 Kuroda Haruhiko became the the head of Bank of Japan in Abe Shinzō's second cabinet.

138 *Aid: development, security and connectivity*

134 Koizumi' economic reforms focused on the revitalisation of the Japanese economy, which included the reduction of public debt and welfare programs, as well as loosening of lifetime employment.
135 Interview with a MOFA official, February 2013.
136 Dennis Yasutomo, 'Japan and the Asian Development Bank,' in *Japan's Foreign Aid: Power and Policy in a New Era*, ed. Robert M. Orr (Boulder, CO: Westview Press, 1993), 307–9, 317.
137 As a reminder, Uzbekistan is uniquely one of the world's two doubly landlocked countries, surrounded by other landlocked states (the other doubly landlocked country is Liechtenstein).
138 Shirin Akiner, Rovshan Ibrahimov, Ariz Huseynov, 'Interregional Cooperation in Eurasia: Transport and Logistics Projects as an Accelerator of Integration Within and Between the Black Sea Region, the South Caucasus and the Central Asia,' *SAM Review*, Center for Strategic Studies, Vols. 9–10, September 2013.
139 In South Asia, the ADB promoted the connections of landlocked Nepal and Bhutan with seaports in India and Bangladesh.
140 Yoneda Hiroshi, *Susumu chūō Ajia to no deai. Bunka kōryū to kokusai kyōryoku* (Hiroshima: Keisuisha, 2012), 205–27.
141 Russia applied for the ADB membership in the mid-2000s, however, its application was neither approved by the United States, nor by Japan. As of June 2012, Russia's application was still pending, according to the officials of the Russian Ministry of Finance (Q&A session at the 2012 St. Petersburg International Economic Forum). In 2015, after more than a year of hesitation, Russia joined the China-led Asian Infrastructure Investment Bank, becoming its 3rd largest shareholder.
142 For a general analysis of Japan's proactive involvement in the ADB as an exception to otherwise passive/reactive foreign policy, please refer to Dennis Yasutomo, *Japan and the Asian Development Bank* (New York: Praeger, 1983).
143 CAREC, From Landlocked to Linked in, ADB 2013.
144 Regional Economic Cooperation in Central Asia, report prepared for the ADB, 1998.
145 CAREC Timeline 1996–2012, http://www.carecprogram.org/uploads/docs/CAREC-Timeline-1996-2012.pdf (Accessed 25 March 2014).
146 Arguably the first diplomatic strategy of a non-CA country to conceptualise CA and the Caucasus as the 'Silk Road.'
147 Address by Prime Minister Hashimoto Ryūtarō to the Japan Association of Corporate Executives, 24 July 1997, http://japan.kantei.go.jp/0731douyukai.html (Accessed 28 March 2014).
148 The New Great Game in Asia. *New York Times*, 2 January 1996, http://www.nytimes.com/1996/01/02/opinion/the-new-great-game-in-asia.html (Accessed 17 March 2014); Kawatō Akio, 'What is Japan up to in Central Asia,' 29.
149 Bakhtiyor Islamov, 'Foreign Economic Relations of Central Asian Independent States: Implications for North-East Asia' in *Northeast Asian Studies* 2 (Sendai, Japan: Tohoku University, 1998), 168–9.
150 Interview with Masuda Gen'ichi, a retired freight professional formerly involved in the Eurasian Land Bridge operations, April 2012.
151 Otsuka Shigeru, 'Central Asia's Rail Network and the Eurasian Land Bridge,' *Japan Railway & Transport Review* 28, no. 9 (2001): 42–9.
152 Zheleznaya doroga Kazahstan-Turkmenistan-Iran ne interesna biznesu [The Kazakhstan-Turkmenistan-Iran railway is not interesting for businesses], *EurAsia Daily*, 19 December 2018, https://eadaily.com/ru/news/2018/12/19/zheleznaya-doroga-kazahstan-turkmenistan-iran-ne-interesna-biznesu (Accessed 30 September 2018).
153 Oksana Reznikova, 'Tsentral'naya Aziya i Aziatsko-Tikhookeanskiy region' [Central Asia and the Asia-Pacific region], *Mirovaya ekonomika i mezhdunarodnye otnosheniya*, #4, 1999.

Aid: development, security and connectivity 139

154 Murat Laumulin, 'U.S. Central Asian Policy under the President Barack Obama,' *Central Asia's Affairs* 1 (2011): 6; CAREC involves six financial institutions: ADB, EBRD, IMF, IsDB, UNDP, and the World Bank.

155 'Afghanistan is not a special case – ADB head,' Philip Blenkinsop, *Reuters*, 1 April 2004, http://www.eariana.com/ariana/eariana.nsf/allDocs/78f8b18f8e68b3b187256 e690064ce4e!OpenDocument&Click= (Accessed 11 March 2014).

156 Akiner et al., 'Interregional Cooperation in Eurasia,' 29; Alan Boyer, 'Recreating the Silk Road: The Challenge of Overcoming Transaction Costs,' *China and Eurasia Forum Quarterly*, 4, no.4 (2006): 71–96.

157 Thomas E. Ricks. 'Fred Starr: Keep on trucking, Afghanistan,' *Foreign Policy*, October 20, 2009.

158 US embassy cable – 06TOKYO5820, EB DAS MOORE COVERS ECONOMIC AGENDA AT FINANCE MINISTRY, Created: 2006 October 2006, http://cables. mrkva.eu/cable.php?id=80876 (Accessed 31 March 2014).

159 New Silk Road Foreign Ministers' Meeting, Remarks by Haruhiko Kuroda, ADB president, at the German House, New York, 22 September 2011, http://www.adb.org/ news/speeches/search/194 (Accessed 14 February 2014).

160 Fatema Z. Sumar, deputy assistant secretary, bureau of South and Central Asian affairs, Remarks, 13th Anniversary CAREC Ministerial Conference, Bishkek, Kyrgyzstan, 6 November 2014.

161 Alexander Knyazev, 'Mify dlya Tsentralnoy i Yuzhnoy Azii stanovyatsya pochti epicheskimi' [Myths for Central and South Asia are becoming almost epic], *Nezavisimaya gazeta*, 16 May 2016, http://www.ng.ru/courier/2016-05-16/11_asia. html (Accessed 24 May 2016).

162 Yoneda, *Susumu chūō ajia to no deai. Bunka kōryū to kokusai kyōryoku*, 250.

163 The communications inside Afghanistan proper include the Ring Road, the North-South corridor, the Kabul to Jalalabad expressway, and the Hairatan to Mazar-e-Shariff railway.

164 'ADB and JICA sign Uzbekistan electrification loans,' *Railway Gazette*, 01 March 2012, http://www.railwaygazette.com/news/projects-infrastructure/single-view/view/ adb-and-jica-sign-uzbekistan-electrification-loans.html (Accessed 10 March 2014).

165 Mitsui has mothballed virtually all its projects in Uzbekistan by the early 2010s owing to a previous corruption scandal with Japanese MP Suzuki Muneo, on the one hand, and gradually deteriorating business climate of Uzbekistan, reducing business operations to merely the ODA. Interview with former senior official of the MOF, March 2012, interview with MOFA officials, January 2012.

166 'Tsutomu Hiraoka zavershil svoyu diplomaticheskuyu missiyu v Uzbekistane' [Tsutomu Hiraoka ended his diplomatic mission in Uzbekistan], *Anons.uz*, 28 September 2010, http://www.anons.uz/article/politics/3103/ (Accessed 20 March 2014).

167 'Uzbekistan na den'gi SShA postroit zheleznuju dorogu iz Termeza v Mazari-Sharif' [Uzbekistan to construct a railway from Termez to Mazar-e-Sharif, funded by the US]. 11 October 2004, http://www.fergananews.com/articles/3233 (Accessed 20 March 2014).

168 'Talimarjan Power Project In Uzbekistan: Talimarjan Thermal Power Plant Expansion Project: Construction Of Two Combined Cycle Gas Turbine Units,' https://www.devex.com/projects/tenders/talimarjan-power-project-in-uzbekistan-talimarjan-thermal-power-plant-expansion-project-construction-of-two-combined-cycle-gas-turbine-units/63008 (Accessed 20 March 2014).

169 Aga Khan Foundation is a private non-profit development agency involved in various social projects targeting Ismaili population: South and Central Asia, Eastern and Western Africa, and the Middle East. The Gorno-Badakhshan region of Tajikistan has a large Ismaili population. More details on JICA-Aga Khan Development Network can be found here: http://www.jica.go.jp/english/news/press/2011/120308. html (Accessed 20 March 2014).

140   *Aid: development, security and connectivity*

170   'Afghanistan-Tajikistan: New bridge to provide key economic link,' *IRI News*, http://www.irinnews.org/report/28681/afghanistan-tajikistan-new-bridge-to-provide-key-economic-link (Accessed 22 March 2014).

171   'Afghan, Tajik, Turkmen heads seek loans for regional railway,' Reuters, 20 March 2013, http://uk.reuters.com/article/2013/03/20/turkmenistan-railway-idUKL6N0C-CEMK20130320 (Accessed 22 April 2014).

172   'Turkmenistan gets $125 million ADB loan for a regional railway project.' *CAREC*, http://www.carecprogram.org/index.php?page=railway-turkmenistan-april-2011 (Accessed 20 March 14).

173   'Afghan, Tajik, Turkmen heads seek loans for regional railway,' Reuters, 20 March 2013, http://uk.reuters.com/article/2013/03/20/turkmenistan-railway-idUKL6N0CCEMK20130320 (Accessed 22 April 2014).

174   Shirin Akiner, 'Silk Road Projects,' Presentation at Cambridge University 26 May 2013.

175   I draw parallels between China's international infrastructure push and Japan's initiatives in the 1980s, when the MITI developed a master plan for Asia, and Japan invested in ports and other infrastructure largely for facilitating trade. Chapter 7 examines this in greater detail.

176   Interview with Japanese ADB officials, January 2012; Interview with EBRD official, March 2013; Cooley, *Great Games, Local Rules: The New Great Power Contest in Central Asia*, 88.

177   Wang Zheng, 'China's Alternative Diplomacy,' *The Diplomat*, 30 January 2015.

178   Lin, Jinbing, 'Japan-Led Asian Development Bank Appoints Chinese Government Official as Vice President,' *Caixin*, 20 November 2018 https://www.caixinglobal.com/2018-11-20/japan-led-asian-development-bank-appoints-chinese-government-official-as-vice-president-101349902.html (Accessed 30 August 2019).

179   Interview, ADB official, 2012.

180   Interview with a senior Chinese official in charge of CA affairs, October 2014.

181   'Infra yushutsu he shikin jinsoku ni tetsudzuki tanshuku, yūrotate kaikin' [Easing of procedures for financing infrastructure exports, euro denomination ban lifted], *Nikkei*, 20 May 2016, www.nikkei.com/article/DGXLASFS19H5T_Z10C16A5MM8000/?n_cid=NMAIL001 (Accessed 20 May 2016).

182   George Obulutsa, 'Japan pledges $30 billion for Africa over next three years,' *Reuters*, 27 August 2016, https://www.reuters.com/article/us-africa-japan/japan-pledges-30-billion-for-africa-over-next-three-years-idUSKCN112077.

183   Masayuki Yuda, 'Abe Pledges $50bn for Infrastructure in Indo-Pacific,' *Nikkei Asian Review*, 11 June 2018.

184   JICA: Shinichi Kitaoka becomes JICA's new president, 1 October 2015, http://www.jica.go.jp/english/news/field/2015/151001_01.html (Accessed 15 October 2015).

185   The multitude of funding contributors under the Japan-led ADB umbrella is in itself more attractive for the Japanese budget than bilateral disbursements, because it allows diversifying credit risks and pooling funds on a much greater scale than Tokyo could do bilaterally.

186   Mawdsley, *From Recipients to Donors. Emerging Powers and the Changing Development Landscape*, 38–9.

187   Matteo Fumagalli, 'Growing Inter-Asian Connections: Links, Rivalries, and Challenges in South Korean–Central Asian relations,' *Journal of Eurasian Studies*, 7, no. 1 (2016): 39–48; MOFA: Uzbekistan Kyōwakoku – Kiso dēta [Republic of Uzbekistan – Basic data], http://www.mofa.go.jp/mofaj/area/uzbekistan/data.html#section1 (Accessed 20 June 2016).

4 Energy Silk Road

Anticipation and adaption in Japan's resource diplomacy

Introduction

Security of resource procurement is a matter of national interest that Tokyo has proactively and consistently pursued over the past century. Given the extreme scarcity of domestic resource endowment and resulting reliance on foreign supplies, Japan particularly prioritised ensuring its energy needs after the 1973 oil crisis. Resource diplomacy (*shigen gaikō*) became a term openly and frequently used by the Japanese government and pundits.[1] Japan's government has further undertaken global efforts in the post-Cold War period promoting new opportunities in the post-Socialist countries, including Central Asia (CA).[2]

The epitome of *shigen gaikō* is Prime Minister Abe's foreign travel to numerous resource-rich countries early in his second premiership (2012–present). Abe's visits sought to boost Japan's international profile and deal with the post-Fukushima reconfiguration of its energy policies. Abe's trip to CA took place in October 2015. Although this delay indicated the region's peripheral importance, it also confirmed that CA still mattered, as Abe was only the second ever Japanese prime minister to visit CA. Abe toured all five states, securing contracts of notable aggregate value, thus confirming the role of infrastructure finance and natural resources in Japan's diplomacy vis-à-vis CA.

Throughout the entire history of its relations with post-Soviet CA, Japan's interest in the region's mineral riches has been acknowledged recurrently as a key rationale for its diplomacy by officials and in the Ministry of Foreign Affairs (MOFA's) Diplomatic Bluebooks.[3] The cooperation between Japan and CA in the exploration of oil and natural gas has intensified in the 1990s and attracted considerable media attention earning clichés such as 'The New Great Game,' sometimes validated by Ministry of Economy, Trade, and Industry (METI) officials.[4] The 2000s 'commodity supercycle' spurred Japan to further diversify both its energy mix and its supply structure. By the mid- and late 2000s, it was CA uranium ore and rare earth metals (REMs) that stole Japan's spotlight away from hydrocarbons. At the same time, differences in CA's economic development made the Japanese companies shift their preference from Uzbekistan to Kazakhstan.

142 *Energy Silk Road: anticipation and adaptation*

Direct procurement was not the sole purpose of CA resources for Japan. These fossil riches were viewed by Japanese officials as a source of prosperity for CA countries in their market transition. Thus, Japan was not only extracting the resources for its self-interest, but also offering its signature contribution: competitive know-how, infrastructure, and environmentally friendly technologies for extraction and commercialisation, including export. Besides, Japan-funded or Japan-inspired infrastructure projects improved the larger international accessibility of CA commodities, benefiting not only Japan, but other buyers of raw materials and CA as sellers. Nonetheless, some Japanese officials with CA expertise and a MOF perspective characterised Tokyo's resource diplomacy in CA as belated and insufficient.[5]

Argument

This chapter aims to provide an account of the history of Japanese resource diplomacy in CA, including the private-sector perspective. Comparing the periods of 1992–2003, 2003–11, and 2011–15, I analyse critical junctures, key cooperation projects, the impact of individuals, and changing risk perceptions on bilateral relations contextualising them in various conceptualisations of Japanese foreign policy.

I argue that the overall strategic importance of CA resources for Japan and Japan's competition for them with other powers is mildly exaggerated by existing scholarship and conventional wisdoms that posit a perpetual zero-sum-game rivalry for scarce commodities stemming from Japan's resource predicament and competition with China and South Korea.

An assumption of Japanese competition with other East Asian countries as a default setting would be static, as it takes the subject rivalry out of the changing global macroeconomics and downplays the evolution of the Japanese commodity diplomacy in CA from 1991 until the present. I argue that this evolution demonstrates that, on balance and in the specific context of CA's resources, Japanese actions in that field were rather successful – with the notable exception of Mitsui's Uzbek uranium operations – and cognizant of cyclical market trends.

Whilst Japanese involvement in Azerbaijan and Turkmenistan is arguably more mercantile than the more state-driven relationship with Kazakhstan and Uzbekistan, the Japanese political and corporate establishment was also considerate of the changing strategic and macroeconomic environment and evolving risk perceptions.

Since this chapter focuses on the actions of companies, I employ the term 'anticipative strategic adaptation' used by Thierry Hommel.[6] Hommel applied the term to the behaviour of firms anticipating changes in the regulatory environment and conducting strategies of adjustment. I use this term in a broader sense and argue that the Japanese government and companies used anticipative strategic adaptation to the changing environment both globally and in CA. I aim to demonstrate that rather than playing a reactive catch-up game, Japan has actually been anticipative in its advent to CA oil and gas exploration. In the case of uranium and rare earths, Japanese companies displayed more adaptiveness and reactivity than anticipation.

Finally and more importantly, tracing this evolution is helpful in answering the question why Japan's relationship with CA plateaued in the late 2000s. The contribution of this chapter is to answer the points of the Japanese response to a changing global commodity environment, the varying degrees of institutional inertia inside Japanese corporations, and Japanese domestic policy. I also examine whether the Japanese political establishment not only had a holistic strategic view with regard to energy security, but also took consistent and efficient necessary measures to implement this vision institutionally through diplomatic and other means.

Namely, Japan managed to secure major oil investments in the region in the favourable conditions of the late 1990s, when low oil prices reduced the bargaining power of CA countries, while Chinese and Korean competitors were temporarily influenced by the outcomes of the 1997 Asian financial crisis. As invasions into Afghanistan and Iraq spurred oil prices from 2002 to 2003 onwards, this shift in the energy environment pushed Japan to diversify its energy mix in favour of nuclear power in 2004–6 and consequently changed its focus in the region in favour of uranium and REMs. The main task of this chapter thus will be to demonstrate how this evolution of Japanese natural resource policies shaped its overall involvement in the region.

I evaluate Japanese policies and commercial activities in CA in the area of natural resources and will argue that as far as energy security is concerned, Japanese corporate strategies had limited success, due to a decrease in risk appetite inside companies. On the one hand, Japanese resource diplomacy had built a fruitful long-term relationship with CA stakeholders, which was compatible with Japan's energy strategy. On the other hand, Japan's regional presence in resources was constrained by reduced government support of the Japanese companies operating in CA (compared to similar government support of other East Asian countries to their companies) and demonstrated elements of reliance on the United States. It also reflected a lack of consistent or comprehensive vision on the part of bureaucrats.[7]

Theory: mercantilism and functionalism vs. internal constraints and personal factor

Richard Samuels (1987) summarised the role of the Japanese state in energy markets as 'guarantor state,' differentiating it from French-style dirigisme: 'although the Japanese state pervades the market, it does not lead, guide or supervise private interests.'[8] The role of the Japanese state in CA resource markets fits this concept, as I will demonstrate.

Japanese post-Cold War energy diplomacy also generally fits within various theoretical interpretations of Japanese foreign policy.[9] For instance, it can be viewed as a rational and pragmatic adaptation to a changing strategic environment suggested by Kenneth Pyle.[10] Furthermore, Japan's resource diplomacy in CA reflects the search for a 'just right' strategy, in that, depending upon governments in Tokyo, the country alternated between elements of realism and 'middle power internationalism,' as well as that of a 'mercantile state' (*tsūshō kokka*) approach.[11]

144 *Energy Silk Road: anticipation and adaptation*

If applied to Japan's relations with CA and the foreign policy priorities of both sides, Kōsaka Masataka's conceptualisation of Japan as 'mercantile state' also – partially – fits the broader international relations paradigm of functionalism. According to functionalists, the primary goal of the states is to ensure peace and prosperity rather than military security as compared to the realist view.[12] Subsequently, states tend to use economic instruments rather than military force to achieve their objectives. In the context of globalisation and the erosion of state sovereignty, states are also inclined to integrate, initially cooperating over functional technical questions and later having this cooperation 'spill over' in political dimensions.

Nonetheless, although it is premature to speak of any integration between Japan and CA, there is certainly a functionalist regionalisation between Central and East Asia. As far as Japan–CA relations are concerned, the prevalence of economic means for foreign policy is more relevant than state sovereignty erosion. When it comes to the foreign policies of CA countries vis-à-vis Japan, their own mercantile facet was strongly pronounced. Kent Calder fitted the 'division of labour' between Japan and CA – Kazakhstan, in particular – into the paradigm of Eurasian producer-consumer complementarity. He called it an 'energy entente' between an energy-insecure consumer and a 'petrostate' in need of development assistance and superior technologies.[13]

I contend, however, that Japan's rationale for resource cooperation with CA goes beyond mercantilism. Although this cooperation had a clearly pragmatic facet, such as reaping the benefits of access to resource-rich areas, it also stressed the importance of contributing towards economic prosperity and peace in the region, both for the sake of democracy promotion and for stabilising the Afghanistan neighbourhood. Such aims were formulated in the strategic conceptualisations of Japan's presence in CA: Hashimoto's 'Eurasian diplomacy' and Asō's concept of Arc of Freedom and Prosperity. The importance of Eurasian diplomacy and Arc of Freedom and Prosperity also reflected the high role of personal factors induced by internal structural features of Japanese bureaucracy.

In the case of CA, the domestic rigidities can be exemplified by METI's mixed record of support of regional affairs, showcasing its reliance on top politicians. At the departmental level, the ministry's expertise was adversely affected by frequent rotations related to METI's role as career pool or trampoline for other cabinet, ministerial, or parliamentary jobs. Some officials assigned to the CA desk did not have sufficient proficiency in regional affairs and viewed their stint as a temporary career interlude. Others were haphazardly seconded or sourced from as far afield as police agencies.[14]

From the perspective of a former MOF official, in its relationship with CA, the METI's attitude was different from that of the MOF and closer to that of the MOFA in its regional prioritisation of Russia.[15] Structurally, this position can be linked to CA's place inside the METI's organisation. Similarly to the MOFA, where CA shares bureaucratic space with Russia inside the European Affairs Bureau, the METI's Trade Policy Bureau locates the region within the Russia, CA, and Caucasus Division. The number of officials with METI, Japan Oil,

Energy Silk Road: anticipation and adaptation 145

Gas, and Metals National Corporation (JOGMEC), or similar economic background was growing in Japanese embassies in CA in the late 2000s, the latest examples being METI-affiliated Ambassador to Uzbekistan Katō Fumihiko (2013–16) and his successor Itō Nobuaki – a career diplomat, but also with a METI experience. MOF-affiliated Japanese ambassadors served in Uzbekistan in 1999–2002 (Nakayama Kyōko) and in Kazakhstan in 2010–13 (Harada Yūzō), although Harada was arguably the only non-career diplomat sent to Kazakhstan as ambassador.

Furthermore, I argue that the oscillations in the Japanese approach towards CA resources can be interpreted through the interplay of various domestic ideological currents. Namely, 'neo-revisionists,' such as Abe, Asō, and Amari Akira (in 2006–7 and 2012–15), and realists, such as Noda Yoshihiko (2011–12), combined a mercantile push for greater uranium and rare metals cooperation with CA with alternating postures of balancing and engaging China.[16]

By contrast, in 2007–8 and 2009–10, 'middle power internationalists' present both in the Liberal Democratic Party of Japan's (LDP's) 'mercantile realists' faction (Fukuda Yasuo) and Democratic Party of Japan's (DPJ's) 'middle power Asianists' (Hatoyama Yukio) considered that it was important to convince South Korea and China that Japan has no great power ambitions, acting in the interest of promoting economic growth and prosperity.

Nevertheless, relations with South Korea and China are at stake in the Japanese quest for CA resources and constitute a competing priority to Japan's own natural resource security, which limits the 'middle power internationalist' approach. Both of Japan's Northeast Asian neighbours have been significantly increasing their presence in CA since 1991 to pursue new commercial opportunities, especially since their competitiveness with Japan in East Asia was lower at that time. The question whether Sino-Japanese–Korean interaction in CA will be cooperative, complementary, and mutually beneficial or will represent a conflicting zero-sum game, remains open.

The scholarship on this subject to date has provided very different opinions, up to mutually exclusive ones. Some scholars argued that Japan and China are bound to cooperate in the nuclear sphere, while others portrayed China as the clear winner of the energy race in CA.[17] Japan External Trade Organization (JETRO) officials argued in favour of a win-win Japanese–Korean teamwork (*nikkan renkei*) in CA.[18] In this chapter, I also attempt to demonstrate that, on balance, to date, this competition appears to be rather situational, intermittent, and not yet fully manifest, as Northeast Asian companies are finding enough niches in CA.

This chapter starts by outlining Japanese energy strategy, corporate risk perceptions, and their correlation with global macroeconomic context and national security after the end of the Cold War. It explains the emphasis of Japanese companies on CA commodities at the expense of other commercial matters. It then proceeds to the Japanese domestic policy in the field of natural resources, where it also identifies the key actors in Japan, such as the MOFA, METI, and Japanese public and private corporations. Evaluating their role is important in understanding the evolution of energy security as part of national security and

146 *Energy Silk Road: anticipation and adaptation*

the reasons for that change. The two main empirical parts of the chapter examine Japanese involvement, respectively, in CA's oil and gas sector, and uranium and REMs.

Part I. Oil and gas: anticipation over adaptation

External environment matters: cheap oil and the new prospects in the 1990s vs. the 'commodity boom' and tighter reserves scrutiny in the 2000s

In this section, I outline the specifics of the global commodity market and Japan's place in it, in order to link CA's resource attractiveness to Japanese domestic policies. I highlight Tokyo's motivation to adapt to – and seize the opportunities of – the global economic cycles of 'commodity depression' (low international prices for raw materials) in the 1990s and contrast it to Tokyo's behaviour during the 'commodity boom' in the 2000s, the era of sustained and rapid rise in these prices.[19]

JAPAN'S RESOURCE PREDICAMENT AND THE 'ASIAN PREMIUM'

The need for stable natural resource supplies for Japan's national security is a well-known problem. Japan relies on imports for most of its primary energy supply. Ensuring procurement is therefore a matter of national survival. During the entire post-war period, Japan has been solving this issue by creating a solid legal and institutional framework and mitigating the risk through improvement of bilateral relations with commodity producers. Their geography principally included the Middle East and Southeast Asia, further expanding into Africa and the ex-Union of Soviet Socialist Republics (USSR), including CA. Japan's soft stance towards Iran, its key oil supplier despite political pressure from Washington, highlighted Japan's autonomy and the importance of the energy card for Tokyo.

Apart from overall resource scarcity, Japan has historically faced another problem rooted in the structure of international political economy: Japanese companies were charged a premium price for Middle Eastern crude oil – a problem also encountered by corporations from China or South Korea.[20] From the late 1980s and throughout the 1990s–2000s, the difference in pricing mechanisms between Asian destinations and American and European destinations has been consistently bringing about a higher cost of hydrocarbon procurement for Asian countries.[21]

In addition, after the 2000s 'shale revolution,' the imperfections in the global gas market structure created the phenomenon of Asian gas premium.[22] As of 2012, while in the post-shale revolution, United States (U.S.) gas was priced according to the changing supply-demand balance eased by the share revolution, in Japan and the rest of Asia, liquified natural gas (LNG) import prices were 'basically linked to crude oil import prices of Japan under long-term LNG import contracts.... LNG prices thus [moved] according to crude oil price changes rather than the gas supply-demand balance.'[23]

Energy Silk Road: anticipation and adaptation 147

Improving these structural inefficiencies was therefore an important incentive for Japanese and other Asian companies to prioritise new prospective sources of oil and gas. When the littoral Caspian Soviet republics of Azerbaijan, Kazakhstan, and Turkmenistan became independent in 1991, their rich hydrocarbon reserves were considered the last available large prospects – a must-seize opportunity for Asian companies. It was only towards the mid- to late 2000s that audit reports on CA reserves brought about their downward revision, proving that the estimate of the early 1990s turned out excessively optimistic, especially about Turkmenistan.[24] The revision, in turn, reduced the commercial attractiveness of CA for external investors, including Japan.

Furthermore, in the 1990s, low oil prices provided an important boost to the attractiveness of overseas prospects for Japan and East Asian countries, as they increased the bargaining power of investors in commodities and decreased that of host governments. While in the 2000s Japanese government officials criticised the 'resource nationalism' of commodity producers, the 1990s could in this logic be retroactively considered the time of 'resource internationalism.'

Meanwhile, CA governments looked at their mineral endowments as sources of economic growth. During the post-Soviet transition, privatisation reduced the state's income from formerly owned enterprises, as they were privatised. The public fiscal base was not yet solidified as the new source of state income, since in the Soviet era its importance was comparatively low and the state received income through its virtual ownership of the entire economy.[25] External sources of income, such as export duties over commodities, were thus of particular value and foreign investors were welcome, including Japan. Together with shifts in the strategies of the Japanese corporations examined below, CA domestic economic policies prioritised commodities over finished goods in Japanese commercial operations in the region.

PREVALENCE OF COMMODITIES OVER OTHER OPPORTUNITIES IN CENTRAL ASIA

The vertical and horizontal integration of Japanese industrial conglomerates and trading houses is common knowledge. In their overseas expansion, manufacturing and extractive industries are often accompanied by financial and trading arms. Yet, in the case of CA, I focus on the commodity sector, leaving the manufacturing and sales of finished goods outside the analysis perimeter. The reason for this emphasis lies in their comparatively modest commercial attractiveness for Japanese corporations in CA, especially when compared to their Chinese and South Korean competitors (Figure 4.1).

In terms of the commercial potential and production prospects, CA remains of marginal attractiveness to Japanese companies for several reasons. The region's overall population is a little over 72 million – significantly lower than most Asian consumer markets. CA also has a comparatively low purchasing power, while customs and other barriers remain stringent. The localisation level of CA investments made by Japanese producers is also low, which means that Japanese products are merely finished, assembled, and polished in the region, using actual parts and components manufactured elsewhere.[26]

148 Energy Silk Road: anticipation and adaptation

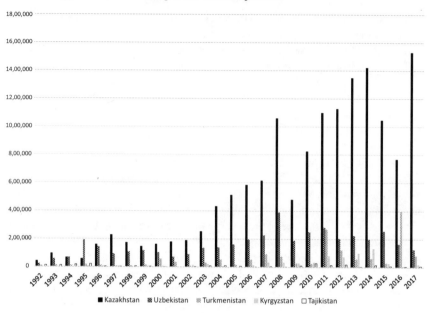

Figure 4.1 Japan–Central Asia two-way trade, USD thousands (from ROTOBO).

In the late 2000s, Kazakhstan stood out as an exception to the rule in terms of purchasing power and a comparatively friendlier business environment, which resulted in growing interest from Japanese companies. Nonetheless, it is still a small market of 18 million inhabitants and an exception confirming the rule in the wider regional context. Much smaller in terms of population, six-million Kyrgyzstan and nine-million Tajikistan suffer from severe poverty and civil instability.[27] Turkmenistan, with a population of nearly six million, still operates in a closed business climate.

Uzbekistan is a special and particularly illustrative case. In the 1990s, this most populous (around 29 million at the time, nearly 33 million as of 2018) regional country was considered CA's best business prospect due to its strong economic growth. Before sanctions were imposed on Iran in 2006, even Uzbekistan's doubly landlocked position did not preclude Japan from viewing it as the key country in the region, since the prospect of exports via the Iranian port of Bandar-Abbas appeared feasible. In 2006, Foreign Minister Asō illustrated the mercantile aspect of Japan's cooperation with Uzbekistan:

> Uzbekistan is the country with the greatest gold resources in the region, with a ranking of 9th in the world in production volume. Next comes Kyrgyzstan, ranked 17th. Japan is one of the world's major importers of gold bullion, importing some 80 tons annually as of 2004. You might want to keep in the back of your mind the fact that 6.7 percent of that – that is, just over five tons of it – came from Uzbekistan.[28]

Energy Silk Road: anticipation and adaptation   149

In the mid-2000s, however, the external environment changed due to international pressure on Iran and conflicts in the Middle East, endangering the prospect of export routes via Bandar-Abbas. Furthermore, despite the investor-friendly rhetoric, the Uzbek business climate gradually deteriorated because of remaining tight currency controls and the repercussions of domestic clan rivalry over investors' property rights, which significantly hindered the operations of foreign companies.

For instance, Mitsui Bussan was the flagship of Japanese business in Uzbekistan since the early 1990s, thanks to its heritage of Soviet-era operations allowing to build a new presence. By the early 2010s, however, the economic environment in Uzbekistan and corruption in Turkmenistan stimulated the company to reorient towards Kazakhstan.[29] Furthermore, Uzbekistan and Japan revealed a mismatch in financing approaches in the mid-2000s, as Uzbekistan increasingly preferred direct equity investment and called upon Japan to adjust its approach accordingly.[30] Japan's priority remained the export of debt capital, as it considered direct investment too risky due to weak protection of property rights. Besides, the government of Uzbekistan reduced the scope and scale of previously abundant guarantees, thus increasing risk aversion on the Japanese side.[31] Uzbekistan's business and political stagnation only started slowly changing in late 2016, with the succession of President Shavkat Mirziyoyev who started gradual economic reforms.[32]

Japan's commercial risk aversion to CA may be contrasted with successful Japanese business operations in the region of the Middle East or with the cases of successful expansion of Chinese and South Korean business operations in CA despite the aforementioned hindrances. There are several justifications provided by Japanese interviewees that account for the limits of Japanese commercial success and are derived from differences in corporate cultures and markets of origin.

RISK PERCEPTIONS OF CENTRAL ASIA IN JAPAN INC.

According to various interviewees, after Japan's 'lost decade' of the 1990s, the strategies of Japanese corporations have been changing globally from expansion to the preservation of attained positions.[33] These strategies, however, varied across individual companies and their corporate cultures, as well as upon the point of view. For instance, energy expert Paik Keun-Wook characterised most Japanese private oil companies as strongly risk-averse and opportunistic, with a notable exception of state-owned JOGMEC being the only risk-taker. According to Paik, the Japanese companies in their Eurasian oil and gas operations did not invest sufficient funds and regularly resorted to the Japanese government for a security umbrella.[34] Once the backing was provided, however, the companies did not always follow suit.

The perspective in the Japanese private sector is different. While acknowledging home government support, Japanese private oil companies were not always satisfied with its quality. According to certain oil company officers, if compared

150 *Energy Silk Road: anticipation and adaptation*

with the state lobbying American or other Western companies benefit from, the Japanese government's promotion of its corporations' interests was comparatively weak and lacking strategic vision, especially if the Japanese companies were operating overseas independently, not being part of an international consortium.[35]

As I show in the section 'Central Asian hydrocarbons: a high-hanging fruit for Japan?,' all four instances of major CA upstream in hydrocarbon projects featured the same Japanese companies (METI-backed International Petroleum Exploration-Teikoku Oil stock company (INPEX), also operating in neighbour Iran, and, with one exception, Itochu), which operated as part of international consortia – unlike most Chinese competitors.[36] In the latest materialisation of Japan–CA resource cooperation, the $20 billion gas-processing plant in Turkmen Galkynysh, Japanese companies also teamed up – with Turkish counterparts.[37] This stable preference for consortia and international partnership stemmed from the intention to share risks and development costs.

Nevertheless, according to a Japanese MOF official, some Japanese companies in CA were risk-takers, such as Itochu or Sumitomo, while Mitsubishi and Mitsui demonstrated a stronger risk aversion.[38] During the early stage of Japan–Kazakhstani nuclear cooperation in 2004–6, it was Sumitomo's initial decision to invest in uranium development in Kazakhstan that triggered subsequent help from the Japanese government. Government support manifested itself in the attraction of the Japanese Bank for International Cooperation (JBIC) and Nippon Export and Investment Insurance (NEXI), a risk insurance body, facilitating the ability of other Japanese companies to share Sumitomo's risk.[39]

This difference in approaches between individual corporations, however, was somewhat paradoxically inversely reflected in bilateral representative business associations. Namely, the success of individual Japanese companies in CA extractive projects did not automatically earn them a higher profile in economic cooperation committees. Although INPEX and Itochu have succeeded in Caspian oil and gas, while Sumitomo prevailed in Kazakhstani uranium and REMs, the Japanese–Kazakhstani economic cooperation committee has been historically chaired by a Mitsubishi representative. A similar Japanese–Uzbek committee has been historically chaired by a Mitsui representative since its creation reflecting this company's long track record of operations in Uzbekistan, even though Mitsui's commercial success declined in the late 2000s, while Itochu's Uzbek projects remain stable to date. In my view, this rigidity in representation may reflect both an honorific element of Japanese corporate culture and a degree of institutional inertia remaining from an initial regional 'division of labour' between Japanese corporations. This allocation dates back to the positions of Japanese companies in the Soviet-Japanese economic cooperation committee at the time of the USSR collapse and no longer reflects their recent performance.[40]

The decision-making of Japanese companies on location choice for their offices in CA reflected both risk-taking and risk-averse approaches. In the early 1990s, when the offices were being established, Tashkent seemed a safer bet,

Energy Silk Road: anticipation and adaptation   151

given its central regional role acquired in the Soviet era, better transport connections with Moscow, and comparatively larger industrial base in Uzbekistan. Mitsui went along with these considerations, while Itochu decided to capitalise on Kazakhstan's future potential, as this republic had a richer mineral endowment and a larger amount of Russian professionals, especially in the northern regions.[41] As I already specified, eventually it was Kazakhstan that became CA business centre by the mid-2000s.[42]

While these nuances in the risk perceptions of individual Japanese companies are noteworthy, all of them still harbour a generally high risk aversion towards CA. This is evidenced by the fact that all Japanese companies in CA are still operating as representative offices rather than full-scale branches, which implies more modest liability and limited capabilities. This structural deficiency has been further complicated by the lack of traditional links between the manufacturing and financial arms of Japanese companies in CA, as Japanese private financial institutions were absent in the entire region except Kazakhstan.[43]

Even within risk-taking companies, the perception of CA was often sceptical and involved elements of historic determinism. For instance, while explaining the slow progress of business operations in CA, some Japanese corporate interviewees brought up several recurrent stereotypes. According to those, the region is defined by the dichotomy of nomadic and sedentary nations and strongly shaped by its transit location and history of conquests by outsiders. In their perceptions, these respondents made a causal link between two individually indisputable phenomena: the above-described heritage and a lack of respect for private property rights with the prevalence of short-term rent-seeking over long-term value-added manufacturing.[44] Silk Road history, as viewed by these Japanese officials, is still entrenched in contemporary CA economy. Consequently, Uzbekistan was viewed as an oasis conducive to agriculture with a modest industrial base, while the historically more nomadic Kazakhstan and Kyrgyzstan were considered cattle farming locations rather than industrial areas (*kōgyōchitai*).[45]

Although the subjective character of these risk perceptions may reduce their value as evidence, they seemingly contributed to the downward revisions of Japanese corporate expectations from CA as a market and manufacturing locale. Ultimately, the Japanese corporate presence focused on state-driven aid projects and commodities.

The commodities, however, required new infrastructure to be delivered from CA to Japan and elsewhere: all transport arteries of these landlocked states led to the 'Third Rome,' (i.e. Russia, their former imperial metropolis). As I explained in Chapter 3, from the 1990s onwards, Japan has been strongly contributing to the modernisation of CA's transport and communication infrastructure to facilitate and diversify the region's export routes from predominantly northwest-bound directions to the east and south. Whilst one cannot rule out the pragmatic mercantile incentive of Japanese corporations improving their access to CA mineral riches, it was accompanied by less pragmatic and more idealist or functionalist considerations of the Japanese government in its financial assistance.

152 *Energy Silk Road: anticipation and adaptation*

JAPANESE ENERGY POLICY

It is a long-established fact that Japan's energy policy is shaped by its low self-sufficiency and extreme dependence on imports of raw materials. Besides general reliance on imports, Japan's energy consumption is still characterised by a high share of oil, although its percentage has been steadily decreasing after the 1973 oil shock.

Oil has consistently made for nearly half the overall energy use in Japan. This situation poses a major problem as it entails a manifold risk chain due to both internal and external factors. Firstly, the reliance on Middle Eastern supplies involves a significant country risk unmitigated in the near future given the ongoing political turbulence in the region. Secondly, it implies a considerable oil price risk, partially mitigated by a strong yen during its appreciation.[46] Thirdly, oil-powered electricity generation has been sensitive to the domestic environmentalist agenda and incompatible with the commitments to greenhouse emissions reduction made by Japan.

Tokyo assumed undertakings on greenhouse emissions under the Kyoto protocol, other international environmental agreements, and its doctrinal energy document, the 2002 Basic Act on Energy Policy.[47] According to the act, Japan committed to increase zero-emission electricity generation from 34 percent to 70 percent by 2030.

In parallel to rising energy prices, the demand for primary energy has also been growing worldwide and especially in emerging and resource-hungry East Asia.[48] Consequently, Japan has been attempting to decrease its oil share in energy consumption, diversify its supply geography, and stockpile resources at home. The examination of the further evolution of Energy Plans in the 2000s is helpful to understand the role of CA resources for Japanese strategic planning.

Strategic Energy Plans: diversification of supplies

The Japanese government outlined its contemporary energy policy in the Basic Act on Energy Policy 2002, which was the first of its kind, remains valid to date, and involved the promulgation of three principles, namely: stability of energy resource supply, environmental harmony, and promotion of market mechanisms.

The development of measures to achieve the strategic aims set out in the Basic Act was undertaken in the Strategic Energy Plan adopted in 2003. The plan followed the Basic Act and proposed to diversify the crude oil supply geography and the sources of primary energy (in favour of nuclear power and new energy types). The forecasts of the time reflected this new logic (Table 4.1).

The government revised the Strategic Energy Plan (SEP) five times: in 2007, in 2010, in 2012 (after 3/11), in 2014 following Abe's reconsideration of the DPJ's nuclear policy, and in 2018. However, Japanese companies – with varying extents of state affiliation and backing – entered into major CA oil projects in 1994–2003 (i.e. *prior* to the introduction of strategic energy planning in 2003). By contrast, Japan's uranium and REM cooperation with CA materialised as part of an energy

Table 4.1 2005 forecast of Japanese energy consumption, percentage

Source type	2000	2010
Crude oil	50	46
Coal	18	18
Natural gas	13	15
Nuclear power	13	14
Other	6	7

Source: Hosoe, Tomoko, *Middle East Econ. Surv.*, 48, 2005.

doctrine established through the SEPs. Therefore, as I elaborate in detail below, Japan showed anticipation in the field of CA oil and gas and adaptation in the mining of uranium and rare earths.

In 2007, the SEP was revised for the first time in three years, with the Japanese government attaching an increased importance to nuclear power through the National Nuclear Energy Plan. The National Nuclear Energy Plan placed an emphasis on CA, securing energy supplies, and helping further conservation alongside other measures. Furthermore, SEP 2007 set an ambitious aim of increasing the share of the so-called 'Hinomaru oil,' or oil produced and imported by Japanese companies (thus avoiding the aforementioned 'Asian premium'), from 15 percent to 40 percent by 2030. However, it was the Middle Eastern and not CA resources that were targeted for Japanese larger self-sufficiency. Two 2007 missions of Japanese top officials evidenced the assignment of niches between regions: the METI head Amari Akira visited CA to boost cooperation regarding uranium and REMs, while Prime Minister Abe Shinzō travelled to the Middle East to strengthen relations with oil producers.[49]

The 2010, 2012, and 2014 plan revisions reflected the change in Japan's nuclear policy before and after 3/11. The DPJ government initially continued the LDP's policy of nuclear renaissance, but changed the stance drastically following the negative consequences of the 2011 nuclear meltdown. After Abe had returned to power in 2012 and consolidated his position, he restored the plan's pro-nuclear orientation in 2014.

Uniquely high reliance on external factors was the main driver behind the adoption of both the Basic Act and the Strategic Energy Plans: Japan's exposure to the risks that are outside its control – political situations in exporting countries, fluctuations of global stock and currency exchanges – is much higher than in other Organisation for Economic Co-operation and Development (OECD) countries.[50] Dependency on the Middle East also represented a significant concern for the Japanese government and public, in particular following the 1990–1 Gulf War, the memory of which was fresh when oil-rich CA countries became independent in 1991.[51]

Japan's post-1973 diversification policy was also oriented towards importing environmentally friendly natural gas. While the level of Japanese reliance

154　*Energy Silk Road: anticipation and adaptation*

on natural gas imports has steadily oscillated around 97 percent, the imports of LNG have progressively increased more than fivefold over the past three decades.[52] Japanese infrastructure is mostly customised for the consumption of LNG only, thus leaving the country without a pipeline system, common in CA, China, and Russia.[53]

These diversification policies brought about tangible results in terms of reducing oil's share in the Japanese energy mix and its partial replacement by natural gas. Diversifying both the type of fuel and its origin brought CA into the geography of Japanese import sources, especially since newly independent CA states wanted a diversification of their own export routes away from Russia.

Central Asian hydrocarbons: a high-hanging fruit for Japan?

In this section, I examine Japan's involvement in CA oil and gas (O&G) development. I point out that the entry of Japanese corporations into Caspian hydrocarbon extraction in 1998–2003 was accomplished thanks to a political and economic window of opportunity that Japan seized, demonstrating anticipative adaptation. Namely, this entry was facilitated by low oil prices, a shift in regional geopolitics – a westward drift in the region – and by the temporary withdrawal of Chinese and South Korean competitors in 1998–2000. I further demonstrate that this early Japanese accomplishment largely 'removed' gas and, especially, oil as prospective agenda items from subsequent relationship development from 2003 onwards. Meanwhile, the increased availability of Russian O&G in the late 2000s, growing resource nationalism in CA, and the region's drift towards China, thanks to Beijing's support of pipeline projects, made CA hydrocarbons less attractive for Japan than previously.

The two questions currently remaining open for Japanese companies present in CA O&G are the daily functioning of the Kashagan oilfield (Kazakhstan) and the future of the TAPI (Turkmenistan–Afghanistan–Pakistan–India) gas pipeline project. I also argue that changes in Japanese corporate behaviour in the 2000s were conditioned by the materialisation of the Asia-oriented oil supply from Russia. The extent of government backing from Tokyo to Japanese companies was steady overall, but variable depending upon the case. Although some experts view these companies (INPEX and Itochu) as comparatively less risk-averse in their strategies than their Japanese peers, these companies' strategic choices of acting as part of an international consortia rather than independently remained constant and differentiated them from Chinese companies.

The O&G relations between Japan and CA can be traced to the early 1990s, predating the comparatively more recent nuclear cooperation. This period was marked by a strong optimism in Japan vis-à-vis CA hydrocarbons. The 1993 Energy White Paper highlighted the importance of natural gas for diversification and mentioned in this regard CA reserves and the adjacent Tarim Basin in China's Xinjiang.

Japan's main focus was Kazakhstan and Turkmenistan and, in line with its multi-lateralism and risk perceptions, it wanted to create several alternative export routes: via China, Turkey, Iran, Afghanistan, and Pakistan. The Japanese

Energy Silk Road: anticipation and adaptation   155

National Oil Company (JNOC, currently JOGMEC) initially expressed interest in Kazakhstan, Turkmenistan, and Uzbekistan. However, due to transportation hindrances and investment policies in Turkmenistan and Uzbekistan, the upstream interests later mostly focused on participation in the Caspian consortia in Azerbaijan and Kazakhstan.

Natural gas: trial and error in two unbuilt pipelines

Although CA is particularly rich in natural gas, this commodity gradually assumed a secondary place to oil in Japan's CA resource involvement. The reasons for the lower priority of gas were both international and domestic: irrelevance for Japanese gas import structure and transportation difficulties. As I mentioned, Japan imports gas mostly in LNG via tankers and does not have a developed pipeline system.

Furthermore, CA gas producers are landlocked and transfer their gas via pipelines, either westward to Russia or eastward to China. In addition, the main ex-Soviet source of natural gas for Japan was long expected to be Russia's Sakhalin-2 project, located much closer to Japan than Kazakhstan, Uzbekistan, or Turkmenistan, although all three countries have abundant gas reserves.[54]

Trans-China pipeline project: a non-event of Sino-Japanese cooperation

In the early 1990s, Mitsubishi and Chinese oil company CNPC visited Turkmenistan and proposed the idea of the so-called Energy Silk Route pipeline that would bring Turkmen and Kazakh gas to China's east coast and then to Japan and South Korea with an overall distance of nearly 9000 km.[55] However, the joint feasibility study carried out in 1993–8 yielded unfavourable results, forecasting low profitability. Furthermore, the Chinese domestic energy policy changed priorities, while the high cost estimate of $11 billion was seen to be insufficiently covered by then-low energy prices.[56] In addition, according to Chinese experts, Chinese companies were interested in the pipeline project, but their Japanese (and South Korean) partners were concerned about possible disruptions of supplies via China.[57] Although the project did not materialise, it provided two important inferences on Japanese foreign energy policy.

Firstly, in the 1990s, Japanese companies were in principle ready to engage in cooperation over CA gas with Chinese counterparts who were ready to reciprocate. Secondly, on balance, it was economic reasons and not so much the awareness of surging Sino-Japanese tensions that prevented the CA–China–Japan project from implementation. Nonetheless, factors external to Sino-Japanese relations also temporarily rendered the Chinese posture more cooperative at the time. While the 1997 Asian economic crisis weakened the positions of Chinese corporations, their actions were conditioned by changes in the Chinese domestic energy policy, while China's relations with CA were still a fresh start after the settlement of border disputes in 1996.

156 *Energy Silk Road: anticipation and adaptation*

About the same time in the mid-1990s, Itochu was considering joining the international pipeline consortium connecting CA gas to Turkey via Iran, but these intentions did not materialise due to a change in American Caspian policy in the second Clinton presidency. U.S. State Department officials, such as Strobe Talbott and Matthew Bryza, pushed for pipeline projects bypassing Arab countries and Iran, whilst the post-Soviet Caspian republics sought to reduce their dependency on Moscow.[58]

After the gas pipeline project from CA to Japan via China was scrapped, the only other option was equally risky: a southward gas pipeline via Afghanistan, also known as TAPI. Nevertheless, it was an international consortium with wider risk-sharing capacities, which implied higher feasibility for Japan.

TAPI and Japan: idealism, pragmatism or helping Washington?

TAPI's origins date back to the mid-1990s, when the idea of a pipeline project bringing Turkmen gas to the Pakistani seaports was first developed by Argentinian company Bridas and involved the Taliban movement by virtue of their de facto control of relevant Afghan provinces.[59] This subsection focuses on Japan's minor, but still illustrative role, which evolved from consortium participant to potential funding contributor via its Asian Development Bank (ADB) involvement. This involvement shows the oscillation between the mercantile and idealist facets of Japanese policy in CA.

After a short leading stint and negotiations with the Turkmen leader and the Afghan Taliban, Bridas was replaced by the U.S.-based Unocal Corporation, which in 1997 formed the Central Asia Gas Consortium (CentGas) involving Japanese and South Korean companies. Unocal's president called CentGas (future TAPI) the 'foundation' of the twenty-first century Silk Road.[60] In this consortium, Japan was represented by INPEX affiliated with the METI and Itochu (each with a 6.5 percent stake), less risk-averse than their Japanese peers because of state backing. This ambition was the first instance of INPEX and Itochu collaboration for CA hydrocarbons, which subsequently materialised twice on the opposite Caspian shore in Azerbaijan (see the section 'Oil: the Goldilocks Consensus reached?'). Russian control of Turkmenistan's pipelines at the time provided the case for an alternative route.

Russian-American relations were highly tense then, however, creating an adverse environment for the consortium. While initial American investment in Caspian energy in the early 1990s was to a large extent driven by Kazakhstan leveraging its nuclear disarmament, further years placed the geopolitics at the forefront. Washington's support of Caspian pipeline projects bypassing Russia in the second Clinton presidency resulted in a very critical reception of the TAPI project in Moscow, even though Gazprom was offered a 10 percent stake in the consortium.

Furthermore, Moscow's criticism of Washington's backing of Unocal's participation in a project was based on the involvement of the Taliban regime in Afghanistan. The Taliban was one of the few regimes to recognise Chechnya's independence and a major supplier of heroin to Russia. Therefore, a hypothetical Russian participation in CentGas would run the risk of endorsing a policy Moscow criticised, especially in the context of its pivot from the West to China and India favoured then by Foreign Minister Yevgeny Primakov (1996–8). Certain Russian experts on CA later claimed that the TAPI pipeline was ultimately a U.S. geopolitical project and went as far calling it a reason for the Taliban's 'creation' by Washington, so as to suggest that the Taliban would be used to ensure the pipeline's safety.[61] Thus, INPEX and Itochu's readiness to join CentGas highlighted their risk-taking attitude, given the important scale of their Russian operations.

During the second Clinton term, however, the White House's stance on the Taliban toughened. Rashid attributed this change to the violent criticism of the Taliban by the powerful women rights movement in the United States.[62] A change of policy resulted in Unocal's withdrawal from the pipeline consortium, which deprived the project of its principal investor. This is where the Asian Development Bank stepped in under Chino Tadao's leadership (1999–2005), pledging funding for the project and spurring speculations of Washington's continued involvement via its ADB clout.

Acting as the TAPI secretariat since 2002, the ADB played the role of coordinator and facilitator, provided its final approval in 2005, and reiterated its support at several instances afterwards, but the instability in Afghanistan and Pakistan delayed the implementation.[63] In 2013, the ADB was appointed transaction adviser by the pipeline participant countries. The bank's mandate included facilitation in setting up an international consortium headed by a company with relevant construction and operation experience in transnational pipelines.[64]

Why was TAPI supported by the ADB and its then-head Chino, who was sympathetic towards CA and known for his proactive support to the region? Firstly, in line with these characteristics examined in Chapter three and linked with Yasutomo's analysis of Japan's influence in the ADB, TAPI would contribute to CA's diversification and reduction of reliance on external players. Transit benefits from TAPI would also improve Afghanistan's economy. These policies were in line with the bank's Asia-centric development mandate and Chino's philosophy of improving CA's connectivity, best illustrated by CAREC. Similarly to the diversified lending pool of CAREC, ADB insisted it would only co-finance TAPI if the participant countries provided their own funding. This policy stimulated the self-reliance of the pipeline participants and their autonomy from external financial players. In addition, Chino's early support for TAPI was interpreted by some MOF-affiliated officials as bandwagoning from the standpoint of organisational behaviour. That is, the ADB's director intended to keep the bank involved in Turkmenistan where otherwise it had little going on in terms of operations and to have its voice heard in key Asian projects that would otherwise materialise independently.[65]

Secondly, although the dimension of Asian development is more strongly pronounced for the ADB, the element of Japan's self-interest should also not be discarded. However remote, TAPI would be the only option for bringing CA gas to southern ports and exporting it to maritime East Asia (including Japan) while also avoiding the Hormuz straits controlled by Iran.

158 *Energy Silk Road: anticipation and adaptation*

TAPI's political importance for Japan and Tokyo's support for it was highlighted in Foreign Minister Asō Tarō's 2006 speech 'Central Asia as a Corridor of Peace and Stability.'[66] Asō said that Japan approached the region from a 'broad-based perspective,' 'contributing a "safety valve" to the "magma" of the region' and emphasised the importance of TAPI as part of the southern route for CA:

> …just becoming possible for such a pipeline to be constructed securely represents in and of itself a target to be attained by the region as a whole. And when it finally becomes reality, the access that the pipeline provides will, along with the southern route to the sea, be for Central Asia a Corridor of Peace and Stability, exactly as the phrase implies.[67]

As I demonstrated in Chapter three, Asō was viewed by some MOF-affiliated officials as having a developmentalist ethos towards the region and close personal ties with regional elites, similarly to Chino. Nonetheless, Asō's take on TAPI can be contextualised within his geopolitical concept of the Arc of Freedom and Prosperity, drafted by key foreign policy advisors to Abe Shinzō. Although antagonism vis-à-vis China or Russia was denied by the authors of the Arc of Freedom and Prosperity concept, Japan's support for Washington-backed TAPI *volens nolens* put Tokyo at odds with Russian, Chinese, and Iranian interests.[68]

Moscow, as was already mentioned, did not want to loosen the grip on CA's gas routes and was generally supportive of Iran, seeing Pakistan as a U.S. ally since the Afghan war. Tehran promoted an alternative to TAPI: the Iran–Pakistan–India pipeline project intended to bring Iranian gas from the Southern Pars field to Pakistan. While a direct rival pipeline from Turkmenistan to China had not been finalised until 2009, Beijing was also long contemplating a China-bound extension of the Iran–Pakistan pipeline alongside the Karakorum highway and, therefore, did not favour TAPI.[69] In addition, Asō's speech coincided with the intensification of the Sino-Japanese rivalry over Iranian oil. Following the U.S. pressure to join the sanctions against Iran, Japan's INPEX relinquished its position as lead developer of Iran's Azadegan oilfield to China's CNPC, although Japan made the initial anchor investment of $2 billion in 2004.[70]

The governments from Asō (2008–9) until Abe II (2012–present), however, did not voice any particular position on TAPI, leaving Japan's ADB influence as the only indirect involvement. The availability of Russian gas improved in 2009 with the launch of the Japan-targeted Sakhalin LNG plant, overshadowing the risky prospects of Turkmen gas. Nevertheless, as 3/11 forced Japan to increase the share of gas in its energy mix and Turkmenistan sought further development of its gas industry in higher value-added segments, there was an increase in the visits of Turkmen officials to Japan in late 2012. This culminated in Turkmen President Berdymukhamedov's second Tokyo trip a year later when JOGMEC and Turkmengaz signed a memorandum of understanding (MoU).[71]

Ultimately, Turkmen state company TurkmenGaz was selected as the new consortium leader and lead investor of the TAPI pipeline in August 2015.[72] Unless the consortium structure undergoes further changes, this outcome indirectly suggests two interpretations of Tokyo's involvement.

Energy Silk Road: anticipation and adaptation   159

The assessment of Japan's involvement in TAPI points, firstly, to a mixture of pragmatism with an idealist and non-politicised facet of the Japan-dominated ADB, as the bank insisted on providing funds to the project subject to significant investment from the participant countries. This policy encouraged the principal responsibility of local stakeholders as opposed to reliance on international majors, as would have been the case with Unocal involved. In terms of international political environment, TurkmenGaz accession to lead role was likely conditioned by Turkmenistan's neutrality policy and a détente in Iran's relations with the West in 2013–15. The reduction of Russia's purchases of Turkmen gas in the mid-2010s left China the dominant buyer and increased Turkmenistan's need to diversify its customer base and TAPI's significance.

Secondly, the ADB's decreased involvement in TAPI reflected deteriorations in the project's political risk profile and low commercial viability. As of August 2019, only the Turkmen section was close to operational, the level of unrest and interethnic violence in Afghanistan remained high, while the U.S. security presence has been decreasing since 2015. Pakistan maintained a wait-and-see position on TAPI, while India started the liberalisation of its domestic gas market which may make gas pricing mechanisms less favourable for Turkmenistan. Moreover, according to some Russian experts, Qatar, India's dominant gas supplier, used its alleged funding of militant groups to destabilise Turkmenistan as a rival gas exporter.[73] In 2018, China indicated interest in TAPI, even though the project is viewed by Turkmenistan as a means of diversifying export routes.

Personalities matter: Abe visits Central Asia

In late 2015, events sparked a somewhat unexpected change in Japan's TAPI involvement by emphasising mercantilism and adjustment to global macroeconomic cycles as key drivers in Japan's resource diplomacy in CA under Abe, while Japan's alliance with Washington played a secondary role. Firstly, in early October, Japanese private companies (Mitsubishi, Chiyoda, Sojitz, and JGC) committed $10 billion to the development of Galkynysh, the giant Turkmen gas field expected to become TAPI's main source. Secondly, the Turkmen leg of Abe's visit to the region in late October was the most lucrative in terms of secured deals – $18 billion or two-thirds out of a total $27 billion splashed during the entire five-country tour. Thirdly, Abe's visit (22–28 October) took place two days before the identical trip of U.S. Secretary of State John Kerry (30 October–2 November) to all five republics – an unprecedented visit, as the last Secretary of State to accomplish a similar feat was James Baker in the early 1990s.

Gas, together with oil in Uzbekistan, became the main commodity highlight of Abe's 2015 trip. The absence of METI-affiliated INPEX among the Japanese entrants into Galkynysh and the particular risk-aversion of the Japanese private sector towards CA implied that the Japanese 'guarantor state' had given a signal of support prior to the entry in Galkynysh. In contrast to the past, the Japanese commercial benefits would come from the export of high value-added

160 *Energy Silk Road: anticipation and adaptation*

gas processing technology rather than from a participation in the risky pipeline. In other words, although Abe declared CA should remain open for various partners (that is, not only China), the Turkmen leg of his trip benefited the commercial interests of Japanese companies not less (or even more) than Japan's political interests.

Since Abe's visit was initially planned for August 2014, then postponed until August 2015, and finally took place in October 2015 for reasons unrelated to CA politics, Japanese private companies were likely to announce their Galkynysh entry either during Abe's visit or even well after it, rather than before, as was eventually the case.

This sequence is important for our understanding of Japan's motivation behind the sudden boost of its support for Turkmen gas. On the one hand, Japanese companies were evidently aware of the plummeting of oil (and linked gas) prices in late 2014–early 2015. The drop reopened an opportune period for O&G importers to acquire foreign assets, as it reduced the bargaining power of producing countries heavily reliant on income from hydrocarbons. In a certain way, that price context was comparable to the 1990s and 'resource internationalism' reclaiming its territory back from the 'resource nationalism' of the 2000s. The Japanese entry into Galkynysh and Abe's supportive visit in 2015 provide evidence for such cycle-driven thinking, albeit qualified by the focus on technology exports.

Although Abe's 2015 visit to CA coincided with that of John Kerry, there is insufficient evidence available to suggest that the trips were coordinated from the outset. A former Japanese diplomat denied any synchronisation.[74] As I already mentioned, Abe was contemplating the visit as early as June 2014. While the TAPI project benefited from U.S. support historically and can be interpreted as a way to reduce Turkmenistan's dependence on China- or Russia-bound gas supplies, Kerry's visit did not devote much attention to the pipeline, except praising the foreign policy diversification of CA – most likely, as an opposition to prospective Russian or Chinese hegemony in the region. Furthermore, Kerry's visit was likely to accompany the American decision to delay the withdrawal of its troops from Afghanistan beyond 2016.

Another notable coincidence in the context of Abe's gas deal with Turkmenistan was the softening of Russia's initially tough stance on TAPI. By 2015, Russian security forces (anti-drug task force) became interested in Russia's participation in the pipeline project and, most importantly, were considering the role of security provider for TAPI's Afghan section.[75] While the possibilities of verifying the level of Japanese awareness of this change in the Russian position are limited, given the topic's sensitivity, its plausibility can be indirectly supported by Tokyo's readiness for technical cooperation with Russia on the securitisation of Tajik-Afghan border. Abe's non-objection to the entry of Japanese companies in Galkynysh is another indicator, although it is qualified by the nature of this involvement, which is a technology export above all. Notwithstanding the success of Abe's 2015 trip, TAPI's future remains unclear due to the security situation in Afghanistan.

Energy Silk Road: anticipation and adaptation 161

The fate of two non-implemented gas pipelines (Trans-China and TAPI) strikes a contrast with Japan's success in Azeri and Kazakh oil projects and helps to understand why Japanese involvement in CA hydrocarbons was more successful in oil, as I examine in the next section.

Oil: the Goldilocks Consensus reached?

In this section, I demonstrate that the Japanese presence in the CA oil sector, including Azerbaijan as a Caspian country, was established early and can be considered an example of anticipative strategic adaptation. The Japanese private sector invested in CA oil assets because they had become available in the first place and were an unmissable opportunity to tackle the above-described 'Asian premium' problem. Nevertheless, these investments were made when the oil price was low, implying a cheaper cost, but also less attractive sales prospects. Therefore, Japanese rationale behind this investment was not only commercial, but also strategic, even if the anticipation of another oil price hike was purely speculative at the time.

As already mentioned, most Japanese oil supplies traditionally come either from the Middle East or from Southeast Asia. Just like natural gas, oil is abundant in CA: Kazakhstan occupies the twelfth place globally in terms of reserves with 30 billion barrels and the largest oilfield in the world, Kashagan, where Japan has a stake. Turkmenistan and Uzbekistan are 42nd and 44th, respectively, with about 600 million barrels each, according to U.S. Energy Information Administration (EIA).

The transportation problem is paramount: Japanese companies removed pipeline projects involving China from the agenda, while transporting CA hydrocarbons via the Middle East would have similar risks, Japan was already facing these in addition to the CA risk chain itself.

In the mid-1990s, however, these hindrances were ultimately outweighed by the attractiveness of cheap oil. Besides, Japanese companies and accompanying governmental agencies, such as JOGMEC or JBIC, were not only active in CA, but also agile in adjusting to the changing strategic environment.

Furthermore, in the 1990s, CA's multi-vectorism – its propensity to deliberately involve multiple external players in regional affairs – worked in Japan's favour for economic and political reasons. An opportune commercial context for Japanese companies in CA was created by the macroeconomic trends and U.S.– Russia geopolitical tectonics described above, as well as by a hiatus in the expansion of competitors from the People's Republic of China (PRC) and Republic of Korea (ROK). Affected by the 1997 Asian financial crisis, many Chinese and Korean companies temporarily curtailed their CA operations, unintentionally creating more space for Japanese presence.[76]

Uzbekistan was the first ever former Soviet state to obtain joint financing from the Japanese Export-Import Bank (later merged with JBIC) and Japan National Oil Corporation (JNOC), supported by the METI. In 1994, these Japanese institutions financed Nissho Iwai's (present-day Sojitz) participation alongside

162 *Energy Silk Road: anticipation and adaptation*

American MW Kellogg and Uzbekneftegaz in the development of Kokdumalak, the biggest O&G field in Uzbekistan, and a priority for Tashkent. Uzbekistan also became the first post-Soviet republic to obtain both Japanese and U.S. funding for the same project, underlining U.S.–Japanese cooperation of the time.[77]

Kazakhstan: the state helps

Whilst JBIC's and JICA's financing tied to Japanese business participation was one of the most affordable at the time, the oil price was very low, thus reducing CA's bargaining power and investment attractiveness.[78] This is when the Kazakh treatment of Japanese officials and business improved from the previously somewhat 'intractable' and less favourable than towards the West or Russia.[79] The intractability in question meant that in the early 1990s, the Japanese commercial proposals were either snubbed by the Kazakh officials or received a lukewarm response, which marked a difference with a smoother reception in Kyrgyzstan and Uzbekistan.[80] Kazakhstan's warmer attitude towards Japan occurred simultaneously with its increased foreign-policy autonomy as Russia's leverage decreased.

The INPEX 1998 entry in the international oil consortium developing the giant Kashagan field in the northern Caspian Sea would be less likely to materialise before or without Kazakhstan's shift toward greater autonomy in foreign policy.[81] INPEX joined the consortium after Kazakhstan's embassy was finally opened in Tokyo in 1996 and before Kazakhstani President Nursultan Nazarbayev paid his second ever visit to Tokyo in December 1999, signing a joint declaration on strategic partnership with Japan. His next trip to Japan would wait until 2008, the heyday of Japanese–Kazakhstani uranium cooperation.

In addition to the above-mentioned unmaterialised CentGas participation in Turkmenistan, INPEX involvement in CA ultimately included three Caspian-related projects: Kashagan, Azeri-Chirag-Gunashli (ACG) oilfields in Azerbaijan, and the Baku-Tbilisi-Ceyhan (BTC) pipeline. INPEX participation in Kashagan is the only case in its CA hydrocarbon enterprises when the company is not flanked with Itochu. This situation reflected the comparatively higher importance of public sector and government backing than in Azerbaijan, the subject of the next subsection.

Financially supported by JNOC (later JOGMEC), INPEX gained a 7.56 percent stake in the Kashagan project. Its entry was welcomed by the Kazakh state aiming to diversify its West/Russia-dominated investor portfolio in favour of East Asia, including Japan. Kazakhstan's benevolence was also stimulated by the prospects of connecting Kashagan to the BTC pipeline in the future.

Whilst Itochu's success in the Azeri section of the Caspian can be attributed to the company's private actions and state support from the JNOC and METI (extended to INPEX as well), INPEX participation in Kashagan is different in that it required a stronger interaction between governments.[82] According to an INPEX official, the METI's initial risk assessment was very conservative, but the MOFA's robust backup for the project seen as important for national interest ultimately persuaded the METI and triggered a go-ahead. Inside INPEX, the key reason to proceed with participation in Kashagan was the oilfield's vast resource

Energy Silk Road: anticipation and adaptation   163

endowment. In order to share the risk, JNOC invited JAPEX, another Japanese oil company, and Mitsubishi Corporation.[83]

Therefore, although it was commercial considerations – reducing Asian oil premiums and being an early comer – that were a primary driver behind the CA involvement of Japanese oil companies, the political dynamics of Russo-Kazakh relations and their repercussions on Kazakhstan's foreign policy were still part of the bigger picture.

In order to further sustain CA's energy security, Japan participated in several projects aimed at upgrading Kazakh infrastructure and introducing advanced energy technologies. In 2002, the Kazakh government and Japan's New Energy and Industrial Technology Development Organization signed a MoU concerning the modernisation of a thermal power plant and demonstrative implementation of energy saving technology. The project cost US$15 million and was related to the Kyoto protocol: as a payment, Kazakhstan would provide to Japan an annual carbon dioxide emission quota of 62,000 tonnes between 2008 and 2012.[84] Thus, Japanese interests in CA went beyond mere pragmatism of resource extraction.[85]

Japanese–Kazakh oil cooperation became part of a larger regional Japanese approach in July 2002, when Japan organised the 'Silk Road Energy Mission.' The mission had a slogan 'Look East!' and invited CA countries to a closer long-term energy cooperation. The level of Japanese delegation was unprecedented as it included high-ranking government officials from the JBIC, JICA, JETRO, JNOC, and major companies. The visit touched upon Japanese participation in the development of Kazakh resources, Japan's contribution towards energy saving and developing alternative power sources in CA, the modernisation of dilapidated Soviet-era infrastructure, and further Japanese investment. The delegation visited Kazakhstan, Uzbekistan, Azerbaijan, and Turkmenistan.[86]

The incident at Fukushima-1 nuclear power plant (NPP) in March 2011 and Kazakhstani private sector development spurred an additional interest from the Japanese government in the Kashagan project and the Kazakhstani petrochemical industry. Firstly, the post-Fukushima nuclear shutdown in Japan required an increased supply of alternative energy sources, including oil, while the instability in the Middle East heightened due to the 2011 Arab Spring. Secondly, the European Bank of Reconstruction and Development (EBRD) held its annual meeting in Astana in May 2011, thus attracting the attention of visiting Japanese finance officials to Kazakhstan and to the local private sector, the most successful in CA. The EBRD's focus on the private sector and growing operations in Kazakhstan implied an improving business climate for direct Japanese corporate involvement with reduced need for state support.[87] The focus on petrochemicals, in parallel, symbolised a more mature cooperation with higher added value going beyond resource extraction.

Azerbaijan: private or public interest?

Among all Caspian countries, Japanese presence is most tangible in Azerbaijan. Although Azerbaijan is not a part of CA *sensu stricto* by virtue of its location in South Caucasus, it is often included in the region by multi-national companies.

164   *Energy Silk Road: anticipation and adaptation*

Azerbaijan is also regularly featured in ideational geopolitical constructs such as 'New Silk Road,' 'Greater Middle East,' or 'Eurasian Balkans' due to the country's vast hydrocarbon resources, geographical situation, and Turco-Persian cultural legacy shared with CA. Azerbaijan was the earliest Silk Road country to start actively attracting foreign investments into its oilfields.

Japanese O&G companies have been operating in Azerbaijan since 1994. According to Russian experts, the Japanese capital played one of the key roles in the development of Caspian Sea shelf projects.[88] In 2002–3, Japanese corporations had finalised their participation in the consortium operating on the highly promising ACG field in the Azeri section of the Caspian Sea.[89] In order to facilitate the transportation of oil from the ACG abroad, the consortium's companies, including Itochu and INPEX, also supported the construction of the BTC pipeline.

While the ACG participation of Japanese companies was supported by JOGMEC's equity financing and loan guarantees, the pipeline construction was financed by the EBRD. Although the BTC construction was in line with the EBRD, the E.U., and the U.S.'s strategy at the time to diversify the export routes of former Soviet republics to reduce their reliance on Russia, there was also a Japan–CA factor at play. As indicated previously, Japanese officials have overseen the EBRD's CA and Caucasus operations since 1991.[90]

Besides, Japan has consistently backed Japanese corporate projects in Azerbaijan by providing financial assistance to the country, not always linked directly to these projects, but connected politically.[91]

According to JOGMEC experts, Japanese participation in the BTC was more business-related than geopolitical, while most decisions were made by the private sector itself. It was initially driven by Itochu and then supported by the JNOC. INPEX joined later, also with the JNOC support, in order to replace Lukoil, a Russian private oil company. On the Azerbaijani side, the project was driven by the state oil company SOCAR, which had the carte blanche from Baku.[92] With hindsight, the turn of the century proved the right time for Japan to seize Azerbaijani opportunities, as oil prices soared following the Afghanistan and Iraq invasions of 2002–3.

Turkmenistan: up the value chain

Until Abe's second premiership and his landmark 2015 visit, Japan's relationship with Turkmenistan had been much less developed than with other CA states, despite INPEX and Itochu participation in CentGas in 1997. The Japanese embassy in Turkmenistan was established only in 2005 – the latest of all Japanese embassies in CA. Most Turkmen oil fields have been developed by Western companies. While gas cooperation remains subject to the TAPI project development, Japanese companies have been promoting higher value-added projects revamping Turkmen energy infrastructure. These culminated in Abe's second premiership, which accounts for ten out of 14 total visits by Japanese officials to Turkmenistan as of November 2019.[93]

Energy Silk Road: anticipation and adaptation   165

Due to geographical remoteness and unmitigated transportation risks, direct import of CA hydrocarbons to Japan has not yet materialised. However, one solution that Japan considered was a swap mechanism. According to this scheme, Japanese companies would produce oil in the Caspian Sea and then swap it with their non-Japanese counterparts for oil produced in another part of the world, for instance, in Southeast Asia, that would be later shipped to Japan.[94]

Caspian oil is of lower quality than its Middle Eastern equivalent, which results in a minor discount. Nevertheless, for Japan, the facilitation of the transportation of Caspian oil to Japanese swap partners – via the BTC – is still commercially beneficial considering the purchase of oil shipped to Japan as a result of the swap.[95] Thus, the involvement of Japanese corporations and governmental agencies in the BTC pipeline served Japanese interests and evidenced a comprehensive strategic approach.

Personalities matter in Russia: the Khodorkovsky affair as game-changer

In a broader context, however, the significance of Caspian oil for Japan was lowered by drastic changes in producer-consumer configuration in another part of Eurasia, namely, in Russia and China. The importance of energy security for Asia increased after the 1997 crisis and 9/11, which was acknowledged at the 2001 Asia-Pacific Economic Cooperation (APEC) summit in Shanghai, where the participants adopted a dedicated resolution.[96] In this context, following a reinvigorated Chinese strategic push for CA O&G, Beijing considered CA a hydrocarbon supplier alternative to Russia, since, unlike Russia, CA states allowed Chinese equity participation. Meanwhile, Moscow intended to make its hydrocarbons available for East Asia, but was reluctant to concede on Chinese equity entry and price, which stalled negotiations with Beijing.[97]

Meanwhile, the competition between China and Japan for East Asia-bound Russian pipelines became fiercer and involved a notable personal factor.[98] From the 1990s and until his arrest in October 2003, the oil magnate Mikhail Khodorkovsky was a strong proponent of a pipeline bound to China only (Angarsk-Daqing). By contrast, the Kremlin's preferred pipeline option allowed access to all of its Northeast Asian neighbours, rather than the PRC alone. From 2003 onwards, the Koizumi government supported and prioritised the Kremlin's pipeline project, which ultimately materialised as the Eastern Siberia-Pacific Ocean (ESPO). The option of the pipeline leading to the Russian port of Nakhodka was mutually beneficial for Russia and Japan. Russia would diversify its consumer pool in East Asia, since the Daqing option implied a Chinese monopsony, whereas Japan would diversify its oil supply sources, crucial in the context of instability in the Middle East, aggravated in 2002–3.

Nonetheless, for a long time, the feasibility of a China-only route was high, due to Khodorkovsky's considerable domestic and international clout as the head of the then-largest Russian oil company Yukos. Until Khodorkovsky's trial in late 2003, the Chinese state oil company CNPC was considering him as its priority

166   *Energy Silk Road: anticipation and adaptation*

partner and the two struck a jumbo $150 billion deal in May 2003.[99] Were the Angarsk-Daqing project to materialise, it would have likely broken the Russian state's monopoly on oil export. Khodorkovsky's imprisonment resulted in the abandonment of the Angarsk-Daqing project and indirectly accelerated the combined ESPO project, which included Japan and, later, China.[100] The availability of Siberian hydrocarbons on top of the Sakhalin ones further lowered the importance of CA O&G as a procurement source for Japan.[101] From the standpoint of counterfactual history, an alternative outcome of the Khodorkovsky affair might have resulted in heightened Japanese interest toward CA projects.

As this section demonstrated, Japanese companies successfully and, to an extent, opportunistically, set up O&G operations in CA, always acting within an international consortium, rather than autonomously. The Japanese government support was robust, although stronger in Kazakhstan than in Azerbaijan. In all Caspian consortia, including the mothballed CentGas in Turkmenistan, the lead Japanese participant was the METI-affiliated INPEX, accompanied only by Itochu in Azerbaijan and Turkmenistan.

Despite the opportunism of Japanese companies, their achievements allowed Japan to secure an important source of hydrocarbons just on time: when the era of cheap oil ended in the early 2000s following an increased instability in the Middle East. The Japanese achievements were, however, qualified by the transportation difficulties, repeated lags in the development of Kashagan, and by the increase of Russia's profile as East Asia's oil supplier following the Khodorkovsky affair.

Consequently, Japanese oil companies in CA mostly focused on downstream operations with higher added value, such as petrochemicals, construction, and revamp of oil refineries in Pavlodar and Atyrau (Kazakhstan), Ferghana and Bukhara (Uzbekistan), and Turkmenbashi and Seydin (Turkmenistan). This focus was in line with Japan's competitive advantages in international trade – quality infrastructure, technology, and advanced manufacturing. As Japanese companies secured their niches in CA oil by the early 2000s, the focus of Japan–CA resource diplomacy shifted to uranium and rare earths, examined in the next section.

Part II. Uranium and rare earths: adaptation over anticipation

Uranium and rare earths: from nuclear renaissance to
Fukushima and beyond

Japan's uranium cooperation with CA was similar to the oil and gas sector in that individuals also played an important role, but differed from it in the greater impact made by the state and by its direct linkage with Japan's Strategic Energy Plans. At least three out of four visits of the METI heads to CA were focused on uranium and REMs rather than O&G.

In this chapter, I demonstrate how the 'nuclear renaissance' in Japan, underpinned by high oil prices in the 2000s, created a context for fostering uranium and REM cooperation between Japan and CA. This section focuses on two related commodities that are abundant in CA, but have a different purpose. While

Energy Silk Road: anticipation and adaptation 167

uranium serves as fuel for Japanese nuclear power generation, REMs are used in Japanese electronics manufacturing and other high-tech industries. A principal source of REMs, however, is uranium ore, which explains the double importance of uranium mining. I argue that Japan's venture into CA uranium was a mix of adaptation and anticipation, affected at times by the policies of Russia and China.

In order to understand the role of CA uranium for Japan in the late 2000s, I start by outlining the Japanese domestic policy of nuclear revival until the 2011 Fukushima incident, explaining uranium's centrality. Then I proceed to Kazakhstan, whose particularly rich uranium endowment made it a natural partner for Japan. After I examine the Japanese–Kazakh nuclear cooperation from the political perspective and demonstrate Japan's sustained proactivity, I proceed to the analysis of Japan's REM cooperation with the region as an alternative to China.

2000–11: 'nuclear renaissance' in Japan and the 2007 uranium bubble

The 1973 oil crisis was the earliest stimulus pushing Japan to seriously consider nuclear power as a major element of its energy diversification strategy. The role of nuclear energy has considerably risen since then, while that of oil has decreased.[102] Japan was one of the key countries where the so-called 'nuclear renaissance' (*genshiryoku runessansu*) was taking place throughout the 2000s.

The 'nuclear renaissance' emerged in response to soaring fossil fuel prices and growing environmental concern over greenhouse gas emissions. It was also a result of improved safety technologies that made public and governmental attitudes towards the nuclear industry less risk-averse than in the aftermath of the Three Mile Island and Chernobyl nuclear accidents.

While being a part of the 2000s global commodity boom, the peak of the nuclear revival was marked by a separate international 'uranium bubble' in 2005–8, with a particular hike in 2007. Uranium prices were reportedly spurred by a 2006 flooding incident at Cigar Lake Mine in Canada, and the resurgence of Indian and Chinese prospects in nuclear power generation.[103] The relevance of the flooding and bubble was direct for Japan, as Japanese companies TEPCO and Idemitsu had shares in the flooded Canadian mine.[104] This change in prices was likely to spur Japanese interest in uranium cooperation with CA at the time, which had just started to materialise.

The pressure for Japan to enhance the nuclear share in its energy mix thus became double: to diversify from high oil prices and to catch up with rising uranium prices, given the country's growing reliance on this mineral. Japan demonstrated an adaptive strategy when it forged a partnership with CA countries as uranium exporters in 2006, after the uranium bubble started forming in 2005. However, this strategy later proved anticipative, as the price for uranium grew exponentially in late 2006 following the flooding in Canada.

In 2001, nuclear energy accounted for 20 percent of Japan's general energy needs and for 35 percent of the power generation. In 2011, these indicators were expected to reach 23 percent and 41 percent, respectively, making Japan more

168 *Energy Silk Road: anticipation and adaptation*

dependent on nuclear energy than the United States, but less than Germany or the United Kingdom. After the DPJ government suspended most reactors following 3/11, the share of the nuclear power generation was reduced to 1.6 percent.[105] However, the consequences of 3/11 did not lead to the scrapping of Japanese uranium projects in CA, only postponing expansion and indicating a potential future resurgence of Japan's nuclear power generation.

Until 3/11, Japan operated 54 reactors (second place globally): 53 light-water reactors and one fast-breeder reactor at Monju. At the time, the government was planning to construct another 14 reactors by 2018.[106] After the accident, all reactors were suspended by the DPJ government, and their future remained a subject of public debate. By contrast, during his second term, Prime Minister Abe backed the idea of restarting nuclear power generation as part of the economy revival.[107]

Japan's rationale for uranium

Prior to the Fukushima disaster, the Japanese government's nuclear policy focused on four aspects: the exploitation of light-water reactors, the creation of a closed nuclear fuel cycle, reprocessing plutonium, and usage of mixed oxide uranium-plutonium fuel.

Through creating a nuclear fuel cycle and reprocessing plutonium, Japan intended to increase its energy security in terms of sourcing nuclear fuel for power plants. This strategy would enable Japan in the long run to regulate the production and stockpiling of plutonium autonomously. Nevertheless, the plutonium reprocessing capacity remained limited and faced domestic controversies and opposition. This shifted Japan's nuclear procurement primary focus towards uranium, where Kazakhstan's positions were particularly strong in terms of reserves and output.

The reserves have been constantly revised through audits in subsequent years, slightly reducing Kazakhstan's share of reserves to 12 percent, still keeping the country at second place globally behind Australia. Kazakhstan's importance is also highlighted by the status of top global producer reached in 2011.[108]

The global structure of uranium demand has consistently favoured new mining developments. The supply-demand gap was covered through existing resources stockpiled in the 1990s due to then-low prices and through secondary uranium sources, such as the impoverishment of highly enriched uranium extracted from warheads. Since 2007, however, the share of production in covering global demand has been increasing at the expense of stockpiles and reached 85 percent in 2014.[109]

According to forecasts, the secondary sources of uranium production were expected to be reduced, while the demand from China, India, and other countries continued surging, therefore a worldwide increase in output was seen as necessary to meet uranium needs. Given the strategic importance of nuclear energy and uranium supply demonstrated above, Japan sought to obtain mining rights in uranium-endowed countries and develop mines.

Kazakhstan and Uzbekistan together have more than 20 percent of global uranium reserves, while Tajik and Kyrgyz prospective reserves are significant as well. In this context, the Japanese government's 2006 National Nuclear Energy

Plan designated CA as a region of strategic importance for securing access to uranium and called for an increase in stable supply through the participation of Japanese companies in uranium mine development, in addition to relying on contractually based imports.[110]

The governmental support in this regard was pronounced and shared between the MOFA and METI. Nuclear energy was designated by the MOFA as one of the key issues of foreign policy, whilst this was not the case for other types of power. The METI's Agency for Natural Resources and Energy promoted and supported the participation of Japanese private corporations in uranium mining activities. The agency aimed at strengthening 'the systems to support overseas exploration projects of private Japanese companies through Japan Oil, Gas, and Metals National Corporation (JOGMEC)' that was created in 2004 via the merger of former Japan National Oil Corporation and Metals National Corporation.[111] The other governmental arm of support to corporations was the JBIC, which provided financing. Several Japanese corporations were involved in Kazakh uranium prospects, the quickest of which materialised for Sumitomo Corporation, another risk-taker known for a relatively aggressive commercial approach in CA, similarly to INPEX and Itochu in oil and gas.

Kazakhstan: Japan's primary partner in uranium and REM

Four of five CA states (except Turkmenistan) have potential in uranium ores and REMs. Kazakhstan is the leader; Uzbekistan is the second largest regional producer, while high security risks marginalise the attractiveness of Kyrgyzstan's and Tajikistan's uranium and REM.[112] Thus, Kazakhstan and Uzbekistan are the main uranium providers in CA and, accordingly, Japan's long-time regional partners, albeit with different motivation: while Kazakhstan is more attractive commercially, Uzbekistan is important geopolitically.

Nuclear cooperation between Japan and Kazakhstan dates back to the post-Soviet denuclearisation of the early 1990s. In the immediate aftermath of the USSR collapse, the United States, Japan, and other parties to the international non-proliferation treaty had to deal with transferring Soviet nuclear arsenals from three newly independent states of Belarus, Kazakhstan, and Ukraine to Russia. Japan then contributed to the Kazakhstani facet of the operation, emphasising its own non-proliferation policy, anti-nuclear sentiment, and grievous experience with nuclear arms. The relationship built in these early independence days between Japanese and Kazakhstani officials became a foundation of subsequent uranium cooperation in the mid-2000s. By 2016, uranium represented the bulk of Japanese cumulative $4.5 billion investment in Kazakhstan.[113]

Japanese–Kazakh joint ventures in uranium

In line with government strategy, the JBIC provided support to Japanese corporations for acquiring interests and participating in uranium mine development in Kazakhstan. The main successful uranium projects involving several Japanese

170 *Energy Silk Road: anticipation and adaptation*

companies were the Appak and Baiken-U joint ventures (JVs) established in 2005–6 with Kazatomprom, the leading corporation of the Kazakhstani nuclear industry.[114]

The combined total of uranium products that the Japanese companies can acquire through these JVs was expected to fulfil up to 40 percent of Japan's annual uranium demand. This cooperation was equally beneficial for Kazakhstan, since it could participate in a technological transfer with Japan, accessing the latest technologies and increasing the added value of domestic industrial output.

While the JBIC's role as government financing arm was fundamental, the projects in question also benefited from increased support at the top of the METI, which shouldered together with the MOFA the responsibility of resource diplomacy in uranium-rich countries. Furthermore, according to Japanese corporate officers, the METI's cohesion with the MOFA improved by the late 2000s, benefiting the heads of the METI, as closer ties between these key ministries enhanced their interoperability and knowledge-sharing.[115]

Personalities matter in Japan: Amari emphasises uranium and geopolitics

Visits by the heads of the METI to CA were rare and started relatively late, counting only four to date, of which three took place during Abe's premierships: Amari Akira in 2007, the DPJ's Edano Yukio in 2012, Motegi Toshimitsu in 2014, and Sekō Hiroshige in 2017. In most instances, the visit coincided with the revisions of the Strategic Energy Plans in respective years. Amari's 2007 'harbinger' trip demonstrated the influence of individual politicians on the overall foreign policy, as can be inferred from related diplomatic correspondence. Kazakhstan was only ever mentioned twice in the White Papers on Nuclear Energy of the Japan Atomic Energy Commission – in 2006, during Amari's tenure at the METI (2006–8), and in 2008, after his successful visit:

> Accordingly, in order to secure stable uranium resources, Japan is actively conducting diplomacy on resources, such as agreement of bilateral cooperation with Kazakhstan, which has the second-largest uranium reserves in the world.[116]

In terms of affiliation with policy constituencies, pragmatism is what all the METI heads visiting CA shared. Both Amari and Motegi are considered conservative neorevisionists.[117] Within the DPJ, Edano was viewed as a pragmatic centrist leaning to realism without clear-cut ideological preferences for foreign affairs, despite instances of criticism of Chinese policies.[118] While Amari and Motegi covered both Kazakhstan and Uzbekistan, Edano only visited the former, reflecting its above-described commercial priority in the region.

It was during Amari's METI leadership that Japanese government bodies and companies reached several agreements with Kazatomprom, including the aforementioned Appak and Baiken JVs. Once again, thanks to the agreements,

Energy Silk Road: anticipation and adaptation 171

Japan secured the rights to ultimately satisfy up to 40 percent of its total uranium demand, while previously Kazakhstan's share was about 1–2 percent. Given the fact that almost two-thirds of the remaining Japanese demand had been covered by Australia and Canada with roughly equal shares, the addition of a relatively politically stable Kazakhstan to the structure of main suppliers served well the objective of diversification and can certainly be viewed as Amari's achievement.[119]

Unlike many METI heads, Amari lasted two years under the first Abe cabinet and succeeding Fukuda cabinet, which can partially explain his ability to engage with CA for a comparatively long period of time. By contrast, his successor and colleague in the second Abe cabinet (2012–present), Motegi Toshimitsu, visited CA in August 2014, at the end of his tenure and before the government reshuffling in October 2014.

In their coverage of Amari's visit, U.S. diplomatic cables directly highlighted uranium as Japan's 'key focus in Kazakhstan':

[MOFA's CA and Caucasus Division Director] Hideki Uyama also labelled Amari's visit 'a great success,' adding that it was an important follow-up to Koizumi's trip in August 2006, during which Japan and Kazakhstan agreed to enhance bilateral cooperation in the peaceful use of nuclear energy, including joint development of uranium mines.... In addition, the Kazakhs are very interested in acquiring Japanese technology to improve their uranium processing industry and hope that in the future Japanese companies will assist them in developing a nuclear power plant. This latest visit involved a package of items involving uranium-for-technology trade, Uyama said.[120]

Amari-era METI official Toyoda addressed the problem of long-term continuity, adding that 'Central Asia is of great interest both to the U.S. and Japan' and called for Washington and Tokyo 'to cooperate in the region':

Toyoda contended that Amari's trip met METI's goal of increasing cooperation between Japan and the countries he visited, but the proof of that assertion will lie in the follow-up. The interest Japan has shown in Central Asia's uranium and its willingness to trade its technology for the mineral contrasts with an apparent lack of interest in trading nuclear know-how for oil and natural gas in the Middle East and indicates a far greater caution toward the Middle East than toward Central Asia.[121]

The importance of Amari as Abe's confidante in resource diplomacy was subsequently reconfirmed, when in 2015, during the second Abe premiership, the official visited Azerbaijan. Serving as minister of economic revitalisation and not head of the METI, Amari negotiated the further promotion of energy projects and synchronised his trip with Abe's tour of five CA states.[122]

The uranium relationship between Japan and Kazakhstan should not be reduced, however, to Tokyo's official actions and its alliance with the United States despite their importance as drivers. It is also possible that the Japanese officials in the

172   *Energy Silk Road: anticipation and adaptation*

cables were telling their American counterparts what the latter wanted to hear. Kazakhstan's own proactivity in Japanese–Kazakh cooperation received a major impetus during the visit of Kazakhstan's President Nazarbayev to Japan in June 2008. This was the third journey to Tokyo for the Kazakhstani leader overall, but the first in nine years, as the last time he visited Japan was in 1999 following INPEX's entry into the Kashagan project, described earlier. The 2008 trip resulted in the creation of a working group for cooperation on the Kyoto protocol, several energy memorandums signed between Kazakhstan and Japanese firms, as well as opening direct air correspondence between Japan and Kazakhstan.[123]

Japan–Kazakhstani rapprochement and its relation to Japan's diplomatic alignment with the United States did not turn out detrimental to Moscow's uranium cooperation with Tokyo and Astana. The examination of this matter points to Japanese pragmatism in its relationship with Russia, Moscow's 'zero-sum-game' perception of the U.S.–Japanese actions in CA at the time, and the influence of Kazakhstani domestic politics on its relationship with Japan.

Personalities matter in Kazakhstan: the Dzhakishev affair as game-changer

In the late 2000s, Tokyo's nuclear cooperation has been progressing not only with Kazakhstan, but also with Russia. This trend challenged the geopolitical conventional wisdoms of the time, according to which Russia, China, and CA states perceived the United States as set on regime change in Eurasia, while Japan was reinforcing its ties with the European Union and the United States through value-oriented diplomacy under Koizumi and Abe.

The potential for trilateral Russo-Kazakh–Japanese cooperation was noteworthy for two reasons. Firstly, its possibility per se demonstrated Japan's ability to maintain a pragmatic posture vis-à-vis Russia despite the Russian–American animosity at the time (2005–8). Secondly, the so-called Dzhakishev affair in Kazakhstan reaffirmed the importance of personal factors and the prevalence of mercantile pragmatism over other considerations in the Japanese uranium strategy.

How did this trilateral cooperation come about? Russia boasted the largest uranium enrichment capacity in the world, but the insufficiency of its own uranium resources for export growth raised the importance of supplies from Kazakhstan and other uranium-rich countries of the region, such as Uzbekistan, Mongolia, and, in the long run, Tajikistan. Kazakhstan, in turn, lacked enrichment capacities that would be satisfactory for Japanese needs, but boasted huge reserves. As for Japan, it covered only 10 percent of its enrichment needs and the maximum level this figure was expected to reach was 30 percent. Therefore, Japan was bound to rely on outsourcing enrichment services overseas. This industry, however, is highly concentrated: over 90 percent of global enrichment facilities were controlled by only four companies – Russian Techsnabexport (a subsidiary of state-run nuclear holding Rosatom), American USEC, French AREVA, and URENCO – a British-Dutch-German conglomerate.

This uneven resource distribution stressed the rationale for Japan's uranium partnership with Russia and CA. Russian nuclear company Techsnabexport has

Energy Silk Road: anticipation and adaptation   173

been operating in Japan since 1991. In 1999, the company started to ship enriched uranium to Japan. After Techsnabexport established its permanent representative office in Tokyo in 2005, it was announced that Russian uranium shipments are expected to reach up to 30 percent of Japan's enrichment needs.[124]

Japan was ready to have all Kazakh uranium enriched in Russia in return for its further transportation through the Russian Far East in order to optimise the supply route; previously, Japan-bound uranium was exported through St. Petersburg, Russia, to the United States, Canada, and France for enrichment, reaching Japan only afterwards.[125]

This Japanese position required both strong pragmatism and a detachment from international politics at the initial stage of Russo-Japanese–Kazakh nuclear cooperation, as Russia's relations with the European Union and the United States significantly soured during Putin's second term (2004–8). As a reminder, Japan under Koizumi and Abe was strengthening the CAJ framework and its value-oriented diplomacy in line with the European Union and the United States, helping to deflect Russian and Chinese influence in CA.

In addition, in 2006 Abe accused Russia of resource nationalism referring to the increase of Gazprom's stake in the Sakhalin O&G projects at the expense of other consortium members, including Mitsui and Mitsubishi. Despite this adverse environment, the Russo-Japanese–Kazakh nuclear cooperation still progressed. Apart from Japanese pragmatism, another driver on the Kazakh–Japanese side was Kazatomprom's top manager Mukhtar Dzhakishev.

Before his trial in 2009 and sentencing in 2010, the media hailed Dzhakishev as a turnaround legend after he had developed competitive and modern uranium production at Kazatomprom from 1998 to 2009. Accomplishing this feat required a considerable change in effort from the giant Soviet-style organisation with a strong potential, but an outdated corporate environment and nearly bankrupt finances.[126] As part of his plan to make Kazatomprom a globally recognised player, Dzhakishev proactively built close ties with core international peers, including Japanese Toshiba, Marubeni, and Sumitomo. This push was successful: besides the aforementioned joint ventures, in 2007, Toshiba even sold to Kazatomprom a 10 percent stake in its American asset Westinghouse, thus forging a strategic partnership with the Kazakh national nuclear company. Both firms have declared they would share the burden of fighting global warming through the development of nuclear energy. Thanks to this transaction, the minority shareholding of Kazatomprom increased Toshiba's clout in the global scale of the industry, while Kazatomprom gained access to new markets.

Nevertheless, somewhat similarly to the Khodorkovsky's case described earlier, the rise of Dzhakishev was stymied by domestic Kazakhstani politics and arguably Russia's intention to preserve its dominant weight. Domestically, Dzhakishev spoiled his relationship with President Nazarbayev by his ties to exiled tycoon Mukhtar Ablyazov, a critic of the regime, and to Nazarbayev's son-in-law Rakhat Aliev, who fell out of the president's favour. According to media reports, formal charges pressed by Kazakhstan's National Security Committee were the following:

174   *Energy Silk Road: anticipation and adaptation*

> [Dzhakishev] and seven other former top officials at Kazatomprom 'alleg-
> edly disposed of the uranium companies' shares for the benefit of a num-
> ber of offshore companies. The specific project in question involves several
> Japanese companies and Canada's Uranium One. When the news broke about
> the arrests, Uranium One's stock dropped briefly by almost 40 percent.[127]

Internationally, Dzhakishev's problems have been attributed to his cooperation
with Toshiba, which was ultimately aimed at Kazatomprom's greater independence from Moscow. Whilst Japanese experts considered possible trilateral
nuclear cooperation between Astana, Tokyo, and Moscow, the last of these
was against Kazatomprom's rise and reportedly contributed to the demise of
Dzhakishev, later replaced by a Russia-backed successor Vladimir Shkolnik.[128]

According to Dzhakishev, Russia wanted to cooperate with Japan separately to
the exclusion of Kazakhstan, but initially, the Japanese refused and demanded to
have Kazakhstan included. The executive was scheduled to discuss trilateral cooperation with the Russian representatives on the day of his eventual arrest.[129] Sumitomo
officials confirmed that although initially Japan was interested in dealing directly
with Kazakhstan without Russia as third party, Kazatomprom's Japanese strategy
has not significantly changed after Dzhakishev's replacement by Shkolnik.[130]

Domestic politics arguably weighed more than foreign ones in Dzhakishev's
case, as his replacement Shkolnik was above all a close ally of President
Nazarbayev, as was evidenced by his later appointment to the helm of the energy
ministry.[131] The affair thus highlighted the link between the control of external
ties in CA and the power base of domestic constituencies. As I argued in previous chapters, this link exposes the foreign relations of CA countries to internal
factional rivalry. The intensity of such rivalries is likely to acutely intensify once
the succession struggle kicks off after more than two decades of one-man rule in
Kazakhstan, Tajikistan, and Uzbekistan.

Despite previous support to the reduction of CA's reliance on larger powers,
Japan, in this case, did not exercise any particular counteraction, pragmatically
accepting the ultimate strengthening of Moscow's weight in the trilateral relationship. The attribution of this attitude to Japan's traditionally limited diplomatic means is qualified by Japan's solid position in global nuclear alliances.
According to Kazakh interviewees, Japanese companies in question were
unhappy with Dzhakishev's fall, but decided not to compromise their Russian
business ties. A more pragmatic and marginally less antagonistic stance on CA's
ties with Russia and China can also be explained by changes in Tokyo's foreign
policy following the DPJ's advent to power under Hatoyama Yukio.

Uzbekistan: politics over economics or public over private?

While not a top global uranium producer like Kazakhstan, Uzbekistan nonetheless occupies an important place internationally. At the time of early Japanese
engagement in the mid-2000s, its reserves accounted for 2.4 percent of the global
amount and ranked 7th globally.[132] Although in later years the rank of its reserves

Energy Silk Road: anticipation and adaptation   175

was revised to 13th position, Uzbekistan's weight is still significant due to its 7th position in global uranium production with a 4 percent share as of 2015.[133] In Uzbekistan, Japan has intensified its efforts in gaining access to uranium resources since the mid-2000s and benefited from Tashkent's rapprochement with the West in 2009. Uzbekistan also showcased the Japanese government's intent to support strategically important countries, despite their stagnant commercial attractiveness for the private sector.

The 2006 Koizumi visit and the 2007 Amari mission turned out fruitful, providing a lasting impetus reaching well into subsequent DPJ premierships. In September 2006, an intergovernmental agreement between Japan and Uzbekistan was signed for the financing of Uzbek uranium development, while in October 2007, Itochu agreed with Navoi Mining and Metallurgy Combinat, the main national uranium miner, to develop a technology to mine and mill the black shale. A 50/50 JV was envisaged to operate on the Rudnoye deposit.[134]

In mid-2008, Mitsui, the long-established Japanese flagship in Uzbekistan, signed a basic agreement with the Uzbek government's State Geology and Mineral Resources Committee (Goscomgeo). The agreement established a JV for geological exploration for the development of black-shale uranium resources at the Zapadno-Kokpatasskaya (West Kokpatas) mine, northwest of Navoi city. Navoi is Uzbekistan's centre for uranium and precious metal mining, especially gold. It hosts one of the main Uzbekistani foreign investment projects – the Navoi free industrial economic zone, supported by Japan and hosting several Japanese companies.

Yet despite Mitsui's long history in Uzbekistan and its high representative status among other Japanese corporations, the late 2000s also marked the stagnation of its commercial success, which included the uranium projects. In particular, the company was only let into uranium development in black shale and denied access into more promising uranium sandstones, even though sandstones are richer in uranium and more abundant in Uzbekistan than black shale.[135] The reasons for this insufficiently favourable treatment were sensitive from Mitsui's standpoint and hard to obtain from either the Japanese or Uzbek side. One plausible hypothetical explanation could lie in the overall deterioration of the Uzbekistani business environment in the late 2000s–early 2010s that affected private investors lacking strong home state support.[136] Gradually, the Uzbek uranium authorities changed their interaction from Mitsui in favour of the state-run JOGMEC, reflecting a preference for public sector involvement.

In mid-2009, and further to a 2007 MoU, Goscomgeo and JOGMEC signed an agreement for uranium and REMs exploration in the Navoi region, focused on leach sandstone deposits and black shale, with a view to a Japanese company taking a 50 percent interest in any resources identified and developing them.

Nevertheless, Itochu, a private company with a reportedly less risk-averse corporate culture than Mitsui, was also allowed exploration rights in Uzbek leach sandstone deposits in the late 2000s. Since Itochu is a private company without government affiliation, Mitsui's misfortunes in Uzbekistan cannot be explained only by the insufficient support from home government and may also be linked with risk perceptions.

176 *Energy Silk Road: anticipation and adaptation*

Japanese cooperation with Uzbekistan received a new impetus at the highest level during the official visit of President Islam Karimov to Japan in February 2011. Tokyo secured a 10-year long uranium supply contract in return for investment in the development of Uzbek uranium ore extraction. In parallel, a new ¥18 billion Official Development Assistance (ODA) loan was approved for a railroad construction project, which would inter alia contribute to the transportation of non-military goods to Afghanistan.

Uzbekistan's proactivity towards Japan was largely motivated by a new iteration of President Karimov's rapprochement with the United States, which started in 2009.[137] Japan followed suit and revitalized its economic ties with Tashkent around the same time, although it had started laying the relevant groundwork in 2008 already.

In January 2009, during Russian President Medvedev's visit to Tashkent, President Karimov declined the prospect of Uzbekistan joining the Russian–Kazakh uranium enrichment centre in Russia. According to Russian expert Azhdar Kurtov, Karimov's decision was made in the anticipation of an unfolding revamp of Japanese–Uzbekistani business ties.[138] Indeed, in November 2009, Tokyo announced plans to substantially boost economic cooperation with Tashkent and invest in Uzbekistani uranium and O&G projects. This meant different perspectives, however, for the private and public sector.

The deterioration in the Uzbekistani business climate was noted by JETRO representatives and Mitsui officials who were not satisfied with the level of uranium development, as they were only allowed into less attractive black shale deposits. By 2013, Mitsui's presence reportedly decreased even further.[139]

By contrast, the state-run JOGMEC had been expanding its Uzbek uranium operations, signing another agreement with Goscomgeo in 2011, and finally receiving a license to explore for uranium in more attractive sandstone deposits – achieving something Mitsui could not. The contrast between JOGMEC's success and Mitsui's misfortune in Uzbekistan confirmed the Uzbek government's inclination for state-to-state interaction rather than state-to-private.

Nevertheless, the visits of DPJ-era Japanese officials to Uzbekistan were scarce – only three in total – and not resource-oriented. In 2010, Finance Minister Kan visited the country for the ADB Annual Meeting and Foreign Minister Okada attended the Central Asia plus Japan meeting. Deputy Foreign Minister Yamane came in May 2012 for political consultations, whereas the METI head Edano visited only Kazakhstan. As at the time of manuscript submission, Abe's return to power struck a contrast with the DPJ, both in terms of a clearer resource diplomacy facet and numbers of trips to CA – 10 to Uzbekistan, 14 to Kazakhstan, and 10 to Turkmenistan.

Watershed: the DPJ and 3/11 switch focus to rare earths

As I mentioned in Chapter two, the DPJ came to power following a political landslide not only in Japan, but also in world politics. The Obama administration announced its 'pivot to Asia,' while also pursuing a reset in Russian-American

Energy Silk Road: anticipation and adaptation 177

relations with President Medvedev. Russia's financial power in CA was eroding due to the 2008 financial crisis and growing Chinese economic inroads in the region, which raised suspicions in Moscow. Meanwhile, two important energy projects were finalised in 2009, reinforcing Russo-Japanese economic ties. Firstly, the Japan-oriented Sakhalin LNG plant was launched in February 2009 and featured the presence of then-Prime Minister Asō at the inauguration.[140] Secondly, the ESPO pipeline, bringing Russian oil to Northeast Asia, was commissioned in December 2009. These projects marked the increased availability of oil and gas in Japan's proximity, thus decreasing the role of distant CA hydrocarbons and prioritising that of CA uranium and REM.

DPJ's policy before 3/11

During the DPJ rule, Japan saw considerable progress in its trilateral Eurasian relationship with Russia and Kazakhstan in natural resources. Firstly, in March 2010, Japan and Kazakhstan signed an agreement on the peaceful use of nuclear power, setting a cornerstone for deeper uranium cooperation. Secondly, later that month, a Japanese–Kazakh joint venture for the exploration of REMs (Summit Atom Rare Earth Company, or SARECO) was created by the Kazakh atomic company Kazatomprom (51 percent) and Sumitomo (49 percent). Thirdly, despite brief Russo-Japanese tensions over President Medvedev's visit to the Kuriles, both countries finalised their bilateral agreement on nuclear cooperation – in January 2011 Medvedev signed the relevant law.

Soon after SARECO's creation, Japan reconfirmed its interest towards CA when, in August 2010, Foreign Minister Okada Katsuya visited the key Japanese resource partners in the region – Kazakhstan and Uzbekistan. As I mentioned earlier, it was the first visit by the MOFA's head to the region since Kawaguchi Yoriko's 2004 trip.

SARECO's establishment quickly proved an important step to reduce Japanese dependence on the Chinese supply of REMs, sourced from uranium ores and crucial for further development of Japanese electronics, semiconductor, and automotive industries. China dominates the world market of REMs with over 90 percent of the world's output and about 57 percent of global resources.[141] This position can be reflected by Deng Xiaoping's 1992 phrase 'The Middle East has its oil, China has rare earths.' Since 2009, China has started to impose export quotas on REMs and did not hesitate to use this trading advantage as political leverage: following the boat incident near the disputed Senkaku Islands in September 2010, China was reported by Japanese companies to have halted its supply of REMs to Japan. Although Beijing promptly denied the imposition of the ban, both Japan and the United States voiced their concern over Chinese resource nationalism in this field and threatened to undertake a World Trade Organisation (WTO) action against China.[142] SARECO's setup was therefore timely and can be viewed as anticipative adaptation – had it occurred after the Senkaku incident, Japan's commercial position would have been weaker.

3/11 and subsequent Japanese visits

The shift in the Japanese government's energy policy triggered by 3/11 is well accounted in existing scholarship.[143] Namely, according to Samuels, major changes took place not so much at the level of national strategy, as at the level of local government and in the energy mix itself after Japan had stepped up its natural gas consumption, compensating for the suspended NPPs.[144] This change in energy mix favoured closer ties with Russia as a favourably located gas producer, but suggested a low profile for Japanese uranium expansion plans in CA, especially given the topic's public sensitivity for the METI.

Edano Yukio's visit to Kazakhstan took place during Noda's premiership one year after Fukushima and was the second time in five years a METI head went to CA after the ambitious Amari mission in 2007. Edano skipped Uzbekistan and visited only Kazakhstan, sticking to business-first ties. The visit materials reflected the METI's post-3/11 sensitivity to all things nuclear, as they showed no mention of uranium, highlighting the shifted focus to REMs and 'technical cooperation for treating radioactive wastes by private companies and Kazakhstan's National Nuclear Center'.[145]

In 2012, energy expert Yu Ka-ho confirmed the continuation of the ascending trend in Japanese–Kazakh cooperation in the field of REMs:

> Japan expects that the Kazakhstan REM venture will undergo rapid growth and they plan to increase the total production to 15,000 tons per year by 2015, this would account for *10 percent of the current entire world supply*. In 2012, the Japanese and Kazakh governments signed an agreement to jointly develop REM critical to electronic applications, weaving a path for partnership between Japanese and Kazakh companies. In this joint development, a REM plant will be built in Stepnogorsk – located in northern Kazakhstan – to produce dysprosium which is crucial to the production of the motors of electric and hybrid vehicles. The agreement ensures Japan will receive 55 tons of dysprosium per year from the plant. This number makes *up around 10 percent of the Japanese annual demand* for dysprosium and is expected to increase yearly.[146]

Although Abe did not rush to CA immediately himself, delaying his trip until October 2015, he boosted resource diplomacy by dispatching the METI head Motegi Toshimitsu to the region. Motegi was only the third ever METI head to visit CA and the second ever to visit Uzbekistan, since Amari's 2007 trip, also organised during Abe's first premiership.

In Kazakhstan, Motegi marked a shift to higher value-added projects in the Japan–Kazakhstan 'energy entente.' He signed a memorandum on nuclear power cooperation with Energy Minister Shkolnik and confirmed future cooperation in resources and energy, which was expected to include oil and the construction of an NPP.[147] The Uzbekistan leg of the trip was somewhat more symbolic and declaratory as it yielded less tangible results, apart from traditional business

Energy Silk Road: anticipation and adaptation 179

committee meetings and agreement on information exchange. Motegi met with three key officials who have been traditional 'gatekeepers' and local counterparts for Japan since 1992 (see Chapter three): President Karimov, Finance Minister Azimov, and Foreign Economic Relations Minister Ganiyev.

During the nuclear renaissance of the 2000s, the Japanese government's outlook for the global nuclear industry's future suggested not only a uranium mining expansion, but also an export strategy for Japanese companies with nuclear technology. Namely, it stated that national companies engaged in construction and operation of NPPs would only survive if they developed strategic alliances with counterparts in other countries.[148] Until 2008, major competition was taking place between four such groups, three of which had a Japanese participant: Japanese–American Toshiba-Westinghouse, French–Japanese Areva-Mitsubishi Heavy Industries, American–Japanese GE Nuclear Energy-Hitachi, and Russian Atomenergoprom.[149] As was mentioned earlier, Toshiba developed an alliance with Westinghouse in which it controlled over 67 percent of shares and subsequently sold a 10 percent stake in Westinghouse to Kazatomprom, indicating how the policy of alliances may be extended to Russia and CA.

A similar cooperation process took place in relations between Russian Rosatom and Toshiba, as well as other Japanese nuclear businesses. In 2007, Russia's former Federal Agency on Atomic Energy was transformed into state corporation Rosatom.[150] Rosatom's vertical integration model, offering both reactor construction and access to primary resources, appeared particularly attractive to Toshiba and resulted in stronger cooperation with Rosatom.

In March 2008, Toshiba and Rosatom's subsidiary Atomenergoprom signed a framework agreement on the peaceful use of nuclear energy. Since Toshiba considered French Areva its main competitor in global NPP construction, it needed a strategic partnership guaranteeing access to uranium enrichment, which made Rosatom attractive. Rosatom, in turn, was interested in Japanese cutting-edge nuclear technologies and in the commercial strength such an alliance would provide. Toshiba's activities in Kazakhstan and Russia were endorsed by the Japanese government.[151] The Russo-Japanese bilateral agreement signed by President Medvedev in January 2011 aimed at strengthening this cooperation.

Although 3/11 suspended the Japanese nuclear industry, Abe's reconsideration of nuclear power may boost Russo-Japanese and Japanese–Kazakh nuclear cooperation further.[152] At the same time, strong anti-nuclear sentiment in Kazakhstan and competition with Rosatom will serve as major impediments for Japan in this field. During his October 2015 visit, Abe robustly lobbied Japan's bid for the upcoming Kazakhstani tender, justifying Japanese technological superiority by the post-3/11 experience. While President Nazarbayev said the tender would be decided by 2017–18, the Kazakh government had not yet made the decision about the construction of the NPP as of August 2019, leaving it unclear which country will be contracted for building it and whether Japan would be in the bidding mix at all. Meanwhile in Uzbekistan, however, the government decided in

180 *Energy Silk Road: anticipation and adaptation*

2018 to contract Russia's Rosatom for the construction of the first Uzbek NPP in Navoi, despite the long history of cooperation with Japanese companies in the field of uranium mining.

Conclusion

Japanese economic involvement in CA represents a multi-faceted and complex picture. The instances of intensification of Japan's oil diplomacy in 1997–2003 and, in particular, uranium diplomacy in 2007–11 turned out to be a timely anticipative adaptation – rather than oscillating between anticipation and adaptation – to the changing global strategic and macroeconomic environment. This is proven by the contextualisation of Japan's resource diplomacy within the evolution of the world energy markets after 9/11 and the Iraq invasion, the implementation of a diversification strategy in the Japanese energy mix and supply structure, nuclear renaissance, as well as such adverse external factors as China's politicisation of its rare earths dominance. Japan's economic efforts made CA resources more accessible not only to Japan, but also to the global market, easing the price pressure which, in turn, benefits Japan as importer.

While the 'energy entente' with Kazakhstan confirmed the mercantile facet of the Japanese resource diplomacy, this aspect was less pronounced in the case of commercially less attractive, but geopolitically important Uzbekistan. Japan's direct (via Asō Tarō in 2006) and indirect (via the ADB in 2002–15) backing of the TAPI pipeline proved both Tokyo's idealism with a minor element of self-interest in direct energy procurement vis-à-vis Turkmenistan and Tokyo's alignment in Washington beyond the traditional alliance scope. The ADB's support for TAPI was parallel to its support for CAREC, engaging multiple parties including China and implying a strong idealist drive in favour of developing CA regionalism per se. Meanwhile, Japan's oil success in Azerbaijan was more a result of the private sector's opportunistic and anticipative proactivity rather than intergovernmental interaction, although it benefited from the geopolitically favourable context of Washington's increased support to the diversification of export routes for Caspian oil.

Japanese resource diplomacy in CA demonstrated the particular importance of individuals and specific policy constituencies: the ADP presidents such as Chino Tadao or Kuroda Haruhiko in their support of TAPI within the bank, conservative 'neorevisionists' such as Abe, his cabinet members Asō Tarō and Amari Akira, and businessmen such as Mikhail Khodorkovsky and Mukhtar Dzhakishev, whose actions and litigations had game-changing effects. The METI's initially insufficient expertise on CA and internal staffing constraints in the 2000s rendered the role of individuals and groups particularly visible, without, however, depriving Japanese companies from the METI's support whenever it was necessary.

The personal factor has been demonstrated again by the resource diplomacy of Abe's second cabinet and, most imminently, by his visit to CA in October 2015, which focused on resources and infrastructure. This time, however, Abe's approach was markedly different from earlier value-oriented diplomacy: mute

Energy Silk Road: anticipation and adaptation 181

on values and not antagonistic to Russia. Moscow, financially weakened by the post-2014 sanctions and 2015 drop in oil prices, became 'outfinanced' by China in CA, while the side effects of sanctions targeting Russia hit the region hard as well. Tokyo's increased financial support to the region is thus likely to indirectly and unintentionally benefit the Kremlin by preventing CA from financial over-reliance on China and from social destabilisation.

Japanese risk-taking and state-affiliated companies (INPEX, JOGMEC, Itochu, and Sumitomo) demonstrated assertiveness by improving the availability of CA resources for the global market and Japanese procurement security. Other Japanese companies, such as Mitsui, shifted from risk-taking in the 1990s to risk-aversion in the late 2000s, accordingly changing their CA strategies from expansion to conservation.

The beginning of military operations in Iraq and Afghanistan in the early 2000s spurred oil prices in the already tangible commodity boom and precondi-tioned the imperative of Japan's energy mix diversification in both sources of fuel and their supply geography. The diversification of power sources implied a shift from hydrocarbons to the increase of nuclear power share, while the improve-ment of supply structure necessitated a deeper cooperation with Russia and post-Soviet states, as well as with other regions outside the turbulent Middle East.

The combination of cyclical market changes, the role of individuals alongside the historic evolution of corporate achievements, and risk perceptions accounted altogether for the stabilisation of resource cooperation between Japan and CA in the late 2000s.

Abe's return to power in 2012 and the subsequent surge in proactive resource diplomacy provided a strong contrast to the previous governments, except Noda. Yet, despite the structural limits of Japanese domestic politics and the DPJ's lack of foreign policy experience, this party also managed to influence Japanese diplomacy in CA by continuing the cooperation in uranium and rare earths min-ing. Furthermore, according to some observers, Abe managed to achieve domes-tically what the DPJ attempted, but failed: wrest control from bureaucrats to elected politicians.[153] If the iron triangles of the past – the LDP, big business, and bureaucrats – remain substituted by the cabinet, big business, individual advisers, and the METI representatives, the nature of Japan as guarantor state is subject to change too, just like its involvement in CA natural resources.

Notes

1 'Abe seiken susumu shigen gaikō, Mekisiko to ha sekiyu gasu kaihatsu' [Abe gov-ernment's advancing resource diplomacy – oil and gas development with Mexico]. *Nikkei Shimbun*, 26 July 2014.

2 Some parts of this chapter rely on a study I have published earlier: Nikolay Murashkin, 'Japan and Central Asia: Do Diplomacy and Business Go Hand-in-Hand?' Etudes de l'Ifri, Ifri, April 2019.

3 Kent E. Calder, 'Japan's Energy Angst: Asia's Changing Energy Prospects and The View from Tokyo,' *Presentation at the National Bureau of Asian Research*, Seattle. WA. 28 September 2004; *MOFA Diplomatic Bluebooks* (Tokyo, 2007–2014).

182 *Energy Silk Road: anticipation and adaptation*

4 Joseph Ferguson, *Japanese-Russian Relations 1907–2007* (London: Routledge, 2008), 148; Hisane Masaki, 'Japan Joins the Energy Race in Central Asia,' *The Asia-Pacific Journal*, 4, no. 8 (August 2006): 1–4, http://apjjf.org/-Hisane-MASAKI/2179/article.pdf (Accessed 1 July 2015); and Zaven Avagyan, 'Novaya bol'shaya igra: komu dostanetsya Tsentral'naya Aziya?' [New Great Game: who will Centra Asia go to?], *Rex*, http://www.iarex.ru/articles/52022.html (Accessed 17 October 2015).

5 Interview with Councillor Nakayama Kyōko, former Ambassador to Uzbekistan and Tajikistan (1999–2002), March 2012.

6 Thierry Hommel, *Stratégies des firmes industrielles et contestation sociale* [Strategies of industrial firms and social contestation] (Versailles: Editions Quae, 2004), 39–50.

7 Interview with Ito Shōichi, energy expert, Institute of Energy Economics Japan, April 2012.

8 Richard Samuels, *The Business of the Japanese State: Energy Markets in Comparative and Historical Perspective* (Ithaca, NY: Cornell University Press, 1987), 260.

9 The aforementioned Samuels' 1987 monograph provides an authoritative and comprehensive account of Cold War-era Japanese energy policy, as well as of the scholarship on the matter.

10 Kenneth Pyle, *Japan Rising: The Resurgence of Japanese Power and Purpose* (New York: Public Affairs, 2007).

11 Richard Samuels, *Japan Rising: The Resurgence of Japanese Power and Purpose* (New York: Public Affairs, 2007). Kōsaka Masataka, '*Kōsaka Masataka gaikō hyōronshū: Nihon no shinro to rekishi no kyōkun*' [Diplomacy review by Kōsaka Masataka: Japan's course and lessons of history] (Tokyo, Japan: Chūō Kōron, 1996), 118–24.

12 John McCormick, *The European Union: Politics and Policies* (Boulder, CO: Westview Press, 1999).

13 Kent Calder, *The New Continentalism: Energy and Twenty-First-Century Eurasian Geopolitics* (New Haven, CT: Yale University Press, 2011).

14 Interview with former Japanese diplomat, January 2012 and Interview with former Mitsubishi official, April 2012.

15 Interview with Nakayama Kyōko, March 2012.

16 In 2006, Foreign Minister Asō pointed out three challenges for Japanese energy security. The first was geopolitical uncertainty in the Middle East, as regional conflicts and U.S. sanctions on Iran increased the price of hydrocarbon exports and challenged their security. Secondly, Asō referred to 'resource nationalism' that resurged in the producing countries due to high prices and could endanger the security of supply by preventing upstream investment. Transportation risks alongside the supply chain, especially in the Straits of Malacca, Singapore, and Hormuz, were named as the third challenge. Consequently, Asō suggested three solutions: close dialogue with the Middle Eastern countries which Japan has been maintaining regularly, free and open markets to counter 'resource nationalism,' and better international cooperation through various mechanisms, including, inter alia, the international energy agency. To an extent, all three of Asō's concerns related to CA. MOFA: Speech by Asō Tarō, Minister for Foreign Affairs on the Occasion of the Japan Institute of International Affairs Seminar. 'Arc of Freedom and Prosperity: Japan's Expanding Diplomatic Horizons,' http://www.mofa.go.jp/announce/fm/aso/speech0611.html (Accessed 25 April 2010).

17 Raquel Shaoul, 'Japan's Evolving Nuclear Energy Policy and the Possibility of Japan-China Nuclear Energy Cooperation,' in *Shaping the EU-China Knowledge Exchange on Energy Security* (Book-Series International Comparative Social Studies, Amsterdam, the Netherlands: Brill Academic Publishers), 2010 and Jacob Townsend and Amy King, 'Sino-Japanese Competition for Central Asian Energy: China's Game to Win,' *China and Eurasia Forum Quarterly*, 5, no. 4 (2007), 23–45.

18 Shimoyashiro Manabu, 'Nikkan no kyōdō sensen ni shōsan ari' [Success in cooperation on the Japanese-Korean collaboration frontline], *JETRO Sensā*, April 2010.

19 For more details on the phenomenon of the 2000s commodity boom, consult Thomas Helbling, Valerie Mercer-Blackman, and Kevin Cheng, 'Commodities boom: Riding a wave,' *Finance & Development*, March 2008.

20 Ogawa Yoshiki, 'Asia Oil Price Analysis 1: Middle Eastern Crude for Asian Market Priced at Comparatively Higher Levels and Switchover of Marker Crude Inevitable to Gain Market's Confidence,' The Institute of Energy Economics, Japan, September 2002, http://eneken.ieej.or.jp/en/data/pdf/133.pdf (Accessed 11 July 2015) and Moon Young-Seok, Lee Dal-Sok, *Asian Premium of Crude Oil*, presentation, International Workshop on 'Cooperative Measures in Northeast Asian Petroleum Sector,' 6 September 2003, Seoul, Korea.

21 Ogawa Yoshiki, *Asian Premium of Crude Oil and Importance on Preparation of Oil Market in Northeast Asia*, presentation, The 26th IAEE International Conference 7 June 2003, Prague, http://www.iaee.org/documents/prague/p03ogawa.pdf (Accessed 11 July 2015).

22 Shale revolution refers to a drastic increase in the usage of shale gas: in the United States, it rose from less than 1 percent of domestic gas production in 2000 to over 20 percent by 2010. For more information, refer to Paul Stevens, 'The "Shale Gas Revolution:" Developments and Changes,' *Chatham House Energy, Environment and Resources Briefing Paper*, August 2012.

23 Koyama Ken, 'An Analysis on Asian Premium for LNG Price,' *A Japanese Perspective on the International Energy Landscape* (79), Special Bulletin, The Institute of Energy Economics, Japan, 9 March 2012.

24 Interview with INPEX official, March 2012.

25 Bakhtiyor Islamov, 'Transformation and Development of Central Asian States in 1991–1997: A comparative analysis of outcomes,' in *Facets of Transformation of the Northeast Asian Countries*, eds. Yoshida Tadashi and Oka Hiroki, Center for Northeast Asian Studies (Sendai, Japan: Tohoku University, 1998), 71.

26 Given that post-Soviet markets share many consumer characteristics, it was easier, for instance, for Japanese carmakers to locate manufacturing in Russia and export it to CA rather than do the opposite. In 2010, this situation changed after the establishment of the Customs Union of Belarus, Russia, and Kazakhstan. It was not until 2013 that Toyota launched its first car production line in Kazakhstan.

27 For instance, the first joint venture with Japanese capital was established in Tajikistan as late as 2011. Motomura Kazuko, 'Tekushaya situatsiya v Tadjikistane' [Current situation in Tajikistan], *Mesyachnyi bulleten' obsledovaniya situatsii v Rossii i NNG* [Monthly bulletin of monitoring the situation in Russia and the NIS], December 2011, 2.

28 MOFA: 'Central Asia as a Corridor of Peace and Stability,' speech by Asō Tarō, Japan National Press Club, 1 June 2006, http://www.mofa.go.jp/region/europe/speech0606.html (Accessed 19 April 2016).

29 Diplomatic cable, U.S. Ashgabat embassy, Turkmenistan: Japan Hopes To Regain Momentum In Commercial Relations, Identifier: 09ASHGABAT1286, Created: 9 October 2009 12:58:00.

30 Interview with Alisher Shaykhov, former ambassador of Uzbekistan to Japan and chairman of Chamber of Commerce and Industry of Uzbekistan, June 2011.

31 Interview with Mitsui officials, June 2011.

32 Murashkin, 'Japan and Central Asia,' 31.

33 Interview with a Kazakhstani former employee of Toyota Motor, May 2011.

34 Private communication with Paik Keun-Wook, September 2014.

35 Interviews with the officials of INPEX, JOGMEC, Idemitsu, January 2011.

184 *Energy Silk Road: anticipation and adaptation*

36 INPEX Corporation is a Japanese oil company, whose largest shareholder is the METI. Itochu is one of the largest Japanese trading houses (*sōgō shōsha*) with interests across various industries. Its approach to CA was identified by the respondents as relatively less risk-averse than that of its Japanese peers.

37 'Consortium offers up to $20bn for Turkmenistan gas project,' *Nikkei Asian Review*, 29 February 2016, http://asia.nikkei.com/Business/Companies/Consortium-offers-up-to-20bn-for-Turkmenistan-gas-project (Accessed 29 February 2016).

38 As I mentioned in Chapter four, Sumitomo demonstrated a great degree of initiative as early as 1998, proposing an integrated regional management system of transport infrastructure. Oksana Reznikova, 'Tsentral'naya Aziya i Aziatsko-Tihookeanskiy region' [Central Asia and the Asia-Pacific region], *Mirovaya ekonomika i mezhdunarodnye otnosheniya*, 4, 1999.

39 Interview with Sumitomo official, June 2011.

40 Interview with Itochu official, April 2012.

41 Ibid.

42 By contrast, the rationale for picking Tashkent as the JETRO's office location reflected Japanese bureaucratic logic. As a METI affiliate, the JETRO would be considered a competitor to the MOFA and would therefore refrain from establishing an office in a city where the MOFA or its affiliates were already established in order to avoid inter-agency competition. For this reason, the JETRO proceeded with settling in the capital of Uzbekistan, rather than Kazakhstani then-capital Almaty – which was already the location of the Japanese embassy and later, a JOGMEC office – or the Azerbaijani capital Baku, which at the time already hosted a JNOC office. Ashgabat, the Turkmen capital, was also considered, but the risks of President Niyazov's authoritarian rule weighed against this option. Interview with JETRO official, April 2012.

43 Interview with a former MOF official, April 2012.

44 Interview with INPEX official, March 2012.

45 Interview with Itochu official, April 2012.

46 For instance, over 2006–16, the exchange rate has fluctuated between 75 \/$ and 124 \/$, according to the xe.com currency converter. The second Abe administration sought to depress the value of the yen to improve the competitiveness of Japanese exports, but benefited from the 2014 and 2015 oil price slumps.

47 Basic Act on Energy Policy, http://www.iea.org/policiesandmeasures/pams/japan/name-24372-en.php (Accessed 20 June 2015).

48 Raquel Shaoul, 'Japan's Evolving Nuclear Energy Policy and the Possibility of Japan-China Nuclear Energy Cooperation,' in *Shaping the EU-China Knowledge Exchange on Energy Security* (Book-Series International Comparative Social Studies-Brill Academic Publishers), 2010.

49 MOFA: Prime Minister Shinzō Abe's Visit to the Middle East Countries, May 2007, http://www.mofa.go.jp/region/middle_e/pmv0704/ (Accessed 19 July 2015).

50 Viktor Pavlyatenko, 'Energeticheskaya bezopasnost' Yaponii i factor rossiysko-yaponskih otnosheniy' [Japan's energy security and the factor of Russo-Japanese relations], in *Energeticheskiye izmereniya mezhdunarodnykh otnosheniy i bezopasnosti v Vostochnoy Azii* [Energy dimensions of international relations and security in East Asia]. (Moscow: MGIMO, 2007), 781. Despite a steady decrease of Japanese dependence on oil (44 percent), its general level is still high, compared with the United States (40 percent), United Kingdom (36 percent), Germany (41 percent), or France (36 percent).

51 Besides, the oil share in Japanese energy consumption per capita is second-largest among the OECD countries after the United States. 'Japan International energy data and analysis,' U.S. Energy Information Administration, 30 January 2015, https://www.eia.gov/beta/international/analysis_includes/countries_long/Japan/japan.pdf (Accessed 15 July 2015).

Energy Silk Road: anticipation and adaptation 185

52 From 16.9 million tonnes in 1980 to 58.47 million tonnes in 2003 and 85.05 million tonnes in 2015. 'Japan LNG imports down 14.1 pct in January,' *LNG World News*, 18 February 2016, http://www.lngworldnews.com/japan-lng-imports-down-14-1-pct-in-january/ (Accessed 3 March 2016).
53 Over the past decade, Japan has also diversified its geography of LNG imports. While in the mid-2000s the bulk of LNG imports came from Southeast Asian countries, in 2013 Indonesia, Malaysia, and Brunei's combined share amounted to 30 percent, 29 percent from the Middle East (Oman, Qatar, UAE), 21 percent from Australia, 10 percent from Russia, the rest being covered by other countries. Japan International Energy Data and Analysis; Pavlyatenko, 'Energeticheskaya bezopasnost' Yaponii i factor rossiysko-yaponskih otnosheniy,' 783.
54 In 1987, Mitsui started the negotiations with the Soviet government on what would become the first Russian LNG plant on Sakhalin in 2009. Source: Mitsui's website https://www.mitsui.com/ru/en/company/message/index.html (Accessed 1 June 2016).
55 Paik Keun-Wook. 'Russian and Central Asian Gas Supply to Asia.' in *Natural Gas in Asia: The Challenges of Growth in China, India, Japan and Korea*, ed. Jonathan Stern (Oxford: Oxford Institute for Energy Studies, 2008).
56 Miyamoto Akira, *Natural Gas in Central Asia: Industries, Markets and Export Options of Kazakhstan, Turkmenistan and Uzbekistan* (London: The Royal Institute of International Affairs, 1997). Quoted from Paik, *Sino-Russian Oil and Gas Cooperation: The Reality and Implications* (Oxford: Oxford University Press, 2012).
57 Interview with Chinese energy expert, Chinese Institute for Contemporary International Relations, October 2014.
58 Interview with a JOGMEC official, March 2012.
59 For detailed historical account, see Ahmed Rashid, *Taliban: Islam, Oil and the New Great Game in Central Asia* (London: I.B. Tauris & Co. Ltd, 2000).
60 'Consortium formed to build Central Asia gas pipeline,' Chevron's press release, 27 October 1997, https://www.chevron.com/stories/consortium-formed-to-build-central-asia-gas-pipeline-turkmenistanafghanistanpakistan (Accessed 17 June 2015).
61 'Aleksandr Knyazev: Afganistan i Sredniy Vostok na poroge "voiny vseh protiv vseh"' [Alexander Knyazev: Afghanistan and the Middle East at the brink of war of everyone against everyone], *Regnum*, 29 November 2013, http://www.regnum.ru/news/polit/1738545.html (Accessed 7 July 2015).
62 Rashid, *Taliban: Islam, Oil and the New Great*, 174.
63 'Historic Agreements Bring Long-Awaited TAPI Pipeline Closer to Reality,' ADB website, 23 May 2012; Keun-Wook Paik, *Sino-Russian Oil and Gas Cooperation: The Reality and Implications* (Oxford: Oxford University Press, 2012), 324–6.
64 John C.K. Daly, 'Will the TAPI Pipeline Ever Be Built?' *Silk Road Reporters*, http://www.silkroadreporters.com/2014/07/24/willtapipipelineeverbuilt/ (Accessed 8 July 2015).
65 Interview with an EBRD official, October 2013.
66 MOFA: Speech by Asō Tarō, at the Japan National Press Club, 'Central Asia as a Corridor of Peace and Stability,' http://www.mofa.go.jp/region/europe/speech0606.html (Accessed 8 July 2015).
67 Ibid.
68 Interview with Yachi Shōtarō, professor at Waseda University, April 2012.
69 'Aleksandr Knyazev: Afganistan i Sredniy Vostok na poroge "voiny vseh protiv vseh",' 2013.
70 Hisane Masaki, 'Japan Joins the Energy Race in Central Asia,' *The Asia-Pacific Journal* 4, no. 8 (August 2006), http://apjjf.org/-Hisane-MASAKI/2179/article.pdf (Accessed 1 July 2015).
71 MOFA. *Japan-Turkmenistan Relations* (Basic Data, 2014), http://www.mofa.go.jp/region/europe/turkmenistan/data.html (Accessed on 20 March 2016).

186 *Energy Silk Road: anticipation and adaptation*

72 'Turkmengaz selected TAPI consortium leader,' *Natural Gas Asia*, http://www.natu-ralgasasia.com/turkmengaz-selected-tapi-consortium-leader-16255 (Accessed on 20 July 2015).

73 Alexander Knyazev, 'Mify dlya Tsentralnoy i Yuzhnoy Azii stanovyatsya pochti epicheskimi' [Myths for Central and South Asia are becoming almost epic], *Nezavisimaya gazeta*, 16 May 2016, http://www.ng.ru/courier/2016-05-16/11_asia.html (Accessed 24 May 2016).

74 Private communication with Kawatō Akio, former ambassador to Uzbekistan and Tajikistan, December 2014.

75 Konstantin Gaaze, 'Silovoy vykhod. V chyom smysl i politicheskiye posledstviya reform spetssluzhb' [Power exit. The meaning and consequences of security services reform], *Carnegie Endowment for International Peace*, 6 April 2016, http://carnegie.ru/commentary/2016/04/06/ru-63253/iwpl (Accessed 7 April 2016).

76 Paik, *Sino-Russian Oil and Gas Cooperation*, 381; Kazantsev, *Bolshaya igra*, 363–4.

77 Uzbekistan – The Main Fields, APS Review Oil Market Trends, 13 October 2008, http://www.highbeam.com/doc/1G1-186836235.html (Accessed 10 July 2015). The Kokdumalak field was discovered in 1986 in the Kashkadarya region, which was governed by Islam Karimov in 1986–9 prior to his appointment to the republic's top position. Nissho Iwai's stake was purchased in 2005 by Zeromax, a Swiss company affiliated with Karimov's daughter Gulnara.

78 Paik Keun-Wook, 'Sino-Russian Gas Cooperation: Regional and Global Implications,' presentation (Cambridge: University of Cambridge, 28 February 2013) and Interview with a JOGMEC official, March 2012.

79 Kawatō Akio, 'Japan's Strategic Thinking Toward Central Asia,' in *Japanese Strategic Thought Toward Asia*, ed. Gilbert Rozman et al. (New York: Palgrave, 2007); Uyama, 'Japanese Policies,' 168.

80 Interview with a JETRO official, April 2012.

81 Initially OKIOC (Offshore Kazakhstan International Oil Consortium), currently NCOC (North Caspian Oil Consortium).

82 Interview with a JOGMEC official, March 2012.

83 Interview with a former JNOC and INPEX official, March 2012.

84 Produced as a result of the new plant installation by Tohoku Electric Power.

85 Irina Nosova, 'Energeticheskaya politika Yaponii' [Japan's energy policy], in *Energeticheskiye izmereniya mezhdunarodnykh otnosheniy i bezopasnosti v Vostochnoy Azii* [Energy dimensions of international relations and security in East Asia] (Moscow: MGIMO, 2007), 767.

86 MOFA, ODA White Paper 2002, http://www.mofa.go.jp/policy/oda/white/2002/part1_2_2_3.html (Accessed 10 July 2015).

87 Interview with INPEX official, June 2011.

88 Nosova, 'Energeticheskaya politika Yaponii,' 768.

89 Itochu has a 4.3 percent stake, while INPEX owns 11 percent, both operating on the basis of the production share agreements (PSA).

90 Interviews with a Japanese EBRD official, February 2010, October 2013.

91 For instance, the construction of the Severnaya thermal power station funded by a $320 million loan, according to Maeda Mitsuhiro, *Kin'yū shokuminchi wo dasshu seyo. Jirihin nihon wo sukuu 'tōshi paradaisu' no hassō* [Even if it comes to seizing financial colonies. Ideas of 'investment paradise' to save dwindling Japan] (Tokyo: Purezidento, 2010), 88–97.

92 Interview with a JOGMEC official, March 2012.

93 The Turkmenbashi refinery, gas chemical facility, oil product plant, and similar objects.

94 Madeleine Laruelle and Sébastien Peyrouse, *L'Asie centrale à l'aune de la mondialisation – Une approche géoéconomique* [Central Asia in the light of globalisation: a geoeconomic approach] (Paris: Armand Colin, 2010).

Energy Silk Road: anticipation and adaptation   187

95 This mechanism's launch was planned for 2014. Interview with a JOGMEC officer, January 2011.
96 Pavlyatenko, 'Energeticheskaya bezopasnost' Yaponii i factor rossiysko-yaponskih otnosheniy,' 789.
97 Paik, *Sino-Russian Oil and Gas Cooperation*, 326.
98 Interview with JOGMEC official, March 2012.
99 Valeria Korchagina, 'Yukos, CNPC Strike a $150Bln Deal,' *The Moscow Times*, 29 May 2003, http://www.themoscowtimes.com/business/article/yukos-cnpc-strike-a-150bln-deal/238180.html; 'Daqing Pipeline Still Most Feasible,' http://www.china.org.cn/english/2004/Mar/89979.htm (Accessed 10 July 2015).
100 Khodorkovsky's trial and imprisonment have been identified as political both by international NGOs and by various Russian politicians, who viewed Khodorkovsky's charges of tax evasion as pretext for his persecution by rival political groups.
101 Despite minor Russo-Japanese tensions over the Sakhalin consortia in 2006.
102 Pavlyatenko, 'Energeticheskaya bezopasnost' Yaponii i factor rossiysko-yaponskih otnosheniy,' 783.
103 Andrew Mickey, 'Uranium Has Bottomed: Two Uranium Bulls to Jump on Now,' *Uranium Seek*, 22 August 2008, http://www.uraniumseek.com/news/UraniumSeek/1219431716.php (Accessed 19 July 2015).
104 TEPCO had 5 percent, and Idemitsu had 8 percent.
105 APEC Energy Overview 2014, Institute of Energy Economics, Japan, 85.
106 Nuclear Power in Japan, World Nuclear Association, 2011, http://www.world-nuclear.org/information-library/country-profiles/countries-g-n/japan-nuclear-power.aspx (Accessed 14 July 2015).
107 'Japan restarts reactor in test of Abe's nuclear policy,' *Reuters*, 11 August 2015, http://www.reuters.com/article/us-japan-nuclear-restarts-idUSKCN0QF0YW20150811 (Accessed 20 August 2015).
108 Meanwhile, Russia's share of uranium reserves, on the contrary, increased from 3.6 percent in 2005 to 9 percent in 2013. Supply of Uranium, June 2015, http://www.world-nuclear.org/info/Nuclear-Fuel-Cycle/Uranium-Resources/Supply-of-Uranium/ (Accessed 10 July 2015).
109 World Uranium Mining Production, 22 May 2015, http://www.world-nuclear.org/info/Nuclear-Fuel-Cycle/Mining-of-Uranium/World-Uranium-Mining-Production/ (Accessed 10 July 2015).
110 Togzhan Kassenova, 'Uranium Production and Nuclear Energy in Central Asia: Assessment of Security Challenges and Risks,' *China and Eurasia Forum Quarterly* 8, no. 2 (2010): 230.
111 Corporate Profile, JOGMEC, http://www.jogmec.go.jp/content/300196198.pdf (Accessed 13 June 2016).
112 Uranium reserves are present in Tajikistan, but their estimate is difficult to verify, while the deposits are located near the Afghan border, thus adversely influencing their commercial viability for both political and technical reasons. Tajik uranium is still considered attractive due to growth projections for the global nuclear industry and uranium demand. REMs are found in Kyrgyzstan, and Japanese interest in them is evidenced by diplomatic cables, but the protracted political instability and weak property rights regime n Kyrgyzstan delayed any tangible developments. U.S. embassy cable – 07TOKYO5539 KYRGYZ PRESIDENT PAYS LOW-KEY VISIT TO JAPAN, Embassy Tokyo, 13 December 2007, http://cables.mrkva.eu/cable.php?id=134066 (Accessed 20 July 2015).
113 Kulpash Konyrova, 'Japan, Kazakhstan to Share Nuclear Technology, Resources,' *New Europe*, 1 July 2016, https://www.neweurope.eu/article/japan-kazakhstan-share-nuclear-technology-resources/ (Accessed 11 July 2016).
114 Appak is a JV developing a uranium mining project in West Mynkuduk of the South Kazakhstan region and involving Kazatomprom (65 percent), Sumitomo Corporation

188 *Energy Silk Road: anticipation and adaptation*

(25 percent), and Kansai Electric Power Co. Inc. (10 percent). Appak was expected to start the commercial production of 1000 tons of uranium concentrate by 2010 and to further supply the produced uranium ore to Japan. In 2006, the JBIC also signed an MoU for a comprehensive partnership to strengthen strategic ties with Kazatomprom. Appak's initial development was funded through $92 million loans from Sumitomo, KEPCO, JBIC (co-financing), Citibank NA, and Mizuho Corporate Bank. All Appak's production is acquired by Japanese companies. Appak funding was followed by another co-financing loan of approximately US$200 million in 2007 to finance another Kazakhstan-based uranium mine development project in Kharassan. This project is operated by Baiken-U, a JV of Kazatomprom and Energy Asia Limited, a consortium including Toshiba (22.5 percent), Marubeni Corporation (32.5 percent), TEPCO (30 percent), Chubu Electric Power (10 percent), and Tohoku Electric Power (5 percent). Nippon Export and Investment Insurance (NEXI), a Japanese export credit agency, provided investment insurance. Bakytzhan Khochshanov, 'Kazatomprom. Powering a cooler planet,' *Halyk Finance*, 21 January 2011: 15.

115 Interview with Itochu official, April 2012.

116 White Paper on Nuclear Energy 2008, http://www.aec.go.jp/jicst/NC/about/hakusho/hakusho2008/wp_e.pdf (Accessed 20 July 2015).

117 This label was assigned to Amari and Motegi on the basis of their membership in the parliamentary association of Nippon Kaigi, a right-wing organisation unrelated to CA. Matthew Penney, 'The Abe Cabinet – an Ideological Breakdown,' *The Asia-Pacific Journal: Japan Focus*, 28 November 2013, http://japanfocus.org/events/view/170 (Accessed 30 April 2014).

118 Weston S. Konishi, *From Rhetoric to Reality: Foreign-Policy Making under the Democratic Party of Japan*, April 2012, 51, http://www.ifpa.org/pdf/fromRhetoric-ToReality.pdf (Accessed 10 June 2015).

119 Masaki, 'New Energy Fuels Japan's Diplomacy: From the Middle East to Central Asia,' *The Asia-Pacific Journal* 5, no. 5 (May 2007), http://apjjf.org/-Hisane-MASAKI/2416/article.html (Accessed 1 July 2015).

120 Diplomatic cable, U.S. Tokyo embassy, 07TOKYO2306, METI Minister's Visit to Central Asia, Middle East Energy-Focused, http://cables.mrkva.eu/cable.php?id=109365 (Accessed 30 March 2015).

121 Ibid.

122 'Yaponskiye kompanii zainteresovany v uchastii v energoproektakh Azerbaydzhana' [Japanese companies are interested in participating in Azerbaijan's energy projects], *Trend*, 27 October 2015, http://www.trend.az/business/energy/2449145.html (Accessed 17 November 2015).

123 The Japanese companies in question were Marubeni, Mitsubishi, Mitsui, and Itochu.

124 Pavlyatenko, 'Energeticheskaya bezopasnost' Yaponii i faktor rossiysko-yaponskih otnosheniy,' 784.

125 Viktoriya Panfilova, 'Uranovyy interes Tokio' [Tokyo's uranium interest], *Nezavisimaya gazeta*, 10 August 2010, http://www.ng.ru/cis/2010-08-10/6_tokio.html (Accessed 18 July 2015).

126 'FSB "podstavil" KNB?' [Did the FSB 'frame' the KNB?], *Respublika*, 14 August 2009, http://www.respublika-kaz.info/news/politics/4849/ (Accessed 20 July 2015).

127 Bruce Pannier, 'Link To Iran Spoils Kazatomprom Party,' *Radio Free Europe/Radio Liberty*, 30 December 2009, http://www.rferl.org/content/Link_To_Iran_Spoils_Kazatomprom_Party/1917808.html (Accessed 20 July 2015).

128 Taisuke Abiru, 'The Tokyo-Moscow-Astana Triangle: Strategic Partnership in Nuclear Energy is Inevitable,' *Security Index* 3 (85), 14 (2008): 117–21 and Asylkhan Mamashuly, 'Kak Mukhtar Dzhakishev stal politicheskim uznikom' [How Mukhtar

Dzhakishev became a political prisoner], *Radio Azattyq*, http://rus.azattyq.org/content/dzhakishev-status-politzaklyuchennogo/25130955.html (Accessed 27 March 2014).

129 'Kazakhstan: Jailed Ex-Nuclear Boss Suspects Russian Machinations,' *Eurasia.net*, 21 May 2013, http://www.eurasianet.org/node/66991 (Accessed 18 July 2015).

130 Interview with a Sumitomo official, June 2011.

131 Igor Savchenko, 'The case of Mukhtar Dzhakishev – The life of the political prisoner is in danger,' *Open Dialog Foundation*, 10 November 2014, http://en.odfoundation.eu/a/5469,the-case-of-mukhtar-dzhakishev-the-life-of-the-political-prisoner-is-in-danger (Accessed 18 July 2015).

132 Uzbekistan then boasted 230 thousand tonnes of uranium reserves.

133 World Uranium Mining Production, 22 May 2015, http://www.world-nuclear.org/info/Nuclear-Fuel-Cycle/Mining-of-Uranium/World-Uranium-Mining-Production/ (Accessed 10 July 2015).

134 The JV aimed at a production level of 300 tons per year.

135 Interview with Mitsui officials, June 2011.

136 'Investitsionnyi potentsial Uzbekistana,' International Institute for Political Expertise, July 2013, http://www.minchenko.ru/netcat_files/File/Uzbekistan%20issl edovanie%2015_07_full.pdf (Accessed 10 March 2013).

137 As a reminder, the Uzbek version of multi-lateralism included regular pivots between Russia and the West. The most recent pivot towards the West started around 2009, when the European Union lifted sanctions and Washington called Tashkent its strategic partner, since Uzbekistan began replacing Pakistan as the main transit partner for the ISAF operations, while the U.S.–Pakistani ties deteriorated.

138 Panfilova Viktoriya, 'Uzbekskii ryvok na Zapad' [Uzbekistan drives towards the West], *Nezavisimaya gazeta*, 11 November 2009.

139 Interview with MOFA officials, March 2013.

140 First Russian LNG plant launched in Sakhalin, Gazprom press-release, http://www.gazprom.com/press/news/2009/february/article64569/ (Accessed 21 April 2016).

141 'China Denies Rare Earth Export Quota Report,' *Reuters*, 20 October 2010, http://www.reuters.com/article/us-china-rareearth-idUSTRE69J30Y20101020 (Accessed 14 May 2012).

142 Jack Perkowski, 'Behind China's Rare Earth Controversy,' *Forbes*, 21 June 2012, http://www.forbes.com/sites/jackperkowski/2012/06/21/behind-chinas-rare-earth-controversy/#7869986916b8 (Accessed 10 July 2015).

143 For instance, Richard Samuels, *3.11: Disaster and Change in Japan* (Cornell University Press, 2013), 110–50; *Yaponiya: 11 marta 2011. Itogi i uroki* [Japan: the 11 March 2011. Results and lessons] (Moscow: Russian Academy of Sciences, 2012).

144 Samuels, *3.11: Disaster and Change in Japan*, 148–50.

145 Official Trip of Yukio Edano, Minister of Economy, Trade and Industry, to India and Kazakhstan, METI: http://www.meti.go.jp/english/press/2012/0510_01.html (Accessed on 30 May 2012).

146 Yu Ka-ho, 'Japan Challenging China's Rare Earth Hegemony,' *Journal of Energy Security*, 21 November 2012.

147 METI Minister Motegi Visited Ukraine, Uzbekistan, and Kazakhstan, http://www.meti.go.jp/english/press/2014/0811_01.html (Accessed 16 July 2015).

148 Nuclear Energy National Plan, METI 2006.

149 Abiru, 'The Tokyo-Moscow-Astana triangle.'

150 Benefiting from significant vertical integration, Rosatom gained control of virtually all nuclear-related sectors of the Russian economy: power holding Atomenergoprom, weapons manufacturers, and research organisations. This structure increased the firm's global competitiveness: when competing for overseas tenders on reactor

190 *Energy Silk Road: anticipation and adaptation*

construction, Rosatom could offer comprehensive packages including financing, power plant construction, fuel supply, and take-back of spent fuel.

151 Abiru, 'The Tokyo-Moscow-Astana triangle.'

152 'Rosatom vstretil konkurenta v Kazahstane' [Rosatom met a competitor in Kazakhstan], *Kommersant*, 23 January 2015, http://www.kommersant.ru/doc/2651479 (Accessed 12 July 2015).

153 Markus Winter, 'Abe and the Bureacracy: Tightening the Reins,' *The Diplomat* 16 June 2016, http://thediplomat.com/2016/06/abe-and-the-bureacracy-tightening-the-reins/ (Accessed 16 June 2016).

5 Japan, China, and Asian connectivity

Competition, cooperation, and the weaponisation of infrastructure finance?

Introduction

Ever since Chinese President Xi Jinping announced the Belt and Road Initiative (BRI) in 2013, the discussion of Sino-Japanese relations in the field of Asian infrastructure exports has been influenced by a flurry of multi-billion dollar promises made by Chinese and Japanese leaders in the style of a 'battle of checkbooks.' After Xi's launch of the BRI, the Asian Infrastructure Investment Bank (AIIB) and the accompanying pledges of monies to participating countries, Prime Minister Abe Shinzō followed suit and promised numerous concessional loans to Asian and African countries, as well as an increase in Japan's funding of the Asian Development Bank (ADB). For instance, in 2014, Abe promised US$33 billion to India alone over the ensuing five years.[1] In 2015, as if to raise the stakes and match China's offer sheet, Abe promised to boost the Japanese funding of Asian infrastructure by US$110 billion.[2] The commitment involved both bilateral aid and Japanese contributions to the ADB, where Japan has been playing a leading role since the bank's foundation in 1966. A year later, in May 2016, the Japanese government raised the US$110 billion promise to US$200 billion.[3] In June 2018, Abe announced plans to establish a $50 billion fund to boost infrastructure investment in Asia over the next three years.[4] In October 2018, Japan and China signed 52 memoranda regarding infrastructure projects in third countries, although their value was rather symbolic than high in terms of substance. In November 2018, Japanese, Australian, and United States government finance agencies signed a trilateral memorandum of understanding to provide joint funding for infrastructure projects in the Indo-Pacific region – a concept viewed as part of balancing China's rise.[5]

These dynamics were interpreted in existing scholarship as mounting tensions, where Japan was reacting to restore a growing imbalance of power by pursuing a tit-for-tat strategy.[6] Although the promised amounts significantly exceeded actual disbursements, several material factors prevent us from discounting Tokyo's infrastructure-themed pronouncements as merely cheap talk and trading barbs between media-savvy leaders. These factors include the multi-billion dollar scale of infrastructure finance, its top-level political support, systemic

192 *Japan and China: connectivity co-opetition?*

institutionalisation of foreign infrastructural policies in Japan over the past seven years, and high-intensity media coverage including strategic communications.

Indeed, Japanese companies competed with Chinese rivals over several high-speed rail projects in several Asian countries, while Japanese officials recurrently hinted at the lack of transparency and sustainability of Chinese infrastructure finance and urged both lenders and borrowers to promote quality infrastructure and respect the creditworthiness considerations.[7] The promotion of infrastructure exports by Japan in Asia is a decade-long phenomenon that can be traced from as far as the pre-World War II era and has involved such drivers as mercantilism, development, and foreign policy considerations.[8] The novelty here is that the strategic dimension and the politicisation of Japan's infrastructural policies in the region were markedly intensified by the advent of the BRI and the AIIB.[9]

However, Japan's foreign policy in international infrastructure finance had featured not only competitive, but also cooperative postures towards China, both bilaterally and within multi-lateral development banks (MDBs). Scholars interpreted this approach as hedging and as deliberate combination of competition at sea and cooperation on land.[10] In the specific case of Central Asia (CA), some argued that Chinese and Japanese infrastructural strategies were not mutually exclusive.[11]

What was puzzling is that Japan kept sending mixed and even contradictory signals by repeatedly alternating conflictual and cooperative stances within short periods of time. In 2013–17, Japanese officials and Japanese centrist and conservative media (Yomiuri, Nikkei, Sankei) promoted risk-averse coverage of the BRI in the form of 'debt trap narrative.'[12] However, from mid-2017 onwards, they started intermittently signalling willingness to cooperate with China over the BRI. At the same time, the ADB officials not only used moderate rhetoric regarding the AIIB consistently, but also participated in several co-financing projects with the AIIB. Furthermore, in June 2018, a revised version of Japan's basic policy on infrastructure exports referenced promoting cooperation with China for the first time, following an agreement between Prime Minister Abe and Chinese Premier Li Keqiang in May 2018, where they pledged to set up a joint public-private committee to coordinate economic cooperation in third world countries.[13] In 2019, Yomiuri de-escalated its narrative on the topic by emphasising the commercial nature of the competition, as opposed to strategic or geopolitical, and by adding Korea to the mix of Japan's infrastructural competitors.[14] During the 2019 Tokyo International Conference on African Development, the final document for the first time acknowledged the concept of the Indo-Pacific.[15]

Some of those postures may be interpreted as the Abe cabinet's diplomatic 'sandwich' parlance used to defuse tensions with Beijing, especially during the 40th anniversary of the 1978 Sino-Japanese Treaty of Peace and Friendship. Others, however, appear to have been consistently manifested at several instances throughout the past 15 years – for instance, involving Japanese officials in the Ministry of Finance (MOF) and the ADB, thus warranting a closer examination.

Japan and China: connectivity co-opetition? 193

This chapter starts by examining the role of systemic-level influences driving infrastructural competition between Japan and China in Asia. There, I expound the role of infrastructure as a tool of economic statecraft between rival powers in Asia and locate it in the current regional political and economic context. I claim that Japan's initial combination of engagement vis-à-vis the AIIB and checking against the BRI, both evidenced by the promotion of the debt-trap narrative and aimed at managing and slowing the ongoing power shift in Asia, was gradually adjusted to a more engaging posture. This adjustment occurred as a result of structural factors, such as the necessity to hedge against the uncertainty of United States President Trump and in order to avoid overbalancing. I also show the relevance of the concept of lender of last resort for understanding Japan and China's behaviour in Asian finance.

The chapter then proceeds to the analysis of factors at the levels of individual policymakers and the internal makeup of states, delving into greater empirical detail. I show that the impact of individual Japanese officials and policy entrepreneurs is essential for the comprehensive understanding of Japan's approach vis-à-vis China in the field of Asian infrastructure. These levels bear a significant explanatory value for the grasp of drivers behind Japan's cooperative postures towards China that an exclusively neorealist paradigm fails to elucidate. I show that Tokyo's response was driven not only by a structural attempt to balance against China as a rising challenger, but also an attempt to socialise Chinese initiatives in the field of development finance and by Japan's mercantilist promotion of infrastructural exports, itself stemming from the Abenomics policy of economic resuscitation.

Infrastructure as statecraft in Asia

The importance of infrastructure for developmental policies was widely recognised by mainstream economists, including Japanese economists with track records in international financial institutions (IFIs).[16] What structural reasons account for infrastructure's rise to prominence as a strategic tool of statecraft? Recent research suggests that long-term investors are well placed to invest in more long-term global infrastructure assets, especially due to the strengthening of the relative value of illiquid asset classes offering an illiquidity premium, such as infrastructure investments.[17] Consequently, the growing role of states – as standalone long-term investors or stakeholders in sovereign wealth funds, private-public partnerships, and so on – can be arguably explained by the capital-intensive nature of infrastructure and related long-term project finance. High risks and uncertainties make private-sector actors reluctant to finance infrastructure independently in the absence of government support. Businesses also tend to prefer utilising the capacity of existing infrastructure before venturing into building a new one, thus indirectly further empowering state actors.[18] Commercial banks from developed economies operating in emerging countries are often reluctant to accept foreign fixed assets as loan collateral due to risks associated with debt recovery in the case of default, such as rule of law, liquidity, and others.[19]

194 *Japan and China: connectivity co-opetition?*

This, in turn, negatively affects borrowing costs for emerging countries, especially in the events of liquidity shortage. During the commodity boom and the so-called 'resource nationalism' of the 2000s, the bargaining power of commodity-exporting borrowers was partially increased by their ability to collateralise commodity exports as loan security. However, the lowering of commodity prices of the mid-2010s offset this debt securitisation capability and, consequently, reduced the bargaining power of borrowers vis-à-vis private lenders. In this context, government finance gained particular importance, especially in East Asian developmental states, as it provided a source of political power for states capable of exporting technology and large-scale funding for a rare public good.

Although Japan, Western Europe, and North America dominated the international donor landscape until the early 2000s, the advent of new donors, such as China, India, Turkey, and South Korea, over the past two decades increased the supply-side competition in development finance, both in bilateral and multilateral formats.[20] Furthermore, BRICS countries (Brazil, Russia, India, China, and South Africa) showed that collective financial statecraft can materialise through new, purpose-built financial institutions.[21] Meanwhile, the existing rules in this field are under stress, especially since formal regional financial institutions are a relatively recent phenomenon in Northeast Asia.[22] Consequently, since many of these countries compete and cooperate with each other in providing financial solutions to recipient or borrower states, while also revising old rules and making new ones, they tend to increase the politicisation of infrastructure and its financing. In turn, borrowers and recipients, such as Southeast Asian states, encourage the competition between infrastructure providers and lenders, such as Japan and China, in order to prevent the monopoly of either.

Some of those rivalries are predominantly commercial and dealing with intra-city urban infrastructure. However, others concern assets of greater strategic value used for international transport: for instance, ports, airports, bridges, roads, pipelines, telecoms, and terminals for oil, coal, and liquefied natural gas. These projects are important not only due to their lucrative value, but also due to long-term effects on major strategic itineraries and trade routes, and, consequently, the international economic order. Historical examples of the twentieth century, such as the Berlin-Baghdad railway or the Chinese Eastern Railway, show how international connectivity projects sought greater prosperity, but ended up contributing to tensions and, ultimately, conflict between major powers. Modern-day connectivity projects in Southeast, South, and CA, epitomised by various New Silk Road initiatives, face a similar challenge, as they bolster the pacifying effects of economic regionalisation and risk spurring great power rivalry.

The increasing role of infrastructure as Japan's statecraft tool is evidenced not only by Japanese foreign policy initiatives, but also by the growing profile of infrastructure in institutional design. While the latest drive for government bolstering of Japanese infrastructural exports dates to the Democratic Party of Japan (DPJ) rule (2009–12), Abe's second premiership crystallised this trend by harnessing infrastructure export promotion to accelerate Abenomics. The cabinet's Japan Revitalisation Strategy emphasised infrastructure development.

In 2013, the Management Council for Infrastructure Strategy was established at the Prime Minister's Office. The Prime Minister's Office is a key government institution that saw its foreign-policy powers increase under Abe's tenure.[23] The Council's work covered a global geography and involved the participation of senior officials, including Abe himself. In the five years since the body's establishment, its sessions have been dedicated to regional and thematic aspects of Japanese infrastructure promotion, including two sessions on CA, four on Association of Southeast Asian Nations (ASEAN), one separately on Indonesia, and three on India. The BRI was regularly brought up, according to the Council's session materials.[24]

In 2014, the Abe government set up another institution to promote Japanese infrastructural exports – Japan Overseas Infrastructure Investment Corporation for Transport and Urban Development (JOIN). JOIN became Japan's first and only private-public sponsored fund, specialising in overseas infrastructure investment and collaborating with companies, banks, and the government. Amendments to the law on the Japan Bank for International Cooperation (JBIC) enabled the government bank to be more risk-taking. According to *Asahi*, construction companies were among the likeliest beneficiaries of Abe's policies.[25]

As I have mentioned in Chapter 1, this neomercantilism of the Abe premiership is likely to be affected by a parallel securitisation of economic issues. In response to perceived challenges stemming from China, in particular the BRI and Huawei's fifth generation of cellular network technology (5G) development, the Liberal Democratic Party of Japan (LDP) and the Japanese government mulled increasing the Prime Minister's Office powers over guiding economic security policy. Initially, former head of the Ministry of Economic Trade and Industry (METI) and LDP heavyweight Amari Akira proposed establishing Japan's version of the United States National Economic Council.[26] In September 2019, following the cabinet reshuffle and the replacement of Yachi Shōtarō by intelligence officer Kitamura Shigeru as Abe's national security adviser, mainstream media announced the government's plans to set up a new unit in charge of the economic security policy under the cabinet Secretariat's National Security Secretariat in 2019–20.[27]

Sino-Japanese interaction in Asian infrastructure in theoretical paradigms of international relations

Kenneth Waltz pointed to the importance of systemic factors in understanding international politics and made a parallel with the behaviour of companies in a given market.[28] The international infrastructural sector fits that paradigm quite well due to the comparatively larger role of governments and state actors in this industry, associated with the long duration and turnaround of projects and high risks. Furthermore, states are unequally endowed in means of building and financing infrastructure. This creates an oligopolistic market where predominantly developed or emerging countries compete to export their infrastructure systems to developing countries. By providing infrastructure solutions funded

196 *Japan and China: connectivity co-opetition?*

via concessional lending, governments not only further their mercantile interests, such as securing lucrative contracts for national companies and associated project-life servicing engagement, importantly, they also maximise their political power, especially soft power when their hard-power capabilities are restrained, as in the case of Japan. Structural forces here affect several external environments, aside from the distribution of political power in the international system: the borrowers' bargaining power is shaped not only by the supply-side competition, but also by their own purchasing power, which is affected by liquidity, the prices and cycles of currencies and commodities, as well as by financial crises.

Soft lending in these cases often implies not only concessional interest rates, but also sometimes a more lenient attitude towards creditworthiness than in purely commercial financing. Such loans receive approval despite either the borrowers' insufficient creditworthiness, for instance, Kyrgyzstan in the early 2000s or, conversely, despite their improved financial standing no longer requiring concessional borrowing, as was the case of Kazakhstan after the 2000s commodity boom or China that kept receiving Japanese development assistance until 2008.[29] In CA, Japan had also used loan aid, among other purposes, to influence the behaviour of borrowers and to cooperate with the United States as its ally.[30]

In this paradigm, Japan's recent responses to China's rise as a concessional lender and infrastructure provider in Asia could be interpreted in two ways: on one hand, as win-lose zero-sum-game, where Japan's loss of infrastructure bid in a third country to China would be both a literal loss of contract and loss of power; and, on the other hand, as the persistence of reactivity as a dominant feature of the Japanese foreign economic policy.[31]

Prima facie, Japan's opposition to the China-led AIIB can thus be viewed as self-serving, since the criticism of a donor's influence inside an MDB can be pointed to Japan itself with regards to its dominance in the ADB.[32] This interpretation, however, has two notable limits. Firstly, Japan has been consistently promoting concessional infrastructure lending and exports to Asia since the late 1960s, both under China-averse and China-friendly governments, including the cabinets of the Democratic Party of Japan. This, in turn, means that China's behaviour is not the only dependable variable for Japan's infrastructure exports, and where it is the case, Japan is, in fact, reacting to another reaction – that is, China's reaction to Japan's dominant position in Asian infrastructure. Secondly, as the next section shows, the actual Sino-Japanese interaction in the field of infrastructure has shown more cooperation to date than was forecasted in interpretations emphasising competition.

Neoliberal institutionalists use the market metaphor differently, but also in the way relevant for the case of Asian infrastructure. According to this paradigm, international regimes are similar to markets for national interests: state actors entering into that 'market' are socialised into the particular ways of behaviour expected of them in that context.[33] In the field of foreign aid, including infrastructural aid, the example of such a regime is the Organisation for Economic Cooperation and Development's (OECD) 1991 Helsinki Agreement. This OECD Agreement stymied the mercantile aspects of foreign aid – and socialised then

Japan and China: connectivity co-opetition? 197

particularly mercantile donors, including Japan – by limiting the tied component of foreign aid. China has been increasing its profile as a concessional lender, has a cooperation mechanism with the OECD, and is currently in the middle stages of internalising norms specific to responsible outbound investment.[34] However, it is neither a member of the OECD and its Development Assistance Committee (DAC), nor a party to the OECD's 1991 Helsinki Agreement. Moreover, China attempted to establish itself as a normative power in this field by creating courts dedicated to BRI projects.[35]

The OECD DAC member states progressed with reducing the percentage of tied foreign aid after the 1991 Helsinki Agreement's drastic shift away from infrastructure and production projects that were sectors typically chosen for export promotion by donors and concessional lenders.[36] In the 1990s and the 2000s, when the donor landscape was dominated by the OECD DAC countries – Western in the broad sense of the term, including Japan – and all its members abided by the commitment to make aid less mercantile, this arrangement created a stable international regime. However, the rise of China and its active promotion of infrastructure exports and associated concessional loans in the 2010s challenged the relevant international system, rendering the donor landscape more competitive. If the OECD DAC's attempts to regulate the provision of foreign aid by donors can be viewed as a collective effort at reducing anarchy in this section of the international system, China's increased profile as concessional lender and infrastructure provider *volens nolens* reinforced anarchy in this field and challenged the dominance of Western countries, including Japan. In this context, Japan's competition with China over Asian infrastructure can be interpreted as an attempt to preserve the status quo – by socialising China – and mitigate the risks stemming from the rise of a new challenger in the field where Japan has regarded itself as regional leader.

China's absence in the OECD implies that countries seeking to socialise China in terms of concessional loan aid can do it either bilaterally or indirectly within other international institutions – for instance, the ADB in the case of Japan. Japan's official rhetoric tended to describe Japan's experience of challenging the international order in the 1930–40s as if it was an example of what a rising challenger should avoid doing.[37] Although Japanese officials avoided parallels between the infamous Greater East Asia Co-Prosperity Sphere and the BRI, this extrapolation would logically flow out of the usage of Japan's own past as warning. Socialisation-style wording could be found in critical and, at times, alarmist rhetoric on the BRI (for instance, the characterisation of China's policies as a potential debt trap), used by Japanese officials (Flores 2018) and publications in the style of strategic communications in major outlets, such as Yomiuri (2017), Nikkei (2017), or Sankei (2018) newspapers. Abe, in his first speech indicating the possibility of Japan's cooperation with the BRI, stressed such prerequisites for it as quality, openness to all, and creditworthiness.[38] These terms were repeatedly and increasingly used in Japanese official rhetoric, including in international institutions where Japan was a member, such as the Group of Seven. Aside from criticising China's infrastructural footprint, this position is likely to seek

198 *Japan and China: connectivity co-opetition?*

to socialise China in this field, to stress Japan's competitive edge in the sector, and to help preserve Japan's central role in the Asian infrastructure section of the international system. The aforementioned emphasis on creditworthiness and repayment capacity, the disregard of which in the current low-liquidity conditions can lead to a financial crisis and necessitate an international response to it, brings us to another structural aspect of the topic – the role of the lender of last resort.

Japan and China: contenders for the position of Asian lender of last resort?

The role of lender of last resort has been widely discussed in the international political economy. Kindleberger stressed the structural importance of this role in the international system, as shown by the hegemonic stability theory.[39] Thies applied Kindleberger's idea to the rise of China and ensuing prospects of Chinese leadership in the global economy, pointing at China's potential of acting as a new lender of last resort.[40] Ultimately, the proof of that supposed ambition and capability remains to be provided by Beijing's future response to an eventual international economic crisis; at this stage, the AIIB essentially provides project finance. Nonetheless, China's initiatives of the BRI and the AIIB marked a milestone in that direction, as they involved concessional foreign lending and emerged several years after the 2008 global financial crisis (GFC), while the above-described illiquid environment makes Chinese sovereign lending *de facto* countercyclical.

Does this imply that Japanese foreign infrastructural lending is informed by the perception of China as competitor of Japan and the ADB for the position of key Asian regional lender? Available data and a closer look at Japan's pre-BRI infrastructural initiatives suggest that Tokyo's response involved miscalculation and subsequent adjustment. On one hand, even if China's concessional lending record is modest to date, it is rapidly growing (see the next section), and the very availability of China as an alternative source of funding reduces Japan's ambitions to the status of the go-to lender in Asia, which were also stymied in the past by opposition from the United States, as I show below. Furthermore, Beijing is competing with Tokyo in its prised niche of lending with softer conditionality than the financing provided by the international institutions with political mandates, such as the World Bank, the International Monetary Fund (IMF), or the European Bank for Reconstruction and Development.

On the other hand, the international economic system's complexity, the growing scale of international financial crises, and increasing complex interdependence prioritise the plurality of lenders of last resort over a single hegemon. While Kindleberger recognised the weakening role of the United States as stabiliser, he also dismissed the arguments in favour of a duumvirate (United States and Japan) or troika (Japan, United States, and Germany) of lenders of last resort, approximating shared responsibility to no responsibility and pointing to the lack of Japan and Germany's inclination to take over the stabilising role.[41] Yet, when Japan subsequently became inclined to act as stabiliser in 1997, this ambition was opposed by the United States. Furthermore, the 2008 GFC necessitated collective countercyclical action, eventually undertaken by the Group of 20 heads of government.[42] This systemic necessity for collective action is likely to facilitate Japan's socialisation of China, as it limits China's supposed ambition to act as the sole stabiliser in case the Chinese government would indeed intend to supplant Japan as Asia's go-to international lender. Furthermore, scholarship suggests that China among other emerging lenders is actually not likelier to lend to recipients of debt relief than Western sovereign lenders – instead, smaller sovereign lenders are likelier than larger ones to free-ride on debt relief provided by other creditors.[43]

Japan's international financial initiatives in the Cold War era and in the Cold War aftermath evidenced its consistent ambition and readiness to assume greater responsibility in that field. Japan's post-BRI infrastructural and related international financial initiatives can be viewed as continuity with earlier proposals from the DPJ period and preceding decades. Although Japan's initiatives did not always materialise, its infrastructure finance proposals appeared at least once every decade in the post-war period. In 1957, Prime Minister Kishi Nobusuke, Abe Shinzō's grandfather, proposed an Asian Development Fund.[44] In 1966, the Asian Development Bank was established, and Japan had played a consistently strong role in it ever since. In 1977, Prime Minister Fukuda Takeo announced a pivotal policy for Tokyo's cooperation with Southeast Asian countries, including the increase of Japan's aid for infrastructure improvement.[45] In 1987, Prime Minister Nakasone Yasuhiro announced the ASEAN-Japan Development Fund. Between 1987 and the 2010s, Japan and the ADB have proposed numerous large-scale Asian financial initiatives either in the field of connectivity infrastructure or as crisis response: the 1987 New Asian Industries Development (AID) plan, the ADB's sub-regional connectivity programs in 1990–2010s, responses to the 1997–8 Asian financial crisis, and to the 2008 GFC. The New AID plan did not materialise due to lack of enthusiasm and readiness in the ASEAN countries, Japanese domestic politics, and opposition from the United States, the World Bank, and the IMF.[46] After the 1998 Asian financial crisis, then-Finance Minister Miyazawa Kiichi announced a US$30 billion package to the region's economies.[47] Tanaka argued that Japan's response to the crisis was that of an economic superpower and could have been even more robust in the event of materialisation of the Tokyo-proposed US$100 billion Asian Monetary Fund initiative.[48] The initiative was neither supported by Beijing nor by Washington; the Western powers saw Japan's proposal as a challenge to American hegemony in Asia or an attempt to cosy up to the crony capitalism of Asia's authoritarian regimes.[49]

In the aftermath of the 2008 GFC, the ASEAN Plus Three and the Tokyo-based ADB Institute (ADBI) were considering a dedicated Asian infrastructure institution in the late 2000s, as part of the Asian Bond Market Initiative (ABMI). High-profile economists under the aegis of the ADBI proposed 'creating an Asian Infrastructure Investment Fund (AIIF) as a mechanism for channelling funds towards meeting the region's various infrastructural needs, which has been one of the key objectives of the ABMI.'[50] Although this proposal did not materialise,

200 *Japan and China: connectivity co-opetition?*

it showed that the ADB was considering an institutional design similar to the AIIB – including the near match of names – several years before Xi's launch of the new MDB.

Another similar idea, albeit with a narrower regional scope, was voiced by ADB-affiliated Japanese financiers in March 2013 – half a year before Xi Jinping's announcement of the BRI and AIIB. The ADBI's Dean Kawai made the case for the establishment of a dedicated Northeast Asian Infrastructure Investment Fund (NEAIIF) and against the creation of a new MDB.[51] It justified the latter argument with the lack of resources and will of dominant lenders – Japan, Europe, and the United States – to do so. Kawai's argument also *volens nolens* played in favour of Japan preserving its status quo role of dominant Asian lender, as it did not openly address or foresee, as we know with the benefit of hindsight, the eventual scenario of China proposing exactly what Kawai advised against – the creation of a new MDB, possibly due to the underestimation of China's resolve.

A counterfactual view suggests that had the AIIF or NEAIIF initiatives materialised in 2009–10 and 2013–14, respectively, they would have had the potential to impact China's 2015 establishment of the AIIB by making the AIIB less relevant through addressing Asian demand for infrastructure. This raises a number of questions about the role of Japan in the AIIB's effective inception. Did China seize the opportunity where Japan and the ADB had failed to promptly act? The examples of United States opposition to Japan's 1987 New AID plan and 1997 Asian Monetary Fund (AMF) proposal were likely to disincentivise China from accepting the status quo. Furthermore, Wang argued that the establishment of the AIIB was partly induced by China's dissatisfaction with the ADB – despite Japan's attempts to accommodate China's growing influence in it, discussed in the following section.[52] Conversely, China's establishment of the AIIB surprised Japan's MOF that, instead, expected Beijing to expand China's share in the ADB.[53]

Alternatively, did Japan and the ADB deliberately pursue the policy of sharing the burden of Asian lender of last resort by encouraging China's increased contribution in the niche of regional infrastructure financing? In 2009, the Asō cabinet had a full plate of dealing with the GFC's domestic consequences, whereas his successors from the Hatoyama and Kan cabinets maintained a China-friendly stance. At the same time, as I have shown in Chapter 1, Asō proposed the Eurasian Crossroads initiative, aimed at developing transport corridors and involving the use of Japanese infrastructure. A detailed exploration of these hypotheses would be outside the scope of this work; however, the link between Japan's either lack of resolve or insufficient action and China's increased profile in the field of Asian infrastructure at the time is highly plausible.

At the same time, sharing payment default risks with China by encouraging Chinese contribution in international lending and reducing Japan's exposure – especially given the latter's giant debt – actually benefits Japan's self-interest. The model of the aforementioned NEAIIF multi-lateral fund is similar in that specific regard to the ADB's Central Asian Regional Economic Cooperation (CAREC). While this model of pooling funds from multiple contributors dilutes

Japan and China: connectivity co-opetition? 201

the political clout of a single funder, it also distributes financing risks among multiple participants. This approach may also be interpreted as risk-averse and contrasted to China's more daring posture, but it is adequate to Japan's position and self-perception in the international economic system. Furthermore, as a closer look into China's financing spree suggests, Beijing may also harbour an increasingly risk-averse lending attitude underneath an expansive surface. Given the above-described trend favouring collective response to financial crises over singular lenders of last resort, China is likelier to act within that collective mechanism than to carry the entire burden and associated risks.

The role of individual officials and policy entrepreneurs

Recent research made the case for considering the sub-national level of policymaking when analysing rising powers, including in the case of the BRI.[54] As regards Japan's infrastructural policies vis-à-vis China, individual-specific factors contributed to making Japan's postures more cooperative. This section will provide three inferences regarding relevant cooperative patterns. Firstly, the AIIB and ADB have, on balance, exhibited more cooperation than competition in the first three years of AIIB's existence. Secondly, both the interaction of Japanese officials with Chinese officials inside the ADB and the ADB's interaction with the AIIB have exhibited cooperative patterns. Thirdly, Tokyo's posture regarding the BRI has softened due to the agency of individual policymakers.

ADB and AIIB: cooperation over competition

On balance, the interaction between the ADB and AIIB to date reflected that cooperative dynamics have been prevailing over competition. As I show below, the history of infrastructure development with the ADB illustrated a propensity towards accommodating China's rise among the bank's Japanese officials. The AIIB's apparent decoupling from the BRI by the Chinese government was echoed in Japan's and the ADB's simultaneous criticism of the BRI and engagement with the AIIB, which can, in turn, be interpreted as Japan's socialisation of China by encouraging multi-lateralism and discouraging self-serving bilateralism.[55] Their cooperation can be exemplified by an existing track record of joint activity, albeit short, by rhetoric and by appointment policies inside the ADB reflecting the bank's accommodation of China's increasing importance over the past decade.

Despite the abundance of promises made by Japan and China for infrastructure finance in Asia, verbal pledges were much larger than actual disbursements, implying that Japan was still maintaining its top position. The AIIB has disbursed US$1.2 billion in the three years since its opening in 2016, below the expected annual lending rate of US$10–15 billion.[56] The AIIB's first seven disbursements were all arranged as co-financing with other development institutions and IFIs, including the ADB. In particular, the ADB's and the AIIB's co-financing included three projects: a highway in Pakistan, the upgrade of a gas field in Bangladesh,

202 *Japan and China: connectivity co-opetition?*

and a ring road in Georgia. In 2018, the ADB's president Nakao said that the two Asian MDBs were exploring further co-financing opportunities, which was in line with the ADB's accommodative posture regarding the AIIB.[57]

As of 2017, China has spent a total of US$50 billion on the BRI, four years into its announcement.[58] Japanese observers estimated China's spending from the Silk Road Fund at US$7 billion, as compared to its initial value of US$40 billion.[59] In Southeast Asia, Japan's completed and on-going infrastructure investment of US$230 billion exceeded China's US$155 billion.[60]

This discrepancy shows that the expected Sino-Japanese infrastructural rivalry appears more modest in reality than in forecasts. It may also point to the fact that the AIIB tends to exercise prudence in lending policies in order to maintain its high credit rating, the importance of which was among the main reasons listed by Kawai in the rationale against the establishment of a new MDB. Furthermore, similarly to the ADB, the AIIB is likely to opt for sharing and diversifying financial risks, rather than solely shouldering the cost. In this case, structural constraints, such as rating and own creditworthiness seem to be limiting the increase of China's power via the AIIB.

However, the relatively modest disbursement within the AIIB and BRI was offset by stronger bilateral lending from China. For instance, the China Development Bank and China's Exim Bank have become key lenders to Kyrgyzstan and Tajikistan, increasing their reliance on China to a very high level: 41.3% of the total Kyrgyz external debt is owed to the Exim bank, whereas in Tajikistan, Chinese loans constituted 88% of the bilateral debt portfolio.[61] In response to Tajikistan's bilateral debt growth, the ADB mooted providing the US$160 million it had committed for 2018 as grants instead of loans, indirectly reflecting Japan's role in the bank as stabiliser.[62] Paradoxically, although Japan would often present itself as disinterested sponsor for CA's development, this approach was misconstrued in CA as passive and uninterested, while Japanese funding was perceived as too expensive or inaccessible.[63] In this regard, the media campaign that accompanied Tokyo's promotion of infrastructural exports should be viewed not only as positioning vis-à-vis rival exporters, but also as a message for potential importers.

The race of financing pledges and accompanying media buzz may have contributed to the perception of the MDBs involved in the construction and financing of Asian infrastructure as tools of statecraft. However, some of the ADB's institutional characteristics may hinder its diplomatic politicisation. Unlike, for instance, the European Bank for Reconstruction and Development (EBRD's) or the World Bank's political mandates with associated conditionality, the ADB's mandate is a development one, aimed at poverty reduction. Prior to the AIIB's emergence, this approach was advantageous, as it created a source of funding for emerging countries, alternatively to politically conditional lending from the EBRD and the Bretton Woods institutions, indirectly reinforcing the bank's competitive position as supplier. Together with support of gradual reforms over shock therapy and Japan's perception of economic prosperity as precondition for political liberalisation, the ADB's approach attracted the governments of several

Japan and China: connectivity co-opetition? 203

countries struggling with political reforms. The AIIB's rise, however, challenged that advantage, as it is likely to involve even more pragmatism on the part of the lender, making China a more accessible alternative to Western countries. This, in turn, may stimulate a change in the ADB's policy, either towards adding conditionality, which is less likely, or towards looser standards. Still, unlike the AIIB, the ADB's structure has another feature that may stymie its eventual inclination to compete with the AIIB. According to Robert Orr, the presence of a board of resident directors inhibited the ADB's dependency on the United States and Japan as key shareholders, despite Japan's influence in the bank.[64]

The ADB's rhetoric vis-à-vis the AIIB has been accommodative. In May 2017, one week before the inaugural BRI Forum in China, the ADB held its 50th annual meeting in Yokohama, where ADB President Nakao said that he viewed the AIIB and the BRICS-led New Development Bank (NDB) as partners, which was confirmed by the incumbent head of the AIIB and former ADB Vice President Jin Liqun.[65] The quoted reason for cooperation was straightforward: the resources of both MDBs are insufficient to cover Asia's need for infrastructure, estimated by the ADB at US$26 trillion for the period of 2016–30. One noteworthy discrepancy in approaches might come from the fact that while the AIIB focuses on new infrastructure and public funding, the ADB also seeks to increase the financial involvement of the private sector, whereas private businesses tend to favour fully utilising existing infrastructure over building a new one.

The AIIB's emergence also seemingly stimulated the ADB to increase its inclusivity. In October 2017, when Nakao pledged to provide US$5.5 billion of ADB funding to CAREC over the next five years, he noted the importance of partnering the ADB with a large number of external partners, including not only the BRI, but also the Shanghai Cooperation Organisation (SCO) – an organisation that Japan previously regarded with suspicion. Furthermore, in 2016, the ADB also signed a framework agreement with the Eurasian Development Bank, led by Russia and Kazakhstan, on co-financing for a total of US$3 billion for projects in Armenia, Kazakhstan, Kyrgyzstan, and Tajikistan.

The role of inter-ministerial differences and policy entrepreneurs inside the ADB

On top of the structural factors outlined above, another important driver of cooperative dynamics between China and Japan inside Asian MDBs is found at the level of individuals, for instance, the ADB's presidents. In turn, this level is a part of larger differences over foreign policy often found in Japan's three-ministerial (*sanshōchō*) policy coordination between the MOF, foreign affairs (MOFA), and METI.

On balance, Japanese officials inside the ADB have been rather accommodating and welcoming of China's increasing participation in Central Asian and South Asian projects, rather than opposing it. This can be evidenced by the ADB's appointments of Chinese vice presidents (2003–present) I have examined in Chapter three. The ADB's Japanese and Chinese officials forged a link of

204 *Japan and China: connectivity co-opetition?*

mutual trust, which has ultimately affected a positive attitude of Japanese finance officials towards the AIIB, as Jin became its president.[66]

The acceptance of the Chinese senior officials' growing role inside the ADB by Japanese officials in the 2000s is consistent with the argument that Japan had been accommodating China's rise in 1978–2011.[67] After the BRI 2013 announcement, the MOF – a key Japanese government body handling the relationship with the ADB and other IFIs – exhibited continuity in this China-friendly approach by adopting a more accommodative posture towards the AIIB than the MOFA.[68] MOF officials perceived the AIIB as an opportunity both for Japanese companies and regional development – similarly to China's mercantilist approach towards the development of Asian infrastructure in the early 1990s.

CAREC's corridors are both latitudinal (East-West) and longitudinal (North-South) and include China, similarly to the ADB's other sub-regional connectivity programmes, such as the Greater Mekong Sub-region. CAREC and Turkmenistan–Afghanistan–Pakistan–India (TAPI) were aimed at diversifying landlocked CA's export routes (including away from China, but not aimed at antagonising it), while CAREC not only involved China, but was also covered by Chinese officials within the ADB from 2003. Furthermore, in 2017 ADB Vice President Zhang said that CAREC would build linkages with a diverse range of organisations: the BRI, the Japan-led Partnership for Quality Infrastructure, the Russia-led Eurasian Economic Union, the Russia- and China-led SCO, and the Economic Cooperation Organisation led by CA states.[69] This newly inclusive approach marked a departure with Japan's previous suspicion towards the SCO and towards cooperation with Russia inside the ADB. This change can be interpreted, firstly, as Japan's gradual reckoning with China's increased weight and, secondly, as an attempt to socialise China by showing an example of openness of infrastructural projects to competing powers.

The rules of the game are still in the making, and, if China's past behaviour in international institutions, such as the World Trade Organisation (WTO), can be a predictor of its future behaviour in the MDBs, then China would go through the stages of rule-taking and rule-shaking before attempting rule-making.[70] According to a number of scholars, with whom this chapter agrees, a competition between the two MDBs would, on balance, do more good than harm.[71]

While Sino-Japanese interaction in infrastructure at the level of Asian MDBs to date reveal tangible cooperative trends, at the bilateral level of interstate relations and relevant individual officials, the picture is more ambivalent and reveals stronger competitive patterns.

Japanese officials between the Indo-Pacific Strategy and the BRI: inconsistency, continuity, or hedging?

Between Xi Jinping's announcement of the BRI in 2013 and the promotion of the Indo-Pacific Strategy by Abe in 2017–18, Tokyo's bilateral response to China's infrastructure initiatives gradually shifted from mostly balancing to the mixture of balancing and engagement. This shift was symbolically reflected in the

Japan and China: connectivity co-opetition? 205

renaming of Indo-Pacific Strategy into Indo-Pacific Vision, thus reducing military connotations of 'strategy' in Chinese and Japanese languages. The shift also challenged the interpretations of Abe's China policy as balancing without hedging and indicated a return of oscillation between Japan's competitive and cooperative postures.[72] This section argues that the change of Japan's position, even if more rhetorical than substantial, had stronger drivers at the level of individual politicians than at the level of international system, although systemic-level drivers were present as well.

Japan's initial 'cold shoulder' rhetoric addressed China's infrastructure advances without naming them directly and stressed the importance of economic feasibility, creditworthiness, and quality as prerequisites for infrastructure development, thereby emphasising Japan's competitive edge and ambition – both mercantile and norm-setting – in this sector. This language is found already in the name of Tokyo's corresponding initiative – Partnership for Quality Infrastructure, which includes three key Japanese ministries: MOF, METI, and MOFA. The partnership was announced simultaneously with Abe's 2015 pledge of US$110 billion for Asian infrastructure in 2015–20. The MOFA stressed infrastructure's quality aspect in its 2018 Diplomatic Bluebook.[73]

These trends were echoed in the language of multi-lateral summits. For example, until 2012, the Leaders' Declarations of Asia-Pacific Economic Cooperation (APEC) summits did not contain many references to infrastructure, however, over the last five years the number of mentions has steadily increased.[74] At the G7 summit hosted by Japan in Ise-Shima, the infrastructure not only increased its presence and was recurrently accompanied by emphasis on quality in the Leaders' Declaration, but also received its own separate document – G7 Ise-Shima Principles for Promoting Quality Infrastructure Investment.[75] Subsequent G7 documents kept the wording on quality infrastructure.

2017 and the first half of 2018 were particularly intensive in terms of the Japanese government's mixed-signal statements on the BRI, alternating direct calls for cooperation with calls for competition and then cooperation with elements of competition. This alternation and its frequent channelling via outlets, considered close to the Abe cabinet, such as Yomiuri and Nikkei, suggested that infrastructure announcements were used as strategic communications instrumentalised for influencing China's foreign policy in the short term, thus fitting the socialisation interpretation. At various stages, the media explained the Japanese government's proposals to partner with the BRI as means to other ends, such as getting Beijing to be more cooperative on the North Korean issue and refocusing on ties with China due to lack of progress in Abe's Russian diplomacy.

In May 2017, two of Japan's 'China hands,' the ruling Liberal Democratic Party's Secretary General Nikai Toshihiro and Abe's Political Secretary Imai Takaya participated in the inaugural BRI Forum and hinted at prospects of Sino-Japanese cooperation over the BRI. In June 2017, Abe himself highlighted the basis upon which Japan would be ready to cooperate with the BRI and the AIIB. He expressed hope that the BRI would fully incorporate a common frame of thinking and come into harmony with the free and fair Trans-Pacific economic

206 *Japan and China: connectivity co-opetition?*

zone and contribute to the peace and prosperity. However, Abe qualified the cooperation prospect by urging that infrastructure should be open to use by all, procurement ought to be transparent and fair, while projects needed to be economically viable, financed by debt that can be repaid, and not harm the soundness of the debtor nation's finances. This rhetoric, apart from stress on creditworthiness and responsibility, also showed continuity with Japan's demands for open regionalism in CA in response to the rise of the SCO in the mid-2000s during the Koizumi premiership.

Salient and long-standing points of Sino-Japanese bilateral rivalry over strategic (rather than urban) infrastructure included several Indian Ocean countries, such as Myanmar, Iran, Sri Lanka, Maldives, and even Pakistan. For instance, during a 2017 meeting with the Myanmar's leader Aung San Suu Kyi in Manila, Abe promised to provide US$1.1 billion in financial assistance for the development of infrastructure and agriculture. This decision was in line with Japan's long-established policy of reducing Myanmar's dependence on China, including through financial assistance. Another vivid example is Japan's assistance to the construction of the Iranian port of Chabahar, a competitor of the Pakistani port of Gwadar that, in turn, is part of China–Pakistan Economic Corridor (CPEC). India is interested in Chabahar as a hub for developing communications with CA bypassing Pakistan, whereas Japan is 'killing two birds with one stone:' continuing to develop its relations with Iran outside the oil sector and helping India as its Indo-Pacific partner to balance China and its ally Pakistan. In early 2018, Foreign Minister Kōno went on a diplomatic tour of Sri Lanka, Maldives, and Pakistan, seeking to promote Japan's infrastructure offer as a means of helping these countries avoid China's 'debt-trap' diplomacy.[76] The new round of United States sanctions on Iran, imposed by the Trump administration, made exceptions for Chabahar and Iran's several Asian counterparts, including Japan.

The most intensive and perhaps the most confusing, whether by miscalculation or by design, period of Japan's communications on the BRI occurred in 2017. Shortly after Abe's announcement of the Indo-Pacific Strategy together with United States President Donald Trump and a new attempt at furthering the quadrilateral partnership between Australia, Japan, India, and the United States, Kōno openly called the Quad anti-thetical to China's BRI-related expansion.[77] In this respect, Tokyo combined strategic and mercantile rationales when it invited its Quad partners to expand the dialogue's agenda by including infrastructure development in Asia and Africa: Japanese companies sought to use India's historical ties in East Africa. The geography of possible infrastructural cooperation between Japan, the United States, Australia, and India may affect the countries of the BRI's maritime segment, the Maritime Silk Road. The continental Silk Road Economic Belt was not mentioned, possibly in line with Abe's avoidance of antagonising Russia. A trilateral infrastructural partnership (without India) was established in 2018, while its quadrilateral version has not materialised as of August 2019.[78]

Furthermore, it is not clear how the export of infrastructure will fit into the cooperation of the Quad countries on the basis of democratic values, in conditions

Japan and China: connectivity co-opetition? 207

when across Asia these values appear to be yielding to the reinforcement of populist and authoritarian regimes and alignment with the Chinese model.[79] For example, Japan would have to reconcile its financial support to Myanmar with the country's democratisation. In that regard, the Sino-Japanese infrastructure competition is likely to benefit the regimes of recipient countries and their patron-client networks, in turn, facilitating elite predation.

More importantly, the reason why Kōno's anti-BRI rhetoric may appear inconsistent or deliberately aimed at hedging was that it struck contrast with both preceding and subsequent pro-cooperation speeches of Abe and Nikai made in 2017. In November, shortly after calls for quadrilateral cooperation, Abe called on China to boost Sino-Japanese cooperation and agree to a trilateral summit between Japan, China, and South Korea. Commenting on Abe's 2017 Manila meeting with the Chinese Prime Minister Li Keqiang, Japanese media noted that Abe wanted to develop economic diplomacy with China, since he had little progress on the peace treaty with Russia.

Abe's November 2017 Diet speech was tacit on both the Indo-Pacific and the Quad. The rationale for this likely stemmed from auspicious opportunities to mend ties with China, as 2018 marked the 40th anniversary of the Sino-Japanese Peace and Friendship Treaty, with expected mutual visits. A week after meeting with Abe in November 2017, Li Keqiang received the 250-strong delegation of Japanese businessmen from the Japan–China Economic Association – the organisation's largest delegation of the kind since 1975. The delegates called for the early conclusion of the Sino-Japanese–South Korean Free Trade Agreement (FTA) and expressed interest in the BRI's infrastructure projects.

However, Japan's reports on the BRI revealed that Abe and Xi had actually reached agreements over loans to joint projects as early as July 2017, therefore before Kōno's and Abe's October–November 'China-balancing' statements on the Indo-Pacific and the Quad, which supported the interpretation of Japan's behaviour as hedging. Furthermore, the prospects of using the Quad and the Indo-Pacific as anti-BRI vehicles are further impeded structurally by hedging behaviours of not only Japan, but also its Indo-Pacific partners: India and Australia, both of which participate simultaneously in the China-led BRI and AIIB (SCO for India), as well as in the China-balancing Quad.

Does Japan's rhetoric on the Quad, Indo-Pacific, and the BRI suggest reactivity and inconsistency? Not necessarily: various incarnations of Abe diplomacy's coalition manoeuvres around China may be aimed not at balancing or competition per se, but rather at stimulating Beijing by carrots and sticks towards greater cooperation over shared international issues, such as security on the Korean Peninsula, or the East China and South China Seas.

The hedging interpretation is supported by continuities in the Japanese foreign policy team between 2007 and 2017. Several key officials in Abe's second premiership played an important role in his first cabinet (2006–7). Albeit holding different offices then, these officials developed the concept of the Arc of Freedom and Prosperity (AFP), seeking to support unstable countries, including those neighbouring China and Russia. The AFP raised

208 *Japan and China: connectivity co-opetition?*

fears in Beijing and Moscow, however, one of its authors claimed that its real purpose was not anti-Chinese or anti-Russian confrontation, but stimulating Moscow to negotiate on the territorial issue by demonstrating the possible influence of Tokyo on Russia's neighbours.[80] By analogy with the AFP, one of the goals of the Indo-Pacific and the Quad announcements in 2017 may have been to raise Japan's bargaining power vis-à-vis Beijing on problem points in Asia.

Another explanation includes an internal divide, evidenced by the presence of two schools of thought in Abe's government as regards Japan's China policy. The 'pessimists' included Yachi, Asō, and MOFA's China experts who altogether emphasised the threat to Japan's security emanating from China, while acknowledging business prospects. Yachi had participated in the past mini-détentes with Beijing in 2006 and 2014.[81]

Conversely, the 'optimists' included Nikai Toshihiro and Imai Takaya, who participated in the 2017 Beijing Silk Road Forum due to their preference for focusing on economic relations with the People's Republic of China (PRC).[82] Imai was also one of officials put by Abe in charge of promoting Japanese infrastructure exports back in 2012.[83] The MOF (apart from Asō) and METI officials, on balance, would tend to prefer engagement over balancing, viewing it as a commercially interesting opportunity for Japan, especially as Japanese companies had already started cooperating with the BRI. One notable example of Japanese BRI-savvy companies is Nippon Express, one of the ten largest global logistic operators, which is involved in the BRI thanks to an agreement with the Kazakhstan Railways for port-to-rail container service Lianyungang–Kazakhstan–Europe.[84]

Former diplomat and scholar Tōgō Kazuhiko suggested another explanation for Japan's thawing towards the BRI in 2017 that involves both individual agency and structural factors.[85] According to Tōgō, Abe's strategic calculation that it is in Tokyo's interests to maintain credible channels of communication with Beijing could have underpinned his decision to engage with the BRI. However, Abe's change of position on the BRI was triggered by United States President's Trump preference for bilateralism over multi-lateralism and departure from the Trans-Pacific Partnership (TPP) trade agreement, while all European members of the G7 were becoming interested in the BRI and joining the AIIB.

In case Tōgō's argument is valid, Trump's impact can be interpreted in two ways. On the one hand, Tokyo's decision to step up cooperation with Beijing can be viewed as hedging as it followed a change in the balance of powers triggered by Washington's departure from the TPP and Europe's interest in the BRI. On the other hand, Washington's decision to leave the TPP was itself predicated on the transactional style of President Trump's policies, which another individual may have pursued with a different outcome for the TPP and, ultimately, for Japan's posture vis-à-vis the BRI. In that respect, Japan's handling of the 2019 G20 summit is likely to shed further light on the future of infrastructure and other economic statecraft in Asia in the era of heightening United States-Chinese tensions.

Conclusion

This chapter nuanced the *realpolitik* interpretation of Sino-Japanese infrastructural rivalry in Asia with the consideration of economic factors shaping the relationship outside the hard-power distribution. China's establishment of the AIIB and the BRI was predated by similar Japan's initiatives which either did not materialise or were successful, but insufficient in meeting regional needs. China's rise in Asian infrastructure has also been exposed to Japan's attempts at the socialisation of China, which underestimated China's resolve in institutional innovation.

I demonstrated that the assessment of the role of policy entrepreneurs and institutional change is indispensable for interpreting Japan's evolving role in Asian infrastructure and its mixed signals on cooperating and competing with China. The underappreciated dynamics of Japan's cooperation with China explained the ambiguity of Japan's posture. These levels also highlighted Japan's accommodation and socialisation of China in concessional lending before and after the BRI's launch, thus contrasting excessively discounted engagement and accommodative postures with overemphasised competitive patterns. When applied to Tokyo's policies in Asian infrastructure, strongly connected to domestic economic revival in Japan, the structuralist perspective elucidated the balancing aspect of Japanese infrastructural hedging. Conversely, the focus on individual decision-makers revealed important cooperative statecraft. This level of analysis showed that Japan's change of stance from checking against China's infrastructural projects to limited cooperation was largely due to differences between individual officials and government agencies and was a part of a longer, two-decade history of Japan's engagement of China in concessional lending.

Notes

1 Schuman, Michael, 'Why India's Modi and Japan's Abe Need Each Other – Badly,' *Time*, 2 September 2014, http://time.com/3255880/japan-india-narendra-modi-shinzo-abe-business-economy-trade-china/ (Accessed 31 September 2019).

2 'The Future of Asia: Be Innovative,' Speech by Prime Minister Shinzō Abe, 21 May 2015, https://japan.kantei.go.jp/97_abe/statement/201505/0521foaspeech.html (Accessed 31 August 2019).

3 Ministry of Economy, Trade, and Industry (METI), 'The "Expanded Partnership for Quality Infrastructure" Initiative Directed Toward the G7 Ise-Shima Summit Meeting Announced,' 23 May 2016, http://www.meti.go.jp/english/press/2016/0523_01.html (Accessed 31 August 2019).

4 Masayuki Yuda, 'Abe Pledges $50bn for Infrastructure in Indo-Pacific,' *Nikkei Asian Review*, 11 June 2018.

5 Prime Minister of Australia, 'Joint Statement of the Governments of Australia, Japan, and the United States,' 17 November 2018, https://www.pm.gov.au/media/joint-statement-governments-australia-japan-and-united-states (Accessed 31 August 2019).

6 Giulio Pugliese and Aurelio Insisa, *Sino-Japanese Power Politics: might, Money and Minds* (Basingstoke: Palgrave Macmillan, 2017); Tony Tai-Ting Liu, 'Japan's Strategic Rivalry with China in the Second Abe Administration: A survey of competitions in and beyond Asia.' *Paper presented at the 59th Annual Convention of the International Studies Association*, San Francisco, CA, April 2018.

210 *Japan and China: connectivity co-opetition?*

7 'The Future of Asia...', 'Asia's Dream: Linking the Pacific and Eurasia,' speech by Prime Minister Shinzō Abe, June 2017, https://japan.kantei.go.jp/97_abe/statement/201706/1222768_11579.html (Accessed 31 August 2019).

8 Nikolay Murashkin, 'Not-so-New Silk Roads: Japan's Foreign Policies on Asian Connectivity Infrastructure under the Radar,' *Australian Journal of International Affairs* 72, no. 5 (2018): 455–72.

9 Hidetaka Yoshimatsu, 'Japan's Export of Infrastructure Systems: Pursuing Twin Goals through Developmental Means,' *The Pacific Review* 30, no. 4 (2017): 494–512; IFRI [French Institute of International Relations], 'Catching Up or Staying Ahead: Japanese Investment in the Mekong Region and the China Factor,' *Asie Visions* 99, May 2018. Paris: Nicolas, Francoise.

10 Aurelia George Mulgan, 'Hardening the Hedge: Japan's Security Strategy Revisited,' *East Asia Forum*, 10 December 2018, http://www.eastasiaforum.org/2018/12/10/hardening-the-hedge-japans-security-strategy-revisited/ (Accessed 31 August 2019); Narushige Michishita, 'Cooperate and Compete: Abe's New Approach to China,' *The Straits Times*, 13 November 2018.

11 Timur Dadabaev, 'Japanese and Chinese Infrastructure Development Strategies in Central Asia,' *Japanese Journal of Political Science* 19, no. 3 (2018): 542–61.

12 Private communication with a foreign diplomat stationed in Tokyo, November 2018.

13 'Govt Seeking Involvement in China's Belt and Road Plans,' *The Japan News*, 18 June 2018, http://the-japan-news.com/news/article/0004520406 (Accessed 31 August 2019).

14 'Infrayushutsu-go mo shūeki... seifu ijikanrikigyō o shien' [Revenue even after infrastructure exports. Government to support maintenance and management companies], *Yomiuri*, 18 February 2019, https://www.yomiuri.co.jp/politics/20190218-OYT1T50051/ (Accessed 31 August 2019).

15 Yuka Takeshita, 'In Barb at China, TICAD Raises Sea Lane Security and Huge Investments,' *Asahi*, 31 August 2019.

16 Joseph Stiglitz and Andrew Charlton, *Fair Trade for All* (Oxford: Oxford University Press, 2007); Yoshiaki Abe, 'Japan and the World Bank, 1951–1966: Japan as a Borrower (3),' *Journal of Asia-Pacific Studies*, 25 (2015): 190; Yoshiaki Abe, 'Japan and the World Bank, 1951–1966: Japan as a Borrower (4),' *Journal of Asia-Pacific Studies*, 28 (2017): 324.

17 Rabah Arezki, Peter Bolton, Sanjay Peters, Frederic Samama, and Joseph Stiglitz, 'From Global Savings Glut to Financing Infrastructure: The Advent of Investment Platforms, IMF Working Paper 2016,' https://www8.gsb.columbia.edu/faculty/jstiglitz/sites/jstiglitz/files/_wp1618.pdf (Accessed 31 August 2019).

18 Personal communication, officer of a Japanese logistical company, 24 October 2017.

19 Personal communication, officer of a multinational bank, 30 September 2008.

20 Emma Mawdsley, *From Recipients to Donors: Emerging Powers and the Changing Development Landscape* (London: Zed Books, 2012).

21 Cynthia Roberts, Leslie Armijo, and Saori Katada, *The BRICS and Collective Financial Statecraft* (Oxford: Oxford University Press, 2017).

22 T. J. Pempel, ed. *The Economy-Security Nexus in Northeast Asia* (London: Routledge, 2013), 146.

23 Giulio Pugliese, 'Kantei Diplomacy? Japan's Hybrid Leadership in Foreign and Security Policy,' *The Pacific Review*, 30 (2016): 152–68.

24 'Keikyō infura senryaku kaigi – kaisai jōkyō' [Management Council for Infrastructure Strategy – meeting status], https://www.kantei.go.jp/jp/singi/keikyou/kaisai.html (Accessed 31 August 2019).

25 'Large Donors to LDP Stand to Benefit most from Abe Policies,' *Asahi*, 28 December 2018.

26 'Jimin Amari shi 'keizai teko ni kakoikomi, kōmyō' taiō e nipponban NEC teigen' [LDP's Amari suggests a Japanese version of the NEC as response for clever enclosure of economic leverage], *Mainichi*, 20 March 2019.

Japan and China: connectivity co-opetition? 211

27 'Kitamura to replace Yachi as Abe's nat'l security adviser: Gov't,' *Mainichi*, 12 September 2019; 'Keizai-gaikō-anpo. Kantei de ichigenka seifu kokka anpo-kyoku ni senmon busho' [Economy, diplomacy, security centralised in a specialised department under the Cabinet's National Security Secretariat], *Nikkei*, 19 September 2019.

28 Kenneth Waltz, *Theory of International Politics* (New York, McGrawHill, 1979), 62–3.

29 Private communication, former ADB official, March 2012; Evgeny Kovrigin, 'Kitaisko-yaponskiye otnosheniya cherez prizmu ofitsialnoy pomoshchi razvitiyu (OPR) v 1980-2000-h godah' [Sino-Japanese relations viewed through the lens of official development assistance (ODA) 1980–2000], in *Yaponiya* [*Japan*] *Yearbook*, ed. E. Molodiakova (Moscow: Russian Academy of Sciences, 2012), 97–122.

30 US embassy cable. 06TOKYO2992, A/S Boucher's May 30 Meeting with European DDG Yagi on Central Asia, 31 May 2006, http://wikileaks.ikiru.ch/cable/06TOKYO2992/ (Accessed 31 August 2019); US embassy cable. 06TOKYO7164. US-Japan Central Asia Dialogue: Part Two, Foreign Assistance and Project Finance, US Embassy in Tokyo, 28 December 2006, http://wikileaks.ikiru.ch/cable/06TOKYO7164/ (Accessed 31 August 2019).

31 Kent Calder, 'Japanese Foreign Economic Policy Formation: Explaining the Reactive State,' *World Politics* 40, no. 4 (1988): 517–41.

32 Christopher Kilby, 'Donor Influence in Multilateral Development Banks: The Case of the Asian Development Bank,' *The Review of International Organisations* 1, no. 2 (2006): 173–95; Dennis T. Yasutomo, *The New Multilateralism in Japan's Foreign Policy* (New York: St. Martin, 1995); Dennis T. Yasutomo, *Japan and the Asian Development Bank* (New York: Praeger, 1983).

33 Andreas Hasenclever et al., *Theories of International Regimes* (Cambridge: Cambridge University Press, 1997), 9–10; Taku Tamaki, 'Levels of Analysis of the International System,' in *Encounters with World Affairs: An Introduction to International Relations*, ed. Kavalski, Emilian (Farnham: Ashgate, 2015), 85–106.

34 Pichamon Yeophantong and Cristelle Maurin, 'China and the Regulation of Outbound Investment: Towards A "Responsible Investment" Policy Framework,' in *The Yearbook on International Investment Law & Policy 2014–2015*, ed. Bjorkland, Andrea (New York: Oxford University Press).

35 Nyshka Chadran, 'China's Plans for Creating New International Courts Are Raising Fears of Bias,' *CNBC*, 1 February 2018, https://www.cnbc.com/2018/02/01/china-to-create-international-courts-for-belt-and-road-disputes.html (Accessed 31 August 2019).

36 Steven Hall, 'Managing Tied Aid Competition: Domestic Politics, Credible Threats, and the Helsinki Disciplines,' *Review of International Political Economy* 18, no. 5 (2011), 651–2.

37 'Statement by Prime Minister Shinzō Abe,' 14 August 2015, https://japan.kantei.go.jp/97_abe/statement/201508/0814statement.html (Accessed 31 August 2019).

38 'Asia's Dream: Linking…'.

39 Charles Kindleberger, *The International Economic Order* (Hemel Hempstead: Harvester-Wheatsheaf, 1988).

40 Cameron G. Thies, Forthcoming. 'The Future of Chinese Leadership in the Global Economy,' in *Debating China in International Order*, eds. Kai He and Huiyun Feng (Ann Arbor, MI: University of Michigan Press).

41 Kindleberger, *The International Economic Order*, 27.

42 Paul Heinbecker, 'The Future of the G20 and its Place in Global Governance,' CIGI G20 Papers, April 2011, 5, http://www.cigionline.org/sites/default/files/g20no5.pdf.

43 Jonas B. Bunte, 'Sovereign Lending After Debt Relief,' *Review of International Political Economy* 25, no. 3 (2018): 317–39.

44 Hiroyuki Hoshiro, 'Co-Prosperity Sphere Again? United States Foreign Policy and Japan's "First" Regionalism in the 1950s,' *Pacific Affairs* 82, no. 3 (2009): 398.

212 *Japan and China: connectivity co-opetition?*

45 Speech by Prime Minister Takeo Fukuda (Fukuda Doctrine Speech), *Manila*, 18 August 1977, The Ministry of Foreign Affairs of Japan, http://worldjpn.grips.ac.jp/documents/texts/docs/19770818.S1E.html (Accessed 21 September 2019).

46 Peter Katzenstein and Martin Rouse, 'Japan as a Regional Power in Asia,' in *Japan and South East Asia*, ed. Wolf Mendl (London: Routledge, 2001), 193–224; Edith Terry, *How Asia Got Rich: Japan, China and the Asian Miracle* (Armonk, NY: M.E. Sharpe, 2002); Takashi Shiraishi, 'Japan and Southeast Asia,' in *Network Power: Japan and Asia*, eds. Peter J. Katzenstein and Takashi Shiraishi (Ithaca, NY: Cornell University Press, 1996), 169–96.

47 Yukako Ono, 'Malaysia Should "Make Best Use" of Belt and Road, Mahathir Says: Prime Minister Vows to Stay Friendly with China,' *Nikkei Asian Review*, 11 June 2018.

48 Akihiko Tanaka, *Japan in Asia: Post-Cold-War Diplomacy* (Tokyo: Japan Publishing Industry Foundation for Culture, 2017), 187–8.

49 Ibid., 188.

50 Christopher M. Dent, Organising the Wider East Asia Region (Working Paper Series on Regional Economic Integration, No. 62), November 2010. Asian Development Bank: Manila, 19, https://aric.adb.org/pdf/workingpaper/WP62_Dent_Organising_the_Wider_East_Asia_Region.pdf (Accessed 31 August 2019).

51 Masahiro Kawai, 'Financing Development Cooperation in Northeast Asia,' *The Northeast Asian Economic Review* 1, no. 1 (2013): 1–40.

52 Zheng Wang, 'China's Alternative Diplomacy,' *The Diplomat*, 30 January 2015.

53 Private communication with a Japanese economist, 5 November 2018.

54 Lee Jones and Jinghan Zeng, 'Understanding China's "Belt and Road Initiative": Beyond "Grand Strategy" to A State Transformation Analysis,' *Third World Quarterly* 40, no. 8 (2019), 1415–39.

55 Martin Weiss, *Asian Infrastructure Investment Bank* (Washington, DC: Congressional Research Service, 2017); Mikhail Flores, 'ADB Chief Warns of Belt and Road Debt Trap: Nakao Urges Countries to Carefully Weigh Viability of China-backed Projects,' *Nikkei Asian Review*, 3 May 2018.

56 Salvatore Babones, 'Is China's AIIB Developing Asia, Or Just Propping Up China's State-Owned Banks with Extra Cash?' *The National Interest*, 11 December 2018, https://nationalinterest.org/feature/chinas-aiib-developing-asia-or-just-propping-chinas-state-owned-banks-extra-cash-38472 (Accessed 31 August 2019).

57 'ADB, China-Backed AIIB to Co-finance More Projects this Year,' *Reuters*, 12 January 2018, https://www.reuters.com/article/adb-asia-aiib/adb-china-backed-aiib-to-co-finance-more-projects-this-year-idUSL4N1P72UI (Accessed 31 August 2019).

58 Jane Perlez and Keith Bradsher, 'Xi Jinping Positions China at Center of New Economic Order,' *New York Times*, 14 May 2017.

59 Takayoshi Fujimura, '"Ittai ichiro" shikin-jinzai ha jūbun ka' [Does One Belt One Road have sufficient capital and human resources], *Sankei*, 13 February 2018.

60 Siegfried Alegado, 'Japan Still Beating China in Southeast Asia Infrastructure Race,' *Bloomberg*, 8 February 2018, https://www.bloomberg.com/news/articles/2018-02-08/japan-still-beating-china-in-southeast-asia-infrastructure-race (Accessed 31 August 2019).

61 Safovudin Jaborov, 'Chinese Loans in Central Asia: Development Assistance or "Predatory Lending"?' in *China's Belt and Road Initiative and Its Impact in Central Asia*, ed. Marlene Laruelle (Washington, DC: The George Washington University, Central Asia Program); John Hurley, Scott Morris, and Gailyn Portelance, 'Examining the Debt Implications of the Belt and Road Initiative from a Policy Perspective,' Center for Global Development Policy Paper 121, March 2018, https://www.cgdev.org/sites/default/files/examining-debt-implications-belt-and-road-initiative-policy-perspective.pdf (Accessed 31 August 2019); 'Chūgoku "ittaiichiro"

Japan and China: connectivity co-opetition? 213

ga umu shakkinjigoku – beikikan ga shiteki-suru "taka risuku" 8kakoku toha' [Debt Hell Born by China's One Belt One Road – The 8 High-Risk Countries Marked by US Organisations as High-Risk], *Sankei*, 13 May 2018.

62 'Dolg Tajikistana vynudil nekotorye finansovye instituty peresmotret' kriterii finansirovaniya' [Tajikistan's debt made some financial institutions review the financing criteria], *Avesta*, 26 March 2018, http://avesta.tj/2018/03/26/dolg-tadzhikistana-vynudil-nekotorye-finansovye-instituty-peresmotret-kriterii-finansirovaniya/ (Accessed 31 August 2019).

63 Jaborov, 'Chinese Loans in Central Asia'; Interview with a JETRO official, August 2018.

64 Robert Orr, 'Why the Asian Infrastructure Investment Bank Needs Resident Directors,' *Chinadialogue*, 23 August 2016, https://www.chinadialogue.net/article/show/single/en/9206-Why-the-Asian-Infrastructure-Investment-Bank-needs-resident-directors (Accessed 31 August 2019).

65 Takehiko Nakao, 'Closing Address at the 50th Annual Meeting of the Board of Governors,' Asian Development Bank, 2017, https://www.adb.org/news/speeches/closing-address-50th-annual-meeting-board-governors-takehiko-nakao (Accessed 31 August 2019); Zhiming Xin, 'Asia Development Banks Share Goals,' *Xinhua*, 5 May 2017, http://usa.chinadaily.com.cn/epaper/2017-05/05/content_29219586.htm (Accessed 31 August 2019).

66 Private communication with a former MOF official, 29 October 2018.

67 Björn Jerdén and Linus Hagström, 'Rethinking Japan's China Policy: Japan as an Accommodator in the Rise of China, 1978–2011,' *Journal of East Asian Studies* 12 (2012): 215–50.

68 Lindsay Black, 'Japan's Aspirations for Regional Leadership – Is the Goose Finally Cooked?' *Japanese Studies* 37, no. 2 (2017): 151–70.

69 Wencai Zhang, 'A Sneak Peek at CAREC's New Strategy.' *Asian Development Blog*, 31 July 2017, https://blogs.adb.org/blog/sneak-peek-carec-s-new-strategy (Accessed 31 August 2019).

70 Henry S. Gao, 'China's Ascent in Global Trade Governance: From Rule Taker to Rule Shaker, and Maybe Rule Maker?' in *Making Global Trade Governance Work For Development*, ed. C. Deere-Birkbeck (Cambridge: Cambridge University Press, 2011), 153–80.

71 Robert M. Orr, 'The Asian Development Bank and the Asian Infrastructure Investment Bank: Conditional collaboration?' *The Ambassadors Review*, Spring 2016, https://www.americanambassadors.org/publications/ambassadors-review/spring-2016/the-asian-development-bank-and-the-asian-infrastructure-investment-bank-conditional-collaboration (Accessed 31 August 2019); Kazushige Kobayashi and Manuel A. J. Teehankee, 'The AIIB's Launch Sets the Stage for Supply-Side Competition in Development Finance,' *Russian International Affairs Council*, 14 July 2015, http://russiancouncil.ru/en/analytics-and-comments/analytics/the-aiib-s-launch-sets-the-stage-for-supply-side-competition/ (Accessed 31 August 2019).

72 'The Outlook for the Abe Doctrine after Japan's Election, An Interview with Christopher W. Hughes,' *National Bureau of Asian Research*, 25 October 2017, http://www.nbr.org/research/activity.aspx?id=812 (Accessed 31 August 2019).

73 MOFA, 'Gaikō seisho' [Diplomatic Bluebook], 2010–18, http://www.mofa.go.jp/mofaj/gaiko/bluebook/index.html (Accessed 31 August 2019).

74 Asia-Pacific Economic Cooperation (APEC), 'Leaders' Declarations 2017,' https://www.apec.org/Meeting-Papers/Leaders-Declarations (Accessed 31 August 2019).

75 Ministry of Foreign Affairs of Japan (MOFA), 'G7 Ise-Shima Summit,' 26–27 May 2016, http://www.mofa.go.jp/ecm/ec/page24e_000148.html (Accessed 31 August 2019).

76 MOFA, 'Foreign Minister Kono Visits Pakistan, Sri Lanka and Maldives,' 3–7 January 2018, http://www.mofa.go.jp/s_sa/sw/page3e_000799.html (Accessed 31 August 2019).

214 *Japan and China: connectivity co-opetition?*

77 Saki Hayashi and Yosuke Onchi, 'Japan to Propose Dialogue with US, India and Australia: Foreign Minister Kono Sees Japan Playing Key Freedom of Navigation Role,' *Asia Nikkei Review*, 26 October 2017.
78 Prime Minister of Australia, 'Joint Statement of the Governments of Australia.'
79 Thomas Pepinsky, 'Democracy Isn't Receding in Southeast Asia, Authoritarianism Is Enduring,' *East Asia Forum*, 4 November 2017, http://www.eastasiaforum.org/2017/11/04/democracy-isnt-receding-in-southeast-asia-authoritarianism-is-enduring/ (Accessed 31 August 2019).
80 Tomohiko Taniguchi, 'Beyond "The Arc of Freedom and Prosperity": Debating Universal Values in Japanese Grand Strategy,' Asia Paper Series, The German Marshall Fund of the United States, 2010, 2.
81 Giulio Pugliese, 'Japan's Kissinger? Yachi Shotaro: The State Behind the Curtain,' *Pacific Affairs* 90, no. 2 (2017): 231–51.
82 'Japanese Government Split over China Policy,' *Nikkei Asian Review*, 8 July 2017.
83 'Abe's "New Mercantilism" Bears Fruit for Japan,' *Nikkei Asian Review*, 4 Januray 2016.
84 'Nippon Express climbs aboard China's Belt and Road Initiative,' *Nikkei Asian Review*, 30 September 2017.
85 Kazuhiko Tōgō, 'Ittai Ichiro kōsō to Nihongaikō' [The Belt and Road Initiative and Japanese Diplomacy], *Bulletin of the Institute for World Affairs* no. 33, March 2018, Kyoto Sangyo University; Kazuhiko Tōgō, 'Japan's Relations with Russia and China and the Implications for the U.S.-Japan Alliance,' *The National Bureau of Asian Research* 16 May 2018, http://www.nbr.org/downloads/pdfs/psa/togo_commentary_051618.pdf (Accessed 31 August 2019); Kazuhiko Tōgō, 'Toranpu seiken no tōjō to nihon no gaikō senryaku' [The Rise of the Trump Administration and Japanese Diplomatic Strategy], *Mondai to Kenkyū* [Issues and Research], National Chengchi University, Centre for International Studies 47, no. 1 (2018): 1–31.

Conclusion

Japanese foreign policy in Central Asia and the New Silk Road is still a new and problematic subject, especially as it is a work-in-progress, and the very idea of the New Silk Road is being redefined by the debates over the Belt and Road and the Indo-Pacific. There is a scarcity of volumes in English, Japanese, or Russian tackling the matter comprehensively, from a cross-regional, multi-disciplinary, linguistically, and culturally nuanced perspective. Moreover, relevant evidence is either unavailable, given the topic's recent nature, or dispersed linguistically and geographically, further complicating its systematisation. This book has attempted to provide an account filling the abovementioned gaps and addressing the challenges, while also navigating the traditional debates on the proactivity and reactivity of Japanese foreign policy and Japan's strategic thinking.

I have analysed five main empirical aspects of Japan's New Silk Road policies: security, party politics, financial assistance, natural resources, and connectivity infrastructure. In the introduction, I called Japan's hesitation between various foreign policy options an oscillation and have used the term 'damping,' implying that hesitations have faded by the early 2010s as Japan's policy towards Central Asia stabilised after 'euphoria' and 'fatigue' stages. Japan's main foreign policy options included: pragmatism, which maximised economic gains; political realism, which fitted the zero-sum-game paradigm of Sino-Japanese rivalry; and idealism, which emphasised the human and developmental dimension of relations with Central Asia. I assessed Japan's behaviour following the choices between those options from the perspectives of both structure – as either anticipation of or adaptation to a changing environment – and agency, as either proactivity or reactivity.

Consequently, I have chronologically and thematically examined the variations of the dependent variable of Japanese foreign policy in a given region in conjunction with independent variables of external political and economic environment, partisan, and domestic politics in both Japan and Central Asia. I have attempted to demonstrate the multiplicity of 'chefs' and 'sous-chefs' involved in the making of Japan's Central Asian policy, to unpack the 'black box' of policy-making on both sides of this relationship, and demonstrate the weight of contingent factors and events.

216   *Conclusion*

I have analysed the evolution of Japan's foreign policy towards Central Asia by contextualising it in the evolution of Japan's security perceptions in the post-Cold War era governments formed by the Liberal Democratic Party. All Japan's major initiatives in the region – Eurasian Diplomacy, Central Asia plus Japan, and Arc of Freedom and Prosperity – reflected the dominant broad strategic thinking at the time and in one way or another were related to China and Russia. Nonetheless, they represented isolated leaps rather than a historically consistent policy course, since there was no clear evidence of close coordination between the different strategic approaches towards Central Asia (CA). Central Asia plus Japan, the most institutionalised of those initiatives and the only one surviving to date, was inspired by Japan's format of multi-lateral engagement with Southeast Asian states and, together with such other replicas as Guam Plus Japan, demonstrated a sometimes inflexible 'template' approach as opposed to more creative 'tailor-made' solutions. However, Central Asia plus Japan's low-key and routine character proved its greater viability compared to more colourful and ambitious grand designs. The examination of individual politicians demonstrated that those with relatively better knowledge of the region, factional support, and ties to key financial actors had a greater advantage, as demonstrated by Prime Minister Hashimoto Ryūtarō and the tandem of Abe Shinzō and Asō Tarō, especially as the latter two returned to power in 2012 with renewed foreign policy approaches. Japan–Central Asia ties were greatly affected by – and not reduced to – Japan's changing relations with China, Russia, and the United States. In fact, as far as Central Asia is concerned, the dynamics of Japan's relations with Russia switched from competitive to cooperative, while relations with China evolved from initially cooperative to competition with elements of cooperation. For the United States, Japan demonstrated its value not only as ally, but also as role model in engaging Central Asia.

Furthermore, the examination of three cabinets formed by the Democratic Party of Japan (2009–12) showed that the differences between intra-party factions and constituencies, including those described by Richard Samuels, mattered more than those between the Liberal Democratic Party (LDP) and Democratic Party of Japan (DPJ). The DPJ cabinets initially attempted to provide policies alternative to those of their LDP predecessors, but, on balance, the continuity with the LDP prevailed over differentiation and could best be visualised through the comparison of pragmatic resource diplomacies pursued by Noda Yoshihiko and the LDP. The 2010 Senkaku incident and the 2011 Fukushima nuclear accident marked an important watershed in the DPJ rule. 3/11 marked a change from the LDP legacy of 'nuclear renaissance' and related uranium expansion to the subsequent modification of Japanese energy mix in favour of natural gas. The 2010 Sino-Japanese tensions expanded into rare earths and crystallised Japan's focus in Central Asia on that commodity.

While Japanese foreign policymaking was at the centre of this study, I have addressed another gap in existing scholarship by avoiding the objectification of Central Asian states and examining the impact of their domestic politics and foreign policies on Japan's New Silk Road involvement. At critical junctures of the relationship, the agency of individual Central Asian states exposed the limits of Japan's hesitant attempts to reconcile three distinct elements: a disinterested posture, pragmatism, and value-oriented diplomacy. In particular, I have asserted the importance of Central Asian multi-vector diplomacies, neopatrimonialism, and factionalism in the form of clan rivalries as key factors shaping their external relations, including those with Japan. As several Central Asian states have experienced leadership in recent years or are facing a leadership transition at present, the significance of these structural features is likely to increase.

A close-up practitioner's perspective on Japan's financial assistance to Central Asia has been instrumental in showcasing the agency of individual non-diplomatic officials. They shaped the donor-recipient relationship into an 'asset' of Japanese foreign policy by advocating gradualist transition policies and supporting the region financially. However, after a generational change occurred among those officials, the problems of patron-client systems and rent-seeking dynamics at the recipient end of the relationship highlighted its 'liability' facet. The motivations of Japanese state financiers displayed a mixture of idealism, sentimentalism, and realism, as their involvement in Central Asian affairs increasingly included monitoring and engaging China. A particularly illustrative case of their agency was the crucial contribution of Japanese financiers inside the Asian Development Bank (ADB) to the creation of Central Asian Regional Economic Cooperation (CAREC), a multi-lateral 'Silk Road' project aimed at the improvement of Central Asia's connectivity and removal of trade barriers. Although functionalist CAREC received considerably less attention than China's ambitious Belt and Road Initiative, it has had tangible results for the member states and has achieved solid institutionalisation. CAREC was inspired by a similar earlier initiative of the Greater Mekong Sub-region, which, in turn, likely had bureaucratic roots in Ministry of International Trade and Industry's New Asian Industries Development AID plan (New AID). This showed the role of Southeast Asia as a comparative model for engagement with other Asian sub-regions, including Central Asia, not only in Japan's making of its regional policy, but also inside the ADB. Nonetheless, it was also a pioneer in Central Asian multi-lateral infrastructure projects and demonstrated pros and cons of prevalence of functionalism over geopolitics.

Japan's financial assistance to Central Asia is a part of a much broader and increasingly topical subject of international infrastructure politics in Asia, which would benefit from further research. Namely, I would suggest a detailed inquiry into the role of infrastructure as the new 'hardware' of incipient regionalisation between East and Central Asia – a process that to date has proven to gain more traction than the United States-led initiatives of Afghanistan–Pakistan, New Silk Road, or the coupling of Central Asia with South Asia. These American projects were arguably less successful because they prioritised geopolitics over private sector motivations and the economically, pragmatically motivated actions of national governments.

Another suggestion for further research would be to investigate the evolution of Japan's foreign infrastructural policy from pre-war 'techno-imperialism'

218   *Conclusion*

and projects related to the Greater East Asia Co-Prosperity Sphere to post-war Japan's developmentalist posture involving the ADB and other projects. Can Japan's turbulent experience in infrastructure and its financing be a lesson for contemporary China not only in terms of exporting excess construction capacity, but also in contributing to economic regionalism? Can a state promote infrastructure development policies which are mutually beneficial to the countries involved and which avoid the danger of excess politicisation?

The answers to those questions are of particular relevance now that Sino-Japanese infrastructure rivalry is at the forefront of Asia's international agenda. As I have shown, we should avoid discounting cooperative patterns between China and Japan as well as distinguish between Japan's neomercantilist and geopolitical drives. Moreover, the demonstrated roles of Central Asian states confirm the importance of avoiding the objectification of smaller states when examining the infrastructural rivalry.

Unlike China, Japan continues to be bound by international norms in its foreign aid. Beijing's Belt and Road and Asian Infrastructure Investment Bank (AIIB) were a significant feat of public diplomacy and investor relations, earning more political mileage than Japan's lower-key posture in Central Asia. Yet the normative framing of China's aid and infrastructure finance remains an open question. If Japan's proven idealism and membership in the Organisation for Economic Co-operation and Development (OECD) Development Assistance Committee (DAC) does not preclude them from strong aid pragmatism, what approaches are available for the normative engagement of China and other non-OECD donors?

As for bilateral aid, Japanese authors have produced research harnessing Japan International Cooperation Agency's (JICA's) expertise in the field.[1] In the case of multi-lateral development banks, however, it is not only the normative aspects that merit further inquiry, but also the decision-making of financial bureaucracy and its developmental ethos. To what extent is aid policymaking based on actual creditworthiness and to what extent is it geopolitical?

Mainstream economists and economic historians have stressed the benefits of infrastructure as a 'public good' for economic development, and generations of financial bureaucrats were trained with that ethos, applying it in international financial institutions. However, the emerging 'weaponisation' of infrastructure and its finance as a political power tool, especially in Asia, requires deeper research through the lens of international political economy, history, and political science.

Does infrastructure finance rivalry channel conflict between nations into the field of economy and away from military confrontation? Or do the donor-recipient and patron-client relations, enhanced by large-scale financing, fuel bloc mentality and zero-sum-game thinking? Can increasingly powerful donors and infrastructure providers run the risk of becoming techno-imperialists like pre-war Japan?

Furthermore, the rise of inter-donor competition improves the bargaining power of small recipient states, but might also entrench the rent-seeking dynamics of authoritarian elites, thus subverting the purpose of development. Japan

Conclusion   219

faced this dilemma in Central Asia. This research demonstrated the mixed results of its engagement, but further avenues, including those stressed above, await exploration.

Existing scholarship and media coverage have regularly pointed out the importance of Central Asian natural resources as a driver of Japan's interest – in line with Japan's Diplomatic Blue Book – but provided a predominantly static image. My contribution to this field was twofold and equally emphasised structure and agency. Namely, I have retraced Japan's resource diplomacy in the fields of oil, gas, uranium, and rare earths metals, while distinguishing between the agencies of the state and private sector, mostly in Japan, but also in Central Asia, in particular Kazakhstan. Furthermore, I have attempted to chart the dynamic evolution of anticipative and adaptive strategies implemented by the Japanese government and corporations throughout the stages of low commodity prices in the wake of the Union of Soviet Socialist Republics (USSR) collapse and subsequent commodity boom in the noughties, with its 'resource nationalism.' The cyclicality of international commodity markets, however, turned out not to be the only determinant factor in this regard, as I have claimed through the examination of equally important and regularly changing risk perceptions of Japan Inc. vis-à-vis Central Asia.

As Abe Shinzō returned to office in 2012, he appeared to soften the value-oriented component of his first term in favour of greater pragmatism in his diplomacy, including Central Asia. Initially, Abe raised the stakes in the Sino-Japanese rivalry over infrastructure and corresponding finance provided through multi-lateral development banks, but subsequently adopted a more hedging posture in the form of infrastructure coopetition with China. He became the second ever Japanese leader to visit Central Asia and the first one to do a tour of all five countries, while his second-term team also happened to be the most 'Central Asia-literate' in terms of having knowledge of the region, as compared to his predecessors. Abe's proactivity and strategic thinking underscored the role of individuals in Japanese foreign policymaking. And his successors, regardless of party affiliation, are likely to oscillate mildly when they take their turn to shape Japan's diplomacy vis-à-vis Central Asia and the New Silk Road.

Note

1 Sakiko Fukuda-Parr and Shiga Hiroaki, 'Normative Framing of Development Cooperation: Japanese Bilateral Aid between the DAC and Southern Donors,' _JICA Research Institute Working Paper_ No. 130, June 2016.

Glossary

chikyūgi wo fukan suru gaikō	diplomacy that takes a panoramic view of the world map
chōtōha	non-partisan group
datsu-a ron	de-Asianisation
fuan	insecurity
fukkō gaikō	revival diplomacy
gaiatsu	external pressure
genpatsu mura	'the atomic village,' pro-nuclear power lobby
genshiryoku runessansu	nuclear renaissance
giinrenmei (giren)	Diet members' caucus, league
habatsu	faction
Heisei Kenkyūkai	Heisei Research Council
hikiwake	hikiwake, a draw in judo
jikan	a vice-minister
jisshi taisei	implementation
jiyū to han'ei no ko	Arc of Freedom and Prosperity
kankeisha nettowāku	network of parties concerned
kanryōshihaikataken'ishugitaisei	bureaucratic authoritarianism
Kasumigaseki	metonym designating the Japanese government bureaucracy as opposed to elected officials of the legislative branch known as Nagatachō
kōgyōchitai	industrial area
kokka senryaku kyoku	National Policy Unit
manadeshi	favourite disciple
Nagatachō	metonym designating elected officials of the legislative branch as opposed to the government bureaucracy
nemawashi	laying the groundwork
nikkan renkei	Japanese-South Korean cooperation, linkage
Nippon Kaigi	Japan Conference

222   *Glossary*

Ōkurashō	the pre-2001 name of the Ministry of Finance
Sanshōchō	three-ministry system referring to the three key ministries in the foreign-policymaking: the Ministry of Foreign Affairs, the Finance Ministry, the Ministry of Economy, Trade, and Industry
Seiwa Seisaku Kenkyūkai	Seiwa Political Analysis Council
senryaku	strategy
shigen gaikō	resource diplomacy
shigen gaikō senryaku kaigi	Strategic Council on Resource Diplomacy
shinseichōsenryaku	New Growth Strategy
shiruku rōdō	Silk Road
shitashimi	closeness
shitsu	division (administrative unit in a ministry)
sōgō anzen hoshō	comprehensive security
tanabota	a godsend, a windfall
tsūshō kokka	mercantile state
yōseishugi	demand-based [aid philosophy]
yūai	fraternity
zaimukan	vice minister of finance for international affairs (in Japan)
zaiseikin'yūkenkyūjo	Financial Policy Institute
zenshinshugi	gradualism

Index

Abe, Shinzō 2–6, 10–12, 20, 33–4, 46, 49–54, 64, 68–9, 74, 80, 82–3, 98, 112–13, 115–16, 127–8, 130, 141, 145, 152–3, 158–60, 164, 168, 170–3, 176, 178–81, 191–5, 197, 199, 204–8, 216, 219
Afghanistan 3, 7, 10, 17, 19, 25, 30–1, 33, 39, 43, 48–9, 51, 70, 72–3, 77, 81, 98, 106–7, 116, 118–19, 122–6, 132, 139–40, 143–4, 154, 156–7, 159–60, 164, 176, 181, 186, 204, 217
Akayev, Askar 32, 73, 100, 112
Akino, Yutaka 29
Amari, Akira 4, 20, 34, 52–3, 115–16, 145, 153, 170–2
anticipative adaptation 142
Appak 170
Arc of Freedom and Prosperity 4, 20, 34, 48–51, 66, 116, 144, 158, 207, 216
ASEAN *see* Association of Southeast Asian Nations
Asian Bond Market Initiative 199
Asian Development Bank 7, 9, 20, 26, 43, 52, 74–5, 89–92, 102, 107–14, 117–19, 123–4, 126–8, 156–9, 176, 180, 191–2, 196–204
Asian Development Bank Institute 199–200
Asian financial crisis 95, 104, 143, 161, 199
Asian Infrastructure Investment Bank 4, 14, 74, 119, 191, 218
Asian Infrastructure Investment Fund 199–200
Asian Monetary Fund 199–200
Asian premium, 146, 153, 161
Asian values 94
Asō, Tarō 4, 20, 34, 49–52, 66, 68, 72, 77, 98, 113, 115–16, 144–5, 148, 158, 177, 180, 200, 208, 216

Association of Southeast Asian Nations, 32, 46, 102–3, 109, 195, 199
Azerbaijan 7, 9, 34, 50, 104–5, 119, 142, 147, 155–6, 161–4, 166, 171, 180
Azimov, Rustam 38–42, 95, 102, 111, 113–15, 179

Baiken 170
Bakiyev, Kurmanbek 73, 112
Baku-Tbilisi-Ceyhan pipeline, 162, 164–5
Bandar-Abbas 148–9
Banno, Yutaka 75
Belt and Road Initiative (also One Belt One Road) ix, 1–2, 10, 13–14, 51, 71, 89–91, 119, 124, 126, 128, 191, 206, 215, 217–18
Berdymukhamedov, Gurbanguly 126
big bang reforms, 94
Bishkek 45

CAREC *see* Central Asian Regional Economic Cooperation
CASA-1000 124
CentGas 156–7, 162, 164, 166
Central Asian Regional Economic Cooperation 3, 11, 52, 90–1, 107, 109, 111, 118–29, 157, 180, 200, 203–4, 217
Chabahar 206
China 1–7, 10–11, 13–15, 17, 19–20, 22, 24–5, 27–37, 40–1, 44–54, 56–7, 60, 62, 66–73, 75–6, 78–9, 83–4, 86–7, 89–91, 102–3, 105–9, 117, 119, 121, 124, 126–30, 135, 138–9, 141–2, 145–6, 154–61, 165–8, 172, 174, 177, 180–2, 184–5, 188, 190, 192–212, 214, 216–19; and infrastructural lending 191–208; Japan and rise of 20, 22, 46–9, 109
Chino Tadao 69, 93, 110–12, 117–18, 122–3, 127–9, 157–8, 180

224 *Index*

commodity boom 146, 167, 181, 194, 196, 219
conditionality 40, 89, 96, 104, 198, 202–3
connectivity infrastructure 1–2, 5, 9, 51, 72, 199, 215

DAC *see* Development Assistance Committee
debt securitisation 194
debt trap 192–3, 197, 206
demand-based aid 102
Democratic Party of Japan 20, 34, 51, 64–83, 116, 145, 152–3, 168, 170, 174–7, 181, 194, 199, 216
democratisation 23, 28, 44, 48, 50, 54, 94, 116, 207
Development Assistance Committee 20, 102, 128, 197, 218
DPJ *see* Democratic Party of Japan
Dzhakishev, Mukhtar 40, 172–4

EBRD *see* European Bank for Reconstruction and Development
Edano, Yukio 52, 68, 80–1, 170, 176, 178
energy diplomacy 143
Eurasian Crossroads 48–52, 200
Eurasian Development Bank 203
Eurasian Diplomacy 11, 13, 27–9
European Bank for Reconstruction and Development 9, 11, 13, 20, 26, 31, 33, 39, 89–90, 92–3, 98, 100, 102–3, 111, 114–15, 117, 126, 163–4, 202
external pressure (*gaiatsu*) 35, 106

factions 36–8, 40–1, 43, 66–70, 76, 82, 216
financial aid 10, 13, 37, 89–130
Fukushima disaster 4–5, 65–6, 77–81, 83, 104, 141, 163, 166–8, 178, 216
functionalism 1, 118, 122, 124, 126, 128–9, 143–4, 151, 217

Gemba, Kōichirō 76–7, 79–80, 116
global financial crisis 52, 73–4, 99, 198
Goscomgeo 175–6
gradualism 95–100, 110
Greater East Asia Co-Prosperity Sphere 197, 218
guarantor state 143, 159, 181

habatsu 43
Hashimoto, Ryūtarō 11, 20, 25, 27–9, 31, 46–8, 50, 68–9, 93, 97, 100, 103, 111, 121, 144, 216
Hatoyama, Yukio 64–6, 68, 70–4, 76–7, 82, 116, 145, 174, 200
Heisei Research Council 49, 68–70, 73

Idemitsu 167
India 27, 48–51, 157, 159, 167–8, 191, 194–5, 206–7
INPEX 17, 104, 132, 134, 150, 154, 156–9, 162, 164, 166, 169, 172, 181, 183–4, 188
intellectual assistance 90
Iran 7, 10, 104, 122, 125, 146, 148–50, 154, 156–9, 206
Iran-Pakistan-India pipeline 158
Itochu 9, 150–1, 154, 156–7, 162, 164, 166, 169, 175, 181

Japan Bank for International Cooperation 89, 92, 104, 124, 150, 161–3, 169–70, 195
Japan External Trade Organization 145, 163, 176
Japan International Cooperation Agency 34, 45, 73, 89–90, 92, 102–6, 109–10, 115, 117, 124–6, 128, 162–3, 218
Japan Oil, Gas and Metals National Corporation 78, 80, 145, 149, 155, 158, 161–2, 164, 169, 175–6, 181
Japan Overseas Infrastructure Investment Corporation for Transport and Urban Development 195
JAPEX 163
JBIC *see* Japan Bank for International Cooperation
JETRO *see* Japan External Trade Organization
JICA *see* Japan International Cooperation Agency
JOGMEC *see* Japan Oil, Gas and Metals National Corporation
JOIN *see* Japan Overseas Infrastructure Investment Corporation for Transport and Urban Development

Kan, Naoto 75–9
Kanehara, Nobukatsu 4, 20, 49
Karimov, Islam 30–1, 36–40, 60, 69, 75–7, 79, 88, 94–5, 103–4, 111–14, 132, 136, 176, 179, 188
Kashagan 30, 104–5, 154, 161–3, 166, 172

Kawaguchi, Yoriko 11, 20, 32–3, 49, 53, 69, 75, 103, 177
Kazakhstan 2, 7, 9–10, 12, 16–17, 19–20, 26, 30, 32, 34–6, 45–7, 57, 59, 64, 70–2, 74–8, 81, 84, 86, 90, 94, 97, 99–100, 103–5, 109, 112–13, 115, 118–19, 122–3, 126, 130–1, 133–5, 137–8, 141–2, 144–5, 147–8, 149–51, 154–6, 161–3, 166–9, 171–4, 176–80, 183, 186, 188–91, 193, 196, 203, 208, 219
Kazakhstan-Turkmenistan-Iran railway 122
Kazatomprom 77, 170, 173–4, 177, 179
Khodorkovsky, Mikhail 165–6, 180
Kishi, Nobusuke 4, 199
Koizumi, Jun'ichirō 2, 29, 35, 46, 48–9, 52–4, 69, 72–3, 80, 98, 106, 115–16, 118, 123, 128, 165, 171–3, 175, 206
Kyrgyzstan 7, 9–10, 32, 36–7, 39, 45–7, 54, 62, 66, 68, 73–4, 81, 87, 97, 100, 103, 105, 109, 112–13, 119, 131, 134–5, 137, 139, 148, 151, 162, 169, 189, 196, 202–3

LDP see Liberal Democratic Party of Japan (LDP)
lender of last resort 193, 198–201
Liberal Democratic Party of Japan (LDP) 4, 12–13, 20, 29, 31, 43, 49–54, 65–70, 72–4, 77, 82, 84, 86, 110–11, 116, 145, 153, 181, 195, 210, 216
liberalisation 94, 96, 98, 104, 110, 159, 202
loan aid 34, 72, 90, 104–5, 117, 196–7

Machimura, Nobutaka 50–1
Maehara, Seiji 68, 76–7, 79–80
Magosaki, Ukeru 94
Management Council for Infrastructure Strategy 195
Marubeni 173
Matsumoto, Takeaki 68, 79
mercantile state 23, 143–4
mercantilism 14, 53, 72, 95, 130, 143–4, 159, 192, 195
METI see Ministry of Economy, Trade and Industry
Ministry of Economy, Trade and Industry 9, 14–16, 20, 24, 34, 48, 52–3, 55, 62, 78, 80–1, 85, 87–8, 96, 102, 115, 134, 137, 141, 144–5, 150, 153, 156, 159, 161–2, 166–71, 176, 178, 180–1, 184, 188–9, 195, 203, 205, 208–9

Ministry of Finance 9, 13–15, 24, 26–7, 31–3, 57, 69, 78, 89–93, 95–6, 98–100, 102–3, 106, 108–12, 115, 117, 123, 127, 129, 131–4, 136–7, 139, 142, 144–5, 150, 157–8, 184, 192, 200, 203–5, 208, 213
Ministry of Foreign Affairs 9–10, 13–15, 20, 24, 27–9, 31–4, 47, 49–51, 53–4, 58–60, 62–3, 66, 69–71, 73, 78–81, 83–7, 89, 93, 96, 102–3, 108, 110, 112, 115, 117, 132, 134–5, 137–41, 144–5, 162, 169–71, 177, 181–6, 189, 203–5, 208, 213
Mirziyoyev, Shavkat 39, 42, 114, 129, 149
Mitsubishi 150, 155, 159, 163, 173, 179
Mitsui 109, 124, 142, 149–51, 173, 175–6, 181
MOF see Ministry of Finance
MOFA see Ministry of Foreign Affairs
Mori, Yoshirō 29, 46–7, 68–9, 82, 103, 111
multi-vectorism 7, 42, 102, 112, 116, 128, 161

Navoi (city and region) 175, 180
Nazarbayev, Nursultan 72, 173
neo-liberalism 95–8, 108, 118
New Silk Road initiative (U.S.) 123–4
NEXI see Nippon Export and Investment Insurance
Nippon Export and Investment Insurance 150
Nippon Express 208
Niyazov, Saparmurat 126
Noda, Yoshihiko 64, 68, 77, 79–82, 145, 178, 181, 216
nomenklatura 42, 113, 116
Northeast Asian Infrastructure Investment Fund 200
nuclear renaissance 78, 104, 153, 166–9, 179–80, 216

Obama, Barack 48, 65, 124, 176
Obuchi, Keizō 11, 20, 29, 46, 68–9, 97, 103
Okada, Katsuya 68, 70, 72–3, 75–6, 116, 176–7
O-Shin 101
Ozawa, Ichirō 21, 66, 68, 70, 73, 75–6, 79–80

Pakistan 7, 10, 48, 51, 119, 123, 125, 154, 156–9, 201, 206, 217
policy entrepreneurs 92, 107, 109–10, 193, 201, 203, 209
post-neo-liberalism 97
Putin, Vladimir 53, 173

226 *Index*

rare earth metals 141, 143, 146, 150, 153, 166–81
reactivity 2, 5–6, 14, 65, 67, 75, 82, 93, 106, 142, 196, 207, 215
resource diplomacy 34, 79–83, 141–81
revival diplomacy 78–9
risk perceptions 1, 142, 145, 149–51, 154, 175, 181, 219
Rosatom 179–80
Russia 4–5, 7, 9–13, 15, 17, 19–21, 24–6, 28–37, 40–5, 47–8, 50–3, 57–63, 65–7, 71–2, 75, 79–81, 83–5, 94, 97, 100–3, 105, 108, 110, 113, 115, 117, 119, 121, 129–31, 136, 138, 144, 151, 154–62, 164–7, 169, 172–4, 176–81, 183, 185, 187, 189, 194, 203–4, 206–8, 214, 216

securitisation 3, 17, 36, 43, 53–4, 73, 160, 195
Seiwa Policy Research Council 4, 68
Sengoku, Yoshito 68, 76
Shanghai Cooperation Organisation 10, 32, 44, 122, 203
Silk Road Action Plan 20, 68, 97
Silk Road Energy Mission 163
Silk Road Strategy Act (U.S.) 11, 122
Sumitomo 77, 122, 150, 169, 173–4, 177, 181

Tajikistan 7, 9–10, 19, 25, 29–30, 32, 36, 45–7, 72, 78, 81, 84, 86, 90, 98–9, 105–6, 109, 113, 119, 122, 124–6, 134–5, 139–40, 148, 169, 172, 174, 182–3, 188–9, 202–3, 214
Taliban, the 31, 156–7
Taniguchi, Tomohiko 49–50
TAPI pipeline *see* Turkmenistan-Afghanistan-Pakistan-India pipeline
TEPCO *see* Tokyo Electric Power Company
tied aid 162, 197

Tokyo Electric Power Company 167
Toshiba 77, 173–4, 179
Turkmenistan 3, 7, 9–10, 17, 36, 45, 59, 75, 90, 97, 99, 105, 107, 113, 119, 122–6, 128, 134, 136, 138, 141–2, 147–9, 154–64, 166, 169, 176, 180, 183–4, 186–7, 204
Turkmenistan-Afghanistan-Pakistan-India pipeline 107, 111, 123–4, 128, 154, 156–61, 164, 180, 204

United States of America 4, 7, 10–11, 13, 15–18, 20, 22–3, 25, 31, 33–4, 36–7, 39–40, 50–2, 55–64, 66–7, 69–71, 74, 83–9, 91, 94, 97, 102, 106–8, 110, 113, 115, 123, 129–41, 146–7, 151–2, 154, 156–7, 161, 165–6, 169, 172–3, 175–8, 181–92, 195, 199–200, 203, 205–7, 209–14, 216–17
uranium 14, 20, 26, 35, 65, 72, 77, 79, 82, 104, 141–6, 150, 153, 162, 166–80, 216, 219
Uzbekistan 3, 5, 7, 9–10, 12, 16–17, 19–20, 30–42, 45–7, 50, 54, 58–9, 65, 68–72, 74–8, 81–4, 86–8, 90–1, 94–7, 99–101, 103–7, 109–17, 119, 123–5, 128–39, 141–2, 145, 148–51, 155, 159, 161–3, 166, 168–9, 171–2, 174–80, 182–4, 186, 188, 191

value-oriented diplomacy 20, 33–4, 49–50, 53–4, 113, 115, 180, 217

Washington Consensus 94–7, 110
Westinghouse 173, 179

Yachi, Shōtarō 4, 20, 33, 49, 52, 195, 208
yōseishugi see demand-based aid

zero-sum game 119, 145

Printed in the United States
by Baker & Taylor Publisher Services